Java for Complete Beginners

Step By Step with Full Explanation for Java Beginners

Mohammed Abdelmoniem Kamel

Java for Complete Beginners

Step By Step with Full Explanation for Java Beginners

Copyright © Mohammed Abdelmoniem Kamel, 2019

NOTICE OF RIGHTS

All right reserved. No part of this publication may be reproduced, stored or introduced into a retrieval system, or transmitted, in an form or by any means (electronic or mechanical form), including photocopy, recording, or otherwise, without the prior written permission by the copyright owner.

For information on getting permission for reprints and excerpts, contact ata4tech@gmail.com.

National Library Cataloging-Sudan

005.1

MJ Mohammed Abdelmoniem Kamel Mohammed, 1980-
      java for complete beginners/ Mohammed Abdelmoniem
    Kamel Mohammed.- Khartoum M.A.K. Mohammed,2019.

    500P. : ill. ;24 cm.

    ISBN : 978-99942-57-87-4

    1.Programming (electric system).   A.Title

DISCLAIMER

The information in this book is distributed on an "As Is" basis, without warranty. While every precaution has been taken in the preparation of the book, neither the authors nor the publisher , shall have any liability to any person or entity with respect to any loss or damage or alleged to be caused directly or indirectly by the instructions contained in the book or the computer software and hardware products described in it.

TRADEMARKS

Many of the designation used by manufacturing and sellers to distinguish their products are claimed as trademarks. Where those designations appear in this book, the designation appear as requested by the owner of the trademark. All other product names and services identified throughout this book are used in editorial fashion only and for the benefit of such companies with no intention of infringement of the trademark. No such use, or the use of any trade name, is intended to convey endorsement or other affiliation with this book.

Contents

Java Fundamentals 1

1. Introduction to Java 3
- Hardware and Software Concepts 3
- Processing of Executing a Program 8
- Programming Languages 9
- What is a Java? 14
- Hardware and Software Platforms 16
- The Java Platforms 19
- Installing The JDK 10 On Windows 10 24
- Summary 36

2. Java First Steps 39
- Phases of Program Creation and Execution 39
- Creating Your First Java Program 40
- Explanation of Your First Java Program (Welcome.java) 47
- Creating Your Second Java Program 50
- Packages in Java 51
- Java Comments 60
- Summary 67

3. Variables, Constants & Data Types 69
- Java Variables 69
- Get Input From The User in a Console-based Java Program 76
- Identifiers in Java 78
- Introduction to Java Data Types 79
- Floating-Point Data Type 83
- char & boolean Data Types 87
- The byte, short, int and long Data Types 90
- String Data Type 91
- Java Literals 92
  - Java Constant 101
  - The Difference Between Variable, Constant, and Literal 102
  - Java Keywords 103
  - Summary 103

4. Expressions and Operators 107
   Operators and operands 107
   Java Arithmetic operators 107
   Java Relational Operators 110
   Java Logical Operators 112
   Java Assignment Operators 114
   Java bitwise Operators 117
   Java Increment and Decrement Operators 120
   Summary 121

5. Control Structure 123
   Introduction to Java Control Structure (a.k.a. Control Flow) 123
   The Selection Structure 124
   Relational Operators 126
   Comparing Characters 129
   if...else Statement 131
   Conditional Operator (? :) 132
   Nested if...else Statements 134
   Logical Operators 135
   The switch Statement 142
      Summary 146

6. Java Arrays 147
   Introduction 147
   Accessing Array Elements 149
   Store Data Inside an Array 151
   Displaying the Content of the Array 152
   Array Initialization (Declaration + Instantiation = Initialization) ... 153
   Processing Array Elements 155
   String Arrays 162
   Two Dimensional Arrays 165
   Arrays with Three or More Dimensions 172
      Java Performing Bounds Checking 174
      Watch out for Off-by-One Errors 175
      Summary 176

7. Java Loops 179
   The Increment (++) and Decrement (--) Operators 179
   The while Loop 183
   The for Loop 191
   Nested Loops 197
   Summary 203

8. Java Methods 205
    Introduction 205
    Create a New Method (defining a void method) 207
    Calling a Method 208
    Passing Arguments to a Method 209
    More About Local Variables 218
    Returning a Value From a Method 221
    Summary 227

Object-Oriented Programming 229

9. Classes and Objects 231
    Introduction 231
    Class Creation 232
    Declaring Fields for a Class 233
    Defining Methods 233
    Notes About Class Creation 234
    Object Creation 235
    Building a Simple Class 238
    Accessor and Mutator 245
    Layout Of Class Members 245
        Summary 249
10. Constructors 251
    Introduction 251
    Uninitialized Local Reference Variables 253
    The Default Constructor 254
    Writing Your no-arg Constructor 255
    Summary 255
11. Scope of Instance Fields 257
    Basics 257
    Shadowing 259
    Summary 260
12. Access & Non-Access Modifiers 261
    Access Modifiers in Java 261
    Non-Access Modifiers in Java 267
    Summary 271
13. Static Class Members 273
    Introduction 273
    Static Fields 274

- Static Methods...........277
- Passing Objects as Arguments to Methods...........279
- Returning Objects from Methods...........285
- The toString Method...........287
- Summary...........288

14. ArrayList in Java...........289
- Introduction...........289
- Initialize and Use an ArrayList...........289
- ArrayList Add/Remove...........290
- Sorting of ArrayList...........300
- Get/Search...........314
- Capacity...........321
- Summary...........322

15. Overloading Methods and Constructors...........325
- Overloading Methods...........325
- Overloading Constructors...........327
- Summary...........328

16. Introduction to Aggregation...........329
- Introduction...........329
- Summary...........335

17. Enumerated Types...........337
- Introduction...........337
- Enumerated Types are Specialized Classes...........341
- toString(), values(), ordinal() and valueOf() methods...........343
- Writing Enumerated Type Inside Its Own File...........348
- Switching On an Enumerated Type...........348
- Enum with Customized Value in Java...........350
- Where You Use Java Enums...........352
- The finalize Method...........352
- Summary...........352

18. The this Reference Variable...........355
- Introduction...........355
- Using this to Overcome Shadowing...........356
- Using this to Call an Overloaded Constructor from Another Constructor...........357

19. Text Processing and Wrap Classes...........359
- Introduction to Wrap Classes...........359
- Character Testing and Conversion with the Character Class...........360

	Searching For SubStrings	365
	Extracting SubStrings	372
	Methods That Returns a Modified String	377
	The static valueOf Methods	379
	The StringBuilder Class	381
	Tokenizing Strings	387
	Wrapper Classes for The Numeric Data Types	395
	Summary	399
20.	Inheritance	403
	What is Inheritance?	403
	Calling the superclass Constructor	405
	The Object Class	408
	Overriding Superclass Methods	408
	Protected Members	413
	Package Access	415
	Summary	416
21.	Polymorphism	421
	Introduction	421
	Polymorphism & Dynamic Binding	425
	The Instanceof Operator	426
	Summary	427
22.	Abstract Classes and Interfaces	429
	Abstract Classes & Abstract Methods	429
	Interfaces	433
	Summary	437
23.	Exceptions	439
	Introduction	439
	Handling Exception	440
	Finding Details of the Exception	447
	Polymorphic References to Exceptions	449
	Handling Multiple Exception	450
	The finally Clauses	452
	The Stack Trace	454
	When an Exception Is Not Caught	456
	Exception Classes	456
	Checked and Unchecked Exceptions	458
	Summary	459
24.	Java File I/O	463

Introduction..463
The File Class...464
Text Files..472
Binary Files..473
Random Access Files..479
Summary...485

Building Graphical User Interface 487

25. JavaFX Layouts..489

Introduction..489
A JavaFX application skeleton...492
JavaFX Layout...497
Summary...522

26. JavaFX Controls..523

JavaFX controls...523
Events and Event Handlers...552
Summary...567

27. JavaFX and Scene Builder..569

JavaFX and Scene Builder...569
Summary...582

28. Login Form Application Using 585

Introduction..585
Create the Main Application Class......................................586
Add User Interface (UI) Controls to the Layout...................586
Add the Handler Code that is Executed on Form Submit (LoginController.java file)..595

29. Calculator Application..599

Introduction..599
Create the Main Application Class......................................600
Add UI Controls to the Layout...601
Adding Events Handling for Calculator...............................607
Summary...614

Code Samples

The sample programs shown in the pages of this book were compiled with IntelliJ IDEA 2019 & JDK 8/9/10. You can download the source code from the below link:

› **learnjava_source.zip:** https://drive.google.com/open?id=19NZbBa8g4A-aDG2z31zhF5n6EA2JS1Wr

› **learnjava_source.7z:** https://drive.google.com/open?id=1wrjtuE48dzSy2ieM6gkAIj2xBHvvIPxE

I'll try to keep the code updated with the latest release of JDK and to fix (and comment) any errors that might have sneaked through.

You can report problems, bugs, or other kinds of feedback about the book or source code by sending it on my email: ata4tech@gmail.com

About the Author

I'm **Mohammed Abdelmoniem** . I'm a web developer who design, currently living in Omdurman, Sudan. I have a Bachelor of Science in Computer Science, and an MBA degree in Information Technology. My primary focus and inspiration about creating beautiful and useful products. I'm constantly experimenting with new technologies and techniques. I am very passionate about Web development, and strive to better myself as a developer, and the development community as a whole.

Preface

Java is one of the preferred languages among developers, used in everything right from games, supercomputers to even home appliances. This book on Java programming aims to instill the reader with an understanding of the object-oriented approach to programming and aims to develop some practical skills along the way. The concepts that will be explained and skills developed are in common use among programmers using many modern object-oriented languages and are thus transferable from one language to another. However, for a practical purpose, these concepts are explored and demonstrated using the Java programming language.

The Java programming language is used to highlight and demonstrate the application of fundamental objects (inc. the use of loops, selection statements, performing calculation, arrays, data types and a basic understanding of file handling), as well as basic concepts of JavaFX.

This book has a practical purpose so that the primary goal is to show how to do. Of course, there is also a more theoretical explanation, but I have tried to minimize the theoretical material in order to quickly reach what you need to write a program. Most of the material is presented through a large number of examples and the explanations, which are associated therewith.

This book is an introduction to programming and the language Java. It requires no special assumptions of the reader and is aimed at anyone who wants or needs to learn about programming. It is thus not a prerequisite that the reader has knowledge of programming, but only that the reader is interested in programming and would have IntelliJ IDEA installed on his computer.

When you finish this book, you'll be comfortable with the basics of Java language and will be able to start using them in your day-to-day Java programming work.

Mohammed Abdelmoniem Kamel
2019
ata4tech@gmail.com

Part 1

Java Fundamentals

"You don't have to be great to start. But you have to start to be great." - Zig Ziglar

Chapter 1

Introduction to Java

Hardware and Software Concepts

What is a computer?

A computer is an electronic device that takes input, processes it, and converts it into meaningful information. All input is called data, and all output is called information.

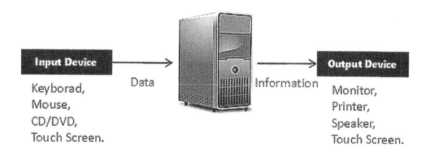

Figure 1.1 | Computer System

The table below describes the difference between the data and information.

Table 1.1 | Difference between data and information

Data	Information
Data is used as input for the computer system.	Information is the output data.
Data is unprocessed figures.	Information is processed data.
Data doesn't depend on information.	Information depends on data.
Data doesn't carry a meanings.	Information must carry a logical meanings.
Data is the raw material.	Information is the product.
Example: 200, B, Sudan	Example: Fred's blood pressure readings

So, data usually refers to raw data, or unprocessed data. It may be in the form of numbers, letters, or a set of characters. And once the data is analyzed, it is considered as information. Information is a sequence of symbols that can be interpreted as a message. It provides knowledge or insight about a certain matter.

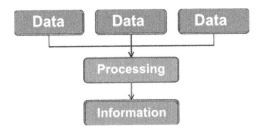

Figure 1.2 | Data and Information

Therefore a computer can now be defined as a fast and accurate data processing system that accepts data, performs various operations on the data, has the capability to store the data and produce the results on the basis of detailed step by step instructions given to it. The terms hardware and software are almost always used in connection with the computer[1].

Computer hardware

Hardware refers to the physical components that a computer is made of. For example, chips, boxes, wires, keyboards, speakers, disks, cables, mice, monitors, and so on.

---

[1] http://www.tmv.edu.in/pdf/Distance_education/BCA%20Books/BCA%20I%20SEM/BCA-121%20Computer%20Fundamental.pdf - Page 2

The major hardware components

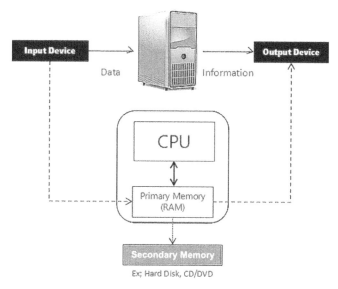

Figure 1.3 | The Major Hardware Components

Input Devices
> Inputs are the signals or data received by the computer or system.
> Input Devices is a hardware used to send signals or data to a computer.
> For example: keyboard, mouse, touch pad, touch screen, and microphone.

Central Processing Unit (CPU) or Processor
> A CPU is the "Brain" of the computer which does most of the work.
> A CPU is used to executes or carry out program instructions.
> After executing the program, a program is copied from secondary memory (e.g., hard disk) and stored in main memory (RAM) with the support of CPU and operating system.
> - Hard disk is slower than RAM. Hard disk drives can't access information nearly as quickly as memory does and it affects the speed at which data can move between the drive and the CPU. So why use hard drive at all? Well, they're cheap and plentiful.
> - RAM speed is near than CPU speed. RAM has a very fast path to the computer's CPU but it is more expensive than Hard disk.

- CPU must be connected to input device, output device and storage device to carry out the activities.
- Examples for CPU manufacturers: Intel and AMD
- Common examples of CPU:
    - Intel: i7-8086K (8th generation Core), i5-8600K (8th generation core)
    - AMD: Carrizo (Excavator core), Kaveri (Steamroller core), Summit Ridge Ryzen.

Cache Memory
- Cache memory is high-speed memory that a processor can access more quickly than it can access regular random access memory (RAM).
- It is purpose is to hold those parts of data and program instructions that are used repeatedly in the operation of programs. The processor can access this data from the cache rather than having to get it from main memory.
- Cache memory is typically located in two general locations: inside the CPU chip and on the motherboard.
    - Primary Cache memory is located inside the CPU chip.
    - Secondary cache memory is located on the motherboard outside the CPU.
- Cache Memory is a very high speed memory which can speed up the CPU. It is faster than main memory, but it has a limited capacity.
- It is very expensive than RAM.
- It is a volatile memory, means that the contents stored in it will be erased if the power is turned off.

Main Memory or Random Access Memory (RAM)
- It faster than secondary memory.
- It acts as a staging post between the hard disk and the processor.
- Main memory is the storage device that holds data and machine code (program instructions or program) CURRENTLY being used, as the program being processed by the CPU.
- It allows a processor to access running execution applications that are temporarily stored in a specific memory location.
- It is a volatile memory, means that the contents stored in it will be erased if the power is turned off. This is why none of your programs or files are still open when turn your computer back on.

> One way computers get around this limitation is to put your computer into hibernation mode. Hibernating a computer just saves the contents of RAM or current state of your computer - open programs and documents - to your hard disk and then turns off your computer. Then when it's time to start it up again all your previous work is back on.

Secondary Memory
> Secondary memory hold saved data when power is turned off (a.k.a. non-volatile memory).
> It is used for long term storage.
> For example: flash memory, hard disk, magnetic tape and optical disks (CD/DVD).

Output Devices
> Outputs are the signals or data sent from the computer or system.
> Output device is any device used to send data from a computer to another device or user.
> For example: monitor, printer, touch screen, speaker, headphones and data projector.

The Hardware components of a computer are essentially useless without instructions or programs to tell them what to do.

Computer software

Software refers to the programs that run on a computer. A program is a set of instructions that the computer (CPU) executes one after another. Software consist of programs and the data those programs use as shown in the image below:

Figure 1.4 | Software Components

For example, the Microsoft Word software consists of limited programs, such as insert images or search for text within a Word document. Data means video, audio, images or text.

General categories of software

> **System software**
>   - System software is a set of programs that manages the computer's hardware devices and provide a platform to other software.
>   - Examples: Operating Systems (Windows, Mac OS X, UNIX/Linux Distribution), and development tools (Compilers, Interpreters, Debuggers).
>
> **Application software**
>   - Application software refers to programs that make the computer useful to the user. These programs solve specific problems or perform general operations that satisfy the needs of the user.
>   - Examples: MS Office, LibreOffice, Paint and Photoshop.

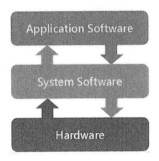

Figure 1.5 | General Categories of Software

The application software is always depends on system software. The System software manages the hardware devices and other application software.

Processing of Executing a Program

Executing a program involves how information moves among the basic hardware components of a computer. Suppose you have an executable program you wish to run (e.g., MS Calculator)

> - The program is stored on some secondary memory device, such as a hard disk.
> - You instruct the computer (double click or click on the MS Word icon) to execute your program.
> - A copy of the program is brought into from secondary memory and stored in main memory (RAM).

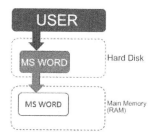

Figure 1.6 | Moving information from hard disk to main memory

> The processor reads the individual program instructions from main memory. The processor then executes the instructions one at a time until the program ends.

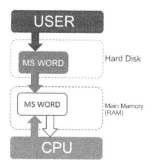

Figure 1.7 | How information move between main memory and the Processor

> The data that the instructions use, such as two numbers that will be added together, are also stored in main memory (RAM). They are either brought in from secondary memory or read from an input devices such as the keyboard.
> During execution, the program may display information to an output device such as monitor.

The process of executing a program is a fundamental to the operation of a computer. All computer systems basically work in the same way.

Programming Languages

A Programming language is a special language programmers use to write computer programs. A program is a series of instructions a computer executes in order to perform a task. A program can be written in one of many programming languages, such as C/C++, C#, and Java.

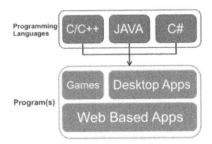

Figure 1.8 | Programs and Programming Languages

Programming language levels

Programming languages can be classified into three categories:

1. Machine Languages
2. Assembly Languages
3. High Level Languages

Machine Languages

Computer CPUs are too primitive to directly run the commands of any language that a human would actually use. They can only run a think called "machine code", which is a binary ones and zeroes. A Machine Language program is made up of a series of binary digits, for example 01011101. Machine language programs can be run directly by the processor.

Every processor or processor family (e.g., Intel, AMD, etc) has its own machine language. Machine language is difficult for programmers to write and read, and also it is time consuming and error prone.

Assembly Languages

The Assembly Language instructions are replaced binary digits with mnemonics short English-like words that represent commands or data (e.g., ADD, MOV). This Assembly languages are also unique to a specific processor. Prior to execution, an Assembly language program requires translation to machine language, using a computer program known as **Assembler** as shown in the following picture.

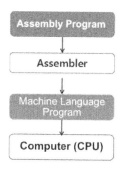

Figure 1.9 | Assembly Languages

It is still tedious to use both machine languages and assemble languages are considered low-level languages.

> **NOTE:** A low-level programming language is a programming language that provides commands or functions in the language closely to processor instructions.

High-Level Languages

High level language is expressed in English-like phrases, and it is easier to read and write. A single high-level language statement can accomplish the equivalent of hundreds-of machine language instructions as shown in the image below.

```
High-Level Language      Assembly Language        Machine Language
--------------------     --------------------     -------------------
a + b                    ld [%fp-20],%o0          ...
                         ld [%fp-24],%o1          1101 0000 0000 0111
                         add %o0,%o1,1..0         1000 1111 0000 1000
                                                  1101 1111 1110 1001
                                                  1001 0000 0000 0000
                                                  ...
```

Figure 1.10 | Programming Language's Instructions

A high level programming language enables a programmer to write programs that are more or less independent of a particular type of processor or computer.

A high level language program must be translated into machine language in order to be executed. This translation is accomplished by either a **compiler** or an **interpreter**.

What is a Compiler?

A compiler is a program that reads a program written in some high-level programming language - the source code- and translate it into an equivalent program in another language - the target language- on our case, it converts it into executable machine code for a CPU.

Figure 1.11 | Compilation of a high level language program using a compiler

After compilation, the machine language program can be executed directly on a specific processor, without the need for a compiler.

Figure 1.12 | Execution of a compiled program

The compiler compiles the entire program at a time, and the resulting code is executed by the computer hardware. This means that, after compilation an autonomous executable file is generated by the compiler and the job of the compiler is over. A compiler does not execute anything. It translates your program into an "executable" version of itself. The change made by this translation is intended to read by computer processor. It is written in what is called "machine code". After that we can run the executable file directly without running the source code.

What is an Interpreter?

An Interpreter is a program that reads a program written in some high-level programming language - the source language - and translate it into an intermediate code. You still need to install the interpreter to every targets well.

Figure 1.13 | Interprets of a high level language program using an interpreter

The resulting code is executed by another program - by interpreter itself - not by the computer hardware. This means that, the interpreter is compulsory for executing an interpreter program or high level language program.

Figure 1.14 | Executing of an interpreted program

So an interpreter is a program that takes in a program written in a source language and executes the instructions as they read them. E.g. Tcl, Lisp, Scheme,

Bash and JavaScript are mostly pure interpreted languages. Interpreters are generally used in cases where flexibility and programmability is the main aim rather than high performance.

There is a third class that has become very common that falls in-between the pure distinctions. They are compiled languages but the result of the compilation is a second interpreted language. e.g. Java and C#.

Compiling and interpreting applications in Java

Java source code is **compiled** by a program called **javac**. It converts source code into an intermediate file known as **Bytecode** file. The Bytecode file is unique for all type of operating system, means bytecode is platform independent.

Now, the Interpreter of java converts Bytecode into a specific operating system compatible machine code. This code will vary according to operating system. Because byte code does not run natively on nearly all CPUs, it must be run on some other program which converts it. In java, this is the Java Virtual Machine, **JVM**.

Java language uses both compiler and interpreter. Compiler translates the Java source code into *Bytecode*, which is executed by JVM. The JVM interprets the Java Bytecode into *Machine Code*.

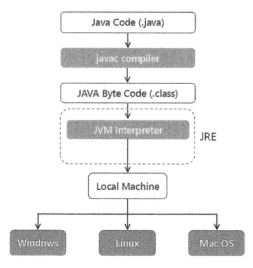

Figure 1.15 | Java Compilation Process

The Java compiler transforms a java source code (.java file) into a Java *bytecode (.class file)*, which is the machine language for the **Java Virtual Machine (JVM)**. The

Java interpreter (**java**) translate or execute a Java bytecode instruction by instruction to code that can be executed natively on the underlying machine.

JVM is a part of Java Development Kit (JDK) and Java Runtime Environment (JRE) and whatever Java program you run using JRE or JDK goes into JVM and is responsible for executing the Java program line by line hence it is known as **Interpreter** (we will discuss in more detail later.)

Why we use both - compiler as well as interpreter in Java?

At the time of C and C++, only compiler was there that converts source code into specific Operating System (OS) machine code. The machine code was OS dependent that varied from OS to OS. That means if a C++ program is compiled on Windows, it will only run on Windows. And if a user wants to execute the same program on Linux, it will not run.

The problem the programmer were facing that they had to design a different compiler for different Operating System that is too difficult, Too time consuming and much Costly. Then Sun Microsystems take the whole Initiative by making:

› a unique compiler that transforms a Java source code into a Java Bytecode (Platform Independent Code)
› the specific JVM (Interpreter) that converts bytecodes into machine code that will vary from Operating System to Operating System.

Different JVM for different Operating System was much easier and economical than the whole compiler.

So, Java compiler generates a bytecode file which is a kind of machine language that only a JVM can understand.

What is a Java?

Java is a general purpose, high-level programming language developed by Sun Microsystems in 1995. In subsequent years, the Java language has become the backbone of millions of applications across multiple platforms, including Windows, Macintosh, and UNIX/Linux.

A general-purpose programming language is a programming language designed to be used for writing software in a wide variety of application domains.[1]

---
[1] https://en.wikipedia.org/wiki/General-purpose_programming_language

Type of Java Applications

1. **Native Applications**, which are stored on, and run directly on, the user's desktop, laptop, or mobile device.
2. **Web Applications**, served by, and run mostly on, a web server.
3. **Embedded Applications**, which are a software that permanently resides in an industrial or consumer device (a.k.a. Embedded Systems), such as washing machine, ATM, Heartbeat monitors and much more.

Java version history

The Java language has undergone several changes since 1995. Many changes and improvements have been made to the technology over the year. The following table summarize all versions of Java Standard Edition (Java SE.)

Table 1.2 | Java version history

Year	Versions
1991	James Gosling, Mike Sheridan, and Patrick Naughton (called Green team) initiated the Java language project in June 1991
1995	JDK Alpha and Beta
1996	JDK 1.0 - Called Oak (The first stable version JDK 1.0.2 is called Java 1)
1997	JDK 1.1.
1998	J2SE 1.2 (The version name "J2SE" (Java 2 Platform, Standard Edition) replaced JDK to distinguish the base platform from J2EE (Java 2 Platform, Enterprise Edition) and J2ME (Java 2 Platform, Micro Edition.)
2000	J2SE 1.3
2002	J2SE 1.4 (The first release that developed under the Java Community).
2004	J2SE 5.0 (originally numbered 1.5, which is still used as the internal version number)
2006	Java SE 6 (Sun replaced the name "J2SE" with Java SE.)

2011	Java SE 7
2014	Java SE 8
2017	Java SE 9
March, 2018	Java SE 10
Sep, 2018	Java SE 11
March, 2019	Java SE 12

From the table above we can see that the naming and the version number have been changing over times:

> Versions 1.0 & 1.1 are named as JDK (Java Development Kit).
> Versions 1.2 & 1.4 are named as J2SE (Java 2 Standard Edition).
> From Versions 1.5, Sun introduces internal and external versions. Internal versions is continuous from previous ones (1.5 after 1.4), but the external version has different numbering (5.0 for 1.5). Version 1.5 and version 5.0 are just different version names for only one thing.

Hardware and Software Platforms

A **platform** is a hardware and/or software environment - that serves as a foundation or base- in which a program runs. For example, when purchasing software, it's important to know what platform (hardware and/or software) the software was written for. The table below describes the different hardware and software requirements for many software.

Table 1.3 | Hardware and Software Requirements for many Software

Software	Hardware Platform	Software Platform
Windows 10	Processor: 1 GHz or faster RAM: 1 GB (32-bit) or 2 GB (64-bit) Hard Disk Space: 16 GB Graphics card: Microsoft DirectX 9 graphics device with WDDM driver	None

Java JDK 8	Processor (min): Pentium 2 (266 MHz)	Oracle Solaris OS, Microsoft Windows, Linux., OS X
	Disk Space (min): 245MB	
	Memory (min): 128MB RAM	
IntelliJ IDEA 2016	1 GB RAM minimum, 2 GB RAM recommended	MS Windows 10/8/7/vista/2003/XP
	300 MB hard disk space + at least 1 GB for caches	JDK 1.8
	1024 x 768 minimum screen resolution	

NOTE: Platform Specific software is platform-specific, means it run on one platform -- Windows or Mac. **Cross-Platform s**oftware means the software intended to be executed on more than one platform -- Windows, Mac OS X, and Linux.

Hardware platform

A hardware platform refers to only a CPU architecture or CPU family. A hardware platform is a set of compatible hardware (processor and associated hardware pieces) on which software applications can be run.

In the computing world, there are many processor manufacturers but the main ones are Intel, AMD and ARM. Intel and AMD are for the desktop, server and PC side, while ARM is for phones, tablets, TVs, fridges and some laptops.

From all these, there are two processor, x86 from Intel which is 32-bit/64-bit and x64 from AMD which is 64-bit. ARM authors the CPU architectures for mobile systems-on-a-chip, to make their 32-bit and 64-bit processors. From these architectures, we have gotten single, dual, tri, quad, hexa core CPUs.

Table 1.4 | A list of the major hardware platforms

Platform	Manufacturer
x86 (32-bit), x64 (64-bit)	Intel
x64 (64-bit)	AMD
ARMv8-A (32/64-bit), ARMv8-R (32-bit)	ARM

Other companies like Qualcomm, Apple, Samsung, Huawei and Mediatek acquire license from ARM in order to make their processors meaning they have to be ARM compatible in order to work.

32-bit vs 64-bit Processor
- Bit is the smallest unit of computer memory. It can be 0 or 1, at any given time. So a 32-bit processor can deal with a sequence like. xxxxxxxx xxxxxxxx xxxxxxxx xxxxxxxx where x can be 0 or 1. Similarly a 64-bit processor can deal with a sequence like: xxxxxxxx xxxxxxxx xxxxxxxx xxxxxxxx xxxxxxx xxxxxxxx xxxxxxx xxxxxxx.
- The architecture of a CPU refers to :
  - The CPU instruction set - how much binary or number of calculations the processor can process per second. 64-bit systems can be much faster and more efficient than 32-bit computers running at the same speed because they can do more at once.
  - The Memory bus - a memory bus carries data between the central processing unit (CPU) and a system memory (or RAM) for calculation. 64-bit systems can carries more data than 32-bit computers running at the same speed.
- Memory Addressing
  - A 32-bit CPU can address only up to 4 GB of memory (RAM).
  - A 64-bit CPU, on the other hand, can theoretically address up to 16 Exabytes (that is, 16 billion gigabytes).
- Operating Systems and Programs
  - A computer with a 64-bit processor can have a 64-bit or 32-bit version of an operating system installed.
  - However, with a 32-bit operating system, the 64-bit processor would not run at its full capability.
  - Many 64-bit programs will work with a 64-bit processor and operating system.

In general, when you increase the number of bits you have some benefits. More bits means that a larger amount of data can be processed in the same time interval. It also means a system can addresses a larger number of locations in physical memory.

So to run a 64-bit operating system you need support from the lower level: the 64-bit CPU. To run a 64-bit application you need support from all lower levels:

the 64-bit OS and the 64-bit CPU. The table below describes the combination and compatibility of 32-bit and 64-bit platforms.

Table 1.5 | Combination and compatibility of 32-bit and 64-bit platforms

CPU (bit)	Operating System	Application	Compatibility
32	32	32	OK
32	32	64	NO
32	64	32	NO
32	64	64	NO
64	64	64	OK
64	64	32	OK
64	32	32	OK
64	32	64	NO

So the newer 64-bit systems are backward-compatible with the 32-bit system.

Software platform

A software platform is computer software on which application programs can run. On personal computers, Windows and Linux are examples of two different platforms.

A software may be considered a platform when it is used as a base for other programs. For example:

› Operating system platforms: Windows, Macintosh, OS/2, and Linux.
› Software framework platforms: .NET Framework, Flash Player (AIR), SQL, and Java Platform (Java ME, Java SE, Java EE).

Since Java has its own Runtime Environment (JRE) it is called **platform**.

The Java Platforms

Java is a programming language and a development platform that helps user to run and develop Java applications. Java platform is a collection of tools that help to develop and run programs, and also help developers work efficiently. There are three platforms of the Java programming language as shown in the following table.

Table 1.6 | Java Platforms

Java Platform	Description
Java Standard Edition (Java SE)	Provides all the essential software tools necessary for writing java applications.
Java Enterprise Edition (Java EE)	Is build on top of the Java SE platform. It provides tools for creating large business applications that employ servers and provide services over the web.
Java Micro Edition (Java ME)	Provides a small highly optimized run-time environment for consumer products such as cell phones, pagers, and appliances.

All Java platforms consist of two essential pieces of software:

> the Java Runtime Environment (JRE), which provides the Libraries, JVM, and other components to you to run applications written in Java language.; and

> the Java Development Kit (JDK), which is needed to develop those Java applications. The JDK comes equipped with a JRE as well. So, for all the purpose of this book, you would only require the JDK.

In this section, we will explore the further detail what these two software components of the Java platform do.

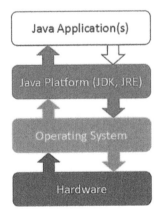

Figure 1.16 | Java Platform

Java Development Kit (JDK)

The Java Development Kit (JDK) is a software development environment used for developing Java applications. It includes the Java Runtime Environment (JRE), plus development tools such as compiler, debugger and other tools that are necessary for developing Java applications.

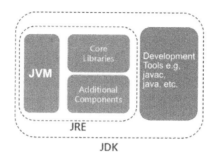

Figure 1.17 | Java Development Kit (JDK)

The Java compiler

The Java compiler tool (named javac in the JDK) is the most important utility found with the JDK. It converts the Java source code (.java) to Java bytecode (.class).

Figure 1.18 | Java Compiler

Java class libraries (JCL)

JCL provide the programmer with a well-known set of standard class libraries containing much of the same reusable functions, such as save data into the database or performing complex number. It's the full featured Software Development Kit to create and compile programs.

Java Runtime Environment (JRE)

Java Runtime Environment (JRE) is part of the Java Development Kit (JDK). It includes the JVM (which actually executes Java programs), core libraries or classes, other additional components to run applications written in java.

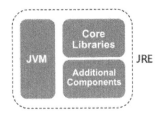

Figure 1.19 | Java Runtime Environment (JRE)

The JRE provides the minimum requirements for executing a Java application. When you only care about running Java programs on your computer you will only install JRE. The JRE does not contain tools and utilities such as compilers or debuggers for developing Java applications.

The JRE acts as a liaison between the underlying platform and that application. It interprets the Java application to run in accordance with the underlying platform, such that upon running the application, it looks and behaves like a native application. The part of the JRE that accomplishes this complex liaison agreement is called the Java Virtual Machine (JVM). Java applications can be Written Once and Run Anywhere. This feature of the Java platform is commonly abbreviated to **WORA** in format Java texts.

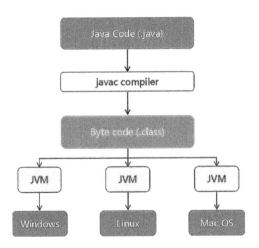

Figure 1.20 | JAVA Program Execution

Java Virtual Machine (JVM)

Java Virtual Machine (JVM) is inbuilt in both JDK and JRE. Whatever java program you using using JRE or JDK goes into JVM and JVM is responsible for executing the java program. The JVM acts like a virtual processor, enabling Java applications to be run on the local system. Its main purpose is to execute the byte code generated by compiler and produce output.

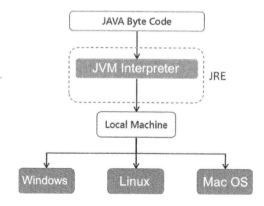

Figure 1.21 | JVM Interpreter

Each operating system has different JVM, however the output they produce after execution of bytecode is same across all operating systems, which means that the bytecode generated on Windows can be run on Linux and vise versa. The JVM is ported to different platforms to provide hardware-and-software-independence.

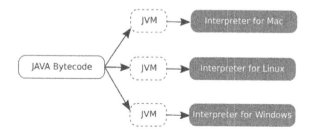

That is why we call Java as platform independent language.

Just-in-Time Compilation[1]

The Just-In-Time (JIT) compiler is a component of the JRE. The JIT compiler improves the performance of Java applications at run time.

During interpretation, a Java application performs more slowly than a native application. The JIT compiler helps improve the performance of Java programs by compiling (not interpreting) bytecodes into machine code at run time. A JIT compiler runs after the program has started and compiles the bytecode on the fly (or just-in-time) into a form that's usually faster, typically the host CPU's native instruction set.

---

[1] http://www.ibm.com/support/knowledgecenter/SSYKE2_8.0.0/com.ibm.java.win.80.doc/diag/understanding/jit_overview.html

When a program has been compiled, the JVM call the compiled code of that method directly instead of interpreting it. Instead of interpreting byte-code, it down-right converts the code straight into equivalent native code for the local system.

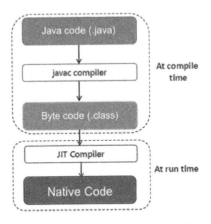

Figure 1.22 | Just-In-Time Compilation

The JIT compiler helps improve the performance of Java programs by compiling bytecodes into native machine code at runtime. When a method has been compiled, the JVM calls the compiled code at that method directly instead of interpreting it. The JIT compilation threshold helps the JVM starts quickly and still have improved performance.

JDK > JRE > JVM

> JRE and JDK are platform dependent because configuration of each OS differs, but Java source code is platform independent. It's allow Java to be a "portable language" (Write Once, Run Anywhere) WORA.
> JDK = JRE + Development Tool
> JRE = JVM + Library Classes

Installing The JDK 10 On Windows 10

In this section we will learn how to download and install Java on Windows 10. Before installing the JDK on your Windows platform, you must verify that it meets the following minimum processor, disk space, and memory requirements.

- Processor: Pentium 2 - 266 MHz (64-bit)
- Free hard disk space: 555 MB
- Memory (RAM): 128

Windows 10 system requirements

- Processor: 1 GHz or faster
- Memory (RAM): 1 GB (32-bit) or 2 GB (64-bit)
- Free hard disk space: 16 GB
- Graphics card: Microsoft DirectX 9 graphics device with WDDM driver

Until unless your Windows 10 environment is setup properly, you will not be able to develop java programs and run them successfully. Setting up Java on Windows 10 is really easy. Just follow the steps as follows:

Step 1: Java download for Windows 10

First step is to download Java installation files from Oracle's website. Java 10 is the latest version, so go to *http://www.oracle.com/technetwork/java/javase/downloads/jdk10-downloads-4416644.html* and accept the license agreement. Then click on the download link for windows as shown in the below image, and save the file.

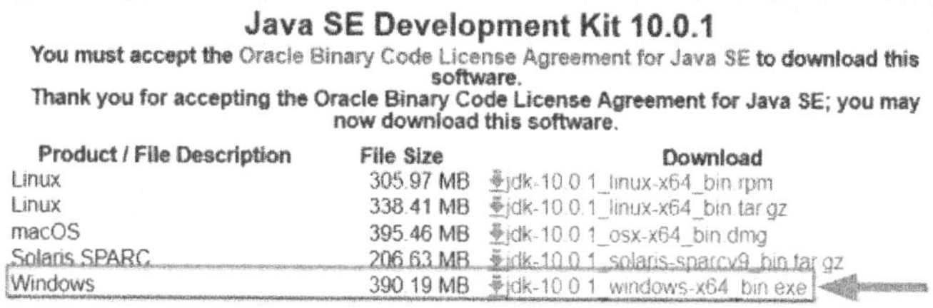
Java SE Development Kit 10.0.1

You must accept the Oracle Binary Code License Agreement for Java SE to download this software.

Thank you for accepting the Oracle Binary Code License Agreement for Java SE; you may now download this software.

Product / File Description	File Size	Download
Linux	305.97 MB	jdk-10.0.1_linux-x64_bin.rpm
Linux	338.41 MB	jdk-10.0.1_linux-x64_bin.tar.gz
macOS	395.46 MB	jdk-10.0.1_osx-x64_bin.dmg
Solaris SPARC	206.63 MB	jdk-10.0.1_solaris-sparcv9_bin.tar.gz
Windows	390.19 MB	jdk-10.0.1_windows-x64_bin.exe

Figure 1.23 | Java SE Development Kit 10 Downloads Page

NOTE: This version of JDK supports only Windows 64-bit operating system. If your Windows 10 is 32 bit OS then download Java 8 or earlier (Windows x86 file for 32-bit and Windows x64 file for 64-bit).

If you are not sure of your Windows version, you can easily check it in **Setting** > **System Settings** > **About**.

Figure 1.24 | Device Specifications Windows

Step 2: Java 10 Installation steps

Next step is to run the downloaded java installer file. Just double click on it and follow the steps. Below are images from my installation screens. They might differ little bit based on your java version installation but mostly it's same as usual.

Allow the application to make changes to your computer. Click **Next**.

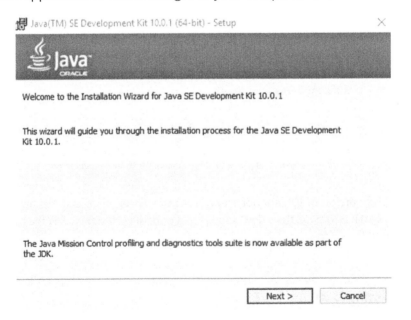

Figure 1.25 | JDK Welcome Screen

By default the JDK will installed in directory `C:\Program Files\Java\jdk-10.0.1\"`. Click **Next** to accept the default installation setting.

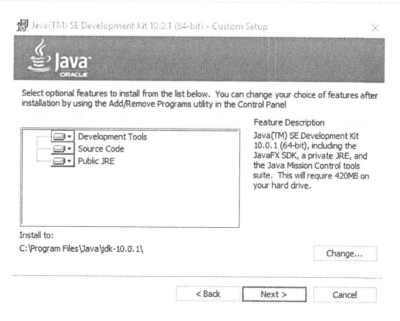

Figure 1.26 | JDK - Custom Setup screen

By default the JRE will be installed in directory `C:\Program Files\Java\jre10.0.1.`(for 64-bit OS and Java10) and `C:\Program Files (x86)\Java\jre1.8.0_144` (for 32-bit OS and Java 8). Click **Next** to accept the default installation folder for JRE.

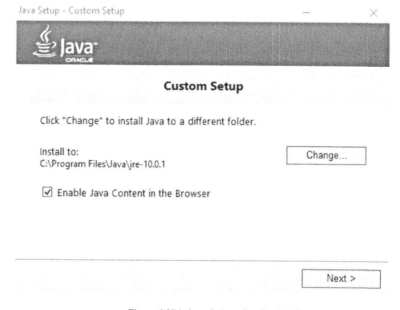

Figure 1.27 | Java Setup - Destination Folder

Click **Close** button when the installation is complete.

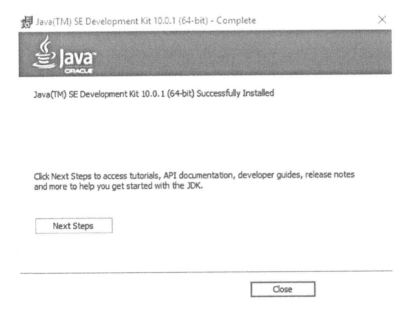

Figure 1.28 | JDK - Complete installation screen

Check the JDK installed directory using File Explorer. Take a note of your JDK installed directory which you will need in the next step.

Step 3: Check Java version on Windows 10

Finally, we have to check if Java is installed property or not. We can do that by using `java -version` command in command prompt, as shown in below image.

```
Microsoft Windows [Version 10.0.17134.48]
(c) 2018 Microsoft Corporation. All rights reserved.

C:\Users\Mohammed>java -version
java version "10.0.1" 2018-04-17
Java(TM) SE Runtime Environment 18.3 (build 10.0.1+10)
Java HotSpot(TM) 64-Bit Server VM 18.3 (build 10.0.1+10, mixed mode)
```

Step 4: Setting up the environment variables for Java

After installing Java on Windows 10, you may still need to do some configuration to get Java ready for compiling and executing Java program. The following instruction will guide you through the process of setting up JDK for software development (Include JDK's "bin" directory in the PATH).

Windows shell searches the current directory and the directories listed in the PATH environment variable (System Variable) for executable programs. JDK's programs (such as Java compiler `javac.exe` and Java runtime `java.exe`) reside in directory "<JAVA_HOME>\bin" (where <JAVA_HOME> denotes the JDK installed directory). You need to include "<JAVA_HOME>\bin" in the PATH to run the JDK programs. To edit the PATH environment variable in Windows 10, do the following steps:

› Launch **Control Panel** > (optional) System and Security > **System** > Click **Advanced System Settings** on the left pane.
› Switch to **Advanced** tab > Push **Environment Variables** button.
› Under **System Variables** scroll down to select **Path** > Click **Edit**.
› Click **New** > Enter the JDK's binary directory `"C:\Program Files\Java\jdk-10.0.1\bin"` *(Replace 10.0.1 with your installation number)* > Select **Move UP** to move this entry all the way to the TOP as shown the following image.

NOTE: Starting from JDK 1.8, the installer created a directory `"C:\ProgramData\Oracle\Java\javapath"` and added to the PATH. It contains only JRE executables (`java.exe, javaw.exe, javaws.exe`) but not the JDK executables.

› Launch a **CMD** shell (**Start** button > **Windows System** > **Command Prompt**) and issue the following commands to verify that JDK/JRE are property installed and display their version.

```
Microsoft Windows [Version 10.0.17134.48]
(c) 2018 Microsoft Corporation. All rights reserved.

C:\Users\Mohammed>java -version
java version "10.0.1" 2018-04-17
Java(TM) SE Runtime Environment 18.3 (build 10.0.1+10)
Java HotSpot(TM) 64-Bit Server VM 18.3 (build 10.0.1+10, mixed mode)

C:\Users\Mohammed>javac -version
javac 10.0.1

C:\Users\Mohammed>
```

```
C:\Users\Mohammed>java -version    //check your JRE version
C:\Users\Mohammed>javac -version   //check your java compiler
(JDK) version
```

Step 5: Download and install IntelliJ IDEA IDE on Windows 10

An integrated development environment (IDE) is a software that provides the basic tools computer developers need to write and test Java programs. Typically, an IDE contains a source code editor, a compiler and/or interpreter and a debugger. From the IntelliJ IDEA you can invoke the JDK compiler/runtime directly. Popular IDE tools include IntelliJ, Visual Studio, Eclipse and NetBeans.

In this book, we are going to use the IntelliJ IDEA IDE to build our Java programs. IntelliJ IDEA is one of the most popular IDEs for Java development. It was developed by JetBrains, and is available in community and ultimate edition. And for this book we are going to use community edition.

To install IntelliJ IDEA, do the following steps:

Download the IntelliJ IDEA IDE Community Edition From *https://www.jetbrains.com/idea/download/#section=windows*

Figure 1.29 | IntelliJ IDEA Download Web site

Run the IntelliJ IDEA Installer file. Click **Next**.

Figure 1.30 | IntelliJ IDEA Community Edition Setup screen

Choose default install location. Click **Next**.

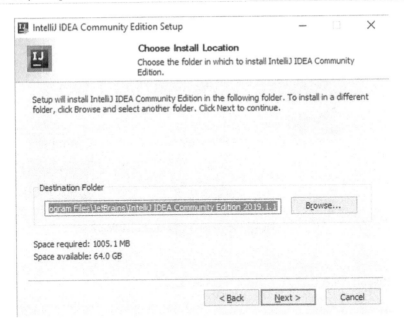

Figure 1.31 | IntelliJ IDEA Install location screen

Choose **32-bit/or 64-bit launcher** under **Create Desktop Shortcut** section, and check **add launchers dir to the PATH** under the **Update PATH variable section**, and check **java** under **Create associations** section. Click **Next**.

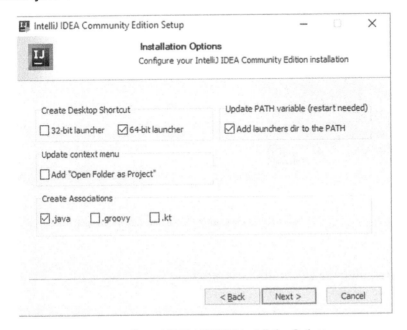

Figure 1.32 | IntelliJ IDEA Installation Options

Click **Install**. Wait while IntelliJ IDEA Community Edition is being installed.

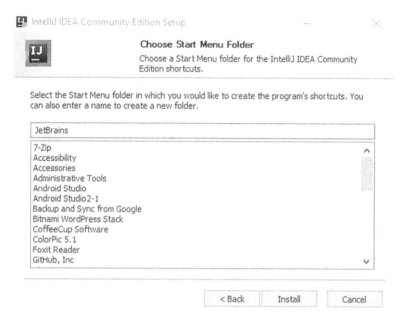

Check **Reboot now** checkbox and click **Finish**.

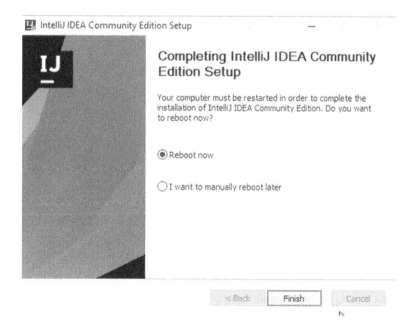

Figure 1.33 | IntelliJ IDEA Complete Installation screen

Run the **IntelliJ IDEA**. Leave the default chosen for importing (again unless you do have files) and click **OK** button.

Figure 1.34 | IntelliJ IDEA - Import Settings screen

Read and accept the terms and conditions. Click **Accept**.

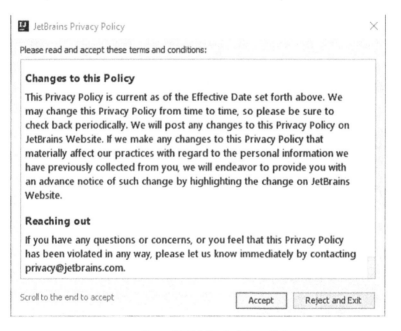

Figure 1.35 | JetBrain Privacy Policy

Choose **IntelliJ** UI theme and click **Next:Default plugins** button.

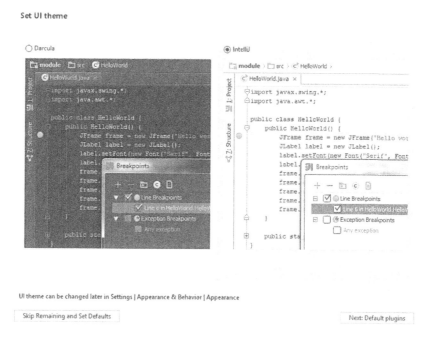

Figure 1.36 | Customizing IntelliJ IDEA window

Click **Skip Remaining and Set Defaults** button. And finally if you get warned about Firewall access. Choose **Allow Access**.

After you have completed initial IntelliJ IDEA configuration, the **Welcome** screen opens that allows you to open an existing project, create a new project, or checkout a project from a version control system, as shown in the following picture.

That's all. In the next chapter, we will learn how to create a new Java project using IntelliJ IDEA.

Summary

- A computer is an electronic device that takes input, processes it, and converts it into meaningful information.
- Data usually refers to raw data. It may be in the form of numbers, letters, or a set of characters.
- Information is a sequence of symbols that can be interpreted as a message.
- Hardware refers to the physical components that a computer is made of.
- Input device is a hardware used to send signals or data to a computer.
- Output device is any device used to send data from a computer to another device or user.
- Processor executes instructions or machine code of a program.
- Main memory is the storage device that holds the program instructions as long as the program being processed by the CPU.
- Secondary memory hold saved data when power is turned off .

- A software is a set of instructions that the computer (CPU) executes one after another.
- System software is a set of programs that manages the computer's hardware devices and other software.
- Application software refers to programs that make the computer useful to the user.
- A programming languages is a special language programmers use to write computer programs.
- A machine language program is made up of a series of binary digits.
- The assembly language instructions are replaced binary digits with mnemonics short English-like words that represent commands or data.
- High level language is expressed in English-like phrases, and it is easier to read and write.
- A high level language program must be translated into machine language in order to be executed. This translation is accomplished by either a compiler or an interpreter.
- Java language use both compiler and interpreter. Compiler translates the Java source code into *Byte code*, which is executed by JRE. The JRE interprets the Java Byte Code into *Machine Code*.
- Java is a general purpose, high-level programming language.
- A platform is a hardware and/or software environment - that serves as a foundation or base- in which a program runs.
- Some software is platform-specific, means it run on one platform -- Windows or Mac.
- Software can also be cross-platform, which means the software intended to be executed on more than one platform -- Windows, Mac OS X, and Linux.
- A hardware platform refers to only a CPU model or computer family. A hardware platform is a set of compatible hardware (processor and associated hardware pieces) on which software applications can be run.
- A software may be considered a platform when it is used as a base for other programs.
- The Java platform is the name given to the computing platform from Oracle that helps users to run and develop Java applications.
- There are three platforms of the Java Programming language: Java Standard Edition (Java SE), Java Enterprise Edition (Java EE), and Java Micro Edition (Java ME).

- Oracle provides two principle software in Java platform, Java Standard Edition (Java SE) family:
    - The Java Runtime Environment (JRE). Provides the libraries, JVM, and other components.
    - The Java Development Kit (JDK), which is needed to develop those Java applications. The JDK comes equipped with a JRE as well.
- Java Runtime Environment (JRE) includes the JVM (Which actually executes Java Programs), Core libraries, Other additional components to run applications written in java.
- The JRE provides the minimum requirements for executing a Java application.
- The JVM acts like a virtual processor, enabling Java applications to be run on the local system. Its main purpose is to interpret the received byte-code and make it appear as native code.
- The Just-In-Time (JIT) compiler is a component of the JRE. It improves the performance of Java applications at run time.
- The Java Development Kit (JDK) is a software development environment used for developing Java applications. It includes the Java Runtime Environment (JRE) plus development tools such as interpreters, compiler, debugger and other tools that are necessary for developing Java applications.
- The Java compiler tool (named javac in the JDK) converts the Java source code (.java) to Java bytecode (.class).
- JVM, JRE and JDK are platform dependent because configuration of each OS differs, but Java source code is platform independent. It's allow Java to be a "portable language" (Write Once, Run Anywhere) WORA.

Chapter 2

Java First Steps

Phases of Program Creation and Execution

During the creation and execution of a Java program, programs normally go through four phases. Phases do not necessarily happen in a sequential order. For example, when writing a program, a programmer may need to repeatedly edit and compile it to ensure sufficient quality before it can be distributed to end users. The execution phases of Java program are:

Phase 1: Edit

Editing or writing a Java program involves the following steps:

- Creating a Java program (a.k.a. source code) using an editor or an IDE (Integrated Development Environment) program, such as IntelliJ IDEA.
- Java source code files are saved with the file extension (**.java**)

Phase 2: Compile

- The Java source code is translated into bytecodes using the Java Compiler (**javac**)
- bytecode file is end with (**.class**) extension.
- Running the Java compiler would compile the Java source file (.java extension), and generate a bytecode class file (.class extension).

Java Byte code is the same on all computers (Highly portable). Portability means the program may be written on one type of computer then run on a wide variety of computers, with little or no modification necessary. A compiled Java program may be run on any computer that has a JVM or JRE.

Phase 3: Execute

> The JVM executes a programs bytecodes, performing the actions specified by the program.
> The JVM execute bytecode using combination of interpretation and what is called "Just-in-Time" compilation.
> Using JIT compilation the JVM analyzes the bytecodes as they are interpreted, and searches for parts of the bytecode that execute frequently. For these parts, a JIT compiler translates the bytecodes into the underlying computer's machine language. When the JVM encounters the compiled parts again, the faster machine language code executes.
> This means that Java programs actually go through two compilation phases, one in which source code is translated to bytecodes (for portability across JVMs) and second, during execution, the bytecodes are translated into machine language for the actual computer on which the program executes.

Phase 4: Debug

> Debug your program (if necessary) and then return to Edit Phase.

IntelliJ IDEA supports editing, compiling, executing and debugging for Java language.

Creating Your First Java Program

It's time to write your first application. In this section, you will create a new Java project using IntelliJ IDEA IDE. The IntelliJ runs on the Java platform, which means that you can use it with any operating system form which there is a JDK available. These operating systems include Microsoft Windows, Linux, and Mac OS X. Any new development starts with creating a project. So let's create one now.

Create a new Java project using IntelliJ IDEA IDE

When you create an IntelliJ IDE project, you create an environment in which to build and run your applications. IDE stands for Integrated Development Environment. In other words IntelliJ IDEA is powerful and advanced text editor with a lot of plug-ins and tools. With IntelliJ you can build your application much faster and execute them with a push of a button. The process of building and executing a Java project involves the following steps:

First: Create a Java Project

› If no project is currently open, click **Create New Project** on the Welcome screen. Otherwise, select **File > New > Project**. This opens the **New Project** dialog box.

› In the left-hand pane, select the project type as **Java.** Then Specify the JDK that you want to use in your project (the **Project SDK** field). Select the JDK from the list. If the desired JDK is already available on your computer (e.g., `C:\Program Files\Java\jdk-10.0.1`) but is missing from the list, click **New** and, in the dialog that opens, select the JDK installation folder. Don't select any of the options under **Additional Libraries and Frameworks**.

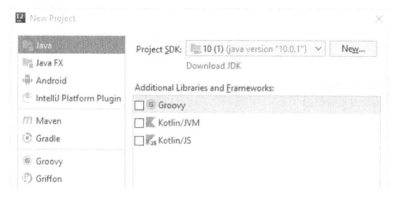

Click **Next**.

› The options on the next page have to do with creating a Java class with a `main()` method. Since we are going to study the very basics of IntelliJ IDEA, and do everything from scratch, we don't need these options at the moment. So, don't select any of the options.

Click **Next**.

› Specify the project name (e.g. **JavaPro1**) beside the Project name text box. If necessary, change the project location suggested by IntelliJ IDE.

Click **Finish**.

› Wait while IntelliJ IDEA is creating the project. When this process is complete, the structure of your new project is shown in the **Project** tool window.

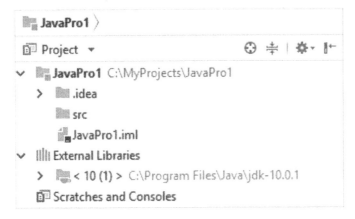

Second: Create a Java Package

Package in Java is a way to organize a set of related code (classes and interfaces) in a single place. The classes in the Java are organized into packages. To manage the large number of classes, packages are used to keep things organized by grouping related classes and interfaces. So let's create a new package named **basics**.

› In the **Project** tool window, right click the **src** folder and select **New > Package**.

At the top you see a directory called "**src**". This is the source root directory. It is not a Java package itself. Inside this directory, all subdirectories correspond to Java packages.

> In the **New Package** dialog that opens, type **basics** in the Name filed, and press enter to create the package. The package **basics** is shown in the **Project** tool window.

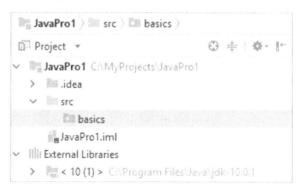

Now we have a directory **basics**, which is a package:

`C:\MyProjects\JavaPro1\src\basics`

Third: Create a Java Class

Every thing in Java has to be part of a **class**. Each class is designed for a specific purpose, and you can use the classes in your own programs. So let the class name be **Welcome**.

> In the **Project** tool window, right click the **basics** package folder and select **New** > **Java Class**.
> In the **Create New Class** dialog that opens, type **Welcome** in the Name filed and press Enter to create the class. The class `Welcome` is shown in the Project tool window.

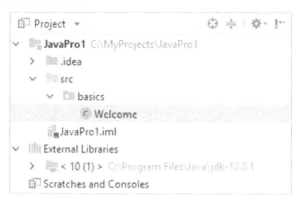

At the same time, the file `Welcome.java` (corresponding to the class) opens in the editor.

```
 Welcome.java
1    package basics;
2
3    public class Welcome {
4    }
5
```

NOTE: When you created the `Welcome.java` file inside the **basics** package, IntelliJ IDEA IDE puts the statement `package basics;` at the top of your `Welcome.java` program. This statement should be used in the beginning of the program to include that program in that particular package. Every class in Java belongs to a package. Package declaration must be the first line in Java source file. At most one package declaration can appear in a source file even before import statement. You can create more than one package in a project.

Forth: Write a Java Program

To demonstrate compilation and execution of a Java program, type the following code inside the `Welcome.java` file.

```java
package basics;
public class Welcome {
    public static void main(String[] args){
        System.out.println("Welcome");
    }
}
```

NOTES: While writing `Welcome` program we must keep in mind that the file name and the name of the class that contains `main` method must be identical. A file can contain only one `public class` at a time; therefore, if a file contains more than one class, the only class can be declared `public` at a time.

Fifth: Compile Java Program

Once the Java program is written and saved, first it has to be compiled. To compile a Java program from IntelliJ IDEA, right click the `Welcome.java` file and select **Build Module JavaPro1**.

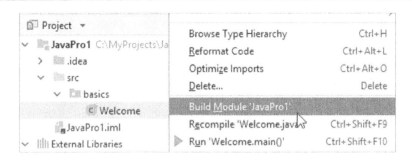

The **javac** compiler creates a file called `Welcome.class` under the "`C:\MyProjects\JavaPro1\out\production\JavaPro1\basics`" directory, that contains the bytecode version of the program, as shown in the following image:

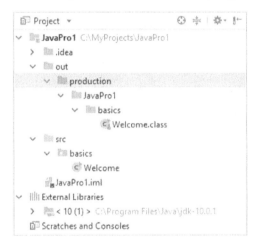

Sixth: Run Java Program

After compilation of `Welcome.java` to `Welcome.class`, we use the Java interpreter, called **java** to run the program. To do so, right click the `Welcome.java` and select "**Run Welcome.main( )**".

The message Welcome will be printed on the screen as a result of the above command.

Exploring the project structure

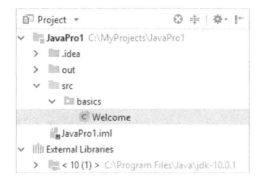

Let's take a quick look at the project structure. There are two top-level nodes, the **JavaPro1** node and the **External Libraries** node:

› The **JavaPro1** node
- This node represents your Java project.
- The **src** folder: This is the location where you will create your Java files such as packages and classes.
- The **.idea** folder: This location is used to store your general information about your workspace. You should not place any of your application files in this folder as it is managed by IntelliJ IDEA.
- The **JavaPro1.iml** file: Is used to store configuration data for your project and module respectively.
- The **out** folder: This location contains the output of your project when you build/compile it (i.e. contains `.class` files).

› The **External Libraries** node
- This is a category that represents all the "external" resources necessary for your development work.

- Currently in this category are the .jar files that make up your JDK.

Package name and the file system directory

Java expects a one-to-one mapping of the package name and the file system directory structure. For example, if we have a package called `basics`, we should have a directory called **basics**, and if we create a class `Welcome` in a package called `basics`; then it will reside under directory **basics** in the source tree (`src/basics`). If we use IntelliJ IDEA, the corresponding directories are automatically created.

Example 2.1: if you create a class `Welcome` in a package called `basics`; then it will reside under directory `basics` in the source tree (`src/basics`), as shown in the following image:

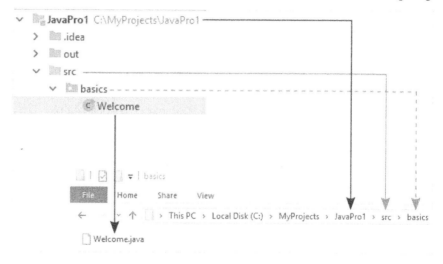

Figure 2.1 | IntelliJ IDEA Directory Structure

Explanation of Your First Java Program (`Welcome.java`)

In this section, we will explain your first Java program `welcome.java` step by step. `Welcome.java` is the name of Java Source code file.

```
01  package basics;
02  public class Welcome {
03      public static void main(String[] args){
04          System.out.println("Welcome");
05      }
```

```
06 }
```

Explanation

Line 01: `Package basics`

> This statement should be used in the beginning of the program to include that program in that particular package. Every class in Java must belong to a package.

Line 02: `public class Welcome`

> This line is known as **class header**. Class header comprised of three words: `public`, `class`, & `<ClassName>`. Class header marks the beginning of a class definition or creation. In Java, everything we're going to be writing is going to be inside a class. Java program must have at least one class definition.

> `public` keyword is an access modifier which represents visibility. It controls where the class may be accessed from. The `public` specifier means access to the class is unrestricted (the class is open to the public). It must be written in all lowercase letters.

> `class` keyword is a Java Keyword (see the next chapter) that used to declare a class in a Java. It indicates the beginning of a class definition or just class. It must be written in lowercase letters.

> `Welcome or any name` is the class name. This name is made up by the programmer. It may be written in lowercase letters, uppercase letters, or a mixture of both.

> `{ and }`: Left brace or an opening brace ({) is associated with the beginning of the class. Right brace or a closing brace (}) is associated with the closing of the class. All of the statements that are part of the class are enclosed in a set of braces. Everything between the braces is the body of the class name `Welcome`.

Line 03: `public static void main(String[ ] args)`

> This line is known as **method header**. Method header marks the beginning of a method definition. Method serve as a starting point for an application. A Java program must have at least one `main` method. The first thing your computer does when it runs a Java program is it looks for a method called `main`, and if it doesn't find the method `main`, it will not start. A method can be thought of a group of one or more statements that collectively has a name.

> `main`: The first thing we're going to make or build inside a class is a method called `main`.

- `public static void`: are required for the method to be properly defined (more in next chapters).
- `(String[ ] args)` is used for command line argument (more details on chapter 6).
- `{ and }`: Opening brace (`{`) is associated with the beginning of the main method. Closing brace (`}`) is associated with the closing of the main method. Everything between these braces is the body of the `main` method. Every Java Application must have a method named `main`. The `main` method is the starting point of an application.

Line 04: `System.out.println("Welcome");`
- This line displays a message on the screen. The group of characters inside the quotation marks is called a **"string literal"**. This is the only line in the program that causes anything to be printed on the screen.
- Semicolon `(;)` marks the end of a sentence in Java. Not every line of code ends with a semicolon.
- `"  and  "` is called quotation marks. It encloses a string of characters, such as a message that is to be printed on the screen.
- `System.out.println()` is used to print statement on the screen.
- `Opening and Closing parentheses ( and )`: Used in a method header.

Key concepts

- Java is a case sensitive language (car != Car != CAR).
- All java programs must be stored in a file with the name that ends with `.java` extension.
- A `.java` file may contain many classes, but may only have one `public` class.
- If `.java` file has a `public` class, the class must have the same name as the file.
- Every Java Application program must have a method named `main`.
- For every left brace, there must be a corresponding right brace.
- Statements are terminated with semicolons. This does not include comments, class headers, method headers, or braces.

Creating Your Second Java Program

Here is a simple example that will create multiple lines using `println()` method

Example 2.2: Welcome2.java - Displaying multiple lines Using `System.out.println()` method

> Right click the **basics** package and select **New** > **Java Class**. Type `Welcome2` in the Name field, and press enter to create the class.
> Open the `Welcome2.java` file and type the following code inside it:

```
01  public class Welcome2
02  {
03      public static void main(String args[])
04      {
05          System.out.println("Welcome to ");
06          System.out.println("Java!.");
07      }
08  }
```

Output

```
Welcome to
Java!.
```

Understanding your second Java program

Lines 05 & 06

> This lines displays a message on the screen (Console).
> The group of characters inside the quotation marks is called a "**string literal**".
> These are the only two lines in the program that causes anything to be printed on the screen.
> Line 05 Executes the method `println()` which displays the message `"Welcome to "` and then throws the cursor to the next line.
> Line 06 Executes the method `println()` which displays the message `"Java!."` and then throws the cursor to the next line.

Semicolon (;)

> Marks the end of a statement in Java.
> Not every line of code ends with a semicolon.

`"Welcome to"` **String**

- › `" "` is called quotation marks. It encloses a string of characters, such as a message that is to be printed on the screen.
- › `System.out.println()` is used print statement. We will learn about the internal working of `System.out.println` statement later.
- › `main` represents start-up of the program.
- › `String[] args` is used for command line argument (we will discuss in more detail later.)

Packages in Java

Package in Java acts as "container" for Java classes, interfaces, and sub-packages (package inside the package). It is a way of grouping related classes, interfaces, and sub-packages together.

The main purpose of the packages:

- › Packages allow us to use other people's code.
- › Packages prevent naming conflicts. It save name clashes with other people. For examples, there can be two classes with name `Student` in two packages, `Course` and `Gym`.
- › Packages provide control access (or security) to the classes and interfaces. So that outside program can't access to classes and interfaces directly.
- › Package can be considered as data encapsulation (or data-hiding). Packages provide a way of "hide" classes thus preventing other programs or packages from accessing classes that are meant for internal use only.

All we need to do is put related classes into packages. After that we can simply import a class from an existing package and use it in our program. We can reuse existing classes from the packages as many time as we need it in our program.

Categories of Java packages

Package in java can be categorized in two forms:

1: User defined packages

The package we created is called user-defined package (e.g., **basics** package under the **Java Pro1** project).

2: Built-in packages

Built-in packages are those which are developed by Oracle and supplied as a part of JDK to simplify the task of java programmers. JDK provides a large number of classes grouped into different packages according to functionality.

Some of the commonly used built-in packages are shown in the table below:

Table 2.1: Some of commonly used built-in packages

Package	Sub-Package	Description
java	lang	`java.lang` package is automatically imported in all java programs. It contains language support classes (e.g. classes which defines primitive data types, exceptions, math operations). These are classes that java compiler itself uses.
java	util	`java.util` package contains language utility classes which implements data structure such as vectors, hash, tables, date etc.
java	io	`java.io` package contains classes for supporting input/output operations.
java	awt	`java.awt` package contains set of classes for implementing Graphical user interface. They include classes for windows, buttons, lists, menus, and so on.
javax	swing	`javax.swing` package is used to create Graphical user interfaces. It is built on the top of AWT (Abstract Windowing Toolkit).
javafx	application	The main class for a JavaFX application extends the `javafx.application.Application` class.
javafx	stage	`javafx.stage` is the top level JavaFX container. It contains all the objects of the JavaFX application.

Creating a package

Creating a package in Java is quite easy. Simply include a `package` keyword followed by name of the package as the first statement in Java source file. This must be the first statement in java source file.

Syntax

```
package <packagename>
public class <classname>
{ ... }
```

After that define all the classes, that someone wants to put in that package.

Creating a new package, sub-package, and class using the IntelliJ IDEA

Let the packages and the class names be `course.java` and `HelloWorld` respectively.

> Uncheck "**Hide Empty Middle Packages**" under the **Project View** settings drop-down:

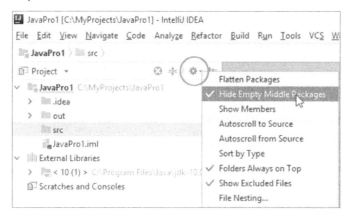

> Create a new Package. in the Project tool window, right click the **src** folder and select **New > Package**.
> In the **New Package** dialog that opens, type **course** in the Name filed, and press enter to create the package.
> In the Project tool window, right click the **course** package and select **New > Package**.
> In the **New Package** dialog that opens, type **java** in the Name filed, and press enter to create the sub-package. The sub-package **java** is shown in the Project tool window.

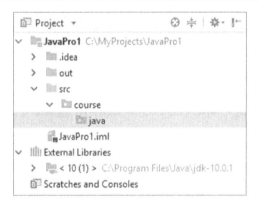

› In the Project tool window, right click the **java** package and select **New > Java Class**.
› In the Create **New Class** dialog that opens, type **HelloWorld** in the Name filed, and press enter to create the class. The class `HelloWorld` is shown in the Project tool window.

A package directive begins with the `package` keyword. An identifier that names a package, `course.java`, immediately follows. If classes are to appear in a sub-package (at some level) within `packageName`, one or more period-separated `sub-packageName` identifiers appear after `packageName`, as shown in the above figure (`course.java.HelloWorld`).

Now we have a directory `C:\MyProjects\JavaPro1\src\course\java`, which is a package.

› Write code for the `HelloWorld` class, as shown in the following code:
```
package course.java;
public class HelloWorld {
    public static void main(String[] args) {
        System.out.println("Hello World");
    }
}
```

› Building and running the application. Classes with a `main()` method can be run right from the editor. To show that, there are the green arrow markers (▶) in the left margin. Click one of the markers and select Run 'HelloWorld.main()'.

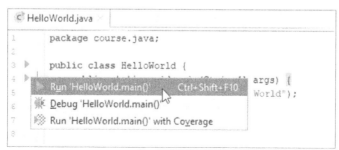

› When the compilation is complete, the **Run** tool window opens at the bottom of the screen.

› And, finally, you see the program output `Hello World` between these lines.

In this example package with **course** name is created. And another sub-package with **java** name under the `course` package is created. `java` package has only one class on its body named `HelloWorld`.

The above steps will create a package with name `course` and sub-package with name `java` in the project directory. Java uses file system directories to store packages. For example the `HelloWorld.java` class for `java` package must be stored in a directory called `java` as shown in the following image.

NOTE: All classes within the package must have the `package` statement as its first line. The packages are organized in a *hierarchical* structure. For example, the package named `course` contain the package `java`, which in turn contains the `HelloWorld`

class. All classes of the package which we wish to access outside the package must be declared `public`. For example:
public class HelloWorld.

How to use a class from a package

`import` keyword is used to import built-in and user-defined packages into your Java source file so that your class can refer to a class that is in another package by directly using its name.

There are three different ways to refer to any class that is present in a different package:

1. Use the fully qualified name of the class (not a good practice)

To import any class into your program, only that particular class of the package will be accessible in your program, other classes in the same package will not be accessible.

No need to use the `import` statement, but you will have to use the fully qualified name every time you are accessing the class. This is generally used when two packages have classes with same names. For example:

```
Hello.java
package course.java;
public class Hello {
    public static void main(String[] args){
        System.out.println("Hello Java");
        course.csharp.Hello.msg();
    }
}

Hello.java
package course.csharp;
public class Hello {
    public static void msg(){
        System.out.println("Hello CSharp");
    }
}
```

You might want to use fully-qualified package names if you have for example, two classes with the same name in different packages. One common example from the standard library are the classes `java.util.Date` and `java.sql.Date`, or `java.util.List` and `java.awt.List`.

2. Use the `import` statement to import only the class or classes you want to use (a.k.a. explicit import statement)

If you import `packagename.classname` then only the class with name `classname` in the package with name `pacakgename` will be available for use. For example:

HelloJava.java
```
package course.java;
import course.csharp.HelloCsharp;
public class HelloJava {
    public static void main(String[] args){
        System.out.println("Hello Java");
        HelloCsharp.msg();
    }
}
```

HelloCsharp.java
```
package course.csharp;
public class HelloCsharp {
    public static void msg(){
        System.out.println("Hello CSharp");
    }
}
```

The `import` statement tells the compiler where to locate the classes. An `import` statement is really just a way to tell the compiler "when I write `HelloCsharp`, I actually mean `course.csharp.HelloCsharp`.

For example, to import the `Scanner` class from the `java.util` package, you use `import java.util.Scanner;`

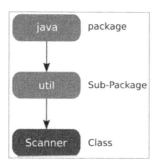

An `import` statement is really just a way to tell the compiler "when I write `Scanner`, I actually mean `java.util.Scanner`".

3. To import all the classes from a particular package (a.k.a. wildcard import statement)

If you use `course.*`, then all the classes of this package will be accessible. But the classes inside the sub packages (such as `java`, or `csharp`) will not be available for use.

The `import` keyword is used to make the classes of another package accessible to the current package. For example, `import java.util.*;`. The `import` statement tells the compiler where to locate the classes.

> **NOTES:** When a package name is not specified, the classes are defined into the default package (the current working directory) and the package itself is given no name. While creating a package, care should be taken that the statement for creating package must be written before any other import statements.
>
> Each package in Java has its unique name. Classes and interfaces with the same name cannot appear in the same package.
>
> Package names are dot separated, e.g., `java.lang`. Package names have a correspondence with directory structure, for example the `lang` is a subdirectory of the `java` directory.
>
> Packages avoid name space collision. There can not be two classes with same name in a same package. But two packages can have a class with same name.
>
> Exact name of the class is identified by its package structure <<Fully Qualified Name>>, For example:
>
>   java.lang.String;
>   java.io.BufferedReader;
>   java.util.Arrays;
>   java.util.Date;
>
> import statement allows the importing of package.

Explicit & wildcard import statements

To use a class from a package, there are two types of import statements:

› Explicit import statement.
› Wildcard import statement.

Explicit import Statement

The explicit import identifies the package location of a single class. For example `import java.util.Scanner;`. Explicit import statement explicitly identifies the location of the `Scanner` class.

For example, `java.util` package contains: `Scanner`, `Random`, and other classes. If the program needs to use `Scanner` and `Random`, it will have to import both of these classes.

```
import java.util.Scanner;
import java.util.Random;
```

Wildcard import Statement

A wildcard import statement tells the compiler to import all of the classes in a package. For example `import java.util.*;` tells the compiler to import all the classes that are part of the `java.util` package.

Wildcard import statement doesn't affect the performance or the size of your program. It merely tells the compiler that you want to make every class in a particular package available to your program.

The best practices and naming conventions for Java packages

Oracle recommends following best practices and naming conventions for Java packages.

> - Packages usually use all lowercase letters.
> - Programmers should use hierarchical structure to define packages and sub-packages, e.g. `java.util`, then `java.util.concurrent`, or `java.util.concurrent.atomic`.
> - If a packages has a hyphen `(-)` in there name, replace them with an underscore `(_)`.

Remember, just like class, you can not have two packages with the same name, but as you can have two classes with the same name in different packages, you can also have the same name of sub-packages inside two different packages. For example:

```
com.xyzschool.student.high.Record
com.xyzschool.stuff.high.Record
```

Conclusion

> - In any Java file there should be only one package statement.
> - In any Java file, the first line should be package statement (if it is available)
> - The proper structure of a Java source file is:

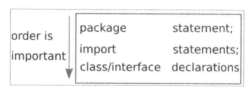

> - An empty source file is a valid Java program.

Java Comments

A Java comment is an explanation in the source code of a computer program which allowing others to better understand what the source code was intended to accomplish and making the source code easier for humans to understand. Comments are part of the program, but Java compiler does not include them in final executable file (.class file). In other words, comments are generally ignored by the Java compiler.

There are three types of Java comments:
1. Single-line Comments
2. Multi-line Comments
3. Documentation Comments

Java's single line and multi-line comments are collectively called **implementation comments**, because they are used to provide additional information that it not available in the code itself.

On the other hand, the documentation comments too inserted into the code but they read by **javadoc** tool in order to generate source code documentation.

Let's start with the single-line comment.

Single-line comments

As the name suggests, it is used to comment out just a single line in the code. It starts with two forward slashes with no white spaces (//) and lasts till the end of line, and can be placed anywhere. It is written usually after termination of statement. The compiler ignores everything written after (not before) the `//` to the end of the line.

Syntax
```
Starts with // (2 forward slashes with no white spaces)
```

Here is a simple two examples showing two different ways of using the single line comment.

Example 2.3: Single line comments on a line by themselves
```
01  public class Welcome
02  {
```

```
    public static void main(String args[])
    {
    // holds the age of the employee.
    int empAge;
    // holds the hours worked
    double hours;
    }
}
```

Example 2.4: Single line comments after termination of statements (at the end of line)
```
public class Welcome
{
    public static void main(String args[])
    {
    int empAge;      // holds the age of the employee.
    double hours;    // holds the hours worked.
    }
}
```

Multi-line comments

Multi-line comment is used to comment out multi-lines in the code. It can be placed anywhere.

Syntax
Start with **/*** *(a forward slash followed by an asterisk)* and end with ***/**.

Everything between these marks is ignored. For example:

Example 2.5: Multi-Line Comment
```
01  /*  Program:       .....................
02      Written by:    ..................
03      This program is:..................
04  */
```

Different ways of using Multiple Line comment

Way 1: Used for program title and documentation.
```
01  /******************************************
02  * Title:   Add Two Numbers
03  * Author:  Mohammed Abdelmoneim
04  ******************************************/
```

Way 2: Used for more detailed comment inside program
```
01  /* Following line is used to get -
02     1. Name of the Customer.
03     2. Return the name of the customer.
04  */
```

Difference between single line and multi-line comment

Table 2.2 | Difference between single line and multi-line comment

Multi-Line Comment	Single-Line Comment
Start with /*	Starts with //
All words and statements written between /* and */ are ignored.	Statement after the symbol // up to the end of the line are ignored.
Comments end when */ occurs.	Comment ends whenever ENTER is pressed and new line starts.
e.g. /* This is Multiple Comment */	e.g. // Single Line Comment

Documentation comment

Javadoc is a tool which comes with JDK and it used for generating Java code documentation in HTML format from **Javadoc** comments in source code. The basic format is a description followed by any number of predefined tags. The description should give a concise summary of the item being commented.

Syntax
```
/** .. */
```

In general, **Javadoc** comment precedes any class, interface, method or field declaration. It must begin with a slash and two stars and it can followed by any number of predefined tags to describe characteristics like methods parameters or return values. The entire comment may contain any valid HTML. Examples of different **Javadoc** comments are listed below.

Normal Javadoc comments

For example, the following simple `Employee` class (`Employee.java`) has several **Javadoc** comments.

```
01  /**
02   * Represents an Employee record in the company.
03   * An Employee can be working in may departments.
04   */
05  public class Employee {
06
07      /**
08       * The first and last name of this employee.
09       */
```

```
       private String empName;
       /**
12      * Creates a new Employee with the given name.
13      * The name should include both first and
14      * last name.
15      */
       public Employee (String name) {
           this.empName = name;
       }
}
```

Using Javadoc Tags

The **Javadoc** tags are used to provide essential information about the code. Each tag has a specific format which we will now look at in the following example.

Example 2.6: `Employee2.java`

```
01  /**
02   * Represents an Employee record in the company.
03   *
04   * @author Mohammed Abdelmoniem
05   * @version 1.0
06   * @since 0.2
07   */
   public class Employee {
09
       /**
11      * The first and last name of this employee.
12      */
       private String empName;
       /**
15      * Creates a new Employee with the given name.
16      * @param name The name of the Employee to accept.
17      */
       public Employee (String name) {
           this.empName = name;
       }
       /**
22      * Gets the name of this Employee.
23      * @return this Employee's name.
24      */
       public String getName (){
           return empName;
       }
       /**
29      * Change the name of this Employee.
30      * This may involve a lengthy process.
31      * @param newName This Employee's new name.
32      *                Should include both first
33      *                and last name.
34      */
       public void setName(String newName){
           empName = newName;
       }
```

```
38    }
```

The table below briefly describes the purpose of the **javadoc** tags used in the sample source code shown above (This table shows the most commonly used Javadoc tags):

Table 2.3 | The most commonly used javadoc tags

Tag	Used Where	Purpose
@author	Interface and Class comments	This tag lets you put the name of the code author into the documentation.
@parameter	Method comments	This tag is used to define parameters that are passed into a method.
@return	Method comments	This tag defines values that are returned from methods.
@version	Interface and Class comments	This tag lets you define the version of the Java code you're developing.
@since	Interface and Class comments	Indicates the version of the source code that this item was introduced.

How It Works

› **Javadoc** comments only have meaning when they appear before a public class, or before public or protected variables and methods.
› The first line in a **javadoc** comment is a summary line.

Generating Documentation Comments for a Project Using IntelliJ IDEA

To generate project documentation

› On the main menu, choose **Tools** > **Generate JavaDoc**. Generate JavaDoc dialog is opened. This dialog invokes JavaDoc utility.
› In the General Java Doc dialog, specify the following options:
  ▪ **Generate JavaDoc scope**. Specify the whole project, files, folders, custom scope for which JavaDoc should be generated.
  ▪ **Include JDK and library sources in -sourcepath**. The paths to the JDK and library sources will be passed to the JavaDoc utility.
  ▪ **Output directory**. Specify the output directory, where the generated documentation will be placed. Click the Browse button to open the Select Path dialog box where you can select the desired location.
  ▪ **Slider**. Specify the visibility level of members to be included in the generated documentation. For example: **Private** means show all classes and members, **Public** means show only public classes and members,

Protected means shows only protected and public classes and members (default). **Package** means shows public, protected and package declarations.
- **Generate hierarchy**. Select it to have the class hierarchy generated.
- **Generate navigator bar**. Select it to have the navigator bar generated.
- **Generate index**. Select it to have the documentation index generated.
- **Separate index per letter**. Select it to have a separate index file for each letter generated.
- **@use**. To have the use of class and package documented.
- **@author**. To have the @author paragraphs included.
- **@version**. To have the @version paragraphs included.
- **@deprecated**. To have the @deprecated information included.
- **@deprecated list**. To have the deprecated list generated.
- **Open generated documentation in browser**. Select it to have the generated JavaDoc automatically opened in the browser.
- **Link to JDK documentation**. If you select it the reference to the classes, packages etc, from JDK will turn into links.

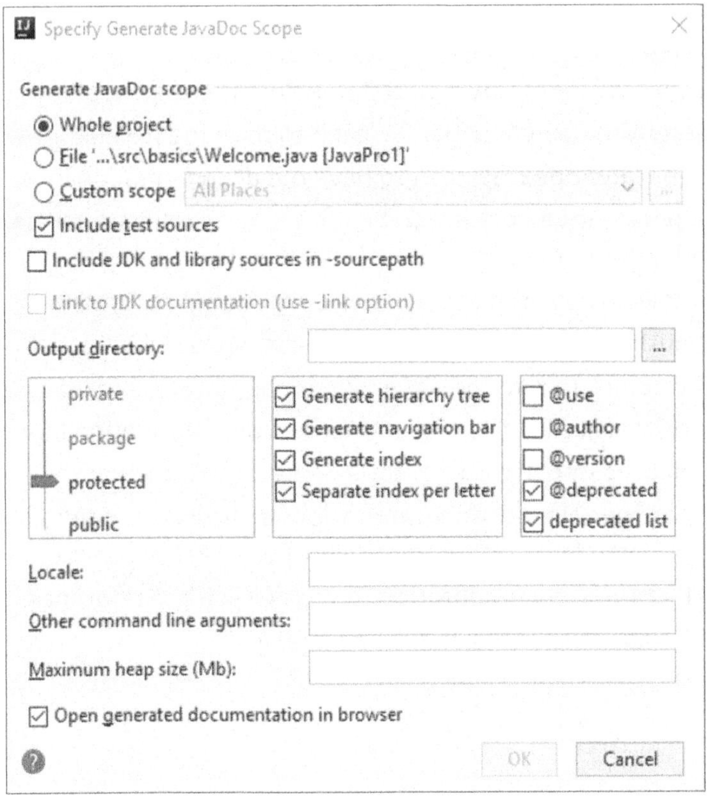

> Click **OK**.

When you do this, **javadoc** generates documentation in HTML format for all of your `public` classes, and your `public` and `protected` methods and variables. Based on the files you submit and the documentation within those files, **javadoc** creates many types of HTML files, as shown below:

Table 2.4 | javadoc documentation file

File	Purpose
basics\Employee.html	There will be one file of this type for each class defined. This file contains the actual documentation for the class.
index-files\index-x.html (where x is the number of file)	This file contains an alphabetical index of the variables (also referred to as fields) and methods you've defined.
basics\package-summary.html	A listing of each package you generated documentation for, and the classes they contain.
basics\package-tree.html	A listing of all the classes you've generated documentation for, and where those classes fit in the class hierarchy.
overview-tree.html	This file listing all packages, plus a hierarchy for each package. Each hierarchy page contains a list of classes and a list of interfaces. The classes are organized by inheritance structure starting with java.lang.Object. The interfaces do not inherit from java.lang.Object.

This table provides brief descriptions of the important files created when the **javadoc** command is run on your Java source files.

I think you'll agree with me after seeing the documentation that **javadoc** creates that, it sure is a lot easier to let **javadoc** do the hard work.

Summary

> During the creation and execution of a Java program, programs normally go through four phases. These are: Edit, Compile, Execute, and Debug.
>   - **Edit** phase: Creating a Java program using an editor or an IDE (.java file).
>   - **Compile** phase: The Java source code is translated into bytecodes using the Java Compiler (javac). bytecode file is end with .class extension.
>   - **Execute** phase: Byte code instructions executed by the JVM.
>   - **Debug** phase: Debug your program (if necessary) and then return to Edit Phase.

- Java expects a one-to-one mapping of the package name and the file system directory structure. For example, if we have a package called basics, we should have a directory or folder called basics.
- Package in java categorized in two form: User defined package and built-in package.
- To use a class from a package, there are two types of import statements: Explicit import statement and Wildcard import statement. The explicit import identifies the package location of a single class. A wildcard import statement tells the compiler to import all of the classes in a package.
- A Comment is an explanation in the source code of a computer program. There are three ways to comment in Java, single-line comments, multi-line comments, and documentation comments.

Chapter 3

Variables, Constants & Data Types

Java Variables

Introduction

A computer program performs processing on data (add, subtract, etc). You can store data in computer memory (RAM) for later purposes. Computer memory is organized as a series of cells. These cells house data, as illustrated below.

10	5	A		
			sea	
	Java			10000

To refer to a particular cell or memory location, you need to assign a name to the computer memory location, say **num**, and then, you can access the contents of this memory location, using the name **num**.

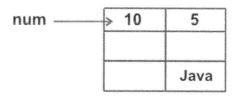

If the data stored in a computer memory location can change, for example if the value in **num** can be changed to 30, such a memory location is called

Variable. The word variable is due to the fact that the contents of such a cell can vary or change during the execution of a program.

What is a variable in Java?

A variable is a unique name for a storage area (memory location) where a value of a particular data type is kept. Variables are typically used to store information which your Java program needs to do its job (add, subtract, divide, etc).

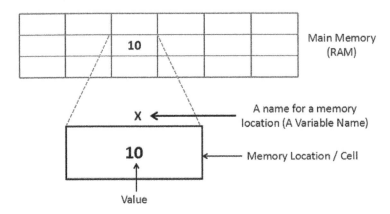

Figure 3.1 | Computer Memory

So, every variable has a name, type, a size and a value.

Java variable types

In Java there are four types of variables (sometimes called a fields):

1. Instance variables.
2. Static variables.
3. Local variables.
4. Parameters.

In this chapter we will talk about local variables.

What is a local variables?

A local variable is a variable that's declared inside the body of a method. Then you can use the variable only within that method. A local variable is only visible within the declared method.

A local variable is destroyed at the moment that the program execution reaches the end of the method in which the local variable is defined. Local variables are created when the method is entered, and destroyed when the method is exited.

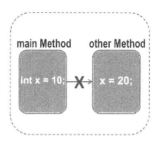

Figure 3.2 | Accessibility of local variable

Creating a local variable

The Java programming language is statically-typed, which means that all variables must first be declared before they can be used. This involves stating the variable's type and name. A variable declaration instructs the compiler to:

› Reserve a portion of main memory space.
› Assign a name to that reserved memory location - called variable's name.
› Assign the type of data it will hold - in Java you call this a data type.

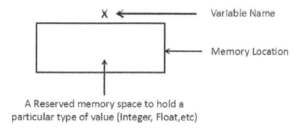

Figure 3.3 | A Reserved Memory Space

So you have to do two things in order to create a local variable:

› Create a variable by giving it a name; and
› Assign a data type for the variable.

Syntax Of Local Variable

```
methodname () {
        <data-type> <variable-name>;
}
```

› `methodname` is the name of method.
› `<data-type>` is the data type of a variable, like `int`, `float`.
› `<variable-name>` is the name you want the local variable to have.

The following code demonstrates how a simple variable can be created. This process is known as **variable declaration**.

Example 3.1: Create a local variable

```
int myNum;
```

(`int`) is the data type of the variable. The identifier `myNum` is the name you want the variable to have. We'll soon discuss the data type `int` for specifying real numbers.

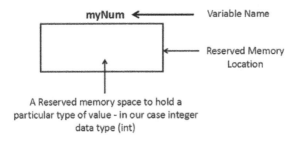

Figure 3.4 | A reserved memory space to hold a particular type of value.

Creating Multiple Variable at the same time

In Java we can declare several variables of the same type by separating their names with commas. For example:

```
int no1, no2, no3;// creating multiple variables of type int, at
the same time
```

Assign an initial value for the variable

There is no default value for local variables, so it should be declared and an initial value should be assigned before the first use.

A variable is a name that refers to a value. An assignment statement creates a new variables and give them values. Variables are assigned a value with an equal sign followed by a constant expression. This process is called an **assignment operation**.

Syntax Of Variable Assignment
```
varName = value;
```

This statement is called an **assignment statement**. In an assignment statement, the name of the variable receiving the assignment must appear on the left side of the operator and the value being assigned must appear on the right side.

The **varName** is the name of a variable. Equal sign (=) is an operator that stores the value of its right side, into the variable named on its left side. The **value** is the variable's value. This line does not print anything on the screen. Here is a simple example.

Examples 3.2: VarEx1.java - Variable assignment
> Delete the `course` package and its sub-packages. In the **Project** tool window, right click the **course** package and select **Delete**. Then, click **Delete** button.
> Create a new Java package named **basics**. Right click the **src** folder and select **New** > **Package**. Type **basics** in the Name field, and press enter to create the package.
> Create a new Java class inside **basics** package. In the Project tool window, right click the **basics** package and select **New** > **Java Class**. Type **VarEx1** in the Name field and press enter to create the class. Type the following code inside the `VarEx1.java` file.

```
01  package ch03;
02  public class VarEx1 {
03      public static void main(String[] args)
04      {
05          int num;
06          num = 0;
07      }
08  }
```

Explanation
> Line 01: Assigns a package called `basics` to the `VarEx1` class. It is a good practice to use names of packages with lower case letters to avoid any conflicts with the names of classes and interfaces.
> Line 02: This line known as class header. Class header marks the beginning of the `VarEx1` class.

- Lines 02 & 08 ({ and }): Everything between the braces is the body of the class `VarEx1`.
- Line 03: In Java, you need to have a method named `main`. This method must appear within a class, but it can any class. So here the above `main` method enclosed in a class named `VarEx1`. A Java program must have one `main` method.
- Lines 04 & 07 ({ and }): Everything between the braces is the body of the `main` method.
- Line 05: Creates a local variable named **num** and assign a data type **int** for it.
- Line 06: Assigns the value **0** to the **num** variable.

Displaying the value of the variable on the screen

To read the value of a variable, we have to use `println()` or `print()` methods. For example, to read the value of a variable using `println()` method, type the following code (`VarEx2.java`):

```
01  package ch03;
02  public class VarEx2 {
03      public static void main(String[] args)
04      {
05          int num;
06          num = 0;
07          System.out.println("Number is " + num);
08      }
09  }
```

Output

```
Number is 0
```

Explanation

- Line 05: Create a variable named **num**.
- Line 06: Assigns the value **0** to the **num** variable.
- Line 07: Sends the variable **num** to the `println()` method. When you send a variable name to `print` or `println` the variable's contents are displayed on the screen

NOTE: No quotation marks around variable's name.

Variable initialization

As you have already seen, a value is put into a variable with an assignment (=) statement. Initialization is assign values to variables as part of the declaration statement.

Initialization = Create variable + Assigning value to a variable

So these are two examples of initialization of integer, double, and String variables:

Example 3.3: VarEx3.java - Assign a value to a variable already when it is declared

```
package ch03;
public class VarEx3 {
    public static void main(String[] args)
    {
        int Num1 = 150;
        double Num2 = 1.4;
        String stringName = "Mohammed";
    }
}
```

Example 3.4: VarEx4.java - Assign a value to a variable when it is declared and display its value on the screen

```
01  package ch03;
02  public class VarEx4 {
03      public static void main(String[] args)
04      {
05          int month = 2;
06          int days = 28;
07          System.out.println("Month " + month);
08          System.out.println(" has " + days + " days");
09      }
10  }
```

Output
```
Month 2
 has 28 days
```

Explanation

› Line 05: Declares the **month** variable and initializes it with the value **2**.
› Line 06: Declare the **days** variable and initializes it with the value **28**.
› Line 07: Display the value of the **month** variable on the screen.
› Line 08: Displays the value of the **days** variable on the screen.

Warning!: When a variable is declared inside a method, it must have a value stored in it before it can be used. If the compiler determines that the program might be using such a variable before a value has been stored in it, an error will occur. You can avoid this type of error by initializing the variable with a value.

Declare several variables and only initialize some of them
```
int flighNum = 60; travelTime, departure = 10, distance;
```

Variables hold only one value at a time

Remember, a variable can hold only one value at a time. When you assign a new value to a variable, the new value takes the place of the variable's previous contents. Here is the `varEx2.java` program that demonstrate this very clearly

Example: VarEx5.java
```
01  package ch03;
02  public class VarEx5 {
03      public static void main(String[] args)
04      {
01          // initialize the variable x with the value 20
02          int x = 20;
03
04          // display the contents of the variable x.
05          System.out.println(x);
06
07          // the variable is assigned the value 99.
08          x = 99;
09
10          // display the contents of the variable x.
11          System.out.println(x);
12      }
13  }
```

Output
```
99
```

Get Input From The User in a Console-based Java Program

A new class called `Scanner` was introduced in Java 1.5 to get simple input values from the user. The simple program below uses the `Scanner` class to read an integer value from the user and then displays the value back to the console to verify the program received the value entered by the user.

Example 3.5: InputUser.java

```
01  package ch03;
02  import java.util.Scanner;
03
04  public class InputUser {
05      public static void main(String[] args){
06          Scanner sc = new Scanner(System.in);
07          System.out.println("Enter an Integer: ");
08          int input = sc.nextInt(); // Suppose the user enter 33 as the input.
09          System.out.println("You entered " + input + ".");
10      }
11
12  }
```

Output
```
Enter an Integer:
33
You entered 33.
```

Explanation

> Line 02: You must import `Scanner` class before you can use it. To do that, you code an `import` statement at the beginning of the program, before the class declaration.

> Line 06: To use the `Scanner` class to read input from the console, you must create an instance or object of the `Scanner` class. To create a `Scanner` object, you use the `new` keyword followed by a call to the `Scanner` class constructor. Note that the `Scanner` class requires a parameter (`System.in`), that indicates the input stream that the input comes from. You can use `System.in` here to specify standard **keyboard** console input.

> Line 07: To let the user know what kind of input the program expects. Calls `System.out.println` to display the message `Enter an Integer:` on the console. That way, the user knows that the program is waiting for input.

> Line 08: Getting input. To read an input value from the user, you can use one of the methods of the `Scanner` class. `nextInt()` method reads an integer **int** value from the user and return the value. Then assignment operator assigns the value returned by the `nextInt()` method to a variable named **input**. When the `nextInt` method is executed, the program waits for the user to enter a value in the console window.

NOTE: If the user enters a value that can't be converted to the correct type, the program terminates abruptly.

> Line 09: This line displays a message on the screen and the value of the **input** variable.

Similarly, we can input values of other data types also. Same as `nextInt()` is used to input an integer value, methods to input values of other data types are listed below.

Table 3.1 | Methods to input values of different data types

Method	Inputs	Method	Inputs
`nextInt()`	Integer	`nextShort()`	Short
`nextFloat()`	Float	`next()`	Single word
`nextDouble()`	Double	`nextLine()`	Line of Strings
`nextLong()`	Long	`nextBoolean()`	Boolean

Identifiers in Java

Identifiers are the names we give to variables, methods, classes, packages and interfaces. In the `Welcome` program:

> `Welcome is a` class name,
> `String is a` predefined class name,
> `args is a` variable name,
> `main is a` method name, and
> `println() is a` method name,

are identifiers.

Rules for naming Java identifiers

There are certain rules for defining a valid Java identifiers. There rules must be followed, otherwise we get compile-time error.

> An identifier's name can be an unlimited-length sequence of alphanumeric characters ([a-z],[A-Z]) and digits (0-9), $(dollar sign), and _ (underscore).
> An identifier's name begin with a letter, or the $ or _ character ("$" or "_" are not recommended). The first letter of an identifier cannot be a digit.
> Identifiers in Java are case sensitive, aBc and aBC are two different identifiers.
> White space is not permitted.
> A Java keyword cannot be used as an identifier. For example "int for = 80;" is invalid statement as **for** is a reserved word.

Java variable naming conventions (*recommended*)

To make the most out of the identifiers you choose, make them meaningful and follow the standard Java naming conventions.

> Variable names are written in lowercase letters.
> If variable names contains more than one word, capitalize the first letter of each word except the first. for instance, `firstName`.
> Use full words to make your code easier to read and understand.
> Names for constants are all uppercase, typically using an underscore character (_) between words. For instance `EXCHANGE_RATE`. By convention, the underscore character is never used elsewhere.

Introduction to Java Data Types

Each variable in Java has a data type. Data type refers to the type of data that can be stored in a variable. For example, if a variable has `int` data type, it can only take integer values.

Java is a strongly typed language

Java is called a *"strongly typed language"* because when you declare a variable, you must specify the variable's type. Then the compiler ensures that you don't try to assign data of the wrong type to the variable. For example, the following code generates a compiler error, because x is declared as a variable of type `int` (which holds whole numbers), you can't assign the value 3.5 to it.

```
01  int x;
02  x = 3.5;
```

Java is a statically typed language. A language is statically typed, if the data type of a variable is known at compile time. This means you must specify the type of the variable (declare the variable) before you can use it.

Categories of data types in Java

In Java we have two categories of data types:

1. **Primitive** data types. *Primitive types* are the data types defined by the language itself.
2. **Object or Reference** data types. Reference types are types defined by classes in the Java or by classes you create rather than by the language itself.

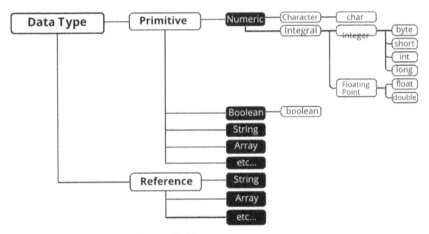

Figure 3.5 | Categories of Data Types in Java

Primitive data types

Primitive data types are those whose variables can hold maximum one value at a time. These data types are called **primitive** because you cannot use them to create objects.

Syntax
```
<data-type> <variable-name);
```

In java we have eight primitive data types which are organized in four groups. They are:

1. Integer data types (Numeric Data Type - Does not allow decimal places): `byte, short, int, long`.

2. Float data types (Numeric Data Type - Numbers with decimal places): `float, double`.

3. Character data types (Numeric Data Type- See Unicode System in Java): `char`.

4. Boolean data types: `boolean`.

Notice that all the data type keywords are in small letters. These are part of the java keywords and every keyword in java is in small letters.

Literals

Now let us look at the values of those variables. A literal is a value that can be assigned to a primitive or string variable, or passed as an argument to a method call. For example:

- boolean literals: `true, false`.
- char literals:
    - `'\n'` - newline ,
    - `'\r'` - return ,
    - `'\t'` - tab
- Floating-point literals:
    - `3.1454` - a decimal point,
    - `4.43E+12` - E or e; scientific notation,
    - `1.343F` - F or f; 32-bit float,
    - `1322D` - D or d; 64-bit double.
- String literals: `String subject = "java";`

When writing a single character, we use single quotes to encapsulate them. Consider the following example:

```
char code = 'a';
```

A string can be initialized as follows:

```
String country = "Sudan";
```

Notice, the use of double quotation marks instead of single quotation marks.

Memory size for data types

Understanding the memory limitations is extremely important in deciding which data type should be used. For example, when you are representing the age of a person, for sure it will not cross 200, so, using short data type is enough instead of long which has very big memory foot print.

The following should be understood for every data type:
- Memory size allocated.
- Default value.
- Range of values it can represent.

Memory size for data types

Every data type has some memory size defined. This enables that whenever a variable is declared, the memory size defined will be blocked irrespective of the value that is going to get assigned. Data types and their memory sizes are listed in the following table.

Table 3.2 | Memory size for data types

Data Type	Default Value (for fields)	Default Size	Range (Min Value)	Range (Max Value)
byte	0	1 byte	-128	127
short	0	2 byte	-32,768	32,767
int	0	4 byte	-2,147,483,648	2,147,483,647
long	0L	8 byte	-9,223,372,036,854,775,808	9,223,372,036,854,775,807
float	0.0f	4 byte	Approximately -3.4E+38 with 7 significant digits	Approximately 3.4E+38 with 7 significant digits
double	0.0d	8 byte	Approximately -1.7E+308 with 15 significant digits	Approximately 1.7E+308 with 15 significant digits
char	'\u0000'	2 byte		
boolean	false	1 bit		

The size of each data type is the same for all hardware platform. When the programmer does not declare to assign any values to the variables, these default values will be assigned by the virtual machine during the object instantiation.

Range of values are what the min and max range of values a data type can be able to hold. All numeric types are signed, meaning that both positive and negative values can be stored in them. In programming zero is considered to be a positive number.

> **WARNING:** Local variables are slightly different; the compiler never assigns a default value to an un-initialized local variable. If you cannot initialize your local variable where it is declared, make sure to assign it a value before you attempt to use it. Accessing an un-initialized local variable will result in a compile-time error.

Here is another example which define two types of numbers in Java, integer and long data types.

Example 3.6: IntLong.java - using `int` and `long` data types

```
01  public static void main(String[] args)
02  {
03      int y = 1090920200;
04      System.out.println(y);
05
06      long x = 10909202929L;
07      System.out.println(x);
08  }
```

Output
```
1090920200
10909202929
```

By default, Java interpret all numeral literals as integer values. If you want to explicitly specify that this is something bigger than integer you should use suffix `L` for long values.

Floating-Point Data Type

In Java, there are two data types that can represent floating-point numbers: `float` and `double`.

Table 3.3 | Floating point data types

Data Type	Default Size	Default Value (for Fields)	Range (min value)	Range (max value)
float	4 byte	0.0f	±3.4X10^-38 OR -3.4E38 (-3.4 * 1038) with 7 significant digits	±3.4X10^38 OR +3.4E38 (3.4 * 1038) with 7 significant digits

double	8 byte	0.0d	±1.7X10^-308	±1.7X10^307
			OR	OR
			-1.7E308 (-1.7 * 10308)	+1.7E308 (+1.7 * 10308)
			with 16 significant digits	with 16 significant digits
			(The smallest non-zero value that you can have is roughly (4.9 * 10-324))	

NOTE: The size of each data type is the same for all hardware platform. Local variables are slightly different; the compiler never assigns a default value to an un-initialized local variable. If you cannot initialize your local variable where it is declared, make sure to assign it a value before you attempt to use it. Accessing an un-initialized local variable will result in a compile-time error.

double data type

The **double** data type is a double-precision floating point. Any value declared with decimal point is by default of type double. When you write a floating point literal in your program code, Java assumes it to be of the double data type. For example: 29.75, 1.76, 31.51 - all treated as double values.

The double data type is considered a double precision data type. It can store a floating point number with 16 digits of accuracy.

> Precision means more digits to the right of the decimal point, than a single precision number.
> The word double derives from the fact that a double-precision number uses twice as many bits as a regular floating-point numbers.

For example, If a single precision number requires 32 bits, its double precision counterpart will be 64 bits long. The extra bits increases not only the precision but also the range of magnitudes that can be represented.

Example 3.7: Double1.java - Using double data type

```
01  package ch03;
02
03  public class Double1 {
04      public static void main(String[] args){
```

```
            double price, tax, total;
            price = 29.75;
            tax = 1.76;
            total = 31.51;
09
            System.out.println("The price of the item is " + price);
            System.out.println("The tax is " + tax);
            System.out.println("The total is " + total);
        }
    }
```

Output

```
The price of the item is 29.75
The tax is 1.76
The total is 31.51
```

Suffixing it with the letter `d or D` is optional.

NOTE: A `double` value is not compatible with a float variable because a `double` can be much larger or much smaller than the allowable range for a `float`.

Here is an example of initialization of two double variables and display their values on the screen.

Example 3.8: Double2.java - double data type

```
01  public static void main(String[] args){
02      double d = 1.1234567891234567891;
03      System.out.println(d);              // Precision: 16 digits
04
05      d = 12.1234567891234567891;
06      System.out.println(d);              // Precision: 15 digits
07  }
```

Output

```
1.1234567891234568
12.123456789123457
```

If we're going to put more values to digit area, we're going to lose it in your output. For example:

```
d = 123.1234567891234567891;   // Precision: 14 digits
d = 1234.1234567891234567891;  // Precision: 13 digits
d = 12345.1234567891234567891; // Precision: 12 digits
```

float data type

A `float` data type is considered a single precision data type. It can store a floating point number with 7 digits of accuracy. Here is how that is done.

Example 3.9: FloatEx.java - using float number (wrong way)
```
float number;
number = 23.5; // error!
```

The Solution is to force a double literal to be treated as a float by suffixing it with the letter F or f

Example 3.10: FloatEx2.java - Using float number (right way)
```
float number = 23.5f;
System.out.println(number);
```

Example 3.11: Float1.java
```
01  package ch03;
02
03  public class Float1 {
04      public static void main(String[] args) {
05          float number = 2.1234567f;
06          System.out.println(number);
07
08          float number2 = 1.12345678f;
09          System.out.println(number2);
10      }
11  }
```

Output
```
2.1234567
1.1234568
```

Scientific and E Notation

Floating point literals can be represented in notation. For example -

```
47,281,97 In Scientific notation 4.728197 X 10^4
10^4 = 10000 & 4.728197 X 10000 is 47,281,97
```

Java Uses **E** notation to represent values in scientific notation. The **E** can be uppercase or lowercase. For example:

```
4.728197 X 10^4 would be 4.728197E4
```

Table 3.4 | Floating point representation

Decimal Notation	Scientific Notation	E Notation
247.91	2.4791 X 10^2	2.48E+02
0.00072	7.2 X 10^-4	7.2 E-4
2,900,000	2.9 X 10^6	2.90E+06

Below is an example of a program that uses the e notation to represent values in scientific notation provided by Java.

Example 3.12: EarthFacts.java

```
01  double distance, mass;
02  distance = 2.389E8;
03  mass = 5.972E24;
04
05  System.out.println("The Earth is " + distance + " Miles away from moon");
06  System.out.println("The Earth's mass is " + mass + " Kilograms.");
```

char & boolean Data Types

boolean data type

The `boolean` data type allows you to create variables that may hold one of two possible values; `true or false`.

Syntax
```
boolean <variable-name>;
```

Here is a simple example.

Example 3.13: BoolEx.java - The declaration and assignment of a boolean variable

```
01  package ch03;
02  public class BoolEx {
03      public static void main(String[] args) {
04          boolean bool;
05          bool = true;
06          System.out.println(bool);
07
08          bool = false;
09          System.out.println(bool);
10      }
11  }
```

Output
```
true
```

88 | Java for Complete Beginners

```
false
```

Remember: Variables of the `boolean` data type are useful for evaluating conditions that are either `true` or `false`. `boolean` variables may only hold the values `true` or `false`. The contents of a boolean variable may not be copied to a variable of any type other than boolean.

char data type

The `char` data type is used to store characters. example: A, B, C...etc. A variable of the char data type can hold one character at a time. Character literals are enclosed in single quotation marks. For example:

Example 3.14: Char.java - Using char data type
```
char grade = 'A'; // only one character at a time
grade = 'B'; // assign different character (only one character)
to a grade variable
```

Syntax
```
char <variable-name>;
```

Example 3.15: CharEx.java - Declaration and assignment of a boolean variable
```
01  package ch03;
02  public class CharEx {
03      public static void main(String[] args) {
04          char letter;
05          letter = 'A';
06          System.out.println(letter);
07
08          letter = 'B';
09          System.out.println(letter);
10      }
11  }
```

NOTE: Do not confuse character literals with string literals, which are enclosed in double quotation marks. String literals cannot be assigned to **char** variables.

Unicode

Characters are internally represented by numbers. Each printable character, as well as many non-printable characters is assigned a unique number.

Java uses **Unicode**, which is a set of numbers that are used as codes for representing characters. Each Unicode number requires two bytes of memory, so char variables occupy two bytes.

When a character is stored in memory, it is actually the numeric code that is stored. When the computer is instructed to print the value on the screen, it displays the character that correspond with the numeric code.

Figure 3.6 | A Portion of the Unicode Character Set

Example 3.16: CharEx2.java - Demonstrates the relationship between characters and integers

```
package ch03;
public class CharEx2 {
    public static void main(String[] args) {
        char letter;
        letter = 65;
        System.out.println(letter);

        letter = 66;
        System.out.println(letter);
    }
}
```

Output

```
A
B
```

Explanation

Figure 3.7 | Characters and how they are stored in memory

---
[1] For more information about Unicode Character Set, see https://unicode-table.com/en/

The byte, short, int and long Data Types

integer data types

An `integer` is a whole number (a number with no fractional or decimal portion.) For example: 7, 34 , -90 (negative number) , 988. Java has four integer types (byte, short, int, and long), which you can use to store numbers of varying sizes as shown in the following table:

Table 3.5 | Primitive Data Types for Numeric Data

Data Type	Size (byte)	Default Value (for Fields)	Range
byte	1	0	-128 to +127
short	2	0	-32,768 to +32,767
int	4	0	-2,147,483,648 to +2,147,483,647
long	8	0L	-9,223,372,036,854,775,808 to +9,223,372,036,854,775,807
float	4	0.0f	±3.4X10^-38 to ±3.4X10^38
double	8	0.0d	±1.7X10^-308 to ±1.7X10^307

The size of each data type is the same for all hardware platform. Local variables are slightly different; the compiler never assigns a default value to an un-initialized local variable. If you cannot initialize your local variable where it is declared, make sure to assign it a value before you attempt to use it. Accessing an un-initialized local variable will result in a compile-time error.

> **NOTE:** The most commonly used integer type is `int`. You can use short or even `byte` when you know the variable won't need to store large values, and you can use `long` when your program will require large values.

Example 3.17: IntegerEx.java

```
01  package ch03;
02  public class IntegerEx {
03      public static void main(String[] args) {
04          int a = 10;        // initial value 10
05          int b = 20;        // initial value 20
06          int result;        // initial value undetermined
07
```

```
            result = a + b;
            System.out.println("Result is " + result);
10
        }
    }
```

Output
```
Result is 30
```

String Data Type

In addition to the eight primitive data types listed above, the Java programming language also provides special support for character strings via the `java.lang.String` class. The String type is a class, however, and is not one of the primitive types of the language.

Because strings are so commonly used, though, Java does have a syntax for including string values literally in a program. The String class is not technically a primitive data type, but considering the special support given to it by the language.

Syntax
```
String <variable-name> = "value";
```

Enclosing your character string within double quotes will automatically create a new String object.

Example 3.18: StringEx.java - Using String data type
```
01  package ch03;
02  public class StringEx {
03      public static void main(String[] args) {
04          String name = "Mohammed";
05          String city = "Omdurman";
06
07          System.out.println("Name : " + name);
08          System.out.println("City : " + city);
09      }
10  }
```

Output
```
Name : Mohammed
City : Omdurman
```

String objects are immutable, which means that once created, their values cannot be changed.

Escape sequences

In Java, a character preceded by a backslash (\) is an escape sequence and has special meaning to the Java. String literals can contain any of the escape sequences that can appear as char literals.

Java Escape Sequences
- \t Insert a tab in the text at this point.
- \b Insert a backspace in the text at this point.
- \n Insert a newline in the text at this point.
- \r Insert a carriage return in the text at this point.
- \f Insert a formfeed in the text at this point.
- \' Insert a single quote character in the text at this point.
- \" Insert a double quote character in the text at this point.
- \\ Insert a backslash character in the text at this point.

Example 3.19: EscapeSequence.java
```
01  public class EscapeSequence {
02      public static void main(String[] args) {
03          System.out.println("Single Quote    : " + "ABCDE\'FGHIJ");
04          System.out.println("Double Quote    : " + "ABCDE\"FGHIJ");
05          System.out.println("Backslash       : " + "ABCDE\\FGHIJ");
06          System.out.println("Horizontal Tab  : " + "ABCDE\tFGHIJ");
07          System.out.println("Carriage Return: " + "ABCDE\rFGHIJ");
08      }
09  }
```

Output
```
Single Quote    : ABCDE'FGHIJ
Double Quote    : ABCDE"FGHIJ
Backslash       : ABCDE\FGHIJ
Horizontal Tab  : ABCDE   FGHIJ
FGHIJ
```

Java Literals

A literal is any digit, letters, text or other characters that directly represents a values to be stored in variable. Literal means what you type is what you get. For example:

```
int year = 2017;
```

The literal is **2017**, because it directly represents the integer value **2017**. The data type is the type of container to hold a literal. For example:

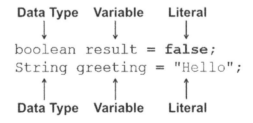

Examples 3.20: LiteralsEx.java - Literals in Java
```
boolean res = true;
char c = 'b';
byte b = 1;
short s = 100;
int i = 1000;
String course = "Java";
```

Types of literals

In Java programming language there are six types of literals. They are: Integer literals, Floating literals, String literals, Character literals, Boolean literals, and Class literals. Let's start with Integer literals.

Integer Literals

Integer data types consist of the following primitive data types: `int`, `long`, `byte`, and `short`. An integer literal is of type long if it ends with the letter L or l; otherwise it is of type `int`. For instance:
```
int val = 350;
long val = 9000;
```

Integer Literals can be assigned by these values:

› **Decimal Literals:** Base 10 (0 - 9)
› **Octal Literals:** Base 8 (0 - 7)
› **Hexadecimal Literals:** Base 16 (0 - 9 and A - F)
› **Binary Literals:** Base 2 (0 and 1)
› **Long Literals:** ends with L or l
› Values with Underscore in between.

Prefix **0** is used to indicate octal, prefix **0x** indicates hexadecimal, and prefix **0b** indicates binary when using these number systems for literals. Let's see an examples for this.

Example 3.21: IntLiteralsEx.java

```
01  package ch03;
02  public class IntLiteralsEx {
03      public static void main(String[] args) {
04          // The number 30 in decimal
05          int decVal = 30;
06          // The number 30 in hexadecimal
07          int hexVal = 0x1E;
08
09          // The number 30 in binary
10          int binVal = 0b11110;
11
12          // the number 30 in octal
13          int octVal = 036;
14      }
15  }
```

Example 3.22: IntLiteralEx2.java

```
01  package ch03;
02  public class IntLiteralEx2 {
03      public static void main (String[] args){
04          long longValue = 100L;
05          System.out.println("Long Value : " + longValue);
06
07          // The number 30 in decimal
08          int decVal = 30;
09          System.out.println("Decimal Value : " + decVal);
10
11          // The number 30 in hexadecimal
12          int hexVal = 0x1E;
13          System.out.println("Hexadecimal value : " + hexVal);
14
15          // The number 30 in binary
16          int binVal = 0b11110;
17          System.out.println("Binary value : " + binVal);
18
19          // the number 30 in octal
20          int octVal = 036;
21          System.out.println("Octal value : " + octVal);
22      }
23  }
```

Output

```
Long Value : 100
Decimal Value : 30
Hexadecimal value : 30
Binary value : 30
Octal value : 30
```

Example 3.23: IntLiteralEx3.java
```java
package ch03;
public class IntLiteralEx3 {
    public static void main (String[] args){
        int num = 10;
        System.out.println("num : " + num);

        num = 100;
        System.out.println("num : " + num);

        num = 0x10;
        System.out.println("num : " + num);

        num = 0b1010;
        System.out.println("num : " + num);

        long number = 399;
        System.out.println("number : " + number);
    }
}
```

Output
```
num : 10
num : 100
num : 16
num : 10
number : 399
```

When you write an integer literal in your program code, Java assumes it to be of the `int` data type. You can force an integer literal to be treated as a `long` by suffixing it with the letter `L`.

```java
long number = 391;
```

We can embed one or more underscores in an Integer Literal (JDK 7 and later). It makes easier to read large integer literals. When the literal is compiled, the underscores are discarded.

Examples 3.24: Integer literal with Underscore
```java
int no  = 800_999_999;   // actual value 800999999
int no2 = 55_00;         // actual value 5500
int no3 = 045_11;        // actual value 04511
int no4 = 0x56_22;       // actual value 0x5622
int no5 = 0b1100_11;     // actual value 0b110011
```

Example 3.25: IntegerLiteralUnderscore.java
```java
package ch03;
public class IntegerLiteralUnderscore {
    public static void main (String[] args){
        int no = 800_888_888;
        System.out.println("no : " + no);
```

```
06
07            int no2 = 55_88;
08            System.out.println("no : " + no2);
09
10            int no3 = 045_55;
11            System.out.println("no : " + no3);
12
13            int no4 = 0x55_11;
14            System.out.println("no : " + no4);
15
16            int no5 = 0b1000_01;
17            System.out.println("no : " + no5);
18        }
19 }
```

Output
```
no : 800888888
no : 5588
no : 2413
no : 21777
no : 33
```

Floating-Point Literals

Java has two kinds of floating-point numbers: `float` and `double`. If the floating point literal ends with the letter `F` or `f`, it is of type `float`; otherwise its type is `double` and it can optionally end with the letter `D` or `d`. For example:

```
float f1 = 12.6f;
```

We can also specify a floating-point literal in scientific notation using Exponent (short E). F or f (32-bit float literal) and D or d (64-bit double literal; this is the default). Here is a simple example to use these literals.

Here is a simple example.

Example 3.26: DoubleFloat.java
```
double d1 = 123.4;
double d2 = 1.234e2; // Same value as d1, but in scientific
notation
float  f1 = 123.4f;
double d3 = 3.4d;
```

Example 3.27: FloatingPointLiteral.java
```
01 package ch03;
02 public class FloatPointLiteral {
03     public static void main(String[] args){
04         double d1 = 123.4;
05         System.out.println("d1 : " + d1);
06
07         double d2 = 1.234e2;
08         System.out.println("d2 : " + d2);
09
```

```
            float f1 = 123.4f;
            System.out.println("f1 : " + f1);
12
            double d3 = 3.4d;
            System.out.println("d3 : " + d3);
15
            double no = 1_587_3_82.0;
            System.out.println("no : " + no);
18
        }
    }
```

Output

```
    d1 : 123.4
    d2 : 123.4
    f1 : 123.4
    d3 : 3.4
    no : 1587382.0
```

Character Literals

Character literals are expressed by a single character in a pair of single quote characters. For instance: `'b'`, `'*'`, and `'7'`.

Java supports thousands of additional characters through the 16-bit Unicode standard. Below table shows a set of these special characters.

Table 3.6 | Character literals[1]

Char	Decimal	Binary	Hex	Octal
"	34	100010	21	41
1	49	110001	31	61
A	65	1000001	41	101
B	66	1000010	42	102

If you want to specify a single quote, a blank slash, or a non-printable character as a character literal use an escape sequence. An escape sequence uses a special syntax to represent a character. The syntax begins with a single backslash character.

Table 3.7 | Character Escape Codes

---

[1] For more information see: https://asecuritysite.com/coding/asc2 (OR) https://en.wikipedia.org/wiki/List_of_Unicode_characters

Escape	Meaning	Escape	Meaning
`\n`	New Line	`\\`	Back slash
`\t`	Tab	`\'`	Single quotation mark
`\b`	Backspace	`\"`	Double quotation mark
`\r`	Carriage return	`\d`	Octal
`\f`	Formfeed	`\rd`	Hexadecimal

The below table views the character literals use the Unicode escape sequence to represent printable and non-printable characters.

Table 3.8 | Unicode Escape Sequences and Printable/non-printable characters

Unicode Escape Sequence	Printable & non-printable characters
`'\u0041'`	Capital letter A
`'\u0030'`	Digit 0
`'\u0022'`	Double quote
`'\u003b'`	Punctuation
`'\0020'`	Space
`'\u0009'`	Horizontal Tab
`'\u004D'`	Capital M

Below is a Java program that illustrates the use of the escape sequence.

Example 3.28: ChataracterLiterals.java

```
01 package ch03;
02 public class CharacterLiterals {
03     public static void main(String[] args){
04         char char_e = 'e';
05         System.out.println("char_e : " + char_e);
06
07         char char_3 = '3';
08         System.out.println("char_3 : " + char_3);
09
10         char singleQuotationMark = '\'';
11         System.out.println("Single Quotation Mark:"+ singleQuotationMark);
12
13         char doubleQuotationMark = '\"';
14         System.out.println("Double Quotation Mark:"+ doubleQuotationMark);
15
16         char capitalM = '\u004D';
17         System.out.println("capitalM : " + capitalM);
```

```
18
            char digitOne = '\u0031';
            System.out.println("digitOne : " + digitOne);
        }
    }
```

Output
```
char_e : e
char_3 : 3
Single Quotation Mark:'
Double Quotation Mark:"
capitalM : M
digitOne : 1
```

String Literals

String literals are set of characters inside double quotation marks. Always use "double quotes" for String literals. For example:

```
String city = "Khartoum"; // a string contains 8 characters
String e = ""; // empty string
```

String literals can include the character escape codes. For example:

```
String value = "Mohammed asked, \" How are you?\" ";
```

Here is a simple example.

Example 3.29: StringLiteralsEx.java
```
01  package ch03;
02  public class StringLiteralsEx{
03      public static void main(String[] args){
04          String welcomeMsg = "Welcome my friend";
05          System.out.println("Welcome Message : " + welcomeMsg);
06
07          String password = "onetwothree";
08          String value = "Mohammed asked, \"How are your?\"";
09          System.out.println("Value :" + value);
10          System.out.println("hi, \n Welcome\n");
11
12          String bookTitle = "Ultimate Java Tutorials\u2122";
13          System.out.println("Title :" + bookTitle);
14      }
15  }
```

Output
```
Welcome Message : Welcome my friend
Value :Mohammed asked, "How are your?"
hi,
 Welcome

Title :Ultimate Java Tutorials™
```

Null Literals

We specify the Null literal to reduce the number of references to an object. The type of the null literal is always null. For instance:

```
s = null;
```

Boolean Literals

The values `true` and `false` are treated as literals in Java. When we assign a value to a boolean variable, we can only use these two values. For example:

```
boolean ans = true;
```

Remember that the literal `true` is not represented by the quotation marks around it. Here is a simple example.

Example 3.30: BooleanliteralsEx.java

```java
01  package ch03;
02  public class BooleanLiteralsEx {
03      public static void main(String[] args){
04          boolean ans = true;
05          System.out.println("Answer :" + ans);
06
07          boolean isSmartAns = false;
08          System.out.println("isSmartAns :" + isSmartAns);
09      }
10  }
```

Output

```
Answer :true
isSmartAns :false
```

Underscore Characters in Numeric Literals

In Java, any number of underscore characters (_) can appear anywhere between digits in a numerical literal. This feature is used to improve the readability of your code. For example:

```
long creditCardNo = 1234_5678_9012_9876L;
float pi = 3.14_15F;
long bytes = 0b11010010_01100111_1111100;
```

Underscore used as a separator. You can place underscores **ONLY BETWEEN DIGITS**. Look at the following examples.

Examples 3.31: WrongStat.java - Wrong Java Statements

```
int val = _20_;          // underscores placed at the beginning &
                         end of a number.
float pi = 3_.1415F;     // underscore placed adjacent to decimal
point.
float pi1 = 3._1415F;    // underscore placed adjacent to decimal
point.
long identityCard = 999_99_999_L; //underscores placed prior to
the L suffix.
```

```
    int x = 2_;              // underscore placed at the end of the
    number.
```

Examples 3.32: RightStat.java - Right Java Statements
```
    long identityCard = 999_99_999L;
    float pi = 3.14_15F;
```

Java Constant

Constants are variables that created to store fixed values. **Named Constant** is a variable whose content is read only and cannot be changed during the program's execution. Constant is a variable that does not change and it should be all UPPERCASE.

Syntax

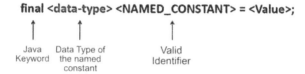

The **final** keyword indicates that the value of this variable or field cannot change. If the name is composed of more than one word, the words are separated by an underscore.

Example
```
    final double INTEREST_RATE = 0.05;
```

INTEREST_RATE: recommended but not required. So they are easily distinguishable from regular variable name.

Benefits:

They make programs more self-documenting. New programmers can read the second statement, and know what is happening.
```
    amount = balance * 0.05;         // wrong way
    amount = balance * INTEREST_RATE; // right way
```

The widespread changes can easily be made to the program. Say interest rate appears in a dozen different statements throughout the program, when the rate changes, the initialization value in the definition of the name of constant is the only value that needs to be modified.

A `static` modifier, in combination with the final keyword is also used to define constants (*more details on chapter 13*). For example:

```
static final int CONSTANT_VALUE = 100;
```

Here is a simple example.

Example 3.33: StaticFinalEx.java - Using static and final keywords

```
01  package ch03;
02  public class StaticFinalEx {
03      static final int CONSTANT_VALUE = 100;
04      public static void main(String[] args){
05          System.out.println("Constant Value : " + CONSTANT_VALUE);
06          // CONSTANT_VALUE = 40
07
08      }
09  }
```

Output
```
Constant Value : 100
```

Example 3.34: FinalEx.java

```
01  package ch03;
02  public class FinalEx {
03      public static void main(String[] args){
04          // char MAX_NUM = 100;
05          // System.out.println(MAX_NUM);
06
07          final int MAX_NUM = 200;
08          System.out.println(MAX_NUM);
09
10      }
11  }
```

Output
```
200
```

The Difference Between Variable, Constant, and Literal

Variables

Variable is a name of location in memory that enables us to store a value for later use. It is called variable because you can change the content in it whenever you want.

Constants

Constant is like variable. The only difference between constants and variable is that it cannot be change once defined.

Literals

Literals are values assigned to variables and constants.

Java Keywords

Keywords are predefined, reserved words used in Java programming that have special meaning to the compiler. For example, int, for, class, package etc. You cannot use keywords as variable or constant name (or identifier). Here's the complete list of all keywords in Java programming.

Table 3.9 | Java Keywords

class	public	default	if	goto	void	protected
while	static	continue	do	const	enum	synchronized
super	assert	boolean	for	float	byte	implements
break	double	private	new	this	throws	strictfp
short	native	package	int	throw	return	volatiles
import	switch	finally	case	long	final	transient
catch	extends	abstract	else	char	interface	

Summary

> - A variable is a name for a memory location used to hold a value of a particular data type.
> - In Java there are four types of variables: non-static variables, static variables, local variables, and parameters.
> - A local variable is a variable declared inside a method.
> - The Java programming language is statically-typed, which means that all variables must first be declared before they can be used.

- A variable declaration instructs the compiler to: reserve a portion of memory space, assign a name to that reserved memory location, and assign the type of data it will hold.
- Initialization is assign values to variables as part of the declaration statement.
- A variable can hold only one value at a time.
- Identifiers are the names we give to variables, methods, classes, packages and interfaces.
- Data type refers to the type of data that can be stored in a variable.
- Java is called a "strongly typed language" because when you declare a variable, you must specify the variable's type.
- Data types divided into two groups: fundamental or primitive data types and object or reference data types.
- Primitive data types are those whose variables can hold maximum one value at a time. These data types are called primitive because you cannot use them to create objects.
- In java we have eight primitive data types which are organized in four groups. They are: Integer data types (byte, short, int, long), Float data types (float, double), Character data types (char), Boolean data types (boolean).
- A literal is a value that can be assigned to a primitive or string variable, or passed as an argument to a method call.
- In Java, a character preceded by a backslash (\) is an escape sequence and has special meaning to the Java.
- String literals can contain any of the escape sequences that can appear as char literals.
- In Java, there are six types of literals. They are: Integer Literals, Floating Literals, String Literals, Character Literals, Boolean Literals, and Class Literals.
- Java has two kinds of floating-point numbers: float and double. If the floating point literal ends with the letter F or f, it is of type float; otherwise its type is double and it can optionally end with the letter D or d.
- Character literals are expressed by a single character in a pair of single quote characters.
- String literals are set of characters inside double quotation marks.
- We specify the Null literal to reduce the number of references to an object.
- The values `true` and `false` are treated as literals in Java. When we assign a value to a boolean variable, we can only use these two values. Remember that the literal `true` is not represented by the quotation marks around it.

- In Java, any number of underscore characters(_) can appear anywhere between digits in a numerical literal.
- Constants are variables that created to store fixed values. Named Constant is a variable whose content is read only and cannot be changed during the program's execution.
- Keywords are predefined, reserved words used in Java programming that have special meaning to the compiler.

Chapter 4

Expressions and Operators

Operators and operands

Expression consist of two types of components: Operators and Operands. The symbol used in an operation is called an operator (e.g., +, -, /). A value involved in an operation is called an operand. For example:

```
5 + x // x and 5 are operands and + is an operator
item = 12; // item and 12 are operand and (=) sign is an opera-
tor
```

Operators are the symbols that represent simple calculations like addition and multiplication. Operators perform operations on data or operands. All expressions have at least one operand.

Java provides a rich set of operators to manipulate variables, such as Arithmetic Operators, Relational Operators, Logical Operators, Assignment Operators, Bitwise Operators, and Misc Operators (conditional operator, instanceOf operator)

Let's start with arithmetic operators.

Java Arithmetic operators

Arithmetic operators are used in mathematical expressions (add, subtract, divide, multiple and so on). Java provides seven Arithmetic operators as shown in the following table.

Table 4.1 | Arithmetic Operators (Assume integer variable A holds 10 and variable B holds 20)

Operator	Description	Example
+ (Addition)	Adds values on either side of the operator.	A + B = 30
- (Subtraction)	Subtracts right-hand operand from left-hand operand.	A - B = -10
* (Multiplication)	Multiplies values on either side of the operator.	A * B = 200
/ (Division)	Divides left-hand operand by right-hand operand.	B / A = 2
% (Modulus)	Divides left-hand operand by right-hand operand and returns remainder.	B % A = 0
++ (Increment)	Increases the value of operand by 1.	B ++ = 21
-- (Decrement)	Decreases the value of operand by 1.	B -- = 19

Here are some examples of arithmetic operators.

Example 4.1: ArithmeticOp1.java

```
01  package ch04;
02  public class ArithmeticOp1 {
03      public static void main(String[] args){
04          int x;
05          int y = 10;
06          int z = 5;
07          x = y + z;
08          System.out.println("+ operator resulted in " + x);//15
09
10          x = y -z;
11          System.out.println("- operator resulted in " + x);//5
12
13          x = y * z;
14          System.out.println("* operator resulted in " + x);//50
15
16          x = y / z;
17          System.out.println("/ operator resulted in " + x);//2
18
19          x = y % z;
20          System.out.println("% operator resulted in " + x);//0
21
22          x = -y;
23          System.out.println("Unary operator resulted in" + x);//-10
24      }
25  }
```

Output

```
+ operator resulted in 15
- operator resulted in 5
* operator resulted in 50
/ operator resulted in 2
% operator resulted in 0
Unary operator resulted in-10
```

Explanation

> Line 04: Create a variable named **x**.
> Line 05: Create a variable named **y** and assign it a value **10**.
> Line 06: Create a variable named **z** and assign it a value **5**.
> Line 07: Add the values of **y** and **z** and assign the result to the **x** variable.
> Line 08: Sends the value of the **x** variable to the `println()` method. The variable's contents are displayed.
> Line 10: Subtract the values of **y** and **z** and assign the result to the **x** variable.
> Line 11: Sends the value of the **x** variable to the the `println()` method. The variable's contents are displayed.
> Line 13: Multiply the values of **y** and **z** and assign the result to the **x** variable.
> Line 14: Sends the value of the **x** variable to the the `println()` method. The variable's contents are displayed.
> Line 16: Divide the values of **y** and **z** and assign the result to the **x** variable.
> Line 17: Sends the value of the **x** variable to the the `println()` method. The variable's contents are displayed.
> Line 19: Convert the value of the **y** variable from 10 to -10. Then assign the result to the **x** variable.
> Line 20: Sends the value of the **x** variable to the the `println()` method. The variable's contents are displayed.

Here is another example.

Example 4.2: ArithmeticOp2.java

```
01  package ch04;
02  public class ArithmeticOp2 {
03      public static void main(String[] args){
04          int a = 10;
05          int b = 20;
06
07          System.out.println("a + b = " + (a+b));
08          System.out.println("a - b = " + (a-b));
09          System.out.println("a * b = " + (a*b));
10          System.out.println("a / b = " + (a/b));
11          System.out.println("a % b = " + (a%b));
12          System.out.println("b % a = " + (b%a));
13          System.out.println("a++ = " + (a++));
14          System.out.println("a-- = " + (a--));
```

```
15
16      }
17 }
```

Output
```
a + b = 30
a - b = -10
a * b = 200
a / b = 0
a % b = 10
b % a = 0
a++ = 10
a-- = 11
```

Explanation

> Line 04: Create a variable named **a** and assign it a value **10**.
> Line 05: Create a variable named **b** and assign it a value **20**.
> Line 07: Both **a** and **b** are added together and the result **30** is displayed.

NOTES: Expressions within the parentheses are evaluated from *left* to *right*. Consider the following example:
    System.out.println("a + b = " + a + b); // 1020
When a String is added to any other data type, the resultant value is a String. The other variable is also converted to a String and then concatenated.
    System.out.println("a + b = " + a + b); // Output: 1020
If the expression within the `println()` method contains parentheses, then the value within the parentheses is evaluated first. Thus, when two integers are operated with a (+) sign, the (+) sign acts as an addition operator and not a concatenation operator. Consider the following example -
    System.out.println("a + b = " + (a+b));   // Output: 30
Parentheses have been used to alter the order in which evaluation is performed. First, the expression within the parentheses is evaluated. Hence, a + b is evaluated to give an integer 30, which is concatenated with the String "a + b = " to give the final String "a + b = 30".

Java Relational Operators

Relational operator in Java is used to compare two values and return a boolean value. For example, the less than operator (<) determines whether one value is less than another. Java provides six relational operators. Table 4.2 lists the Java relational operators, and shows examples of several relational expressions that compare the variable A and B.

Table 4.2 | Relational Operators (Assume integer variable A holds 10 and variable B holds 20)

Operator	Description	Relational Expression
== (equals-to)	Checks if the values of A and B are equal or not, if yes then condition becomes true.	(A==B) is not true
!= (not equal to)	Checks if the values of A and B are equal or not, if yes then condition becomes true.	(A!=B) is true
> (greater than)	Checks if the value of A is greater than the value of B, if yes then condition becomes true.	(A>B) is not true
< (less than)	Checks if the value of A is less than the value of B, if yes then condition becomes true.	(A<B) is true
>= (greater than or equal to)	Checks if the value of A is greater than or equal to the value of B, if yes then condition becomes true.	(A>=B) is not true
<= (less than or equal to)	Checks if the value of A is less than or equal to the value of B, if yes then condition becomes true.	(A<=B) is true

All relational operators are binary, which means they use two operands. For example:

$$A > B$$

This expression is called a relational expression. This relational expression is used to determine whether A is greater than B. The example below Shows how to use relational operators using Java.

Example 4.3: RelationalOp.java

```
01  package ch04;
02  public class RelationalOp {
03      public static void main(String[] args){
04          int a = 10;
05          int b = 20;
06
07          System.out.println("a == b = " + (a == b));
08          System.out.println("a != b = " + (a != b));
09          System.out.println("a > b = " + (a > b));
10          System.out.println("a < b = " + (a < b));
11          System.out.println("a >= b = " + (a >= b));
```

```
12            System.out.println("b <= a = " + (b <= a));
13      }
14 }
```

Output

```
a == b = false
a != b = true
a >  b = false
a <  b = true
a >= b = false
b <= a = false
```

Explanation

> Line 04: Create a variable named **a** and assign it a value **10**.
> Line 05: Create a variable named **b** and assign it a value **20**.
> Line 07: `println()` method display "a == b = false" because (a == b) returns `true` if **a** and **b** are equal, and returns `false` if **a** and **b** are not equal.
> Line 08: `println()` method display "a != b = true" because (a != b) returns `true` of **a** and **b** are not equal, and returns `false` if **a** and **b** are equal.
> and so on.

Java Logical Operators

The relational operators are sufficient when you only need to check one condition. However what if a particular action is to be taken only if several conditions are true? Answer is the logic operators. The following table lists the logical operators:

Table 4.3 | Logical Operators (Assume Boolean variables A holds true and variable B holds false)

Operator	Description	Example
`&&` (logical AND)	It combines two boolean values and returns a boolean which is true if and only if both of its operands are true.	(A && B) is false
`||` (logical OR)	It combines two boolean variables or expressions and returns a result that is true if either or both of its operands are true.	(A || B) is true
`!` (logical NOT)	It reverses the value of a boolean expression. Thus if b is true !b is false. If b is false !b is true.	!(A && B) is true

Given that `x` and `y` represent boolean expressions, the boolean logical operators are defined in the table below:

x	y	!x	x & y x && y	x | y x || y	x ^ y
T	T	F	T	T	F
T	F	F	F	T	T
F	T	T	F	T	T
F	F	T	F	F	F

Example 4.4: LogicalOp1.java

```
01  package ch04;
02  public class LogicalOp1 {
03      public static void main(String[] args) {
04          boolean a = true;
05          boolean b = false;
06          System.out.println("a && b = " + (a&&b));
07          System.out.println("a || b = " + (a || b));
08          System.out.println("!(a&&b) = " + !(a && b));
09      }
10  }
```

Output

```
a && b = false
a || b = true
!(a&&b) = true
```

Explanation

› Line 04: Create a variable named **a** and assign it a value `true`.
› Line 05: Create a variable named **b** and assign it a value `false`.
› Line 06: The logical AND operator combines two boolean variables (a && b) and returns `false`. The `println()` method display `a && b = false` on the screen.
› Line 07: The logical OR operator combines two boolean variables (a || b) and returns `true`. The `println()` method display `a || b = true` on the screen.
› Line 08: The logical NOT operator reverses the value of a boolean expression (a && b). Then, the `!(a && b)` is `true`. The `println()` method display `!(a&&b) = true` on the screen.

Java Assignment Operators

Assignment operators are used in Java to assign values to variables. The Assignment operators takes the value of the right operand and puts it in the variable identified by the left operand. Right operand may be a literal or a variable.

Syntax
```
<left-side-operand> = <right-side-operand>
```

The operand on the left side of the (=) operator must be a variable name. The operand on the right side of the (=) operator must be an expression that has a value.

Example 4.5: AssignmentOp1.java
```
01  public class AssignmentOp1{
02      public static void main(String[] args) {
03          int length = 10;
04          int width;
05          // change the content of length to 20.
06          length = 20;
07
08          // assigns the value of the length variable to the width variable.
09          // length still has the same value 20.
10          width = length;
11
12          System.out.println("Length value is " + length);
13          System.out.println("Width value is " + width);
14      }
15  }
```

Output
```
Length value is 20
Width value is 20
```

Important: The assignment operator only changes the contents of its left operand.

Following are the assignment operators supported by Java language –

Table 4.4 | Assignment Operators (Assume Boolean variables A holds true and variable B holds false)

Operator	Description	Example
=	Simple assignment operator. Assigns values from right side operands to left side operand.	C = A + B will assign value of A + B into C
+=	Add AND assignment operator. It adds right operand to the left operand and assign the result to left operand.	C += A is equivalent to C = C + A
-=	Subtract AND assignment operator. It subtracts right operand from the left operand and assign the result to left operand.	C -= A is equivalent to C = C - A
*=	Multiply AND assignment operator. It multiplies right operand with the left operand and assign the result to left operand.	C *= A is equivalent to C = C * A
/=	Divide AND assignment operator. It divides left operand with the right operand and assign the result to left operand.	C /= A is equivalent to C = C / A
%=	Modulus AND assignment operator. It takes modulus using two operands and assign the result to left operand.	C %= A is equivalent to C = C % A
<<=	Left shift AND assignment operator.	C <<= 2 is same as C = C << 2
>>=	Bitwise AND assignment operator.	C &= 2 is same as C = C & 2
&=	Right shift AND assignment operator.	C >>= 2 is same as C = C >> 2
^=	bitwise exclusive OR and assignment operator.	C ^= 2 is same as C = C ^ 2
|=	Bitwise inclusive OR and assignment operator.	C |= 2 is same as C = C | 2

Example 4.6: AssignmentOp2.java

```
package ch04;
public class AssignmentOp1 {
    public static void main(String[] args) {
        int a =   , b =   , c =   ;
        c = a + b;
```

```
06            System.out.println("c = a + b = " + c);
07
08            c += a;
09            System.out.println("c+= a = " + c);
10
11            c -= a;
12            System.out.println("c -= a = " + c);
13
14            c *= a;
15            System.out.println("c *= a = " + c);
16            a = 10;
17            c = 15;
18            c /= a;
19        }
20    }
```

Output

```
c = a + b = 30
c+= a = 40
c -= a = 30
c *= a = 300
```

Explanation

> Line 04: Create a variable named **a** and assign it a value **10**.
> Line 04: Create a variable named **b** and assign it a value **20**.
> Line 04: Create a variable named **c** and assign it a value **0**.
> Line 05: Add the values of **a** and **b** and assign the result to the **c** variable.
> Line 06: Sends the value of the **c** variable to the `println()` method. The contents are displayed as: c = a + b = 30
> Line 08: Add the values of **c** and **a** and assign the result to the **c** variable.
> Line 09: Sends the value of the **c** variable to the `println()` method. The contents are displayed as: c+= a = 40
> Line 11: Subtract the values of **c** and **a** and assign the result to the **c** variable.
> Line 12: Sends the value of the **c** variable to the `println()` method. The contents are displayed as: c -= a = 30
> Line 14: Multiply the values of **c** and **a** and assign the result to the **c** variable.
> Line 15: Sends the value of the **c** variable to the `println()` method. The contents are displayed as: c *= a = 300
> Line 18: Divide the values of **c** and **a** and assign the result to the **c** variable.

Java bitwise Operators

Java provides Bit wise operators to manipulate the contents of variables at the bit level. These variables must be of numeric data type (`char, short, int, or long`). Java provides seven bitwise operators.

Table 4.5 | Bitwise Operators. (Assume integer variable A holds 60 and variable B holds 15)

Operator	Description	Example
& (bitwise AND)	Performs the AND operation on each pair of bits. a AND b yields 1 only if both a and b are 1.	a = 60 (0011 1100) b = 15 (0000 1111) ---- a & b (0000 1100) 12
| (bitwise OR)	Performs the OR operation on each pair of bits. a OR b yields 1 if either a or b is 1.	a = 60 (0011 1100) b = 15 (0000 1111) ---- a | b (0011 1111) 63
^ (bitwise XOR)	Performs the XOR operation on each pair of bits. a XOR b yields 1 if a and b are different.	a = 60 (0011 1100) b = 15 (0000 1111) ---- a ^ b (0011 0011) 51
~ (bitwise compliment)	Performs the NOT operator on each bit. NOT a yields the inverted value (a.k.a. one's complement) of a.	a = 60 (0011 1100) ---- ~a -61 (1100 0011)

bitwise shift operators

The bitwise shift operators take two operands: the first is a quantity to be shifted, and the second specifies the number of bit positions by which the first operand is to be shifted.

Table 4.6 | bitwise shift operators

Operator	Description	Example
<< (left shift)	In the < < Left Shift Operator all bytes are moved to the left by the number of bits specified by the right operand.	a << 2; a = 60 (0011 1100) The no of bits to shift: 2 ---------------- Result : 11110000 Result : 240 (dec)
>> (right shift) Positive numbers	Binary Right Shift Operator. The left operands value is moved right by the number of bits specified by the right operand.	a >> 2; a = 60 (0011 1100) The no of bits to shift: 2 ---------------- Result : 1111 Result : 15
>> (right shift) Negative numbers	>> shifts the bits to the right using zeros to fill the leftmost bits, and when it finishes, it resets the left bit to 1 to keep the result negative.	a = -99 >> 2 ; looks: 10011101 result:11100111
>>> (zero fill right shift) Positive number	Shift right zero fill operator. The left operands value is moved right by the number of bits specified by the right operand and shifted values are filled up with zeros.	a >>> 2; a = 60 (0011 1100) The no of bits to shift: 2 ---------------- Result : 00001111 Result : 15
>>> (zero fill right shift) Negative number	With >>> , all bits are shifted to the right, and zeros fill in the leftmost bits.	a = -1; a >>> 2 ; The operand -1 : 11111111 Becomes: 00111111

Example 4.7: BitwiseOp1.java

Assume if a = 40 and b = 10; now in binary format they will be as follows:

```
01  package ch04;
02  public class BitwiseOp1 {
03      public static void main(String[] args) {
04          int a = 40; // 40 = 0010 1000
05          int b = 10; // 10 = 0000 1010
06          int c = 0;
07          c = a & b;   // 8 = 0000 1000
08          System.out.println("a & b = " + c);
09          c = a | b;   // 42 = 0010 1010
10          System.out.println("a | b = " + c);
11          c = a ^ b;   // 34 = 0010 0010
12          System.out.println("a ^ b = " + c);
```

```
            c = ~a;
            System.out.println("        ~a = " + c);
            c = a <<  ;    // 160 = 1010 0000
            System.out.println("a >> b = " + c);
            c = a >>>  ;// 10 = 0000 1010
            System.out.println("a >>> 2 = " + c);
        }
    }
```

Output

```
a & b = 8
a | b = 42
a ^ b = 34
       ~a = -41
a >> b = 160
a >>> 2 = 10
```

Example 4.8: BitwiseOp2.java

```
package ch04;
public class BitwiseOp2 {
    public static void main(String[] args){
        int x =       ; // 1111101011101111
        int y =       ; // 1111100011101001
        int z;
        System.out.println("x & y : " + (x & y));
        System.out.println("x ^ y : " + (x ^ y));
        System.out.println("~x : " + (~x));
        System.out.println("x << y : " + (x << y));
        System.out.println("x >> y : " + (x >> y));
        System.out.println("x >>> y : " + (x >>> y));
        // There is no unsigned left shift operator
    }
}
```

Output

```
x & y : 63721
x ^ y : 518
~x : -64240
x << y : 32890368
x >> y : 125
x >>> y : 125
```

The result of applying bitwise operators between two corresponding bits in the operands is shown in the table below:

A	B	~A	A & B	A | B	A ^ B
1	1	0	1	1	0
1	0	0	0	1	1
0	1	1	0	1	1
0	0	1	0	0	0

Java Increment and Decrement Operators

The increment and decrement operators are belongs to arithmetic operators.
- (++) Increases the value of operand by 1.
- (--) Decreases the value of operand by 1.

Table 4.7 | Increment and Decrement Operators. (assume integer variable B holds 20)

Operator	Description	Example
++(Increment)	Increases the value of operand by 1.	B++ gives 21
--(Decrement)	Decreases the value of operand by 1.	B-- gives 19

Example 4.9: IncDecOp.java

```
01  package ch04;
02  public class IncDecOp {
03      public static void main(String[] args) {
04          int a = 1;
05          a++;
06          int b = 2;
07          b++;
08
09          System.out.println("a = " + a);
10          System.out.println("b = " + b);
11      }
12  }
```

Output
```
a = 2
b = 3
```

Explanation
- Line 05: Increases the value of **a** variable by 1.
- Line 07: Increases the value of **b** variable by 1.
- Line 09:   Displays the value of the variable **a** on the screen.
- Line 10: Displays the value of the variable **b** on the screen.

Note. For more information, see the loops chapter.

Summary

> Expression consist of two types of components: Operators and Operands. The symbol used in an operation is called an operator (e.g., +, -, /). A value involved in an operation is called an operand.

> Operators perform operations on data or operands. Operators are the symbols that represent simple calculations like addition and multiplication. All expressions have at least one operand.

> Java provides a rich set of operators to manipulate variables, such as Arithmetic Operators, Relational Operators, Logical Operators, Assignment Operators, Bitwise Operators, and Misc Operators (conditional operator, instanceOf operator).

> Arithmetic operators are used in mathematical expressions (add, subtract, divide, multiple and so on).

> Relational operators in Java are used to compare two or more objects or numbers and return a boolean value. Java provides six relational operators: ==, !=, >, <, >=, <=.

> Logical operators in Java are used to compare two or more conditions. Java provides three relational operators: &&, ||, !.

> The Assignment operators takes the value of the right operand and puts it in the variable identified by the left operand. Right operand may be a literal or a variable.

> Java provides Bit wise operators to manipulate the contents of variables at the bit level. These variables must be of numeric data type (char, short, int, or long). Java provides seven bitwise operators: &, |, ^, ~, <<, >>, >>>.

> The increment and decrement operators are belongs to Arithmetic Operators. The (++) operator increases the value of operand by 1, and the (--) operator decreases the value of operand by 1.

Chapter 5

Control Structure

Introduction to Java Control Structure (a.k.a. Control Flow)

When a program is running, the code is being read by the computer line by line, from top to bottom. Now as the code is being read from top to bottom, it may hit a point where it needs to make a decision, this decision could make the code jump to a completely different part of the program. So, this decision that must be made is known as a **control structure**.

Types of Java control structure (or control flow)
1. The Sequence Structure.
2. The Decision (or Selection) Structure.
3. The Repetition (or Looping) Structure.

The sequence structure

A program is a sequence of instructions. Statements are executed one after the other in the order in which they are written. It is the default execution process. For example -

```
01  public class ClassName {
02      public static void main(String[] args)
03      {
04          System.out.println("First statement");
05          System.out.println("Second statement");
06      }
07  }
```

The computer executes the instructions one after the other, from line number **01** to line number **07** (from up to bottom). However, this is very limited. **Loops** and **selections** are special instructions that can change the flow of control.

The Selection Structure

A selection statement (a.k.a. conditional structure) causes the program control to be transferred to a specific flow based on whether a condition is **true** or **false**. Selection structures use relational operators to test conditions.

There are different types of selection structures that can be used to achieve different outcomes.

Types of Selection Structures

> The `if` selection statement
> The `if...else` selection statement
> The conditional operator `(? :)`
> The `if...else...if` selection statement
> Nested `if` selection statement
> The `switch` selection statement

The if selection statement

It performs (selects) an action if a condition is `true`, and skips the action if the condition is `false`. The `if` statement causes one or more statements to execute only when a condition is `true`.

Syntax
```
01  if (condition)
02  {
03      // statement(s) will execute if
04      // the boolean_expression (condition) is true
05  }
06  // statement(s) will execute if the boolean expression (con-
    dition) is false
```

Explanation
> The condition should always be enclosed in parentheses.

> A boolean expression (condition) is one that is either true, or false. If the condition is true, the next statements between { and } are executed. Otherwise, it is skipped. The statement is conditionally executed (it only executes under the condition that the expression in the parentheses is true.)
> If the condition is false, the next statement(s) after the { and } are executed (line 06).

The control flow in the `if` statement is shown in the following figure.

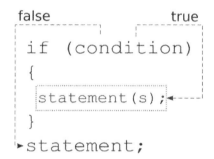

Figure 1.2 | Control flow in if statement

The program `IfSelect.java` illustrates the use of **if** statement for making a decision.

Example 5.1: IfSelect.java

```
01  package ch05;
02  public class IfSelect {
03      public static void main(String[] args) {
04          int x = 11;
05          if (x > 10)
06          {
07              System.out.println("x is greater than 10.");
08          }
09          System.out.println("First statement after the body of if condition");
10      }
11  }
```

Output

```
x is greater than 10.
First statement after the body of if condition
```

Explanation

> Line 05: The condition (x > 10) is true, so the next statement between { and } is executed.
> Line 07: Displays the message "x is greater than 10." on the screen.

> Line 09: Executes the next statement(s) after the `{ and }` (if exists), which display the `"First statement after the body of if condition"` message on the screen.

A decision can be based on any expression - if the expression evaluates to **0**, it is treated as false, and if the expression evaluates to nonzero, it is treated as true.

Relational Operators

Typically, the condition that is tested by an `if` statement is formed with a relational operator. A relational operator determines whether a specific relationship exists between two values. The table below summarizes the relational operators:

Table 5.1 | Java Relational Operators Table

Precedence	Relational Operator	Meaning
1	>	Greater Than
2	<	Less Than
3	>=	Greater Than or Equal to
4	<=	Less Than or Equal to
5	==	Equal to
6	!=	Not Equal to

All of the relational operators are binary, which means they use two operands.

Examples of Several of conditions that compare the variable A and B

Expression	Meaning
A > B	Is A greater than B? - Returns true if A is greater than B
A < B	Is A less than B? - Returns true if A is less than B
A >= B	Is A greater than or equal to B? - Returns true if A is greater than or equal to B
A <= B	Is A less than or equal to B? - Returns true if A is less than or equal to B
A == B	Is A equal to B? - Returns true if A and B are equal
A != B	Is A not equal to B? - Returns true of A and B are not equal

Following is an example, `GreaterT.java`, that defines one integer number and uses the relational operators to determine if its value is greater than 40 or not. Because the expression can be only true or false, it is a boolean expression.

Example 5.2: GreaterT.java - Using the greater than operator (>) with `if` statement

```
01 package ch05;
02 public class GreaterT {
03     public static void main(String[] args) {
04         int x = ;
05         if (x > )
06         {
07             System.out.println("Welcome");
08         }
09     }
10 }
```

Output

```
Welcome
```

Explanation

> Line 05: The `>` operator determines whether one value is greater than another. So if `x` value is greater than 40, return `true`. Then execute the body of `if` statement.
> Line 09-10: If `x` value is not greater than 40, return `false`. Then skip the body of `if` statement and execute the first statement after the body of the `if` statement.

Here is another example that use >= and <=.

Example 5.3: GreaterEqual.java - Using >= and <= (*no space between > or < and = sign*)

```
01 package ch05;
02 public class GreaterEqual {
03     public static void main(String[] args){
04         int a = , b = , c = ;
05         if (b >= a)    // true
06         {
07             System.out.println("B is greater than a ");
08         }
09         if ( a >= c)  // true
10         {
11             System.out.println("A is equal to c");
12         }
13         if (a > )      // false
14         {
15             System.out.println("A is less than 5");
16         }
17     }
18 }
```

Output

```
    B is greater than a
    A is equal to c
```

Explanation

> \>= and <= test for more than one relationship.

> The >= determines whether the operand on the left is greater than or equal to the operand on its right.

Here is a simple example that use equal operator.

Example 5.4: EqualTo.java - Using equal to operator (= =) with if statement

```
01  package ch05;
02  public class EqualTo {
03      public static void main(String[] args) {
04          int a = 4, b = 5;
05          if (a == b) {
06              System.out.println("a is equal to b");
07          }
08          System.out.println("a is not equal to b");
09      }
10  }
```

Output

```
    a is not equal to b
```

Explanation

> Line 05: The `(==)` operator determines whether the operand on its left (value of a) is equal to the operand on its right (value of b). If `a` value is not equal to `b` value, return `false`.

> Line 08: If (a) value is not equal to (b) value, skip the body of `if` statement and execute the first statement after the body of `if` statement.

Here is another example that use != operator.

Example 5.5: NotEqual.java - Using (!=) operator

```
01  package ch05;
02  public class NotEqual {
03      public static void main(String[] args) {
04          int a = 4, b = 5, c = 4;
05          if (a != b)      // true
06              System.out.println("a is not equal to b");
07          if (b != c)      // true
08              System.out.println("b is not equal to c");
09          if (a != c)      // false
10              System.out.println("a = " + a + " b = " + b);
11      }
12  }
```

Output

```
    a is not equal to b
```

```
    b is not equal to c
```

Explanation

> The `(!=)` operator determines whether the operand on its left is not equal to the operand on its right, which is the opposite of the `(==)` operator.

Comparing Characters

The operators `==` and `!=` can be used to compare boolean values. For example, can you figure out what these examples does:

Example 5.6: Compare1.java - Use == with character to test for equality

```
01  public class Compare1 {
02      public static void main(String[] args) {
03          char ch = 'C';
04          if (ch == 'A')
05          {
06              System.out.println("The letter is A");
07          }
08      }
09  }
```

Output
```
    Nothing
```

Explanation

> Line 04: Checks if the value of `ch` variable is equal to `A` or not. It returns false.
> So nothing will appear on the screen.

Example 5.7: Compare2.java - Use != with characters to test for inequality

```
01  // determine whether the char variable ch
02  // is not equal to the letter 'A'
03  char ch = 'A';
04  if (ch != 'A')
05  {
06      System.out.println("Not the letter A");
07  }
```

Output
```
    Nothing
```

You can use the `<`, `>`, `<=`, `>=` operators to compare characters.

One thing that you cannot do with relational operators is to use them to compare values of type String. (The `==` operator checks whether two objects are stored in the same memory location, rather than whether they contain the same value.)

REMEMBER: Computers do not actually store characters, such as A, B, C and so on, in memory instead, they store numeric codes that represent the characters. Java uses Unicode, which is a set of numbers that represents all the letters of the alphabet (both lowercase and uppercase), the printable digits 0-9, punctuation symbols, and special characters.

Unicode System[1]

0	NUL	1	SOH	2	STX	3	ETX	4	EOT	5	ENQ	6	ACK	7	BEL
8	BS	9	HT	10	LF	11	VT	12	FF	13	CR	14	SO	15	SI
16	DLE	17	DCI	18	DC2	19	DC3	20	DC4	21	NAK	22	SYN	23	ETB
24	CAN	25	EM	26	SUB	27	ESC	28	FS	29	GS	30	RS	31	US
32	SP	33	!	34	"	35	#	36	$	37	%	38	&	39	'
40	(	41	)	42	*	43	+	44	,	45	-	46	.	47	/
48	0	49	1	50	2	51	3	52	4	53	5	54	6	55	7
56	8	57	9	58	:	59	;	60	<	61	=	62	>	63	?
64	@	65	A	66	B	67	C	68	D	69	E	70	F	71	G
72	H	73	I	74	J	75	K	76	L	77	M	78	N	79	O
80	P	81	Q	82	R	83	S	84	T	85	U	86	V	87	W
88	X	89	Y	90	Z	91	[	92	\	93	]	94	^	95	_
96	`	97	a	98	b	99	c	100	d	101	e	102	f	103	g
104	h	105	i	106	j	107	k	108	l	109	m	110	n	111	o
112	p	113	q	114	r	115	s	116	t	117	u	118	v	119	w
120	x	121	y	122	z	123	{	124			125	}	126	~	127	DEL

When a character is stored in memory, it is actually the Unicode number that is stored. When the computer is instructed to print the value on the screen, it displays the character that corresponds with the numeric code.

In Unicode, letters are arranged in alphabetic order. A comes before B, the numeric code for the character A is less than the code for the character B (A -> 65, B-> 66). Here is a simple example to understand unicode characters.

Example 5.8: unicode1.java - understanding unicode characters

```
01  public class unicode1 {
02      public static void main(String[] args) {
03          char A, B;
04          if ('A' < 'B')
05              System.out.println("A is less than B.");
06      }
07  }
```

Output
    A is less than B.

In Unicode, the uppercase letters come before the lowercase letters. The space character (code 32) comes before all the alphabetic characters. Here is another simple unicode example.

Example 5.9: unicode2.java - Understanding Unicode Characters

---
[1] https://www.trainside.de/Tutorial%20Java/Konstanten%20Variablen%20Bezeichner/

```
01  class unicode2
02  {
03      public static void main(String[] args)
04      {
05          char ch1 = 67;
06          char ch2 = 104;
07          System.out.println("ch1 = " + ch1);  //ch1=C
08          System.out.println("ch2 = " + ch2);  //ch2-h
09      }
10  }
```

Output
```
ch1 = C
ch2 = h
```

if...else Statement

if...else statement allow you to specify that different actions are to be performed when the condition is true than when the condition is false. It is called a double-selection statement because it selects between two different actions.

Syntax
```
if (condition)
{
    // statement(s) will execute if the condition is true
} else
{
    // statement(s) will execute if the condition is false
}
```

Explanation

- A boolean expression (condition) is one that is either true, or false. If the condition is true, the next statements between { and } are executed.
- If the condition is false, the else statement(s) between { and } are executed.

The control flow in the if-else statement is shown in the following figure.

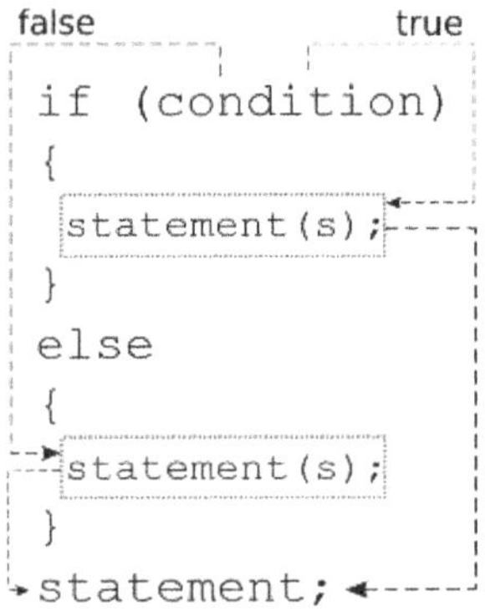

```
         false              true
           ┌─────────────────┐
           │ if (condition)  │
           │ {               │
           │   statement(s); │◄───┐
           │ }               │    │
           │ else            │    │
           │ {               │    │
       ┌──►│   statement(s); │    │
       │   │ }               │    │
       │   └─────────────────┘    │
       └──► statement; ◄──────────┘
```

Figure 1.3 | Control flow in if-else condition

The program `if.java` illustrates the use of the `if-else` statement.

Example 5.10: if.java - Using if-else statement

```
01  package ch05;
02  public class If {
03      public static void main(String[] args) {
04          int x = 10;
05          if (x >= 10)
06          {
07              System.out.println("OK");
08          } else
09          {
10              System.out.println("False");
11          }
12      }
13  }
```

Output

OK

Explanation

› The condition `(x >=10)` is `true`, so the next statement between `{` and `}` is executed (line 07).

Conditional Operator (? :)

It is closely related to the `if...else` statement. It is Java's only ternary operator. The goal of the operator is to decide, which value should be assigned to the variable.

Ternary operator

It is the only conditional operator that takes three operands (3 `Operands` + `Conditional Operator = Conditional Expression`).

Syntax
```
variable x = (expression) ? value if true : value if false;
```
Explanation

> First Operand is a condition `(expression)`.
> Second Operand is the value for the entire conditional expression if the condition is `true`.
> Third Operand is the value for the entire conditional expression if the condition is `false`.

Let's see java ternary operator example in a simple java program.

Example 5.11: Ternary1.java
```
01  package ch05;
02  public class Ternary1 {
03      public static void main(String[] args) {
04          int x = 10;
05          System.out.println(x >= 10 ? "OK" : "Failed");
06      }
07  }
```
Output
```
OK
```
Explanation

> Line 04: `x >= 10` is the condition (1st Operand).
> Line 05: `"OK"` is displayed if the condition is `true` (2nd Operand).
> Line 05: `"Failed"` is displayed if the condition is `false` (3rd Operand).
> Line 05: The `println()` method displays `"OK"` message on the screen.

The conditional expression can either be a simple boolean value, or it can be an action to be executed (a statement that evaluates to a boolean value), like the `(a < 0)` statement. Here is one more example that demonstrate this very clearly.

Example 5.12: Ternary2.java
```
01  package ch05;
02  public class Ternary2 {
03      public static void main(String[] args) {
```

```
04              int x = 60;
05              x = (x > 100) ? 20 : 30;
06              System.out.println(x);
07          }
08      }
```

Output

```
30
```

Explanation (Line 05)

> - `x > 100` is the condition (1st Operand).
> - `20` is displayed if the condition is `true` (2nd Operand).
> - `30` is displayed if the condition is `false` (3rd Operand).

As you can see that we are using java ternary operator to avoid `if-else` and `switch` case statements. This way we are reducing the number of lines of code in java program. That's all for a quick roundup of ternary operator in java.

Nested if...else Statements

Nested `if...else` statements test for multiple cases or conditions by placing `if...else` statements inside `if...else` statements. Here's a program that demonstrates the concept of outer and inner `if` statement.

Example 5.13: OuterInnerIf.java

```
01  package ch05;
02  public class OuterInnerIf {
03      public static void main(String[] args) {
04          int x = 50;
05          if (x > 0) // outer if
06          {
07              if (x < 100) // inner if
08              {
09                  System.out.println("X is between 0 and 100");
10              }
11          }
12      }
13  }
```

Output

```
X is between 0 and 100
```

Explanation (What does Java do when it runs this code?)

> - Evaluates the condition of the outer `if`. If it evaluates to `false`, don't run the code in the `if` body (which is the inner `if`).

> Evaluates the outer `if` condition. If it evaluates to `true`, run its `if` body (the `println()` statement).
> So basically it evaluates the OUTER condition, and only when it succeeds does it evaluate the inner condition.

Example 5.14: IfEsle.java

You can also have an inner `if` statement that is contained in the `if` body of an outer `if` but isn't the `if` body.

```java
package ch05;
public class IfElse {
    public static void main(String[] args) {
        int x = 90;
        if (x > 0)          // outer if
        {
            System.out.println("Outer If");
            if ( x < 100 ) // Innter if
            {
                System.out.println("X is between 0 and 100");
            }
        }
    }
}
```

Output

```
Outer If
X is between 0 and 100
```

Explanation

> In this case, the `if` body of the outer `if` contains two statements, one of which is the inner `if` body.
> This can't be rewritten using `&&` because the first `println()` statement only depends on the outer condition.

Logical Operators

Java Provides two binary logical Operators: `&&` and `||`. A logical operator is an operator that returns a boolean result (`True` or `False`). Logical operators are used to combine two or more boolean expressions into one or single expression. A logical operator is also called a **Boolean Operator**.

A Boolean expression is a three-part clause that consists of two items to be compared, separated by a comparison operator. The logical operators are described in the following table:

Table 5.2 | Logical Operators

Operator	Name	Type	Description
&&	Logical AND	Binary	Returns `true` if the both of the operands evaluate to `true`. Both operands are evaluated before the AND operator is applied. But if the operand on the left returns `false`, it returns `false` without evaluating the operand on the right.
||	Logical OR	Binary	Returns `true` if at least one of the operands evaluates to `true`. Both operands are evaluated before the OR operator is applied. But if the operand on the left returns `true`, it returns `true` without evaluating the operand on the right.
!	Logical NOT	Unary	Returns `true` if the operand to the right evaluates to `false`. Returns `false` if the operand to the right is `true`.

The following table show the result of combining any two boolean expressions using the `AND` operator and the `OR` operator (or the `NOT` operator.)

Table 5.3 | Boolean Expression Using Logical Operators

Expression	Meaning
`x > y && a < b`	Is `x` greater than `y` AND is `a` less than `b`?
`x == y || x==z`	Is `x` equal to `y` OR is `x` equal to `z`?
`!(x>y)`	Is the expression `x > y` NOT `true`?

The && operator

Is knows as the logical `AND` operator. It takes or combines two *Boolean* expressions and create a boolean expression that is true only when both sub-conditions are `TRUE`.

Syntax

```
if ( firstExpression && secondExpression ){
    // statement
}
```

Example 5.15: LogicalAnd.java

```
01  package ch05;
02  public class LogicalAnd {
03      public static void main(String[] args) {
04          int temp = 10;
05          int minutes = 15;
06          if (temp > 20 && minutes > 12) {
07              System.out.println("The Temperature is in the danger zone");
08          }
09      }
10  }
```

Output
```
Nothing
```

Explanation

› Line 06: The two boolean expressions are combined into a single expression.
- 1st expression `temp > 20` is `true`.
- 2nd expression `minutes > 12` is `false`.
- So, the result of the boolean expression is false
  (TRUE && FALSE = FALSE)

› So, the entire expression is `false` and the message is not displayed.

Table 5.4 | Truth Table for the && Operator

Expression	Value of the Expression	
T && T	T	Both sides of the && operator must be TRUE for the operator to return a true value.
F && F	F	
F && T	F	
F && T	F	

The && Operator performs short-circuit evaluation (How it works?):

› If the expression on the left side of the `&&` operator is `false`, the expression on the right side will not be checked.
› Because the entire expression is `false` if only one of the sub-expression is `false`, it would waste CPU time to check the remaining expression.
› So, when the `&&` operator finds that the expression on its left is `false`, it short-circuit and does not evaluate the expression on its right.

The || operator

Is known as the logical OR operator. It takes two boolean expressions and creates a boolean expression that is true when either of the sub-expressions is true. Let's see an example for this.

Example 5.16: LogicalOr.java

```
01 package ch05;
02 public class LogicalOr {
03     public static void main(String[] args) {
04
05         int temp = 101;
06         if (temp < 20 || temp > 100)
07         {
08             System.out.println("The Temperature is in the danger zone");
09         }
10     }
11 }
```

Output

```
The Temperature is in the danger zone
```

Explanation

> The message will be displayed if temperature is less than 20 OR temperature is greater than 100.
> If either relational test is true, the entire expression is true.

Table 5.5 | Truth table for the || Operator

Expression	Value
T || F	T
F || T	T
F || F	F
T || T	T

The ! operator

Performs a logical NOT operation. It is a Unary operator that takes a Boolean expression and reverse its logical value. Means if the expression is `true`, the `!` operator returns `false`, and if the expression is `false`, it returns `true`. Here is a simple example.

Example 5.17: LogicalNot.java

```
01  package ch05;
02  public class LogicalNot {
03      public static void main(String[] args) {
04          int temp = 90;
05          if (!(temp > 100))
06          {
07              System.out.println("This is below the maximum temperature");
08          }
09      }
10  }
```

Output

```
This is below the maximum temperature
```

Explanation

- First, the expression (`temp > 100`) is tested and a value of either true or false is the result.
- Second, the ! operator is applied to that value.
- If the expression (`temp > 100`) is true, the ! operator returns false.
- If the expression (`temp > 100`) is false, the ! operator returns the true.

Table 5.6 | Truth table for the ! Operator

Expression	Value
!true	0
!false	1

The precedence and associativity of logical operators

Like other operator, the logical operators have orders of precedence and associativity.

Logical Operators in order of precedence

!	Higher precedence
&&	
||	Lower Precedence

NOTE: (!) Always enclose its operand in parentheses unless you intend to apply it to a variable or a simple expression with no other operators.

Example: LogicalNot2.java - wrong way

```
01  package ch05;
02  public class LogicalNot2 {
03      public static void main(String[] args) {
04          int x = 20;
05          if !(x > 2) // wrong way
06          {
07              System.out.println("Hi");
08          }
09      }
10  }
```

Output

```
C:\MyProjects\JavaPro1\src\chapter5\LogicalNot2.java
Error:(6, 11) java: '(' expected
Error:(6, 20) java: ')' expected
```

Explanation

> Line 05: Applies the ! operator to the expression x greater than 2
> Line 05: Attempts to apply the ! operator to x only. It is asking "is the logical complement of x greater than 2?"
> Because the ! operator can only be applied to boolean expressions, this statement would cause a compiler error.
> The right way is (change Line 05):
> `(!(x > 2))`

Always use parentheses

> `(a > b) && (x< y)` is the same as: `a > b && x < y`
> `(x == y) || (b > a)` is the same as: `x==y || b > a`

The logical operators evaluate the expressions from left to right. For example:

`a < b || y == 2; // y == 2 is evaluated first`

`a < b || y == 2 && m > j; //` This expression is evaluated to: `(a < b) || (y == 2) (m > j)`

Example 5.18: NotOp.java

```
01  public class NotOp {
02      public static void main(String[] args){
03          int x = 10;
04          if (!(x > 2)){
05              System.out.println("True");
06          }
07          System.out.println("False");
08      }
09  }
```

Table 5.7 | Precedence of all operators

Order of Precedence	Operators	Description
1	- (Unary Operator)	Unary negative, logical NOT
2	* / %	Multiplication, subtraction, modulus
3	+ -	Addition, subtraction
4	< > <= >=	Less than, greater than, less than or equal to, greater than or equal to
5	== !=	Equal to, not equal to
6	&&	Logical AND
7	||	Logical OR
8	= += -= *= /= %=	Assignment and combined assignment

Checking numeric ranges with logical operators

When determining whether a number is inside a range it's best to use the `&&` operator.

Example 5.19: CheckNo1.java - *Write code that determines whether a numeric value is within a specific range of values or outside a specific range of values*

```
01  package ch05;
02  public class CheckNo1 {
03      public static void main(String[] args) {
04          int x = 35;
05          if (x >= 20 && x <= 40)
06          {
07              System.out.println( x + " is in the acceptable range.");
08          }
09      }
10  }
```

Output
```
35 is in the acceptable range.
```

Explanation
> The boolean expression will be `true` only when `x` is >= 20 AND <= 40.
> The value in `x` must be within the range of 20 to 40 for this expression to be `true`.

When determining whether a number is outside a range, it's best to use the (||) operator.

Example 5.20: CheckNo2.java - *Determining whether x is outside the range of 20 through 40*

```
01  package ch05;
02  public class CheckNo2 {
03      public static void main(String[] args) {
04          int a = 10;
05          if (a < 20 || a > 40)
06          {
07              System.out.println( a + " is in the acceptable range.");
08          }
09      }
10  }
```

Output
```
10 is in the acceptable range.
```

It's important not to get the logic of these logical operators confused.

Example 5.21: CheckNo3.java - *the boolean expression in the following if statement would never test true.*

```
01  package ch05;
02  public class CheckNo2 {
03      public static void main(String[] args) {
04          int a = 10;
05          if (a < 20 && a > 40)
06          {
07              System.out.println( a + " is in the acceptable range.");
08          }
09      }
10  }
```

x cannot be less than 20 and at the same time be greater than 40.

The switch Statement

Java provides the `switch` statement to handle a series of decisions in which a variable or expression is tested separately for each of the constant integer values it may assume, and different actions are taken.

A branch occurs when one part of a program causes another part to execute. The switch statement tests the value of an integer or character expression and then uses that value to determine which set of statement to branch to.

Syntax

The switch statement consists of a series of case labels and an optional default case.

```
01  switch (switchExpression)
02  {
03      case caseExpression:
04          // statement(s)
05          break;
06      case caseExpression:
07          // statement(s)
08          break;
09      case caseExpression:
10          // statement(s)
11          break;
12      // case statements may be repeated as many
13      // times as necessary
14      default:
15          // statement(s)
16  }
```

The default section is optional. If you have it out, however, your program will have nowhere to branch to if the switchExpression doesn't match any of the caseExpression. The body of a switch statement is known as a **switch block**. Let's see an example for this.

Example 5.22: Switch.java

```
01  import java.util.Scanner;
02
03  public class Switch {
04      public static void main(String[] args) {
05          Scanner sc = new Scanner(System.in);
06          System.out.println("Enter Your Age: ");
07          int input = sc.nextInt();
08
09          switch (input)
10          {
11              case 20:
12                  System.out.println("You're 20");
13                  break;
14              case 21:
15                  System.out.println("You're 21");
16                  break;
17              case 22:
18                  System.out.println("You're 22");
19                  break;
20              default:
21                  System.out.println("You're not 20, 21, or 22");
22          }
23      }
24  }
```

Explanation

› case 20, case 21, case 22: These statements mark where the program is to branch to if the variable `user` contains the values 21, 22 or 23.

- Default section is branched to if the user enters anything other than 20, 21, or 22.
- Case statements show the program where to start executing in the block.
- `break` statement show the program where to stop. Without the `break` statement, the program would execute all the lines from the matching case statement to the end of the break.
- The default section (or the last case section if there is no default) does not need a break statement. Some programmers prefer to put one there anyway for consistency.

Consider below example for omitting the break statement.

Example 5.23: Switch2.java - Omitting the **break** statement

```java
import java.util.Scanner;
public class Switch2 {
    public static void main(String[] args)
    {
        Scanner input = new Scanner(System.in);
        int aCount = 0;
        int bCount = 0;
        int cCount = 0;
        System.out.println("Enter the letter grades");
        int grade = input.nextInt();
        switch (grade){
        case 'A':
        case 'a': ++aCount; break;
        case 'B':
        case 'b': ++bCount; break;
        case 'C':
        case 'c': ++cCount; break;
        case '\n':
        case '\t':
        case ' ' : break;
        default:
            System.out.println("Incorrect letter grade entered");
            System.out.println("Enter a new grade.");
        }
        System.out.println("Totals for each grade are: \n");
        System.out.println("A: " + aCount);
        System.out.println("B: " + bCount);
        System.out.println("C: " + cCount);
        input.close();
    }
}
```

Explanation
- As break statement is optional. If we omit the break, execution will continue on into the next case.

> It is sometimes desirable to have multiple cases without break statements between them. For example, consider the above program, it increments the value of `aCount` variable whether `grade` value is `A` or `a`. It also increment the value of `bCount` variable whether `grade` value is `B` or `b`, and so on.

Example 5.24: Switch3.java

Consider the following java program, it declares an `int` named `month` whose value represents a `month` (1 to 12). The code displays the name of the month, based on the value of `month`, using the switch statement.

```java
package ch05;
public class Switch3 {
    public static void main(String[] args){
        int month = 5;
        String monthString;

        switch (month)
        {
            case 1: monthString = "January"; break;
            case 2: monthString = "February"; break;
            case 3: monthString = "March"; break;
            case 4: monthString = "April"; break;
            case 5: monthString = "May"; break;
            case 6: monthString = "June"; break;
            case 7: monthString = "July"; break;
            case 8: monthString = "August"; break;
            case 9: monthString = "September"; break;
            case 10: monthString = "October"; break;
            case 11: monthString = "November"; break;
            case 12: monthString = "December";break;
            default: monthString = "Invalid Month"; break;
        }
        System.out.println(monthString);
    }
}
```

Output

```
May
```

Some Important rules for switch statements

> Duplicate case values are not allowed.
> Only one case is selected per execution of the switch statement.
> The value of expression determines which case is selected.
> The value for a case must be the same data type as the variable in the switch.
> The value for a case must be a constant or a literal. Variables are not allowed.

- The break statement is used inside the switch to terminate a statement sequence.
- The break statement is optional. If omitted, execution will continue on into the next case.
- The default statement is optional, and it must appear at the end of the switch.
- When a break statement is reached, the switch terminates, and the flow of control jumps to the next line following the switch statement.
- Not every case needs to contain a break. If no break appears, the flow of control will fall through to subsequent cases until a break is reached.
- A switch works with the byte, short, char, and int primitive data types. It also works with enumerated types, the String class, and a few special classes that wrap certain primitive types such as, Character, Byte, Short, and Integer.

Summary

- When a program is running, the code is being read by the computer line by line, from top to bottom.
- A program is a sequence of instructions. Statements are executed one after the other in the order in which they are written. It is the default execution process.
- A selection statement (a.k.a. conditional structure) causes the program control to be transferred to a specific flow based on whether a condition is true or false. Selection structures use relational operators to test conditions.
- The if statement causes one or more statements to execute only when a condition is true.
- The operators `==` and `!=` can be used to compare boolean values.
- if...else statement allow you to specify that different actions are to be performed when the condition is true than when the condition is false. It is called a double-selection statement because it selects between two different actions.
- Conditional Operator is closely related to the if ...else statement. It is Java's only ternary operator. It is decide which value should be assigned to the variable.
- Java provides the switch statement to handle a series of decisions in which a variable or expression is tested separately for each of the constant integer values it may assume, and different actions are taken.

Chapter 6

Java Arrays

Introduction

Recalls from the previous chapter, a variable is a name for a memory location used to hold one value at a time of a particular data type.

An array is a variable that can hold multiple values (data or variables) of the same data type simultaneously. Array in java is index based, first element of the array is stored at 0 index, as shown in the following figure:

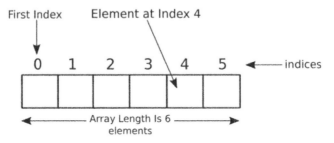

Figure 6.1 | Array in Java

Array declaration

To use an array in program, you must declare a variable to reference the array.

Syntax
```
datatype[] arrayRefVar = new datatype[size];
OR
datatype [] arrayRefVar; // declare an array reference variable
```

148 | Java for Complete Beginners

```
arrayRefVar = new datatype[size]; // initialize an array refer-
ence variable
```

Explanation

> `datatype[ ] arrayRefVar`: Declaring an array reference variable.
> `new datatype[size]`: Creating an array.
> `(=)`: Assigning the address of the array to the reference variable array `arrayRefVar`.

Declaring an array reference variable does not create an array. You declare a reference variable and use the `new` keyword to create an array and assigns its address to the reference variable. For example (Array declaration)

```
int[] numbers; // declare an array reference variable
// Creating an array and assigns the reference variable to the
array.
numbers = new int[6];
```

Explanation

> Declares `numbers` as a reference variable. The `numbers` variable can reference an array of `int` values.
> When executed, `numbers` will reference an array that can hold 6 elements, each one (1 `int`). The `[6]` is the array's size declarator. It indicates the number of the elements or values, the array can hold.
> The brackets indicate that this variable is a reference to an `int` array.

Figure 6.2 | The numbers array

> Now you can store 6 values or variables in a single array named `arrayRefVar`.

As an example, the following program creates four arrays with elements of the type `int`, `float`, `char` and `double`.

Example 6.1: Array1.java - Creation of an array in Java

```
01  package ch06;
02  public class Array1 {
03      public static void main(String[] args){
04          int[] numbers = new int[6];
05          float[] temp = new float[100];
06          char[] letters = new char[41];
07          long[] units = new long[50];
08          double[] sizes = new double[1200];
```

Explanation

> Line 04: Declares `numbers` as a reference variable. The `numbers` variable can reference an array of `int` values, that can hold **6** elements.
> Line 05: Declares `temp` as a reference variable. The `temp` variable can reference an array of `float` values, that can hold **100** elements.
> Line 06: Declares `letters` as a reference variable. The `letters` variable can reference an array of `char` values, that can hold **41** elements.
> Line 07: Declares `units` as a reference variable. The `units` variable can reference an array of `long` values, that can hold **50** elements.
> Line 08: Declares `sizes` as a reference variable. The `sizes` variable can reference an array of `double` values, that can hold **1200** elements.

An array's `size` declarator must be a non-negative integer expression. It can be a literal value (literal value like 50, 1200), or a variable. It is a common practice to use a final variable as a size declarator. For Example:

```
final int NUM_ELEMENTS = 6;
int[] numbers = new int[NUM_ELEMENTS];
```

This practice can make programs easier to maintain. When we store the size of an array in a variable, we can use the variable instead of a literal number when we refer to the size of the array. If we ever need to change the array's size, we need only to change the value of the variable.

The variable should be final so its contents cannot be changed during the program's execution.

> **NOTE:** Once an array is created, its size cannot be changed.

Accessing Array Elements

An array has only one name, the elements in the array may be accessed and used as individual variables. This is possible because each element is assigned a number known as a **subscript**.

A **subscript** is used as an index to pin point a specific element within an array. The first element is assigned the subscript **0**. And the second element is assigned the subscript **1**, and so forth. The **6** elements in the numbers array would have the subscripts (0 to 5).

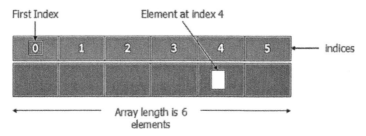

Figure 6.3 | The numbers array

Subscript numbering always starts at **zero**. The subscript of the last element in an array is one less than the total number of elements in the array.

This means that the `numbers` array, which has 6 elements, 5 is the subscript for the last element. Each element in the `numbers` array, when accessed by its subscript, can be used as an `int` variable. For example:

```
01  numbers[0] = 20;
02  numbers[3] = 30;
```

Explanation

> Line 01: Stores 20 in the first element of the array (element 1 - subscript 0)
> Line 02: Stores 30 in the forth element (element 4 - subscript 3)

NOTE: The expression `numbers[0]` is pronounced **"numbers sub zero"**. You read theses assignment statements as "numbers sub zero is assigned twenty" and "numbers sub three is assigned thirty".

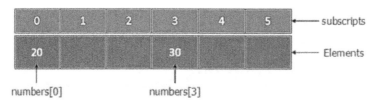

Figure 6.4 | The content of the numbers array

> By default, Java initializes array elements with **0**. In previous figure, values have not been stored in element 1, 2, 4, & 5, so they are shown as `0s`.

REMEMBER: When you use the `new` keyword to create an array object, the number inside the brackets is the size declarator. It indicates the number of elements in the array. The number inside the brackets in an assignment statement or any statement that works with the contents of an array is a subscript. It is used to access a specific element in the array.

Store Data Inside an Array

After you've created an array in Java, you can store values into the array's elements.

Syntax
```
ArrayName [index] = value;
```

For example:
```
// Creating an array
int a [] = new int[ ]; // length: 5 , index: 0 to 4
// To insert a data into array, write the following
a[ ] = ;
a[ ] = ;
a[ ] = ;
a[ ] = ;
a[ ] = ;
```

The following program shows the contents of the `hours` array with the values entered by the user.

Example 6.2: ArrayDemo1.java
```
   package ch06;
   import java.util.Scanner;
   public class ArrayDemo1 {
      public static void main(String[] args) {
         final int EMPLOYEES = ;
         int[] hours = new int[EMPLOYEES];
         Scanner keyboard = new Scanner(System.in);
08
         System.out.println("Enter the hours worked by " +
            EMPLOYEES + " employees");
         System.out.println("Employee 1: ");
         hours[ ] = keyboard.nextInt();
13
         System.out.println("Employee 2: ");
         hours[ ] = keyboard.nextInt();
16
         System.out.println("Employee 3: ");
         hours[ ] = keyboard.nextInt();
19
         System.out.println("The hours you entered are: ");
         System.out.println(hours[ ]);
         System.out.println(hours[ ]);
```

```
23            System.out.println(hours[2]);
24      }
25  }
```

Output

```
Enter the hours worked by 3 employees
Employee 1:
5
Employee 2:
10
Employee 3:
15
The hours you entered are:
5
10
15
```

The contents of the `hours` Array

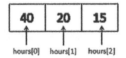

Subscript numbers can be stored in variables. This makes it possible to use a loop to **cycle through** an entire array, performing the same operation on each element.

Displaying the Content of the Array

In this area, you will learn how to display the contents of an array element with `println()`. For example (in `ArrayDemo1.java`) could be simplified by using two for loops: one for inputting the values into the array and the other for displaying the contents of the array. Here is a simple example.

Example 6.3: ArrayDemo2.java

```
01  package ch06s;
02  import java.util.Scanner;
03  public class ArrayDemo2 {
04      public static void main(String[] args){
05          final int EMPLOYEES = 3;
06          int[] hours = new int[EMPLOYEES];
07          Scanner keyboard = new Scanner(System.in);
08
09          System.out.println("Enter the hours worked by " +
10                  EMPLOYEES + " employees");
11          for (int index = 0; index < EMPLOYEES; index++) {
```

```
            System.out.print("Employee " + (index + 1) + ": ");
            hours[index] = keyboard.nextInt();
        }
        System.out.println("The hours you entered are: ");
        for (int index = 0; index < EMPLOYEES; index++)
            System.out.println(hours[index]);
    }
}
```

Output

```
Enter the hours worked by 3 employees
Employee 1: 5
Employee 2: 10
Employee 3: 15
The hours you entered are:
5
10
15
```

Explanation (Line 11: First Loop)

› The loop's control variable, index, is used as as subscript in `hours[index] = keyboard.nextInt()`.

› The variable index starts at **0** which is the valid subscript value. During the loop's first iteration, the user's input is stored in `hours[0]`.

› The loop ends before the variable index reaches **3**, which is the first valid subscript value.

› Then index is incremented, so its value becomes 1.

› During the next iteration, the user's input is stored in `hours[1]`.

› This continues until values have been stored in all of the elements of the array.

Notice: The loop correctly starts and ends the control variable with valid subscript values `(0 -> 2)`. This ensures that only valid subscripts are used.

Array Initialization (Declaration + Instantiation = Initialization)

Like regular variables, Java allows you to initialize an array's elements when you create the array. For example; we can declare, instantiate and initialize the java array together by:

```
int[] days = {31, 28, 31, 30, 31, 30, 31, 31, 30, 31, 30, 31};
```

Explanation

- Declare the reference variable `days`
- Stores initial values in the array.
- The series of values inside the braces and separated with commas is called an **initialization** list. These values are stored in the array elements in the order they appear in the list (first value 31, is stored in `days[0]`, the second value 28, is stored in `days[1]`, and so forth).
- You do not use the `new` keyword when you use an initialization list. Java automatically creates the array and stores the values in the initialization list in it.
- The Java compiler determines the size of the array by the number of items in the initialization list.
- Because there are 12 items in the example statement's initialization list, the array will have 12 elements.

Below is an example of a program that initialize an integer array and displays its content using for loop.

Example 6.4: ArrayInitialization.java

```
01  package ch06;
02  public class ArrayInitialization {
03      public static void main(String[] args) {
04          int[] days = {31, 28, 31, 30, 31, 30, 31, 31, 30, 31, 30, 31};
05          for (int index = 0; index < 12; index++)
06          {
07              System.out.println("Month " + (index + 1) +
08                  " has " + days[index] + " days.");
09          }
10      }
11  }
```

Output

```
Month 1 has 31 days.
Month 2 has 28 days.
Month 3 has 31 days.
Month 4 has 30 days.
Month 5 has 31 days.
Month 6 has 30 days.
Month 7 has 31 days.
Month 8 has 31 days.
Month 9 has 30 days.
Month 10 has 31 days.
Month 11 has 30 days.
Month 12 has 31 days.
```

Java Allows you to spread the initialization list across multiple lines. For example, both the following array declarations are equivalent

```
double[] coins = {    ,    ,    };
double[] coins = {    ,
                      ,
                      };
```

Processing Array Elements

Individual array elements are processed like any other data of variable. For example:
```
grossPay = hours[ ] * payRate;
```

Example 6.5: Pro-increment and Post-increment operations on array elements
```
int[] score = { ,  ,  ,   ,   };
++score[ ];
score[ ]++;
```

Be careful not to use the operator on the subscript when you intend to use it on the array element.

Example 6.6: Decrements the variable count, but does nothing to the values stored in the array element- `amount[count]`.
```
amount [count--];
```

Example 6.7: PayArray.java
```
   package ch06;
   import java.util.Scanner;   // Needed for Scanner Class
   public class PayArray {
      public static void main(String[] args){
         final int EMPLOYEES =  ;
         double payRate;
         double grossPay;
         int[] hours = new int[EMPLOYEES];
         Scanner keyboard = new Scanner(System.in);
         System.out.println("Enter the hours worked by " +
               EMPLOYEES + " employees who all earn " +
               "the same hourly rate.");
         for (int index= ; index < EMPLOYEES; index++)
         {
            System.out.print("Employee #" + (index+ ) + ": ");
            hours[index] = keyboard.nextInt();
         }
         System.out.print("Enter the hourly pay rate " +
               " for each employee: ");
         payRate = keyboard.nextInt();
         System.out.println("Here is each employee's gross pay: ");
         for (int index =  ; index < EMPLOYEES; index++)
         {
```

```
                grossPay = hours[index] * payRate;
                System.out.println("Employee #" + (index + 1) +
                    ": $" + grossPay);
            }
28
        }
    }
```

Output

```
Enter the hours worked by 5 employees who all earn the same
hourly rate.
Employee #1: 1
Employee #2: 2
Employee #3: 3
Employee #4: 4
Employee #5: 5
Enter the hourly pay rate  for each employee: 2
Here is each employee's gross pay:
Employee #1: $2.0
Employee #2: $4.0
Employee #3: $6.0
Employee #4: $8.0
Employee #5: $10.0
```

Assigns the value of `hours[index]` times `payRate` to the `grossPay` variable. Array elements may also be used in relational expressions.

Example 6.8: While loop iterates as long as the `value[count]` does not equal to 0

```
01  if (cost[20] < cost[0])
02  while (value[count] != 0)
03  {
04      // statement(s)
05  }
```

Array length

Each array in Java has a public field named `length`. This field contains the number of elements in the array. For example:

```
                        Create a new array         The temperatures array
                                                   has 25 elements

        double[] temperatures = new double[25];
        // Assign 25 to the variable size
        size = temperatures.length;
```

The `length` field can be useful when processing the entire contents of an array. For example:

```
01  for (int i = 0; i < temperature.length; i++)
02  {
03      System.out.println(temperature[i]);
04  }
```

Explanation

> The loop steps through an array and displays the contents of each elements.
> The arrays length field is used in the `test` expression as the upper limit for the loop control variable.

WARNING: Be careful not to cause an **off-by-one error** when using the length field as the upper limit of a subscript. The length field contains the number of elements in an array. The largest subscript in an array is length -1.

NOTE: You can not change the value of an array's Length field.

The enhanced for loop

Java provides a specialized version of the for loop that simplifies array processing. It is known as the **"enhanced for loop"**.

Syntax
```
for (datatype elementVariable : array) {
    // Statement(s)
}
```

Explanation

> The enhanced for loop is designed to iterate once for every element in an array. Each time the loop iterate, it copies an array element on a variable.
> `datatype elementVariable` is a variable declaration. This variable will receive the value of a different array element during each loop iteration. During the first loop iteration, it receives the value of the first element; during the second iteration, it receives the value of the second element, and so on. This variable must be of the same data type as the array element, or a type that the elements can automatically be converted to.
> `Array` is the name of an array on which you wish the loop to operate. The loop will iterate once for every element in the array.
> `Statement(s)` is a statement(s) that executes during a loop iteration.

Example 6.9: Assume we have the following array declaration

```
int[] numbers = {3, 6, 9};
```

We can use the following enhanced for loop to display the contents of the numbers array

```
for (int val : numbers){
    System.out.println(val);
}
```

Because the numbers array has three elements, this loop will iterate three times.

> First Loop: The `val` variable will receive the value in `numbers[0]`.
> Second Loop: The `val` variable will receive the value in `numbers[1]`.
> Third Loop: The `val` variable will receive the value in `numbers[2]`.

To execute more than one statement in the enhanced for loop:

```
01  int[] numbers = {3, 6, 9};
02  for (int val : numbers)
03  {
04      System.out.println("The new value is ");
05      System.out.println(val);
06  }
```

The enhanced for loop versus The traditional for loop

When you need to access the values that are stored in array, from the first element to the last element, you do not have to create an `"index"` variable to hold subscripts. You cannot use the enhanced for loop as follows:

> If you need to change the contents of an array element.
> If you need to work through the array elements in reverse order.
> If you need to access some of the array elements, but not all of them.
> If you need to simultaneously work with two or more arrays within the loop.
> If you need to refer to the subscripts number of a particular element.

In any of these circumstances, you should use the traditional for loop to process the array.

Letting the user specify an array's size

Java allows you to use an integer variable to specify an array's size declarator. This makes it possible to allow the user to specify an array's size. Here is how that is done.

Example 6.10: DisplayTestScores.java

This program allows the user to determines the size of the array. It stores a number of test scores in an array and then displays them.

```java
package ch06;
import java.util.Scanner;
public class DisplayTestScores {
    public static void main(String[] args) {
        int numTests; //The number of tests
        int[] tests;  //Array of test scores
        Scanner keyboard = new Scanner(System.in);
        System.out.print("How many tests do you have? ");
        numTests = keyboard.nextInt();
        tests = new int[numTests];
        for (int index = 0; index < tests.length; index++)
        {
            System.out.print("Enter last score " +
                    (index + 1) + ": ");
            tests[index] = keyboard.nextInt();
        }
        System.out.println();
        System.out.println("Here are the scores you entered: ");
        for (int index = 0; index < tests.length; index++)
            System.out.print(tests[index] + " ");
    }
}
```

Output

```
How many tests do you have? 5
Enter last score 1: 50
Enter last score 2: 60
Enter last score 3: 70
Enter last score 4: 80
Enter last score 5: 90

Here are the scores you entered:
50 60 70 80 90
```

Explanation

> - Line 10: Creates the array, using the `numTests` variable to determine its size.
> - Lines 11 to 16: First for loop allows the user to input each test score.
> - Lines 19 to 22: Second for loop displays all of the test scores.
> - Both loops use the `length` number to control their number of iterations.

Re-assigning array reference variables

It is possible to reassign an array reference variable to a different array. For example:

Example 6.11: CreateArray.java - Create an array referenced by the number variable
```
01  int[] numbers = new int[10];
02  // reassign numbers to a new array
03  numbers = new int[5];
```

Explanation

› First statement creates a ten-elements integer array and assign its address to the `numbers`.

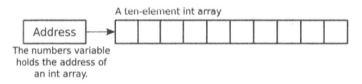

Figure 6.5 | An Array referenced by the number variable

› Second statement allocates a five-element integer array and assigns its address to the `numbers` variables. The address of the five-element array takes the place of the address of the ten-element array. After this statement executes, the `numbers` variables references the five-element array instead of the ten-element array, as shown in the following figure.

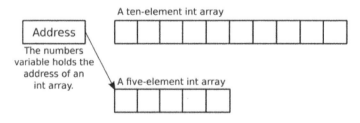

Figure 6.6 | The numbers variables references a five-element array

Copying arrays

Because an array is an object, there is a distinction between an array and the variable that references it. The array and the reference variable are two separate entities. For example:

```
01  int[] array1 = {2, 4, 6, 8, 10};
02  int[] array2 = array1; // this does not copy array1
```

Explanation

› Line 01: Creates an array and assign its address to the `array1` variable.
› Line 02: Assigns `array1` to `array2`. This does not make a copy of the array referenced by `array1`. Rather, it makes a copy of the address that is stored in `array1` and stores it in `array2`.
› After this statement executes, both the `array1`, and `array2` variables will reference the same array.
› This type of assignment operation is called a "**reference copy**".
› Only the address of the array object is copied, not the contents of the array object.

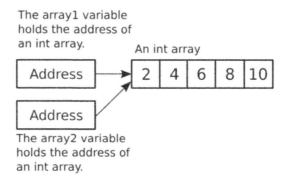

Figure 6.7 | Assigning arrays to two reference variables

Regardless of which variable the program uses, it is working with same array. Here is an example for that.

Example 6.12: SameArray.java

```
01  public class SameArray
02  {
03      public static void main(String[] args)
04      {
05          int[] array1 = {2, 4, 6, 8, 10};
06          int[] array2 = array1;
07          array1[0] = 200;
08          array2[4] = 1000;
09          System.out.println("The contents of array1: ");
10          for (int index = 0; index < array1.length; index++)
11              System.out.println(array1[index] + " ");
12          System.out.println();
13          System.out.println("The contents of array2: ");
14          for (int index = 0; index < array2.length; index++)
```

```
            System.out.println(array2[index] + " ");
        System.out.println();
    }
}
```

Output
```
The contents of array1:
200
4
6
8
1000

The contents of array2:
200
4
6
8
1000
```

You cannot copy an array by merely assigning one reference variable to another. To copy an array you need to copy the individual elements of one array to another. Usually, this is best done with a loop, such as the following:

```
int[] firstArray = {5, 10, 15, 20, 25};
int[] secondArray = new int[5];
for (int index = 0; index < firstArray.length; index++)
    secondArray[index] = firstArray[index];
```

The loop copies each element of `firstArray` to the corresponding element of `secondArray`.

String Arrays

A Java string array is an object that holds a fixed number of string values. An array of String objects may be created, but if the array un-initialized, each string in the array must be created individually. Java allows you to create arrays of string object. The `Names.java` program demonstrates that concept.

Example 6.13: Names.java - Create an array of string object initialized with values

```
package ch06;
public class Names {
    public static void main(String[] args) {
        String[] names = {"Bill", "Susan", "Steven", "Jean"};
    }
}
```

In memory, an array of String objects is arranged differently than an array of a primitive data type. In order to use a String object, you must have a reference to the String object. So, an array of String objects is really an array of references to String objects.

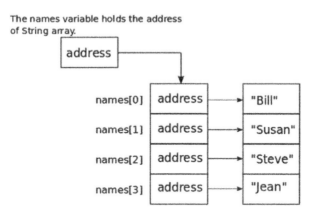

Figure 6.8 | The names variable references a String array

Each element in the names array is reference to a String object. The `names[0]` element references a String object containing `"Bill"`. The `names[1]` element references a String object containing `"Susan"`, and so forth. Below is an example that uses the for loop to display the contents of two arrays `months`, and `days`.

Example 6.14: MonthDays.java

```
01  package ch06;
02  public class MonthDays {
03      public static void main(String[] args) {
04          String[] months = {"January", "February", "March",
05          "April", "May","June", "July", "August",
06          "September", "October","November", "December"};
07          for (int index = 0; index < months.length; index++)
08          {
09              System.out.println(months[index] + " has " +
10                  days[index] + " days.");
11          }
12      }
13  }
```

Output

```
January has 31 days.
February has 28 days.
March has 31 days.
April has 30 days.
May has 31 days.
June has 30 days.
July has 31 days.
August has 31 days.
```

```
September has 30 days.
October has 31 days.
November has 30 days.
December has 31 days.
```

As with the primitive data types, an initialization list automatically causes an array of String objects to be created in memory. If you do not provide an initialization list, you must use the new keyword to create the array. For example:

```
01 final int SIZE = 4;
02 String[] names = new String[SIZE];
```

The above example creates an array of four references to String objects.

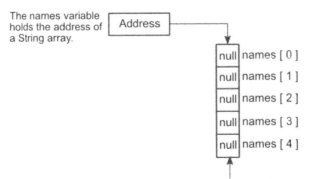

The array is an array of four uninitialized String references. Because they do not reference any objects, they are set to null.

Figure 6.9 | An Array of four references to String objects

When you create an un-initialized array of objects, you must assign a value to each element in the array that you intend to use. For example:

```
01 final int SIZE = 4;
02 String[] names = new String[SIZE];
03 names[0] = "Bill";
05 names[1] = "Susan";
06 names[2] = "Steven";
07 names[3] = "Jean";
```

After execution, each element of the `names` array will reference a `String` object.

Calling string methods from an array element

String objects have several methods. For example, `toUpperCase` method returns the uppercase equivalent of a `String` object. Because each element of a String array is a String object, you can use an element to call a `String` method. For example:

```
System.out.println(names[0].toUpperCase());
```

Uses element **0** of the names array to call the `toUpperCase` method. For example:

```
01  // declare a char variable named letter
02  char letter;
03
04  // assigns the first character in names[3] to letter
05  letter = names[3].charAll(0);
```

It uses element 3 of the `names` array to call the `charAll` method. After execution, the first character of the string stored in `names[3]` will be assigned to the `letter` variable.

TIP: Arrays have a field named `length` and String objects have a method named `length`. For example:
for (int i = 0; i < names.length; i++){
   System.out.println(names[i].length());
}
Explanation
☐ Display the length of each String held in `names`, which is assumed to be a String array.

NOTE: The loop uses both the array's `length` field and each element's `length` method. Because the array's length member is a field, you do not write a lot of parentheses after its name. You do write the parentheses after the name of the String class's `length` method.

Two Dimensional Arrays

A two-dimensional array is an array of arrays. It can be thought of as having rows and columns. Two-Dimensional arrays, which are sometimes called 2D arrays, can hold multiple sets of data. Although a two-dimensional array is actually an array of arrays, it's best to think of it as having rows and columns of elements as shown in the below image.

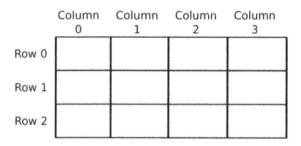

Figure 6.10 | Rows and Columns

There are a total of 12 elements in the above array (3 rows and 4 columns).

Two dimensional array declaration

To declare a 2-dimensional array, two sets of brackets and two size declarations are required: The first one is for the number of rows and the second one is for the number of columns.

Syntax
```
data-type[ ][ ] arrayname = new datatype[no_of_rows
][no_of_columns ];
```

Example 6.15: Declaration of a two-dimensional array with 3 rows and 4 columns
```
double[][] scores = new double[3][4];
```

› The two sets of brackets in the data type indicate that the score variable will reference a two-dimensional array.
› The numbers 3 and 4 are size declarators.
› The first size declarator specifies the number of rows, and the second size declarator specifies the number of columns.

Figure 6.11 | Declaration of a 2D Array with 3 rows and 4 columns

When passing the data in a two-dimensional array, each element has two subscripts: one for its row and another for its column.

In the scores array, the elements in row 0 are referenced as follows:

```
scores[ ][ ];
scores[ ][ ];
scores[ ][ ];
scores[ ][ ];
```

The elements in row 1 are as follow.

```
scores[ ][ ];
scores[ ][ ];
scores[ ][ ];
scores[ ][ ];
```

And the elements in row 2 are as follow.

```
scores[ ][ ];
scores[ ][ ];
scores[ ][ ];
scores[ ][ ];
```

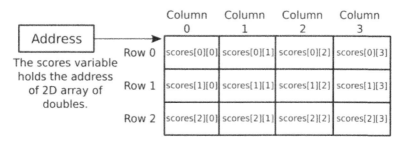

Figure 6.12 | Subscripts for each element of the scores array

To access one of the elements in a two-dimensional array, you must use both subscripts. For example, to store the number 95 in `scores[2][1]`:

```
scores[ ][ ] =  ;
```

Programs that process two-dimensional arrays can do so with nested loops. Consider the below example for that.

Example 6.16: TwoDimArray.java - Prompts the user to enter a score, once for each element in the array.

```
    package ch06;
    import java.util.Scanner;
    public class TwoDimArray {
        public static void main(String[] args) {
            final int ROWS =  ;
            final int COLS =  ;
            Scanner keyboard = new Scanner(System.in);
08
            double[][] scores = new double[ROWS][COLS];
            for (int row =  ; row < ROWS; row++)
            {
                for (int col =  ; col < COLS; col++)
                {
```

```
14                System.out.println("Enter a Score: ");
15                scores[row][col] = keyboard.nextDouble();
16            }
17        }
18    }
19 }
```

Output

```
Enter a Score:
1
Enter a Score:
2
Enter a Score:
3
Enter a Score:
4
Enter a Score:
5
Enter a Score:
6
```

Displays all the elements in the scores array: (TwoArray.java)

```
01 package ch06;
02 import java.util.Scanner;
03 public class TwoArray {
04     public static void main(String[] args) {
05         final int ROWS = 2;
06         final int COLS = 3;
07         Scanner keyboard = new Scanner(System.in);
08
09         double[][] scores = new double[ROWS][COLS];
10         for (int row = 0; row < ROWS; row++)
11         {
12             for (int col = 0; col < COLS; col++)
13             {
14                 System.out.println("Enter a Score: ");
15                 scores[row][col] = keyboard.nextDouble();
16             }
17         }
18         System.out.println("The Scores are:");
19         for (int row = 0; row < ROWS; row++)
20         {
21             for (int col = 0; col < COLS; col++)
22             {
23                 System.out.println(scores[row][col]);
24             }
25         }
26     }
27 }
```

Output

```
Enter a Score:
1
Enter a Score:
```

```
2
Enter a Score:
3
Enter a Score:
4
Enter a Score:
5
Enter a Score:
6
The Scores are:
1.0
2.0
3.0
4.0
5.0
6.0
```

Initializing a two-dimensional array

When initializing a two-dimensional array, you enclose each row's initialization list in its own set of braces.

Syntax
```
int[][] twoDimArray = new int[row][col];
```

Note that every element will be initialized to the default value for `int`, 0, so the above are also equivalent to:

```
int[][] twoDimArray = new int[][]{
    { 0, 0, 0, 0, 0, 0, 0, 0, 0, 0 },
    { 0, 0, 0, 0, 0, 0, 0, 0, 0, 0 },
    { 0, 0, 0, 0, 0, 0, 0, 0, 0, 0 },
    { 0, 0, 0, 0, 0, 0, 0, 0, 0, 0 },
    { 0, 0, 0, 0, 0, 0, 0, 0, 0, 0 }
};
```

Example 6.17
```
int [][] numbers = {{1,2,3},{4,5,6},{7,8,9}};
```

Explanation

› As with one-dimensional arrays, you do not use the `new` keyword when you provide an initialization list. Java automatically creates the array and fills its elements with the initialization values.

› In this example, the initialization values for row **0** are {1,2,3}, the initialization values for row **1** are {4,5,6}, the initialization values for row **2** are {7,8,9}. So this statement declares an array with 3 rows and 3 columns.

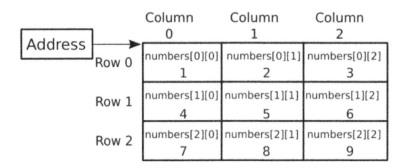

Figure 6.13 | The Numbers Array

The length field in a two-dimensional array

A one-dimensional array has a `length` field that holds the number of elements in the array. A Two-dimensional array, however, has multiple `length` fields. It has a `length` field that holds the number of rows, and then each row has a `length` field that holds the number of columns.

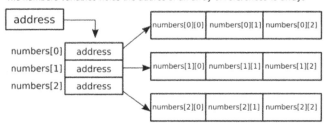

Figure 6.14 | The numbers array is an array of an arrays

> The `numbers` variable references a one-dimensional array with three elements.
> Each of the three elements is a reference to another one-dimensional array.
> The elements in the array referenced by `numbers[0]` are `numbers[0][0]`, `numbers[0][1]`, and `numbers[0][2]`. This pattern continues with `numbers[1]`, and `numbers[2]`.

The following example shows how to get the number of rows and columns of an array.

Example 6.18: Length.java
```
01  package ch06;
02  public class Length {
```

```
        public static void main(String[] args) {
            int[][] numbers = { {1,2,3,4},
                                {5,6,7,8},
                                {9,10,11,12,13}};
            System.out.println("The number of " +
                    "row(s) is " + numbers.length);
            for (int index = 0; index < numbers.length; index++) {
                System.out.println("The number of " +
                        "columns in row " + index + " is " +
                        numbers[index].length);
            }
        }
    }
```

Output

```
The number of row(s) is 3
The number of columns in row 0 is 4
The number of columns in row 1 is 4
The number of columns in row 2 is 5
```

Displaying all the elements of a two-dimensional array

A pair of nested loops are be used to display all the elements of a two-dimensional array. Here is how that is done.

Example 6.19: Length2.java - Create the numbers array with 3 rows and 4 columns, and then displays all the elements in the array.

```
package ch06;
public class Length2 {
    public static void main(String[] args) {
        int[][] numbers = { {1,2,3,4},
                            {5,6,7,8},
                            {9,10,11,12}};
        for (int row = 0; row < 3; row++)
        {
            for (int col = 0; col < 4; col++)
                System.out.println(numbers[row][col]);
        }
    }
}
```

Output

```
1
2
3
4
5
6
7
8
```

```
    9
   10
   11
   12
```

Although this code will display all of the elements, it is limited in the following way: The loops are specifically written to display an array with three rows and four columns.

A better approach is to use the array's `length` fields for the upper limit of the subscripts in the loop test expressions.

Code: Modified Loop
```
01  for (int row = 0; row < numbers.length; row++)
02  {
03      for (int col = 0; col < numbers[row].length; col++)
04          System.out.println(numbers[row][col]);
05  }
```

The header of the outer loop:
```
01  for (int row = 0; row < numbers.length; row++)
```

This loop controls the subscript for the number array's rows. Because `numbers.length` holds the number of rows in the array, we have used it as the upper limit for the row subscripts.

Here is the header for the inner loop:
```
    for (int col = 0; col < numbers[row].length; col++)
```

This loop controls the subscript for the number array's columns. Because each row's `length` field holds the number of columns in the row, we, have used it as the upper limit for the column subscript.

Arrays with Three or More Dimensions

Java does not limit the number of dimensions that an array may have. Java allows you to create arrays with virtually any number of dimensions.

Figure: A three-dimensional array

(Illustrates the concept of a three-dimensional array as "pages" of two-dimensional arrays)

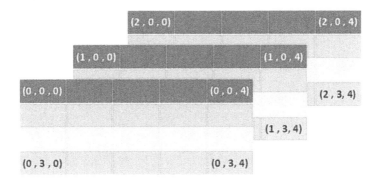

Figure 6.15 | Three Dimensional Array

To declare an array with more than two dimensions, you just specify as many sets of empty brackets as you need. For example:

```
int[][][] threeD = new int[ ][ ][ ];
```

Here, a three-dimensional array is created, with each dimension having five elements. Each element requires three indexes to access. You can access an element in a multidimensional array by specifying as many indexes as the array needs. For example:

```
threeD[ ][ ][ ] =  ;
```

This statement sets element 2 in column 1 of row `0` to `100`. You can nest initializers as deep as necessary, too. For example:

```
int[][][] threeD =
{   { {  ,    ,   }, {  ,   ,   }, {  ,   ,   } },
    { {  ,   ,   }, {  ,   ,   }, {  ,   ,   } },
    { {  ,   ,   }, {  ,   ,   }, {  ,   ,   } }
};
```

Here, a three-dimensional array is initialized with the numbers 1 through 27.

Example 6.20: ThreeDimArray.java - Use multiple nested `if` statements to process an array with three or more dimensions

You can also use multiple nested `if` statements to process an array with three or more dimensions. Here's another way to initialize a three-dimensional array with the numbers 1 to 27:

```
01  package ch06;
02  public class ThreeDimArray {
03      public static void main(String[] args) {
04          int[][][] threeD = new int[ ][ ][ ];
05          int value =  ;
06          for (int i =  ; i <  ; i++)
07          {
08              for (int j =  ; j <  ; j++)
09              {
```

```
10                      for (int k = 0; k < 5; k++)
11                      {
12                          threeD[i][j][k] = value++;
13                          System.out.println(value);
14                      }
15                  }
16              }
17          }
18  }
```

Output
```
2
3
4
5
6
. . .
124
125
126
```

Arrays with more than three dimensions are difficult to visualize, but can be useful in some programming problems.

Java Performing Bounds Checking

Java performs array bounds checking, which means that it does not allow a statement to use a subscript that is outside the range of valid subscripts for an array. For example:

```
int[] values = new int[10];
```

Explanation

› Creates an array with 10 elements.
› The valid subscripts for the array are `0 -> 9`.
› Java will not allow a statement to use a subscript that is less than 0 or greater than 9 with this array.

Bounds checking occurs at runtime

The Java compiler does not display an error message when it processes a statement that uses an invalid subscript. Instead, when the statement executes, the program throws an execution and immediately terminates. Consider the following code example.

Example 6.21: InvalidSubscript.java

```
01  public class InvalidSubscript
02  {
03      public static void main(String[] args)
04      {
05          int[] values = new int[3];
06          System.out.println("I will attempt to store four " +
07                  "numbers in a three-element array.");
08          for (int index=0; index < 4; index++)
09          {
10              System.out.println("Now processing element " + index);
11              values[index] = 10;
12          }
13      }
14  }
```

Output

```
I will attempt to store four numbers in a three-element array.
Now processing element 0
Exception in thread "main"
java.lang.ArrayIndexOutOfBoundsException: 3
Now processing element 1
    at chapter5.InvalidSubscript.main(InvalidSubscript.java:12)
Now processing element 2
Now processing element 3
```

Explanation

> Declares a three-element array, but attempts to store four values in the array.
> When the program attempts to store a value in values[3], it halts and an error message is displayed.

Watch out for Off-by-One Errors

Because array subscripts start at 0 rather than 1, you have to be careful not to perform an off-by-one error. Off by one error occurs when we have "<=" instead of "<" when we are checking the expression in the loop. The example below will illustrate the problem(Example 6.22):

```
01  final int SIZE = 100;
02  int[] numbers = new int[SIZE];
03  for (int index = 0; index <= SIZE; index++)
04  {
05      numbers[index] = 0;
06  }
```

Output

```
Exception in thread "main"
java.lang.ArrayIndexOutOfBoundsException: 100
```

```
    at chapter5.InvalidSubscript.main(InvalidSubscript.java:10)
```

Explanation

› Create an array of integers with 100 elements and store the value 0 in each element. However, this code has an off-by-one error.
› The loop uses its control variable, `index`, as a subscript with the `numbers` array.
› During the loop's execution, the variable `index` takes on the value 1 through 100, when it should take on the values `0-99`. As a result, the first element, which is at subscript 0, is skipped.
› In addition, the loop attempts to use 100 as a subscript during the last iteration. Because 100 is an invalid subscript, the program will result in an array of bounds exception and halt.

Summary

› An array is a variable that can hold multiple values of the same data type simultaneously.
› Declaring an array reference variable does not create an array. You declare a reference variable and use the **new** keyword to create an array and assigns its address to the reference variable.
› An array has only one name, the elements in the array may be accessed and used as individual variables. This is possible because each element is assigned a number known as a subscript.
› A subscript is used as an index to pin point a specific element within an array. The first element is assigned the subscript 0. And the second element is assigned the subscript 1, and so forth.
› Subscript numbering always starts at zero. The subscript of the last element in an array is one less than the total number of elements in the array.
› Java allows you to initialize an array's elements when you create the array.
› Each array in Java has a public field named length. This field contains the number of elements in the array.
› Java provides a specialized version of the for loop that simplifies array processing. It is known as the "enhanced for loop".
› A Java string array is an object that holds a fixed number of string values.

- A two-dimensional array is an array of arrays. It can be thought of as having rows and columns.
- Java allows you to create arrays with virtually any number of dimensions. To declare an array with more than two dimensions, you just specify as many sets of empty brackets as you need.

Chapter 7

Java Loops

The Increment (++) and Decrement (--) Operators

The increment and decrement operators add and subtract one from their operands. Increment and decrement operators are unary operators. Unary operator operates on one operand.

Types of increment and decrement operator

- Pre-Increment / Pre-Decrement Operator (Prefix Mode). The operator is placed before the variable.
- Post-Increment / Post-Decrement Operator (Postfix Mode). The operator is placed after the variable.

Syntax
```
++ increment operator   : increments a value by
-- decrement operator   : decrements a value by
```

Pre-increment / pre-decrement operator

- `(++)` and `(--)` is written before Variable name.
- Value is incremented / decremented first and then incremented / decremented value is used in expression.
- `(++)` and `(--)` cannot be used over "**Constant**" or "**final Variable**".

› Pre-incrementing (pre-decrementing) a variable causes the variable to be increment (decrement) by 1, then the new value of the variable is used in the expression in which it appears.
› If increment or decrement operators are before a variable (i.e. prefix), they referenced to as the pre-increment or pre-decrement operators.

The behavior can be easily illustrated with an example:

Example 7.1: PreInc.java - Increment & decrement the variable by one

```
01  package ch07;
02  public class PreInc {
03      public static void main(String[] args){
04          int no1 = 1;
05          int no2 = 1;
06          ++no1;
07          --no2;
08          System.out.println("Number 1 = " + no1);
09          System.out.println("Number 2 = " + no2);
10      }
11  }
```

Output

```
Number 1 = 2
Number 2 = 0
```

Explanation

› Line 06: Increment value of no1 by one and then assign the new value to variable no1.
› Line 07: Decrement the value of no2 by one, and then assign the new value to the variable no2.
› Line 08: Display the value of no1 using `println()` method on the screen.
› Line 09: Display the value of no2 using `println()` method on the screen.

Post-increment / post-decrement operator

› `(++)` and `(--)` is written after Variable name.
› Value is used in expression first and then incremented (or decremented).
› `(++)` and `(--)` cannot be used over **Constant** of **final Variable**.
› Post-incrementing (post-decrementing) the variable causes the current value of the variable to be used in the expression in which it appears, then the variable value is incremented (decremented) by 1.

The behavior can be easily illustrated with an examples.

Example 7.2: PostInc.java - Increment the variables no1 & no2 by one

```
package ch07;
public class PostInc {
    public static void main(String[] args) {
        int no1 = 1;
        int no2 = 10;
        no1++;
        no2++;
        System.out.println("Number 1 = " + no1);
        System.out.println("Number 2 = " + no2);
    }
}
```

Output

```
Number 1 = 2
Number 2 = 11
```

Explanation

› Lines 06-07: Increment values of variables no1 & no2 after assigning.

Example 7.3: IncrementDecrement.java

```
package ch07;
public class IncrementDecrement{
    public static void main(String[] args){
        int no = 5;
        System.out.println("Number is " + no);
        no++;
        System.out.println("Number is " + no);
        no--;
        System.out.println("Number is " + no);
    }
}
```

Output

```
Number is 5
Number is 6
Number is 5
```

Explanation

› Line 05: Display the value of the variable no on the screen.
› Line 06: Increment the value of the `no` by one.
› Line 07: Display the new value of the variable `no` on the screen.
› Line 08: Decrement the value of the `no` by one.
› Line 09: Display the new value of the variable `no` on the screen.

The difference between postfix and prefix modes

The difference between postfix and prefix modes happen when the operators are used in statements that do more than just increment or decrement. Here is a simple example.

Example 7.4: Postfix mode 1
```
int no1 = 4;
System.out.println(no1++);
```

Explanation
> First, calls `println()` method to display the value of `no1` variable.
> Second, increments `no1` but which happen first? The answer depends upon the mode of the increment operator. Postfix mode causes the increment to happen after the value of the variable is used in the expression. The `println()` method will display 4 and then `no1` will be incremented to 5.

Example 7.5: Prefix mode 1
```
int no1 = 4;
System.out.println(++no1);
```

Explanation
> Prefix mode causes the increment to happen first. `no1` is incremented to 5.
> Then `println()` method will display the value in `no1` (which is 5).

Example 7.6: Postfix mode 2
```
01  int x = 1, y;
02  y = x++;
03  System.out.println(y);
```

Explanation
> Line 02: Assigns the value of x to the variable y. The variable x is incremented. The value that will be stored in y depends on when the increment takes place. Because the ++ operator is used in postfix mode, it acts after the assignment takes place. So y = 1. After the Line 02 code has executed, x will contain 2.

Example 7.7: Prefix mode 2
```
01  int x = 1, y;
02  y = ++x;
03  System.out.println(y);
```

++x acts on the variable before the assignment takes place. So store 2 in y. After the code has executed, x will also contain 2.

The while Loop

A Loop is a control structure that causes a statement(s) to repeat. Java has three looping control structures:

- The `while` loop.
- The `do-while` loop.
- The `for` loop.

Introduction to while loop

The while loop has two important parts:

- A **condition** (boolean expression) that is tested for a `true` or `false` value.
- A **statement(s)** that is repeated as long as the condition (expression) is `true`.

The repetition statement allow you to specify that an action is to be repeated while some condition remain true.

Syntax
```
while (condition)
{
    // statement(s)
}
```

Explanation

- First line is sometimes called the loop header. It consist of the keyword `while` followed by the condition enclosed in parentheses. Condition or boolean-expression is any valid boolean expression.
- The condition is tested, and if it is true, the statement(s) is executed. Then the condition is tested again, if it is true, the statement(s) is executed. This cycle repeats until the condition is false.
- The statement(s) that is repeated is known as the body of the loop. It is also considered a conditionally executed code, because it is only executed under the condition that the condition is true.

The control flow in the while loop is shown in the following figure.

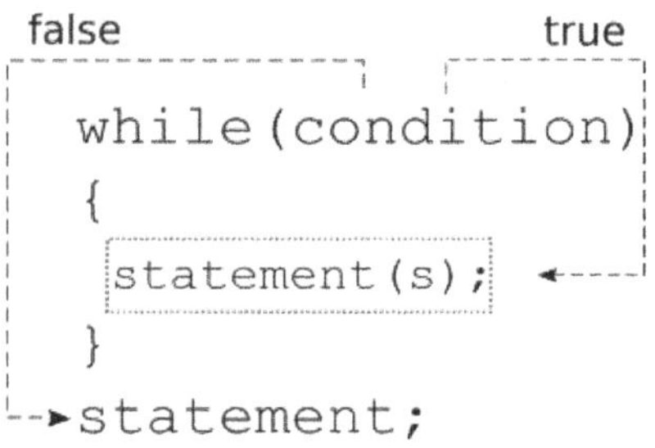

```
                false                    true
        ┌─ ─ ─ ─ ─ ─ ─ ─ ─┐  ┌ ─ ─ ─ ─ ─ ─ ─ ─┐
        │          while (condition)          │
        │          {                          │
        │             statement(s);      ◄────┘
        │          }
        └──► statement;
```

Figure 7.1 | Control flow in while loop

The While loop is a Pretest Loop

The while loop is known as a **pretest loop**, which means it tests its condition before each iteration. The loop will never iterate if the condition is false. If you want to be sure that a while loop executes the first time, you must initialize the relevant data in such a way that the condition starts out as true.

The program `WhileLoop1.java` illustrates the use of the while loop or perform the same function as the for loop.

Example 7.8: WhileLoop1.java

```
01  package ch07;
02  public class WhileLoop1 {
03      public static void main(String[] args) {
04          int num = 1;
05          while (num <= 5)
06          {
07              System.out.println("welcome");
08              num++;
09          }
10          System.out.println("That's all!");
11      }
12  }
```

Output

```
welcome
welcome
welcome
welcome
welcome
That's all!
```

Explanation

> Line 04: An integer variable, `num`, is declared and initialized with the value 1.

> Line 05: The while loop begins. The statement tests the variable `num` to determine whether it is less than or equal to 5. If it is less than 5, then the statements in the body of the loop are executed.

> Line 07: First statement in the body of the loop prints the word `Welcome`.
> Line 08: Second statement in the body of the loop uses the increment operator to add one to `num`. This is the last statements in the body of the loop. So after it executes, the loop starts over.
> Line 05: It tests the condition again, and if it `true`, the statements in the body of the loop are executed.
> This cycle repeats until the condition `num <= 5` is false. The loop will terminate and the program will resume execution at the statement that immediately follows the loop, which is line 10.

Here is another example of while ..loop.

Example 7.8: WhileLoop2.java

```
01  int num = 1;
02  while (num <= 5)
03  {
04      System.out.println("Welcome");
05      num++;
06  }
```

Explanation

> Line 02: First test this condition `num <= 5`. If the condition is true, perform the body of the while loop. After executing the body of the loop, start over.
> Each repetition of a loop is known as an **iteration**. This loop perform 5 iterations. The variable `num` is initialized with the value 1, and it is incremented each time the body of the loop is executed.
> When the expression `num<=5` is tested and found to be `false`, the loop will terminate and the program will resume execution at the statement that immediately follows the loop.
> The `num` variable is referenced to as the **loop control variable** because it controls the number of times that the loop iterates.

Infinite loops

Loop must contain a way to terminate within themselves. This means that something inside the loop must eventually make the condition `false`. For example 7.9:

```
01  int num = 1;
02  while (num <= 5)
03  {
04      System.out.println("welcome");
```

05   }
```

The loop stops when the condition `num<=5` false. It doesn't contain a statement that changes the value of the `num` variable. Each time the condition is tested, `num` will contain the value 1. If a loop does not have a way of stopping, it is called an **infinite loop**. An infinite loop continues to repeat until the program is interrupted.

## Counter-controlled repetition

Counter-controlled repetition requires:

> a control or counter variable (or loop counter) to specify the number of times a set of statement(s) should execute;
> the initial value of the control variable;
> the increment (or decrement) by which the control/counter variable is modified each time through the loop (a.k.a. each iteration of the loop);
> the condition that determines if looping should continue.

Counter controlled repetition is often called **definite repetition** because the number of repetitions is known before the loop begins executing. Here is a simple example.

**Example 7.10:** WhileCounter.java - Counter-controlled repetition with the while repetition statement

```java
01  package ch07;
02  public class WhileCounter {
03      public static void main(String[] args) {
04          int counter = 1; // declare and initialize counter variable
05          while (counter <= 10)
06          {
07              System.out.println(counter);
08              ++counter;  // increment counter variable by 1
09          }
10          System.out.println();
11      }
12  }
```

Output

```
1
2
3
4
5
6
7
```
```

8
9
10

Here is another example of while loop.

Example 7.11: WhileCounter2.java

```
01  package ch07;
02  import java.util.Scanner;
03  public class WhileCounter2 {
04      public static void main(String[] args) {
05          Scanner input = new Scanner(System.in);
06          int counter = 1;      // number of grades to be entered next
07          int total = 0;        // Sum of grades input by user
08          int grade;            // grade value
09          int average;          // Average of grades
10
11          // Processing Phase
12          while (counter <= 5)
13          {
14              System.out.println("Enter Grade");
15              grade = input.nextInt();
16              total = total + grade;
17              counter++;
18          }
19
20          // Termination Phase
21          average = total / 5; // integer division
22          System.out.println("Class Average is " + average);
23      }
24  }
```

Output

```
Enter Grade
90
Enter Grade
80
Enter Grade
70
Enter Grade
60
Enter Grade
50
Class Average is 70
```

Explanation

> › A `total` is a variable used to accumulate the sum of a series of values.
> › A `counter` is a variable used to count - in this case , to count the number of grades entered.

> Variables used to store totals should normally be initialized to zero before being used in a program; otherwise the `sum` would include the previous value stored in the `total`'s memory location.
> `Counter` variables are normally initialized to zero or one.

NOTE: Initialize all counters and totals.

Sentinel-controlled repetition

Sentinel-Controlled repetition is often called **Indefinite Repetition** because the number of repetition is not known before the loop begins executing.

A **sentinel value** (also called a signal value) is used in a sentinel controlled loop to indicate the **end of data entry**. The sentinel value must be chosen so that it cannot be confused with an acceptable input value. It is simply any constant of your choosing that you can use it to mark the end of sequence.

NOTE: This type of repetition allowing the user to end the loop.

Consider the below example.

Example 7.12: WhileSentinel.java

```
01  package ch07;
02  import java.util.Scanner;
03
04  public class WhileSentinel {
05      public static void main(String[] args) {
06
07          int total = 0;
08          int number = 1;
09
10          while (number != 0)
11          {
12              System.out.println("Please enter a number, or 0 to exit");
13              Scanner input = new Scanner(System.in);
14              number = input.nextInt();
15              total = total + number;
16          }
17          System.out.println("Total is: " + total);
18      }
19  }
```

Output

```
Please enter a number, or 0 to exit
5
Please enter a number, or 0 to exit
5
Please enter a number, or 0 to exit
5
Please enter a number, or 0 to exit
0
Total is: 15
```

Using the while loop for Input validation

Input validation is the process of inspecting data given by the user and determine if it is valid. A while loop is especially useful for validating input. If an invalid value is entered, a loop can require that the user re-enter it as many times as necessary. Let's see an example for this.

Example 7.13: InputValidiation.java

```java
01  package ch07;
02
03  import java.util.Scanner;
04
05  public class InputValidiation {
06      String input;
07      public static void main(String[] args) {
08          Scanner sc = new Scanner(System.in);
09          System.out.println("Enter a number in the range of 1 through 100");
10          String input = sc.nextLine();
11
12          int number = Integer.parseInt(input);
13
14          while (number < 1 || number > 100) {
15              System.out.println("Invalid input. " +
16                  "Enter a number in the range of 1 through 100.");
17              input = sc.nextLine();
18              number = Integer.parseInt(input);
19          }
20      }
21  }
```

Output

```
Enter a number in the range of 1 through 100
1000
Invalid input. Enter a number in the range of 1 through 100.
250
Invalid input. Enter a number in the range of 1 through 100.
101
Invalid input. Enter a number in the range of 1 through 100.
100
Process finished with exit code 0
```

Explanation

> - Lines 09 to 12: Allow the user to enter a number (before the loop).
> - Line 14: If the input is valid, the loop will not execute.
> - Line 15: If the input is invalid, however, the loop will display an error message and require the user to enter another number. The loop will continue to execute until the user enters a valid number.

The do-while Loop

The do-while loop is a **post test loop**, which means its condition is tested after each iteration.

Syntax

```
01  do
02  {
03      // statement(s)
04  }while (Condition);
```

The do-while loop is a post test loop:

> - This means it does not test its condition until it has completed an iteration.
> - As a result, the do-while loop always performs at least one iteration, even if the condition is false to begin with.

The control flow in the `do...while` loop is shown in the following figure.

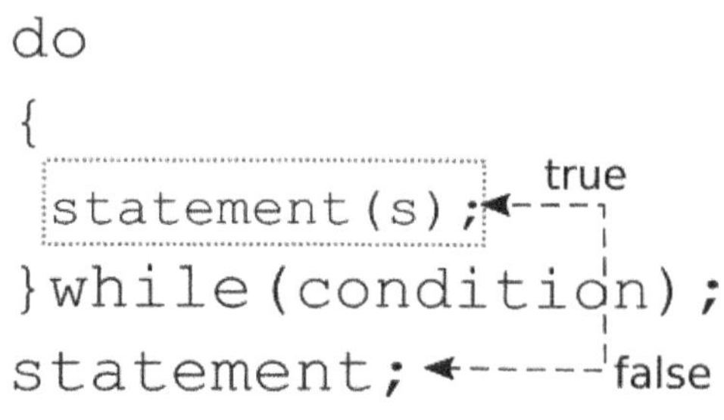

```
do
{
    statement(s); ◄---┐
                     true
}while (condition);   │
statement; ◄------false
```

Figure 7.2 | Control flow in do ..while loop

The program `DoWhile2.java` illustrates the use of the `do ...while` loop.

Example 7.14: DoWhile1.java

```
01  package ch07;
02  public class DoWhile1 {
03      public static void main(String[] args) {
04          int x = 1;
05          while (x < 0)
06          {
```

```
            System.out.println(x);
        }
    }
}
```

The `println()` statement will not execute at all. Here is another example.

Example 7.15: DoWhile2.java
```
package ch07;
public class DoWhile2 {
    public static void main(String[] args) {
        int x = 1;
        do
        {
            System.out.println(x);
        }while (x < 0);
    }
}
```

Output
```
1
```

Explanation

`println` statement will execute once because the `do-while` loop not evaluate the expression (`x < 0`) until the end of iteration. Use the `do-while` loop when you want to make sure the loop executes at least once.

The for Loop

The for loop is ideal for performing a known number of iterations. There are two categories of loops:

1. Conditional Loops.
2. Count-Controlled Loops.

A conditional loop executes as long as a particular condition exists. For example; an input validation loop executes as long as the input value is invalid. When you write a conditional loop, you have no way of knowing the number of times it will iterate.

A count-controlled loop is repeats as specific number of times. For example; A loop asks the user to enter the sales amounts for each month in the year; it will iterate 12 times.

A count-controlled loop must process three elements:
› It must initialize a control variable to starting value.

> It must test the control variable by comparing it to a maximum value. When the control variable reaches its maximum value, the loop terminates.
> It must update the control variable during each iteration. This is usually done by incrementing the variable.

In Java, the for loop is ideal for for writing count-controlled loops. It is specifically designed to initialize, test, and update a loop control variable.

Syntax

```
for (initialization ; condition ; update)
{
    // statement(s)
}
```

Explanation

> **Initialization**: Used to initialize a control variable to its starting value. This is the first action performed by the loop and it is only done once.
> **Condition**: This is a condition that controls the execution of the loop. As long as this condition is true, the body of the for loop will repeat. The for loop is a pretest loop, so it evaluates the condition before each iteration.
> **Update**: It executes at the end of each iteration. Typically, this is statement that increments the loop's control variable.

Sequence of Events in the for Loop

```
          (1)              (2)              (4)
for (int count = 1; count <= 5; count++)
{
    System.out.println("Welcome");  (3)
}
```

Figure 7.3 | Sequence of Events in the for Loop

Step 1: Perform the initialization expression.

Step 2: Evaluate the condition. If it is `true`, go to Step 3, otherwise, terminate the loop.

Step 3: Execute the body of the loop.

Step 4: Perform the update expression, then go back to Step 2.

The count variable

> `count` variable is used only in the loop header.
> `count` variable is used to control the number of times that the loop iterates.

> Because this variable keeps a count of the number of iterations, it is often called a **counter variable**.
> It is not used for any other purpose. It is also possible to use the control variable within the body of the loop.

The control flow in the for loop is shown in the following figure:

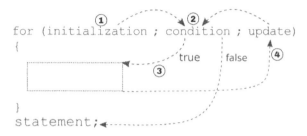

Figure 7.4 | Control flow in for loop

The `ForLoop1.java` program illustrates the use of `for` loop statement.

Example 7.16: ForLoop1.java

```
01  package ch07;
02  public class ForLoop1 {
03      public static void main(String[] args) {
04          int no;
05          for (no = 1; no <= 10; no++)
06          {
07              System.out.println(no + " ");
08          }
09      }
10  }
```

Output

```
1
2
3
4
5
6
7
8
9
10
```

Explanation
> The control variable `no`, controlling the number of iterations. It is also used in the body of the loop.
> The loop displays the contents of the `no` variable during each iteration.

Below is another example of a program that illustrates the use of `for` loop statement.

Example 7.17: ForLoop2.java

```
01  package ch07;
02  public class ForLoop2 {
03      public static void main(String[] args) {
04          int no;
05          System.out.println("no   no squared");
06          System.out.println("---------------");
07          for (no = 1; no <= 10; no++)
08          {
09              System.out.println(no + "\t" + no*no);
10          }
11      }
12  }
```

Output

```
no   no squared
---------------
1    1
2    4
3    9
4    16
5    25
6    36
7    49
8    64
9    81
10   100
```

Explanation (Lines 07 - 10)

› Step 1: Perform the initialization expression `no=1`.
› Step 2: Evaluate the condition, if it is `true`, go to Step 3. Otherwise, terminate the loop.
› Step 3: Execute the body of the loop.
› Step 4: Perform the update expression (`no++`), then go back to step 2.

NOTES
☐ Avoid modifying the control variable in the body of the for loop.
☐ All modifications of the control variable should take place in the update expression, which is automatically executed at the end of each iteration.

If a statement in the body of the loop also modifies the control variable, the loop will not terminate when you expect it to. Here is a simple example:

Example 7.18: ForLoop3.java

```
package ch07;
public class ForLoop3 {
    public static void main(String[] args) {
        int x;
        for (x = 1; x <= 10; x++)
        {
            System.out.println(x);
            x++; // wrong
        }
    }
}
```

Output

```
1
3
5
7
9
```

For other forms of the update expression, see the example below.

Example 7.19: ForLoop4.java

Display all even numbers from 2 through 100 by adding 2 to its counter

```
package ch07;
public class ForLoop4 {
    public static void main(String[] args) {
        int x;
        for (x = 2; x <= 100; x += 2)
        {
            System.out.print(x + ".");
        }
        System.out.println(" ");
        // Counts backward from 100 to 0
        int y;
        for (y = 100; y >= 2; y -= 2)
        {
            System.out.print(y + ".");
        }
    }
}
```

Output

2.4.6.8.10.12.14.16...........92.94.96.98.100.
100.98.96.94.92...........16.14.12.10.8.6.4.2.

Declaring a variable in the for Loop's initialization expression

Example 7.20: ForLoop41.java

```
01  for (int x = 1; x <= 10; x++)
02  {
03      System.out.println(x + "\t\t" + x*x);
04  }
```

Explanation

> Line 01: The **x** variable is both declared and initialized in the initialization expression.
> Line 03: The control variable (**x**) used in the body of the for loop.
> If the control variable is used only in the loop, it makes sense to declare it in the loop header. This makes the variable's purpose clearer.

When a variable is declared in the initialization expression of a for loop, the scope of the variable is limited to the loop. This means you cannot access the variable in statements outside the loop. Here is how that is done.

Example 7.21: ForLoop6.java
```
01  public class ForLoop5 {
02      public static void main(String[] args) {
03          for (int x = 1; x <= 10; x++)
04          {
05              System.out.println(x + "\t\t" + x*x);
06          }
07          System.out.println("x is now " + x);
08      }
09  }
```

Output
```
Error:Error:line (7)java: cannot find symbol
  symbol:   variable x
  location: class ch07.ForLoop5
```

The program will not compile because the last `println()` statement cannot access the variable **x**, because its outside the body of the for loop.

Using multiple statement in the initialization and update expression

It is possible to execute more than one statement in the initialization expression and the update expression.

Syntax
```
for (initExp1, initExp2,..., initExpN; condition ;
     updateExp1, updateExp2,..., updateExpN )
{
    // statement(s)
```

}

Separate the statement with comma.

Example 7.22: ForLoop7.java - Two statements in the initialization expression

```
int x, y;
for (x = 1, y = 1; x <= 5; x++)
{
    System.out.println(x + " plus " + y + " equals " + (x + y));
}
```

Output
```
1 plus 1 equals 2
2 plus 1 equals 3
3 plus 1 equals 4
4 plus 1 equals 5
5 plus 1 equals 6
```

Example 7.23: ForLoop8.java - Execute two statements in the update expression

```
int x, y;
for (x = 1, y = 1; x <= 5; x++, y++)
{
    System.out.println(x + " Plus " + y + " equals "+ (x + y));
}
```

NOTE: With test expression use the `&&` or `||` operators.

Nested Loops

A loop that is inside another loop is called a nested loop. Nested loops are necessary when a task performs a repetitive operation and that task itself must be repeated. For example, here's a simple program for printing each value of a 2D array.

Example 7.24: NestedLoops.java - Print each value of a 2D array

```
package ch07;
public class NestedLoops {
    public static void main(String[] args) {
        int[][] array = { {1, 2, 3},
                          {4, 5, 6},
                          {7, 8, 9} };
        for (int x = 0; x < array.length; x++) {
            for (int y = 0; y < array[x].length; y++){
                System.out.print(array[x][y] + " ");
            }
```

```
11                  System.out.println();
12              }
13          }
14  }
```

Output

```
1 2 3
4 5 6
7 8 9
```

Explanation

> The innermost loop (Line 08) will iterate 3 times for each single iteration of the outer loop (line 07.)

> When the outermost loop (begins at Line 07) has iterated 3 times, the innermost loop will have iterated 9 times.

NOTES
☐ An inner loop goes through all of its iterations for each iteration of one outer loop.
☐ Inner loops complete their iterations before outer loops do.
☐ To get the total number of iterations of a nested loop, multiple the number of iterations of all the loops.

Introduction to break statement

The `break` statement terminates the execution of a loop (`for`, `while` and `do...while` loop) or a `switch` statement immediately when it is encountered. Statements in the loop after the break statement do not execute. The `break` statement is used with decision making statement such as `if...else`.

When it is encountered, the loop stops and the program jumps to the statement or code immediately following the loop. The control flow in `for, while, and do-while` loop statements with break statement embedded within their body is shown in the following Figure.

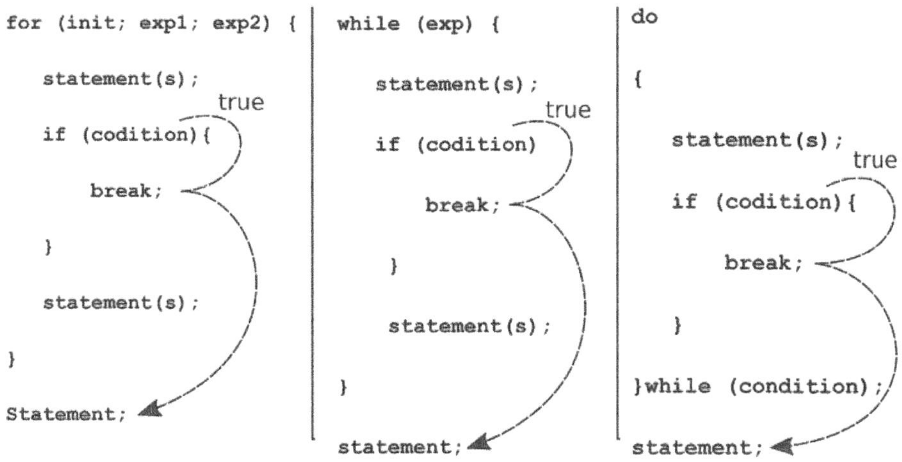

```
                  for (init; exp1; exp2) {    while (exp) {           do
                                                                      {
                       statement(s);               statement(s);
                                      true                     true      statement(s);
                       if (codition){             if (codition)                       true
                                                                         if (codition){
                          break;                     break;
                                                                             break;
                       }                          }
                                                                         }
                       statement(s);
                                                  statement(s);          }
                  }
                                                                         }while (condition);
                  Statement;                     }
                                                 statement;              statement;
```

Figure 7.5 | break statement in loops

Below is a program to calculate the sum of maximum of 20 numbers. Calculates **sum** until user enters negative number.

Example 7.25: BreakFor.java

```
01  package ch07;
02  import java.util.Scanner;
03  public class Break {
04      public static void main(String[] args){
05          int i;
06          double number, sum = 0.0;
07          for (i = 1 ; i <= 20 ; i++){
08              System.out.println("Enter a number");
09              Scanner in = new Scanner(System.in);
10              String num = in.nextLine();
11              number = Double.parseDouble(num);
12
13              // If user enters negative number, loop is terminated
14              if (number < 0.0){
15                  break;
16              }
17              sum += number; // sum = sum + number;
18          }
19          System.out.println("Sum = " + sum);
20      }
21  }
```

Output

```
Enter a number
1
Enter a number
1
..
```

```
Enter a number
1
Sum = 20.0
```

This program calculates the sum of maximum of 20 numbers. When the user enters negative number, the `break` statement is executed and loop is terminated.

Explanation

> Line 05: Create a control variable named i. (controlling the number of iterations)
> Line 06: Create a variable named `number`. Also create a variable named `sum` and assign it a value `0.0`.
> Lines 07 - 18: for loop
> - Step 1: Perform the initialization expression (i = 1).
> - Step 2: Evaluate the condition, if it is `true` - *if i <= 20* - go to next step.
> - Step 3: Execute the body of the loop.
> - Step 4: Perform the update expression (`i++`), then go back to step 2, evaluate the condition.
> Line 08: Displays the message, `"Enter a number"` on the screen (console).
> Line 09: Instantiating a new `Scanner` object.
> Line 10: Reading a line of input (until the user hits enter) from the keyboard and putting it in a String variable called `num`.
> Line 11: Convert the value of the `num` variable from string to double data type - to use it inside the `if` statement (Line 13). Then assign the value to the `number` variable.
> Line 14: `if` Statement. If the `number`'s value is less than 0.0, execute the body of `if` statement.
> Line 15: Execute `break` statement. When a `break` statement is encountered inside a loop, the loop is immediately terminated and the program control resumes at the next statement following the loop. If the `number`'s value is greater than `0.0`, go to the line 17.
> Line 17: Add the value entered by the user to the value of the `sum` variable. Then assign the result to the `sum` variable.
> Line 19: Displaying the value of the `sum` variable on the screen `(console)`.

Below is a program to display the value of **(a)** on the screen, until its value is greater than 15.

Examplev 7.26: Break2.java

```
package ch07;
public class Break2 {
    public static void main(String[] args) {
        int a = 10;
        while (a < 20) {
            System.out.println("Value of a is " + a);
            a++;
            if (a > 15) {
                // terminate the loop using break statement
                break;
            }
        }
    }
}
```

Output

```
Value of a is 10
Value of a is 11
Value of a is 12
Value of a is 13
Value of a is 14
Value of a is 15
```

Introduction to continue statement

The `continue` statement causes the current iteration of a loop to end immediately. The program continues execution from the next iteration. However, when the `continue` statement is executed, it behaves differently for different types of loops.

In a for loop, `continue` causes the update expression to be executed, and then the test expression is executed. The control flow in `for` loop with `continue` statement embedded within their body is shown in the following Figure.

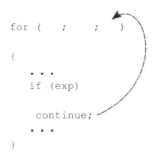

Figure 7.6 | Continue statement in for loop

For the `while` and `do...while` loops, `continue` statement causes the program control to pass to the conditional test. In a `while` loop, this means the program jumps to the boolean expression at the top of the loop. As usual, if the expression is still true, the next iteration begins. In a `do-while` loop, the program jumps to the boolean expression at the bottom of the loop, which determines whether the next iteration will begin.

The control flow in `while` and `d...while` loops with `continue` statement embedded within their body is shown in the following figure.

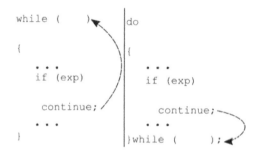

Figure 7.7 | Continue statement in while and do...while loops

The programs `ContinueFor.java` and `ContinueWhile.java` demonstrates the use of `continue` statement.

Example: 7.27 ContinueFor.java

```
01 package ch07;
02 public class ContinueFor {
03     public static void main(String[] args) {
04         int[] num = {1, 2, 3, 4, 5};
05         for(int x : num ) {
06             if( x == 2 ) {
07                 continue;
08             }
09             System.out.print( x + "\n" );
10         }
11     }
12 }
```

Output
```
1
3
4
5
```

Example 7.28: ContinueWhile.java

```
01 package ch07;
02 public class ContinueWhile {
03     public static void main(String[] args) {
04         int a = 10;
05         do {
06             if (a == 15) {
```

```
                // skip the iteration
                a = a + 1;
                continue;
            }
            System.out.println("Value of a = " + a);
            a++;
        }while (a < 20);
    }
}
```

Output
```
Value of a = 10
Value of a = 11
Value of a = 12
Value of a = 13
Value of a = 14
Value of a = 16
Value of a = 17
Value of a = 18
Value of a = 19
```

Summary

> Pre-Increment/Pre-Decrement operator is placed before the variable name. Value is incremented (or decremented) first and then incremented (or decremented) value is used in expression.
> Post-Increment/Post-Decrement operator is written after variable name. Value is used in expression first and then incremented or decremented.
> The difference between Postfix and Prefix modes happen when the operators are used in statements that do more than just increment or decrement. Postfix mode causes the increment to happen after the value of the variable is used in the expression. Prefix mode causes the increment to happen first.
> A Loop is a control structure that causes a statement(s) to repeat. Java has three looping control structures: the while loop, the do-while loop, and the for loop.
> The while loop statement allow you to specify that an action is to be repeated while some condition remain true.
> The while loop is known as a pretest loop, which means it tests its condition before each iteration.
> Loop must contain a way to terminate within themselves. This means that something inside the loop must eventually make the condition false.

- Counter-controlled repetition requires a control or counter variable (or loop counter) to specify the number of times a set of statement(s) should execute, the initial value of the control variable, the increment (or decrement) by which the control/counter variable is modified each time through the loop (a.k.a. each iteration of the loop), and the condition that determines if looping should continue.
- Counter controlled repetition is often called definite repetition because the number of repetitions is known before the loop begins executing.
- Sentinel-Controlled repetition is often called indefinite repetition because the number of repetition is not known before the loop begins executing.
- A sentinel value (also called a signal value, a dummy value, or a flat value) is used in a sentinel controlled loop to indicate the end of data entry. The sentinel value must be chosen so that it cannot be confused with an acceptable input value.
- The do-while loop is a post test loop, which means its condition is tested after each iteration. This means it does not test its condition until it has completed an iteration. As a result, the do-while loop always performs at least one iteration, even if the condition is false to begin with.
- The for loop is ideal for performing a known number of iterations. There are two categories of loops: conditional loops, and count-controlled loops. A conditional loop executes as long as a particular condition exists. A count-controlled loop is repeats as specific number of times.
- A count-controlled loop must process three elements: It must initialize a control variable to starting value, it must test the control variable by comparing it to a maximum value. When the control variable reaches its maximum value, the loop terminates, and it must update the control variable during each iteration. This is usually done by incrementing the variable.
- In Java, the for loop is ideal for writing count-controlled loops. It is specifically designed to initialize, test, and update a loop control variable.
- A loop that is inside another loop is called a nested loop. Nested loops are necessary when a task performs a repetitive operation and that task itself must be repeated.
- The break statement causes a LOOP to terminate early.
- The continue statement causes the CURRENT iteration of a loop to end immediately.

Chapter 8

Java Methods

Introduction

What is a method?

A method is a collection of statements that are grouped together to performs a specific task. Tasks like display message and calculate numbers of days between dates. Methods allow us to reuse the code without retyping the code (Write Once and Reuse Many Times). In Java, every method must be part of some class.

A method has a name. When that name is encountered in a program, the execution of the program branches to the body of that method. When the method is finished, execution returns to the area of the program code from which it was called.

Categories of methods

Java has two different types of methods:
- void methods.
- value returning methods.

A void Methods

`void` methods is one that simple performs a task and then terminates. For example: `println()` method is void method.

```
01  int num = 0;
02  System.out.println(num);
```

```
03
04  num = 1;
05  System.out.println(num);
```

Explanation

> Line 01: declares the `num` variable and initializes it with the value 8.
> Line 02: calls the `println()` method. Passing **num** as argument to it, and the method display a value on the screen.
> Line 04: assigna a new value 1, to the `num` variable.
> Line 05: calls the `println()` method. Passing `num` as argument, and the method display a value on the screen.

A Value Returning Method

A value returning method not only perform a task, but also sends a value back to the code that called it.

Example 8.1:
```
01  int num;
02  String str = "1000";
03  num = Integer.parseInt(str);
04  System.out.println(num);
```

Explanation

> Line 01: declares the `num` variable.
> Line 02: creates a String object with the value 1000, and assigns its address to the `str` variable.
> Line 03: assigns a value to the `num` variable. Right side of the = operator is a call to the `Integer.parseInt` method.
>   - Passing `str` as an argument to the `Integer.parseInt()` method.
>   - The method executes and then return a value to this line of code (Line 03).
>   - The value that is returned from the `parseInt()` method is assigned to the `num` variable.
> Line 04: display the value of `num` variable on the screen using `System.out.println` method.

Value returning methods return a value to the calling statement. The calling statement normally does something with this value, such as assign it to a variable.

Create a New Method (defining a void method)

To create a method you must write its definition, which consists of two general parts:

› The **method header**, which appears at the beginning of a method definition, list several important things about the method, including the method's name.
› The **method body** is a collection of statements that are performed when the method is executed. These statements are enclosed inside a set of curly braces { and }.

Here is a simple example for that.

Example 8.2: The header and body of the main method
```java
public static void main(String[] args)   // header
{
    System.out.println("Welcome");    // body
}
```

As you already know, every complete Java programs must have a `main` method. Java program can have other methods as well. For example:

Example 8.3: The header and body of the displayMessage method
```java
public static void displayMessage()
{
    System.out.println("Welcome from displayMessage method.");
}
```

Parts of the method header

```
             Return
Method Modifiers  Type   Method Name
public static  void  displayMessage()
{
    System.out.println("Welcome from displayMessage method.");
}
```

Figure 8.1 | Method Header

Method Modifiers - for this lesson, every method that we write will begin with `public static`. `public` means that the method is publicity available to code outside the class. `static` means that the method belong to the class, not a specific object *(more on chapter 12)*.

return type - `void` means that the method is a void method and does not return a value.

Method name: Give a descriptive name. The same rules that apply to variable names also apply to method names (*see chapter 3*).

Parentheses: In the header, the method name is always followed by a set of parentheses. The method in this example does not receive any arguments, so the parentheses are empty.

You will learn later - methods can be capable of receiving arguments - a list of one or more variable declaration will appear inside the parentheses.

Calling a Method

A method executes when it is called. The `main` method is automatically called when a program starts, but other methods are executed by method call statements.

In Java, we call a method by stating its name, and the JVM branches to that method and executes the statements in its body.

For example, here's a simple program for calling the `displayMessage()` method from the `main` method

Example 8.4: CallMethod.java

```
01  package ch08;
02  public class CallMethod {
03      public static void main(String[] args) {
04          displayMessage();
05      }
06      public static void displayMessage() {
07          System.out.println("Welcome");
08      }
09  }
```

Output

```
Welcome
```

Explanation

> Line 03: The program starts in the `main` method.
> Line 04: The method modifiers and the `void` return type are not written in the method call statement. They only written in the method header.

> Line 04: When the call to the `displayMessage()` method is encountered, the JVM branches to that method (Lines 06, 07, 08) and performs the statement in its body.
> Once the `displayMessage` method has finished executing, the JVM branches back to the `main` method and resume with the statement that follows the method call (Line 05).

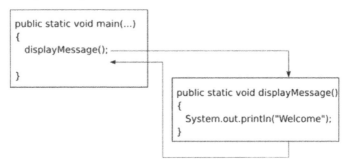

Figure 8.2 | Execution path of one call

Passing Arguments to a Method

A method may be written so it accepts arguments. Values that are sent into a method are called **arguments**. Data can then be passed into the method when it is called.

In the header of the method, the items are termed **parameters**. For example:

```
System.out.println("Welcome"); // Welcome is an argument (data-
values)
```

This statement calls the `System.out.println()` method, and passes `"Welcome"` as an argument.

Parameter variables

By using parameter variables, you can design your own methods that accept data this way. A parameter variable, sometimes referred to as a **parameter**, is a special variable that holds a value being passed into a method.

The definition of a method that uses a parameters

```
public static void displayValue (int num)
{
  System.out.println("The value is " + num);
```

}

`int num` - This is the declaration of a parameter variable, which enables the `displayValue()` method to accept an integer value as an argument.

For example, here's a simple program for calling the `displayValue` method, passing 100 as an argument to the `displayValue` method.

Example 8.5: ParaVar1.java - A call to the `displayValue` method, passing 100 as an argument to the `displayValue` method

```
01  package ch08;
02  public class ParaVar1 {
03      public static void main(String[] args) {
04          displayValue(100);        // 100 is an argument
05      }
06      public static void displayValue(int num) // num is a parameter
07      {
08          System.out.println("The value is " + num);
09      }
10  }
```

Output

```
The value is 100
```

Explanation

> Line 04: Executes or calls the `displayValue` method. The argument that is listed inside the parentheses is copied into the method's parameter variable, `num`.

> Line 08: Inside the body of the `displayValue()` method, the variable `num` will contain the value of whatever argument was passed into it. If we pass 100 as the argument, the method will display as follows: `"The Value is 100"`. You may also pass contents of variables and the values of expression as arguments.

Below is an another example that call the `displayValue()` method with various arguments passed.

Example 8.6: ParaVar2.java - call the `displayValue` method with various arguments passed

```
01  public static void main(String[] args)
02  {
03      int x = 5;
04      displayValue(100);
05      displayValue(x);
06      displayValue(x * 5);
07      displayValue(Integer.parseInt("700"));
08  }
09  public static void displayValue(int num)
10  {
```

```
          System.out.println("The value is " + num);
```

Output
```
The value is 100
The value is 5
The value is 25
The value is 700
```

Explanation

> Line 03: Declares a variable **x**, and initialize it with 5.
> Line 04: It passes the value, 100, as the argument to the `displayValue()` method.
> Line 05: It passes the variable **x** as the argument to the `displayValue()` method.
> Line 06: It passes the result of the expression (`x * 5`) as the argument to the `displayValue()` method.
> Line 07: It passes the value returned from the `Integer.parseInt` method as the argument to the `displayValue()` method. The `Integer.parseInt` method is called first, and its value is passed to the `displayValue()` method.
> Lines 09 - 12: Executing the `displayValue` method when called from the *main* method.

Warning

> When processing a variable as an argument, simply write the variable name inside the parentheses of the method call. Do not write the data type of the argument variable in the method call. For example:
> `displayValue(int x); // error`

> The method call should appear as follow:
> `displayValue(x); // correct`

NOTES

☐ The values that are passed into a method are called **arguments**, and the variables that receive those values are called **parameters**.

☐ There are several variations of these terms in use. Some call the arguments **actual parameters** and call the parameters **formal parameters**. Others use the term **actual argument** and **formal argument**.

☐ Regardless of which set of terms you use, it is important to be consistent.

Arguments and parameters data types compatibility

When you pass an argument to a method, be sure that the argument's data type is compatible with the parameter variable's data type. Java will automatically perform a widening conversion if the argument's data type is ranked lower than the parameter variable's data type. Consider below example for that.

Example 8.7: ParaVar3.java - The `displayValue` method has an `int` parameter variable

Both of the following code segments will work because the `short` and `byte` arguments are automatically converted to an `int`.

```java
01  package ch08;
02  public class ParaVar3 {
03      public static void main(String[] args)
04      {
05          short s = 1;
06          displayValue(s);
07          byte b  = 2;
08          displayValue(b);
09      }
10      public static void displayValue(int num)
11      {
12          System.out.println("The value is " + num);
13      }
14  }
```

Output
```
The value is 1
The value is 2
```

However, Java will not automatically convert an argument to a lower-ranking data type. This means that a long, float, or double value cannot be passed to a method that has an `int` parameter variable. Here is a simple example.

Example 8.8: ParaVar4.java - The following code will cause a compiler error

```java
01  package ch08;
02  public class ParaVar4 {
03      public static void main(String[] args)
04      {
05          double d = 42.5;
06          displayValue(d); // error! cannot double to int
07      }
08      public static void displayValue(int num)
09      {
10          System.out.println("The value is " + num);
11      }
12  }
```

Output

```
Error:(7, 22) java: incompatible types: possible lossy conver-
sion from double to int
```

TIP: You can use a cast operator to convert a value manually to a lower ranking data type. Here is how that is done.

Example 8.9: ParaVar5.java - the following code will compile

```
package ch08;
public class ParaVar5 {
    public static void main(String[] args)
    {
        double d = 2.5;
        displayValue((int)d);
    }
    public static void displayValue(int num)
    {
        System.out.println("The value is " + num);
    }
}
```

Output

```
The value is 2
```

NOTES: Parameter Variable Scope
☐ A variable's scope is the part of the program where the variable may be accessed by its name.
☐ A variable is visible only to statements inside the variable's scope.
☐ A parameter variable's scope in the method is which the parameter is declared. No statement outside the method can access the parameter variable by its name.

Passing multiple arguments to methods

You can pass more than one value over to your methods. The declaration for a method declares the number and the type of the arguments for that method. For example, the following is a method that computes the sum of two numbers, and display the sum on the screen.

Example 8.10: Total1.java - A method that accepts two arguments:

```
package ch08;
public class Total1 {
    public static void main(String[] args)
    {
        showSum(10.5, 14.5); // calling method
    }
    public static void showSum(double num1, double num2)
```

```
08      {
09          double sum; // to hold the sum
10          sum = num1 + num2;
11          System.out.println("The sum is " + sum);
12      }
13  }
```

Output

```
The sum is 56.5
```

Explanation

> Line 07: Two parameter variables, `num1`, and `num2` are declared inside the parentheses in the method header.

> Line 05: This statement `showSum(12.5, 44.0)` passes the arguments (12.5 and 44.0) into the method.

> The arguments are passed into the parameter variables in the order that they appear in the method call. The first argument is passed into the first parameter variable. The second argument is passed into the second parameter variable, and so forth. So, this statement causes `12.5` to be passed into the `sum1` parameter and `44.0` to be passed into the `num2` parameters.

Suppose we were to reverse the order in which the arguments are listed in the method call as shown here:

```
showSum(44.0, 12.5);
```

Cause `44.0` to be passed into the `num1` parameter and `12.5` to be passed into the `num2` parameter. Here is a simple example.

Example 8.11: Total2.java - Passing variables as arguments

```
01  package ch08;
02  public class Total2 {
03      public static void main(String[] args)
04      {
05          double value1 = 5.5;
06          double value2 = 3.5;
07          showSum(value1, value2);   // calling method
08      }
09      public static void showSum(double num1, double num2)
10      {
11          double sum; // to hold the sum
12          sum = num1 + num2;
13          System.out.println("The sum is " + sum);
14      }
15  }
```

Output

```
The sum is 9.0
```

Explanation

› Line 09: The `num1` parameter will contain 5.5
› Line 09: The `num2` parameter will contain 3.5

Warning: Each parameter variable in a parameter list must have data type listed before its name.

Example 8.12: A compiler error would occur if the parameter list for the `showSum` method were defined as shown:

```
public static void showSum(double num1, num2) // error
```

A data type for both the `num1` and `num2` parameter variables must be listed as follow:

```
public static void showSum(double num1, double num2)
```

Arguments are passed by value

In Java, all arguments of the primitive data types are passed by value, which means that only a copy of an argument's value is passed into a parameter variable.

A method's parameter variables are separate and distinct from the arguments that are listed inside the parentheses of a method call. If a parameter variable is changed inside a method, it has no effect on the original argument. Let's see a simple example for that.

Example 8.13: PassByVal.java

```
01  package ch08;
02  public class PassByVal {
03      public static void main(String[] args)
04      {
05          int num = 100;
06          System.out.println("Number is " + num);
07          changeNow(num);
08          System.out.println("Number is " + num);
09      }
10      public static void changeNow(int value)
11      {
12          System.out.println("I am changing the value");
13          value = 0;
14          System.out.println("Now the value is " + value);
15      }
16  }
```

Output

```
Number is 100
I am changing the value
Now the value is 0
```

```
Number is 100
```

Even though the parameter variable `value` is changed in the `changeNow` method, the argument `num` is not modified. The value variable contains only a copy of the `num` variable.

Passing string object references to a method

Now we are going to write methods that accept reference to String objects as arguments. The `PassByRef.java` program demonstrates this concept.

Example 8.14: PassByRef.java

```
01  package ch08;
02  public class ShowLength {
03      public static void main(String[] args){
04          String name = "Mohammed";
05          showLength(name);
06      }
07      public static void showLength(String str){
08          System.out.println(str + " is " + str.length() + " Characters long");
09      }
10  }
```

Output
```
Mohammed is 8 Characters long
```

Explanation

> Line 05: The `showLength()` method accepts a String object references as its argument.
> Line 08: The `showLength()` method displays a message showing the number of characters in the object.
> When an object, such as a `String`, is passed as an argument, it is actually a reference to the object that is passed. So the `name` variable is a String reference variable. It is passed as an argument to the `showLength` method.
> The `showLength` method has a parameter variable `str`, which is also a String reference variable, that receives the argument.
> A reference variable holds the memory address of an object.
> When the `showLength` method is called, the string that is stored in name is passed into the `str` parameter variable.

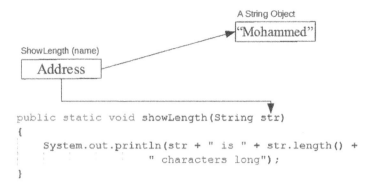

Figure 8.3 | Passing a Reference as an Argument

The parameter variable references the same object as the argument.

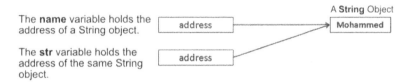

Figure 8.4 | Both name and str reference the same object.

However, String objects in Java are immutable, which means that they cannot be changed. See the following example.

Example 8.15: PassString.java

```
01  package ch08;
02  public class PassString {
03      public static void main(String[] args){
04          String city = "London";
05          System.out.println("Main Method: " + city);
06
07          changeCity(city);
08          System.out.println("Main Method: " + city);
09      }
10      public static void changeCity(String ci){
11          ci = "Khartoum";
12          System.out.println("changeCity Method: " + ci);
13      }
14  }
```

Output

```
Main Method: London
changeCity Method: Khartoum
Main Method: London
```

Explanation

> Line 04: Create a string object containing `"London"`. The `city` reference the object.
> Line 05: Display the String referenced by the `city` variable.
> Line 07: Call the `changeCity` method, passing the contents of the `city` variable as an argument.
> Line 10: The `changeCity` method accepts a String as its argument and assigns the `ci` parameter to a new string.
> Line 11: Create a String object containing `"Khartoum"`, and assigns its address to the `ci` parameter variable.
> Line 12: Display the String referenced by `ci`.

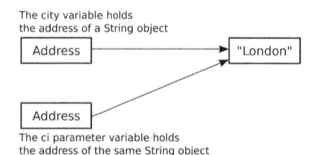

Figure 8.5 | Before line 10 executes both city and ci reference the same object

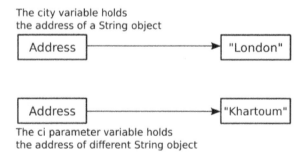

Figure 8.6 | After line 10 executes, city and ci reference different objects

More About Local Variables

Introduction

A local variables are variables that are declared inside a method and is not accessible to statements outside the method. They are called local because they are local to the method in which they are declared. Statements outside a method cannot access that method's local variables.

Because a method's local variables are hidden from other methods, the other methods may have their own local variables with the same name. Let's see an example.

Example 8.16: LocalVar.java

```
package ch08;
public class LocalVar {
    public static void main(String[] args) {
        london();
        khartoum();
    }
    public static void london()
    {
        int birds = 9000;
        System.out.println("In London there are " + birds + " birds");
    }
    public static void khartoum()
    {
        int birds = 5000;
        System.out.println("In Khartoum there are " + birds + " birds");
    }
}
```

Output

```
In omdurman there are 9000 birds
In khartoum there are 5000 birds
```

Explanation

› In addition to the *main* method, this program has two other methods (`london` and `khartoum`)
› These two methods each have a local variable named `birds`.
› The program can only see one of them at a time because they are in different methods.
› When an `london` method is executing, the `birds` variable declared inside `london` is visible.
› When the `khartoum` method is executing, the `birds` variable declared inside `khartoum` is visible.

Local variable lifetime

A method's local variables exists only while the methods is executing. This is known as the *lifetime of a local variable*. When the method begins, its local variables and its parameter variables are created in memory and when the method ends, the local variables and parameter variables are destroyed, and any value stored in a local variable is lost.

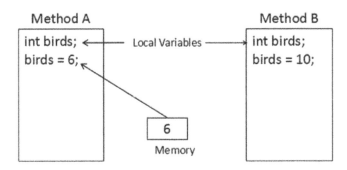

Initializing local variables with parameter values

Use a parameter variable to initialize a local variable. For example 8.17 (LocalVar2.java):

```
01  package ch08;
02  public class LocalVar2 {
03      public static void main(String[] args)
04      {
05          double x = 10;
06          double y = 200;
07          showSum(x, y);
08      }
09      public static void showSum(double num1, double num2)
10      {
11          double sum = num1 + num2;
12          System.out.println("The sum is " + sum);
13      }
14  }
```

Output
```
The sum is 210.0
```

Because the scope of a parameter variable is the entire method in which it is declared, we can use parameter variables to initialize local variables.

WARNING

Local variables are not automatically initialized with a default value. They must be given a value before they can be used. If you attempt to use a local variable before it has been given a value, a compiler error will result. For example 8.18:

```
01  public static void myMethod()
02  {
03      int x;
04      System.out.println(x)  // error! x has no value
05  }
```

This code will cause a compiler error because the variable **x** has not been given a value, and it is being used as an argument to the `System.out.println()` method.

Returning a Value From a Method

You have seen that data may be passed into a method by way of parameter variables. Data may also be returned from a method, back to the statement that call it. For example 8.19:

```
01  int x;
02  x = Integer.parseInt("1000");
03  System.out.println(x);
```

Explanation

> Line 01: Declares an `int` variable called **x**.
> Line 02: Calls the `Integer.parseInt()` method. Passing **1000** as the argument. The method returns the integer value **1000**. The integer value 1000, assigned to the `sum` variable.
> Line 03: Display the value of **x** on the screen.

In this section we will discuss how you can write your own value returning methods.

Defining a value returning method

When you are writing a **value returning method**, you must decide what type of value the method will return. This is because you must specify the data type of the return value in the method header.

Syntax

```
public static <data-type> <method-name> (args....)
{
    // statement(s)
}
```

When `<data_type>` = `void`: A void method does not return a value.

When `<data_type>` = `int, double, boolean,` or any other valid data type in its header: a method will return a value. Consider below example for that.

Example 8.20: ReturnMethod.java - Defining a value returning method

```
01  package ch08;
02  public class ReturnMethod {
03      public static void main(String[] args)
04      {
05          int sum;
06          sum = sum(10, 20);
07          System.out.println(sum);
08      }
09      public static int sum(int num1, int num2)
10      {
11          int result;
12          result = num1 + num2;
13          return result;
14      }
15  }
```

Output

```
30
```

Explanation

- Line 09: Method name `sum`.
- Line 09: `sum` method accepts two `int` arguments (10 and 20). The arguments are passed into the parameter variables `num1` and `num2`.
- Line 11: A local variable `result`, is declared.
- Line 12: The parameter variables `num1` and `num2` are added. This sum is assigned to the `result` variable
- Line 13: This is a `return` statement. You must have a `return` statement in a value-returning method. It causes the method to end execution and it returns a value to the statement that called the method.

General format of the return statements

```
return expression;
```

Expression is a value to be returned. It can be any expression that has a value, such as a variable, literal, or mathematical expression. In this case, the `sum` method returns the value in the `result` variable.

However, we could have eliminate the result variable and returned the expression num1 + num2:

```
01  public static int sum(int num1, int num2)
02  {
03      result = num1 + num2;
04  }
```

NOTE: The `return` statement's expression must be of the same data type as the return type specified in the method header, or compatible with it. Otherwise, a compiler error will occur. Java will automatically widen the value of the `return` expression, if necessary, but it will not automatically narrow it.

Calling a value returning method

The `ValueReturn.java` program demonstrates the concept of calling a value returning method.

Example 8.21: ValueReturn.java

```
01  package ch08;
02  public class ValueReturn {
03      public static void main(String[] args)
04      {
05          int total, value1 = 50, value2 = 40;
06          total = sum(value1, value2);
07          System.out.println("The sum of " + value1 +
08                  " and " + value2 + " is " + total);
09      }
10      public static int sum(int no1, int no2)
11      {
12          int result;
13          result = no1 + no2;
14          return result;
15      }
16  }
```

Output

```
The sum of 50 and 40 is 90
```

Explanation

Line 06: Calls the `sum` method, passing `value1` and `value2` as argument. It assigns the value returned by the `sum` method to the `total` variable. In this case, the method will return 90.

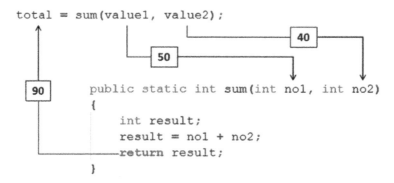

Figure 8.7 | How the args are passed into the method and how a value is passed back from the method

The `ValueReturn.java` shows a method's return value being assigned to a variable. This is commonly how return values are used, but you can do many other things with them. Here is a simple example.

Example 8.22: ValueReturn2.java

```
01  package ch08;
02  public class ValueReturn2 {
03      public static void main(String[] args) {
04          int x = 10, y = 20;
05          double average;
06          average = sum(x, y) / 2.0;
07          System.out.println(average);
08      }
09
10      public static int sum(int no1, int no2) {
11          int result;
12          result = no1 + no2;
13          return result;
14      }
15  }
```

Output

```
15.0
```

Explanation

> Line 06: The `sum` method is called with **x** and **y** as its arguments. The method's return value, which is 25, is divided by 2.0. The result, 12.5 is assigned to `average`.

Here is another example.

Example 8.23: ValueReturn3.java - Calling a value returning method
```
01  package ch08;
02  public class ValueReturn3 {
03      public static void main(String[] args) {
04          int x = 10, y = 20;
05          System.out.println("The sum is " + sum(x, y));
06      }
07
08      public static int sum(int no1, int no2) {
09          int result;
10          result = no1 + no2;
11          return result;
12      }
13  }
```

Output

```
The sum is 30
```

Explanation

> Line 05: Sends the `sum` method's return value to `System.out.println()`, so it can displayed on the screen. The message `"The sum is 30"` will be displayed.

REMEMBER: A value returning method returns a value of a specific data type. You can use the method's `return` value anywhere that you can use a regular value of the same data type. This means that anywhere an `int` value can be used, a call to an `int` value - returning method can be used. Likewise, anywhere a `double` value can be used, a call to a double value returning method can be used. The same is true for all data types.

Returning a boolean value

Sometimes there is a need for a method that tests an argument and returns a `true` or `false` value indicating whether or not a condition exists. Such a method would return a `boolean` value.

Example 8.24: BoolReturn.java
```
01  package ch08;
02  public class BoolReturn {
03      public static void main(String[] args)
04      {
05          int value = 20;
06          if (isValid(value))
07              System.out.println("The value is within range.");
08          else
```

```
09                System.out.println("The value is out of range.");
10        }
11        public static boolean isValid(int num)
12        {
13            boolean status;
14            if (num >= 1 && num <= 100)
15                status = true;
16            else
17                status = false;
18
19            return status;
20        }
21 }
```

Output
```
The value is within range.
```

Returning a reference to a String object

A value-returning method can also return a reference to a non-primitive type, such as a String object.

Example 8.25: ReturnString.java
```
01 package ch08;
02 public class ReturnString {
03     public static void main(String[] args)
04     {
05         String empName;
06         empName = fullName("Mohammed", "Mansour");
07         System.out.println(empName);
08     }
09     public static String fullName(String first, String last)
10     {
11         String name;
12         name =  first + " " + last;
13         return name;
14     }
15 }
```

Output
```
Mohammed Mansour
```

```
customerName = fullName("Mohammed", "Mansour");

A String Object
 "Mohammed
  Mansour"           public static String fullName(String first, String last)
                     {
     address             String name;
                         name  first + " " + last;
                         return name;
                     }
```

Figure 8.8 | The fullName method returning a reference to a String object

Summary

> A method is a collection of statements that are grouped together to performs a specific task.
> Java has two different types of methods, the **void** methods and the **value returning** methods. **void** methods is one that simple performs a task and then terminates. A value returning method not only perform a task, but also sends a value back to the code that called it.
> To create a method you must write its definition, which consists of two general parts, the **method header** and the **method body**.
> A method executes when it is called. In Java, we call a method by stating its name.
> A method may be written so it accepts arguments. Values that are sent into a method are called arguments. In the header of the method, the items are termed parameters.
> In Java, all arguments of the primitive data types are passed by value, which means that only a copy of an argument's value is passed into a parameter variable.
> In Java, we can write methods that accept reference to String objects as arguments.
> String objects in Java are immutable, which means that they cannot be changed.
> A local variables are variables that are declared inside a method and is not accessible to statements outside the method.
> A method's local variables exists only while the methods is executing. This is known as the lifetime of a local variable.
> When you are writing a value returning method, you must decide what type of value the method will return. This is because you must specify the data type of the return value in the method header.

Part 2

Object-Oriented Programming Using Java

"A language that doesn't affect the way you think about programming is not worth knowing." - Alan J. Perlis

Chapter 9

Classes and Objects

Introduction

Java is an Object-Oriented programming language. Object Oriented programming is a programming style which is associated with the concepts like class, object, inheritance, encapsulation, abstraction, polymorphism. Classes and objects are basic concepts of Object Oriented Programming. So let us look deep into what are objects.

If we consider the real-world, we can find many objects around us, cats, cars humans, etc. All these objects have a property (a.k.a. state) and a function (a.k.a. behavior). If we consider a human, its properties are - name, weight, color, and the functions are - walking, eating, talking.

Software objects also have a property and a function. A software objects's property is stored in **fields** and function is shown via **methods**. A **class** is a blueprint for creating **objects**. And from the class, one or more objects may be created. Following is an illustration of a class and objects:

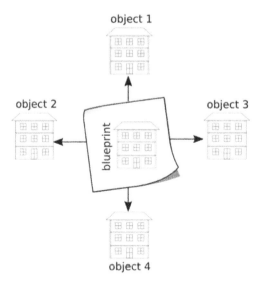

Figure 9.1 | Class and Objects

Each Class has -

> **Properties** (a.k.a. fields or attributes) associated with a class. For example: name, size, location, and color.
> **Methods** (functionality) of a class. For example: walking, talking, eating, and openDoor.

Class Creation

As I said, a class is sort of a blueprint for an object. When you create a class, you must tell Java about the class's characteristics. You define a class by using the **class** keyword along with the **class name** as shown below.

Syntax
```
01   class ClassName {
02
03   }
```

Explanation

> The class definition begins with the keyword `class` followed by the name of the class.
> The body of the class is marked off by curly braces { and } just like any other program block. In this case, the class's body is empty.

If you save the lines in a file called `MyClass.java`, you could even compile the class into a `.class` file, although the file won't actually do anything if you tried to run it.

Declaring Fields for a Class

You declare fields for your class in much the same way you declare any variable in a program.

Syntax

```
class ClassName{

    type instance-variable1;
    type instance-variable2
}
```

Here is a simple example.

Example 9.1: Declare a data type of type integer

```
class ClassName {

    int fieldOne;
}
```

Explanation

> Line 03 declares a field of type integer. Now `fieldOne` is a field of `MyClass` class. This field is by default accessible only by methods in the same package. You can change the rules of this access by using the `public`, `protected`, and `private` keywords.
> A `public` data field can be accessed by any part of a program, inside or outside of the class in which it's define.
> A `protected` data field can only be accessed from within the class or from within a derived class (a subclass).
> A `private` data field cannot even be accessed by a derived class.

Defining Methods

A method's declaration provides a lot of information about the method to the compiler. The method declaration carries information such as the name of the method, the return type of the method, the number and type of the arguments required by the method, and what other classes and objects can call the method.

The only two required elements of a method declaration are the method name and the data type returned by the method.

Syntax
```
01  class ClassName{
02
03      type instance-variable1;
04      type instance-variable2;
05
06      type method-name1 (parameter-list){
07          // body of method.
08      }
09      type method-name2 (parameter-list){
10          // body of method.
11      }
12  }
```

Example 9.2: The following code declares a method named `SetField` in the `MyClass` class that doesn't returns a value
```
01  class MyClass
02  {
03      private int fieldOne;
04
05      public void SetField(int value)
06      {
07          fieldOne = value;
08      }
09  }
```

Explanation
> Line 01: Defining the `MyClass` class.
> Line 03: Declare the class's `fieldOne` field.
> Line 05: Defining the `SetField()` method.
> Line 07: Set the field to the value passed to `SetField()`.

NOTE: All class fields should be declared as `private`.

Notes About Class Creation

> `class` is keyword in Java used to create class in Java.

- `Class name` is name of the user defined class. When a number of objects are created for the same class, the same copy of instance variable is provided to all.
- Access specifier can be applied to instance variable i.e. `public`, `private`.
- **Instance variables** are class variables of the class.
- Instance variables have different value for different objects.
- Instance variables are also called `Fields`.
- Instance methods are methods associated with a class. Class methods can be declared `public` or `private`. These methods are meant for operating on class data i.e. class variable.

Another Example.

Example 9.3: Class Concept

```
public class Rectangle{
    // two fields
    public int breadth;         ⎤  Instance Variables
    public int length;          ⎦

    // two methods
    public void setLength(int newValue){   ⎤
        length = newValue;
    }
    public void setBreadth(int newValue){  ⎥  Class Methods
        breadth = newValue;
    }                                      ⎦
}
```

NOTE: A class is not an object, but a description of an object. Once a class has been written you can use the class to create as many objects as needed. Each object is considered an *instance* of the class.

Object Creation

To create an object from a class, you type the class's name followed by the name of the object.

Syntax
```
<ClassName> object = new <ClassName>();
```

For example, the line below creates an object (myObject) from the MyClass class:

```
MyClass myObject = new MyClass();
```

The following program creates a rectangle.

Example 9.4: `Rectanle.java`

```
01  package ch09;
02  class Rectangle
03  {
04      double length;
05      double breadth;
06  }
07  class RectangleDemo
08  {
09      public static void main(String args[])
10      {
11          Rectangle rect = new Rectangle();
12          double area;
13
14          // Assigns values to rect's instance variables.
15          rect.length = 10;
16          rect.breadth = 20;
17
18          // Compute area of Rectangle
19          area = rect.length * rect.breadth;
20          System.out.println("Area is " + area);
21      }
22  }
```

Output

```
Area is 200.0
```

Explanation

Lines 02 - 06: Class Declaration

> Class defines a new data type `"Rectangle"`.
> `"Rectangle"` will be used to declare objects of type `Rectangle`.

Line 11: Actual creation of object

> Memory is allocated for an object after executing this statement.
> This statement will create instance of the class `"Rectangle"` and name of instance is nothing but actual object `"rect"`.
> Fresh copy of instance variables gets created for fresh instance [`rect` now have its own instance variables - `length` and `breadth`]

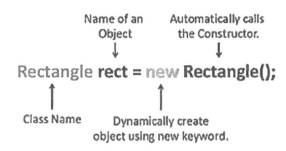

Figure 9.2 | Object Creation

Accessing instance variables of object using DOT operator

Each instance or object gets their own copy of instance variables i.e. `length` and `breadth`. We can access `rect's` copy of instance variable using **DOT** operator. For example:

Example 9.5: Instance Variables
```
rect.length = 10;
rect.breadth = 20;
```

Objects versus primitive variables

A primitive data type is called "**primitive**" because a variable created with a primitive data type has no built-in capabilities other than storing a value.

A primitive data type uses a small amount of memory to represent a single item of data. All data of the same primitive type are the same size. For example, primitive type `int` represents integers using 32 bits. All variables of type `int` use 32 bits.

There are only eight primitive data types in Java: `byte`, `short`, `int`, `long`, `float`, `double`, `char`, and `boolean`. A Java program cannot define any other primitive data types.

An object is a large chunk of memory that can potentially contain a great deal of *data* along with *methods* to process that data.

Building a Simple Class

Step 1: Design a class

Class Name: `Rectangle (inside Rectangle.java file)`

Fields:

- `length:` Hold the rectangle's length.
- `width:` Hold the rectangle's width.

Methods:

- `setLength:` Store a value in an object's length field.
- `setWidth:` Store a value in an object's width field.
- `getLength:` Return the value in an object's length field.
- `getWidth:` Return the value in an object's width field.
- `getArea:` Return the area of the rectangle, which is the result of an object's length multiplied by its width.

Step 2: Writing the code for a class (e.g., `Rectangle.java`)

The General Format of a class definition:

```
01  <access-specifier> class <class-name>
02  {
03      // Members
04  }
```

The fields and methods that belong to a class are referred to as the class's members.

Step 1: Writing a General Class "Skeleton"

```
01  public static Rectangle
02  {
03
04  }
```

Explanation

- `public` access specifier indicates that the class will be publicly available to code that is written outside the `Rectangle.java` file.

- › `Rectangle` is the class name.
- › `class` is a Java keyword.
- › `{ and }`: The contents of the class, which are fields and methods.

Step 2: Writing the `length` and `width` Fields

```
01  public static Rectangle
02  {
03      private double length;
04      private double width;
05  }
```

Explanation (Lines 03 & 04)

- › `private` is an access specifier. It indicates that these variables may not be accessed by statements outside the class.
- › Recall that an object can perform data hiding, which means that critical data stored inside the object is protected from code outside the object. In Java, a class's private members are hidden and can be accessed only by methods that are members of the same class.
- › When an object internal data is hidden from outside code and access to that data is restricted to the object's methods, the data is protected from accidental corruption.
- › It is a common practice in object-oriented programming to make all of a class's fields `private` and to provide access to those fields through methods.
- › When writing classes, you will primarily use the `private` and `public` access specifiers for class members.

Table 9.1 | Summary for the private and public access specifies for class members

Access Specifier	Description
private	When the access specifier is applied to a class member, the member cannot be accessed by code outside the class, The member can be accessed only by methods that are members of the same class.
public	When the public access specifier is applied to a class member, the member can be accessed by code inside the class or outside.

Step 3: Writing the `SetLength` Method

This method will allow code outside the class to store a value in the `length` field.

```
01  public class Rectangle
02  {
03      private double length;
```

```
04      private double width;
05      public void setLength(double len)
06      {
07          length = len;
08      }
09  }
```

`public void setLength(double len)`: Header of the `setLength` Method

› The keyword `public` is an access specifier. It indicates that the method may be called by statements outside the class.
› The keyword `void` indicates that the method returns no data to the statement that called it.
› The `setLength` is the name of the method.
› The `(double len)` is the declaration of a parameter variable of the `double` data type.
› Assigns the value of `len` to the `length` field. When the method executes, the `len` parameter variable will hold the value of an argument that is passed to the method. That value is assigned to the `length` field.

NOTE: The word `static` does not appear in the method header. When a method is designed to work on an instance of a class, it is referred to as an instance method, and you do not write the word `static` in the header, because method will store a value in the `length` field of an instance of the `Rectangle` class, it is an instance method (Discussed Later)

Step 4: Demonstrate how the `setLength` method works

First: `Rectangle` class doesn't have a `main` method

This class is not a complete program, but is a blueprint that `Rectangle` objects may be created from. Other programs will use the `Rectangle` class to create objects. The programs that create and use these objects will have their own `main` methods.

Second: Create the program - `RectangleDemo.java`

(Must be saved as `RectangleDemo.java` in the same folder or directory as the file `Rectangle.java`)

```
01  public class RectangleDemo
02  {
03      public static void main(String[] args)
```

```
        {
            Rectangle box = new Rectangle();
            System.out.println("Sending the value 10.0 " +
                "to the setLength method.");
            box.setLength(10.0);
            System.out.println("Done.");
        }
    }
```

Third: Compile the Program

    Build > Recompile RectangleDemo.java

Steps:

> The compiler reads the source code and sees that a class named `Rectangle` is being used.
> It looks in the current folder or directory for the file `Rectangle.class`. That file does not exist, however, because we have not yet compiled `Rectangle.java`.
> The compiler searches for the file `Rectangle.java` and compile it. This creates the file `Rectangle.class`, which makes the `Rectangle.class` available.

Forth: Run the RectangleDemo file

    Run > RectangleDemo

Fifth: Look at each statement in this program's main method

    Rectangle box = new Rectangle();
    // To create a Rectangle object and associate it with a variable
    Rectangle box

> Declares a variable named `box`.
> The data type of the variable is `Rectangle` (Because the word `Rectangle` is not the name of a primitive data type, Java assumes it to be the name of a class).
> Recall that a variable of a class type is a reference variable, and it holds the memory address of an object. When a reference object holds an object's memory address, it is said that the variable references the object. So the variable `box` will be used to reference a `Rectangle` object.

    new Rectangle();

> `new` creates an object in memory.
> This specifies the class that the object should be created from (In this class, an object of the `Rectangle` class is created.)

> The memory address of the object is then assigned (by the = operator) to the variable `box`.

After execution

> The variable `box` will reference the object that was created in memory.

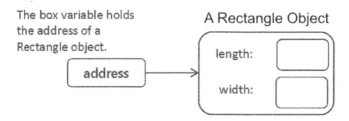

Figure 9.3 | The box variable references a Rectangle class object

```
System.out.println("Sending the value 10.0 " +
            "to the setLength method.");
```

> Display a message on the screen.

`box.setLength(10.0);`

> Calls the `box` object's `length` method.
> Passes the argument (10.0) to the `length` method.
> Method executes, the value 10.0 is copied into the `len` parameter variable.
> The method assigns the value of `len` to the `length` field and then terminates.

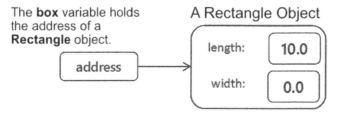

Figure 9.4 | The statement of the box object after the setLength method executes

Sixth: Writing the `setWidth` method

(Add the `setWidth` method to the `Rectangle.class`)

```
public void setWidth(double w) {
    width = w;
}
```

It accepts an argument, which is assigned to the `width` field. Update the `Rectangle` class:

Assumes (inside `LengthDemo.java` file): `box` references a `Rectangle` object and the following statement is executed.

```
box.setWidth(20.0);
```

After this statement executes, the `box` object's `width` field will be set to 20.0.

Seventh: Writing the `getLength` and `getWidth` methods

Because the `length` and `width` fields are private, we wrote the `setLength` and `setWidth` methods to allow code outside the `Rectangle` class to store values in the fields.

We must also write methods that allow code outside the class to get the values that are stored in these fields. That's what the `getLength` and `getWidth` methods will do.

› The `getLength` method will return the value stored in the `Length` field.
› The `getWidth` method will return the value stored in the `width` field.

Code for the `getLength` Method.

```
public double getLength()
{
    return length;
}
```

Assume size is a `double` variable and that `box` references a `Rectangle` object and the following statement is executed (inside `RectangleDemo.java` file):

```
size = box.getLength();
```

So it assigns the value that is returned from the `getLength` method to the `size` variable. After executes, `size` variable will contain the same value as `box` object's `Length` field.

Code for the `getWidth` Method

```
public double getWidth()
{
    return width;
}
```

Explanation

› This method returns the value that is stored in the `width` field.
› Assume: `size` is a variable and that `box` references a `Rectangle` object, and the following statement:
`size = box.getWidth();`

assigns the value that is returned from the `getWidth` method to the `size` variable.

› After Execution, the `size` variable will contain the same value as the `box` object's `width` field.

Eighth: Writing the `getArea` Method as shown in the following highlighted code

Rectangle.java

```
01  public static Rectangle
02  {
03      private double length;
04      private double width;
05  }
06  public void setLength(double len)
07  {
08      length = len;
09  }
10  public double getLength()
11  {
12      return length;
13  }
14  public double getWidth()
15  {
16      return width;
17  }
18  public double getArea()
19  {
20      return length * width;
21  }
```

RectangleDemo.java

```
01  public class RectangleDemo
02  {
03      public static void main(String[] args)
04      {
05          Rectangle box = new Rectangle();
06          box.setLength(10.0);
07          box.setwidth(20.0);
08
09          System.out.println("The box's is length is " + box.getLength());
10          System.out.println("The box's width is " + box.getWidth());
11          System.out.println("The box's area is " + box.getArea);
12      }
13  }
```

Output
```
The box is length is 10.0
The box's width is 20.0
The box's area is 200.0
```

It returns the `area` of a rectangle, which is its `length` multiplied by its `width`.

Code

```
18  public double getArea()
19  {
20      return length * width;
```

Explanation

> Assume `area` is a double variable and that `box` references a `Rectangle` object, and the following code is executed:
> ```
> box.setLength(10.0);
> box.setWidth(20.0);
> area = box.getArea();
> ```
> this code assigns the value that is returned from the `getArea` method to the `area` variable.

> After execution, `area` variable will contain the value **200.0**.

Accessor and Mutator

Recall from the previous lessons, it is common practice to make all of a class's fields `private`, and to provide `public` methods for accessing and changing these fields. This ensures that the object owning those fields is in control of all changes being made to them.

A method that stores a value in a field or changes the value of a field in some other may is known as a *mutator* method. A method that gets a value from a class's field but does not change, it is known as an *accessor* method.

In the `Rectangle` class - the methods `getLength` and `getWidth` are accessors and the methods `setLength` and `setWidth` are mutators.

NOTE: Mutator methods are sometimes called "**setters**". Accessor Methods are sometimes called "**getters**".

Layout Of Class Members

Each instance of a class (or object) has its own set of fields, which are known as **instance fields**. You can create several instances of a class and store different values in each instance's fields. The method that operate on an instance of a class are known as **instance methods**.

In the Rectangle class - The field variables are declared first, then the methods are defined.

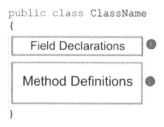

Figure 9.5 | Typical Layout of Class Members (Recommended)

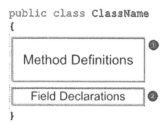

Figure 9.6 | Typical Layout of Class Members (not recommended)

Here is a program that create two Rectangle objects, Square and Rectangle. Then get and store the dimensions of the Square and Rectangle.

Example 9.6: ShapeAreas.java

```
01  package ch09;
02  import java.util.Scanner;
03
04  public class ShapeAreas
05  {
06      public static void main(String[] args)
07      {
08          double number;        // To hold a number
09          double totalRec;      // The total area of Rectangle
10          double totalSquare;   // The total area of Square
11          String input;         // To hold user input
12
13          // Create two Rectangle objects.
14          Rectangle rec = new Rectangle();
15          Rectangle square = new Rectangle();
16
17          Scanner sc = new Scanner(System.in);
18
19          // Get and store the dimensions of the rectangle.
20          System.out.println("What is the rectangle's length?");
21          input = sc.nextLine();
22          number = Double.parseDouble(input);
23          rec.setLength(number);
```

```
24
           System.out.println("What is the Rectangle's width?");
           input = sc.nextLine();
           number = Double.parseDouble(input);
           rec.setWidth(number);
29
           // Get and store the dimensions of the square.
           System.out.println("What is the Square's length?");
           input = sc.nextLine();
           number = Double.parseDouble(input);
           square.setLength(number);

           System.out.println("What is the Square's width?");
           input = sc.nextLine();
           number = Double.parseDouble(input);
           square.setWidth(number);
40
           // Calculate the total area of the Rectangle.
           totalRec = rec.getWidth() + rec.getLength();
43
           // Calculate the total area of the Square.
           totalSquare = square.getWidth() + square.getLength();
46
           // Display the total area of the Square and Rectangle.
           System.out.println("The total area of the rectangle is " + totalRec);
           System.out.println("The total area of the square is " + totalSquare);
       }
   }
```

Output
```
What is the rectangle's length?
10
What is the Rectangle's width?
14
What is the Square's length?
15
What is the Square's width?
12
The total area of the rectangle is 2
The total area of the square is
```

Illustration

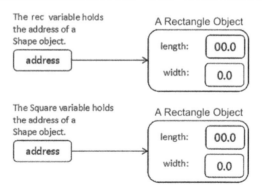

Figure 9.7 | The Shape Object

States of the objects after data has been stored in them.

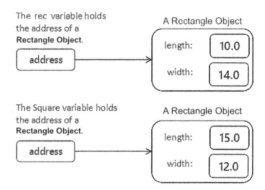

Figure 9.8 | States of the objects after data has been stored in them

Each instance of the `Rectangle` class has its own `length` and `width` variables. For this reason, the variable are known as **instance variables**, or **instance fields**. Each instance of a class has its own set of instance fields, and can store it sown values in those fields.

The methods that operate on an instance of a class are known as "**instance methods**. All of the methods in the Rectangle class are instance methods because they performs operations on specific instance of the class.

Examples

Example
```
rect.setLength(number);
```

`setLength(number)` method calls the `setLength` method which stores a value in the first `rec` object's `length` field.

Example
```
square.setLength(number);
```

Calls the `setLength` method, which stores a values in the `square` object's length field.

Recall that an instance methods do not have the keyword `static` in their headers.

Summary

> Classes and objects are basic concepts of Object Oriented Programming.
> Software objects have a property and a function. A software objects's property is stored in fields and function is shown via methods.
> A class is a blueprint for creating objects. And from the class, one or more objects may be created.
> The class definition begins with the keyword `class` followed by the name of the class.
> The body of the class is marked off by curly braces just like any other program block.
> To create an object from a class, you type the class's name followed by the name of the object.
> A primitive data type is called "primitive" because a variable created with a primitive data type has no built-in capabilities other than storing a value.
> An object is a large chunk of memory that can potentially contain a great deal of data along with methods to process that data.
> A method that stores a value in a field or changes the value of a field in some other may is known as a mutator method. A method that gets a value from a class's field but does not change it is known as an accessor method.
> Each instance of a class (or object) has its own set of fields, which are known as instance fields. You can create several instances of a class and store different values in each instance's fields. The method that operate on an instance of a class are known as instance methods.

Chapter 10

Constructors

Introduction

A Constructor is a special type of method that is automatically called when an object (or an instance of a class) is created. They are called **constructors** because they help construct an object.

Constructors normally perform initialization or setup operations, such as storing initial values in instance fields. A constructor method has the same name as the class. The following example shows the `Rectangle` class with its constructor in place.

Example 10.1: Rectangle.java - Adding a Constructor to a Class

```
01  public class Rectangle
02  {
03      private double length;
04      private double width;
05      public Rectangle(double len, double w)
06      {
07          length = len;
08          width = w;
09      }
10      public void setLength(double len)
11      {
12          length = len;
13      }
14      public void setWidth(double w)
15      {
16          width = w;
17      }
18      public double getLength()
19      {
20          return length;
```

```
21      }
22      public double getWidth()
23      {
24          return width;
25      }
26      public double getArea()
27      {
28          return length * width;
29      }
30  }
```

A constructor is a `public` method (a method that can be accessed anywhere itself when it's created), because you want to be able to create an object from the class anywhere in your program, and when you create an object, you're actually calling its constructor. This constructor accepts two arguments, which are passed into the `len` and `w` parameter variables. The parameter variables are then assigned to the `length` and `width` fields.

Syntax - method header

```
AccessSpecifier  ClassName(parameters…)
```

The constructor's header doesn't specify a return type - no even `void`. This is because constructors are not executed by explicit method calls and cannot return a value.

Example 10.2: Creating an object by calling a constructor

```
Rectangle box = new Rectangle(7.0, 14.0);
```

Explanation

> Declares the variable `box`.
> Creates a `Rectangle` object.
> Passes the value 7.0 and 14.0 to the constructor.
> After Execution: `box` will reference a `Rectangle` object whose `Length` field is set to 7 and whose `width` field is set to 14.

The `ConstructorDemo` class implements the Rectangle class as follow:

Example 10.3: ConstructorDemo.java - to implement Rectangle class

```
01  public class ConstructorDemo
02  {
03      public static void main(String[] args)
04      {
05          Rectangle box = new Rectangle(5.0, 15.0);
06          //Display the length.
07          System.out.println("The box's length is " +
08              box.getLength());
09
10          //Display the width
```

```
            System.out.println("The box's width is " +
                box.getWidth());

            //Display the area.
            System.out.println("The box's area is " +
                box.getArea());
    }
}
```

Output
```
The box's length is 5.0
The box's width is 15.0
The box's area is 75.0
```

Both `Rectangle.java` and `ConsructorDemo.java` classes must exist under the same package name.

Uninitialized Local Reference Variables

In `ConstructorDemo.java` file we initializes the `box` variable with the address of a `Rectangle` object. Reference variables can also be declared without being initialized, for example:

```
Rectangle box;
```

This statement does not create a `Rectangle` object. It only declares a variable named `box` that can be used to reference a `Rectangle` object. Because the `box` variable does not yet hold an object's address, it is an uninitialized reference variable.

After Declaring the reference variable, the following statement can be used to assign it the address of an object.

```
box = new Rectangle(7.0 , 14.0);
```

> This statement creates a `Rectangle` object.
> Passes the value 7.0 and 14.0 to its constructor.
> Assigns the object's address to the `box` variable.
> After execution, the `box` variable will reference a `Rectangle` object.

REMEMBER: You need to be careful when using uninitialized reference variable. Recall that the local variable must be initialized or assigned a value before they can be used. Also a local reference variable must reference an object before it can be used. Otherwise a compiler error will occur.

The Default Constructor

When an object is created, its constructor is always called. But what if we do not write a constructor in the object's class? if you do not write a constructor in a class, Java automatically provides one when the class is compiled. The constructor that Java provides is known as the **default constructor**.

Notes About the Default Constructor
› The default constructor doesn't accept arguments.
› It sets all of the object's numeric field to (0) and boolean fields to false.
› If the object has any fields that are reference variables, the default constructor set them to the special value `null`, which means that they do not reference anything.

Here is an example for default constructors.

Example 10.4: Rectangle.java file - first version without constructor method
```
01  public class Rectangle
02  {
03      private double length;
04      private double width;
05      public void getLength(double len)
06      {
07          length = len;
08      }
09  }
```

Explanation

› When you compiled it a compiler generated a default constructor that set both the `length` and `width` fields to 0.0.
› Assume we wrote no constructor for the `Rectangle` class:
   `Rectangle r = new Rectangle(); //call the default constructor`

We did not pass any size to the default constructor because the default constructor doesn't accept arguments.

Writing Your no-arg Constructor

A constructor that does not accept arguments is known as a "**no-arg**" constructor. The default constructor doesn't accept arguments, so it is considered a **no-arg** constructor. In addition, you can write your own **no-arg** constructor.

Example 10.5: suppose we wrote the following constructor for the `Rectangle` class:
```
public Rectangle()
{
    length = 1.0;
    width = 1.0;
}
```

Create a `Rectangle` object:
```
//call a no-arg constructor
Rectangle r = new Rectangle();
```

The rectangle object's `length` and `width` fields would both be set to 1.0.

Summary

- A Constructor is a special type of method that is automatically called when an object (or an instance of a class) is created.
- A constructor method has the same name as the class.
- Constructors normally perform initialization or setup operations, such as storing initial values in instance fields.
- If you do not write a constructor in a class, Java automatically provides one when the class is compiled. The constructor that Java provides is known as the default constructor.
- A constructor that does not accept arguments is known as a `"no-arg"` constructor. The default constructor doesn't accept arguments, so it is considered a `no-arg` constructor.

Chapter 11

Scope of Instance Fields

Basics

Variables declared as instance fields in a class. An instance field can be accessed by any instance method in the same class as the field. Instance fields are visible to all of the class's instance methods and constructors, as shown in the below image:

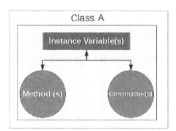

Figure 11.1 | An Instance Fields and Instance Methods inside the same class

If an instance field is declared with the `public` access specifier, it can also be accessed by code outside the class, , as shown in the below image:

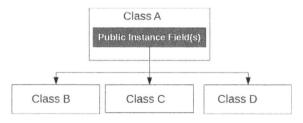

Figure 11.2 | Public Instance Fields

A variable's scope is the part of a program where the variable may be accessed by its name. A variable's name is visible only to statements inside the variable's scope. The location of a variable's declaration determines the variable's scope. Let's see an example for local variable.

Example 11.1: LocalVarEx.java - A local variable

```
package ch11;

public class LocalVarEx1 {
    public static void main(String[] args) {
        // A local variable is defined within the scope of a block.
        // It cannot be used outside of that block.
        int x = 0;
        if(x < 100) {
            // You cannot use name outside of that if block.
            String name = "Local name";
            System.out.println(name);
        }
        // You cannot use name outside of that if block.
        // System.out.println(name);
    }
}
```

Output
```
Local name
```

Here is another example for an instance variable.

Example 11.2: InstanceVArEx.java - An Instance variable (field)

```
package ch11;

public class InstanceVArEx {
    private int x; // x is a field

    public static void main(String[] args) {
        InstanceVArEx ev = new InstanceVArEx();
        ev.displayX();
    }
    public void displayX(){
        System.out.println("X is: " + x);
    }
}
```

Output
```
X is: 0
```

An **instance variable**, or **field**, is a variable that's bound to the object itself. You can use it in the object without the need to use *accessors*, and any method contained within the object may use it.

Shadowing

Previously you cannot have two local variables with the same name in the same scope. This applies to parameter variables as well. A parameter variable is a local variable. So you cannot give a parameter variable and a local variable in the same method the same name. Here is a simple example.

Example 11.3
```
01  static int add(int val1, int val2){
02      // variable val1 is already defined in method add(int val1, int val2)
03      int val1; // error!
04  }
```

However you can have a local variable or a parameter variable with the same name as a field. When you do, the name of the local or parameter variable **shadows** the name of the field. This means that the field name is hidden by the name of the local or parameter variable. Here is how that is done.

Example 11.4: Shadow.java
```
01  public class Shadow {
02      private int balance; // field balance is not used.
03
04      public void processDeposit(int amount) {
05          int balance = 0; // local variable hides a field.
06          balance = balance + amount;
07      }
08  }
```

Shadowing refers to the using two variables with the same name within scopes that overlap. When you do that, the field is hidden because the local or parameter variable overrides it. The field is then **shadowed**.

You can access a shadowed class or instance variable by fully qualifying it — that is, by providing the name of the class that contains it. For example.

Example 11.5
```
01  public class Shadow2 {
02      static int no;
03
04      public static void main(String[] args) {
05          no = 5; // field
06          System.out.println("no = " + no);
07          int no; // local variable hides a field.
08          no = 10;
```

```
09              System.out.println("no = " + no);
10              System.out.println("Shadow2.no = " + Shadow2.no);
11          }
12      }
```

Output
```
no = 5
no = 10
Shadow2.no = 5
```

Explanation

> Line 06: Prints the value of the class variable `no`.
> Line 07: The class variable `no` is shadowed by the local variable `no`, whose value is printed by the second `System.out.println` statement.
> Line 10: The third `System.out.println` statement prints the shadowed class variable by providing its fully qualified name `Shadow2.no`.

WARNING: Because shadowing is a common source for errors, you will want to avoid using it as much as possible.

Summary

> Variables declared as instance fields in a class. An instance field can be accessed by any instance method in the same class as the field.
> Instance fields are visible to all of the class's instance methods and constructors.
> If an instance field is declared with the public access specifier, it can also be accessed by code outside the class.
> A variable's scope is the part of a program where the variable may be accessed by its name.
> You cannot give a parameter variable and a local variable in the same method the same name.
> You can have a local variable or a parameter variable with the same name as a field. When you do, the name of the local or parameter variable shadows the name of the field.
> Shadowing refers to the using two variables with the same name within scopes that overlap.

Chapter 12

Access & Non-Access Modifiers

Access Modifiers in Java

In Java, the term access modifiers refer to the keywords which are used to control accessibility to interfaces, classes, methods, constructors and fields. That means we can protect data and behaviors from the outside world.

There are two types of access modifiers:
- **Top-level access modifiers:** These access modifiers apply to types only (classes, interfaces, enums and annotations). Examples: `public and default` (`default` is when no access modifier is used).
- **Member-level access modifiers:** These access modifiers apply to fields, constructors and methods. Examples: `public, protected, default and private`.

Here's the order of the access modifiers from the least restrictive (left side) to the most restrictive (right side):

`public > protected > default > private`

So, access modifiers help you set the level of access you want for your classes, variables as well as methods.

Access modifiers for class

Classes in Java can use only `public` and `default` access modifiers.
- **public.** The class will be accessible to all the classes available in the Java world.

> **default.** The class will be accessible to the classes which are defined in the same package.

Table 12.1 | Java Access Modifiers for Class

Visibility	Public Access Modifier	Default Access Modifier
Within Same package	Yes	Yes
From outside the same package	Yes	No

Now let's see an examples in which we define the access modifiers for the `Cat` and `Trainer` classes.

Example 12.1: `Cat.java`

```
01  package animal;
02
03  public class Cat{
04      public String name;
05
06      public void meow(){
07          System.out.print("rat rat!");
08      }
09  }
```

Example 12.2: Trainer.java class

```
01  package training;
02
03  import animal.Cat;
04
05  public class Trainer {
06      public void teach(Cat cat) {
07          cat.name = "Oscar";
08          cat.meow();
09      }
10  }
```

Here, the `Cat` and `Trainer` classes are in two different packages: `animal` and `training`, respectively. Because the **Cat** class is declared as `public`, and also its member `name` field and `meow()` method, the **Trainer** class can invoke them:

```
07          cat.name = "Oscar";
08          cat.meow();
```

Access modifiers for instance & static variables

Variables are eligible for all of the above mentioned modifiers.

> **default.** A variable will be accessible to the classes which are defined in the same package. Any method in any class which is defined in the same package can access the variable via inheritance or direct access.
> **public.** A variable can be accessible from any class available in the Java world. Any method in any class can access the given variable via inheritance or direct access.
> **protected.** A variable will be accessible from its sub classes defined in the same or different package only via inheritance.

NOTE: The only difference between protected and default is that protected access modifiers respect class subclass relation while default does not.

> **private.** A variable will be accessible only from within the class in which it is defined. Such variables are not accessible from outside the defined class, not even in its subclass.

NOTE: Visibility of the class should be checked before checking the visibility of the variable defined inside that class. If the class is visible then the variables defined inside that class will be visible. If the class is not visible then no variable will be accessible, even if it is set to public.

Table 12.2 | Java Access Modifiers for Variable

Visibility	Public Access Modifier	Private Access Modifier	Protected Access Modifier	Default Access Modifier
Within same slass	Yes	Yes	Yes	Yes
From any class in same package	Yes	No	Yes	No
From any sub class in same package	Yes	No	Yes	Yes
From any sub class from different package	Yes	No	Yes (only By Inheritance)	No
From any non sub class in different package	Yes	No	No	No

Access modifiers for methods

Methods are eligible for all of the following modifiers.

> **default.** A method will be accessible to the classes which are defined in the same package. Any method in any class which is defined in the same package can access the given method via inheritance or direct access.

> **public.** A method will be accessible from any class available in the Java world. Any method in any class can access the given method via inheritance or direct access depending on Class level access.

> **protected.** A method will be accessible from its sub classes defined in the same or different package.

NOTE: The only difference between protected and default is that protected access modifiers respect class subclass relation, while default does not.

> **private.** A method will be accessible only from within the class in which it is defined. Such methods are not accessible from outside the defined class, not even its subclass.

Table 12.3 | Java Access Modifiers for Method

Visibility	Public Access Modifier	Private Access Modifier	Protected Access Modifier	Default Access Modifier
Within same class	Yes	Yes	Yes	Yes
From any class in same package	Yes	No	Yes	No
From any sub class in same package	Yes	No	Yes	Yes
From any sub class from different package	Yes	No	Yes (only By Inheritance)	No
From any non sub class in different package	Yes	No	No	No

Access modifier for local variable

No access modifiers can be applied to local variables. Only `final` can be applied to a local variable which is a non access modifier.

Difference between inheritance or direct access

Super Class
```
package ch12.abc;
public class FirstClass {
    public int i;
    protected int j;
    private int k;
}
```

Sub Class
```
package ch12.abc;
import abc.FirstClass;
class SecondClass extends FirstClass {
    void method() {
    System.out.println(i);
    /*
     * Here you are trying to access protected variable directly.
     * So it will not be accessible and compile will give an
     * error.
     */
    System.out.println(j);
    /*
     * As k is private so it will not be accessible to subclass
  neither way.
     * Neither it can be accessed via Inheritance nor direct.
     */
    System.out.println(k); // Compilation Error
    FirstClass cls = new FirstClass();
    /*
     * Here property j is accessed via Inheritance hence it will
     * be accessible. But same variable can not be accessed if you
     * try to access via instance because modifier used here is
     * protected so it will be available to sub class only via
     * inheritance.
     */
    System.out.println(cls.j);
    // Private variable will not be accessible here also.
    System.out.println(cls.k); // Compilation error
    }
}
```

Cheat sheet (access modifiers)

- There are four access levels in Java: `public`, `private`, `protected` & `default`.
- A Class can have only `public` and `default` access level
- Methods and instance variable (non local) can use all four access levels
- If a class is not visible to other class there is no question of accessing member of that class, even when access level of that member is public (important)
- Class visibility should be checked before member visibility
- If a super class has `public` member then it will be inherited by subclasses even if it is in other package
- A `public` member can be accessed by all other class even from other package
- `private` members can be accessed only by the code in the same class
- `default` members are not visible to subclasses outside package while protected members are visible to subclasses even when they are in different package
- Different between `protected` and `default` comes into picture only in the case of subclass outside package
- Local variables can not have access modifiers
- Local variables can have only `final` non access modifiers that can be applied

Let's understand the access modifiers with the help of following table

Table 12.4 | Access Modifiers

Access Modifier	Within Class	Within Package	Outside a package by subclass only	Outside a package
Private	Yes	No	No	No
Default	Yes	Yes	No	No
Protected	Yes	Yes	Yes	No
Public	Yes	Yes	Yes	Yes

Non-Access Modifiers in Java

Non-access modifiers do not change the accessibility of variables and methods, but they do provide them special properties. Non access modifiers can alter the behavior of elements in java.

The Non Access Modifiers available in Java: `final`, `abstract`, `static`, `strictfp`, `native`, `synchronized`, and `transient`. Now lets dig into these non access modifiers briefly.

final

Final modifiers are applicable to:

› Class;
› Method;
› Instance variable;
› Local variable and
› Method arguments.

Final Class : A class when set to `final` cannot be extended by any other class. No class can inherit any feature from the final class. For example 12.3:

```
final class Animal{
    // some code
}
```

Final Method : A method when set to `final` cannot be overridden by any subclass. For example 12.4:

```
class Animal{
    public final void displayColor(){
        // body of method
    }
}
```

Final Variable : When a variable is set to `final`, its value cannot be changed. For example 12.5:

```
class Animal{
    public static final String color = "Blue";
    public final void displayColor(){
        // body of method
    }
}
```

abstract

Abstract modifiers are applicable to:

- Class and
- Method

Abstract Class: If a class is declared as abstract, then that class can never be instantiated. An abstract class may contain both abstract methods as well normal methods. A class can also be an abstract class without having any abstract methods in it. If a class has an abstract method, the class becomes an abstract class.

The sole purpose for using abstract is for the class to be extended.

Abstract Method: Abstract methods are those methods which does not have a body but only a signature. The method body is provided by sub class. Abstract methods can never be `final`. For example 12.6:

```
public abstract class SuperAnimal{
    abstract void displayColor(); // abstract method
}
```

NOTE: The abstract method ends with a semicolon.

(more on next chapter)

static

static modifiers are applicable to:

- Class,
- Method and,
- Variable.

The `static` variable and method will exist independently of any instance created for the class. One copy of a `static` variable and method exist regardless of number of instances of the class (*For more details see next chapter.*)

synchronized

`Synchronized` modifiers are applicable to **method**. Synchronized methods can be accessed by only one thread at a time. For example: 12.7

```
public synchronized void displayColor() { ... }
```

The synchronized modifier can be applied with any of the four access level modifiers.

volatile

Declaring a `volatile` Java variable means, the value of this variable will never be cached thread-locally, all reads and writes will go straight to "main memory". Volatile can only be applied to instance variables, which are of type `object` or `private`. A volatile object reference can be `null`.

```
public volatile int speed = 60; //volatile value
```

native

`native` modifiers are applicable to method. Naive methods indicate that the method is implemented on a platform dependent code. Native methods are currently needed when you need to call a library or access system resources from Java that is written in other language.

strictfp

`strictfp` modifiers are applicable to class and method. `strictfp` is a keyword in the Java programming language that restricts floating-point calculations to ensure same result on every platform (portability). If you don't use strictfp, different output (floating-point values) is achieved when a class file is run on different platforms (16/32/64 bit processors), and the JVM implementation is free to use extra precision where available.

`strictfp` can be used on classes, interfaces and non-abstract methods. When applied to a method, it causes all calculations inside the method to use strict floating-point math. When applied to a class, all calculations inside the class use strict floating-point math.

```
public strictfp class MyFclass {
    // class contents
}
```

Here is a simple example.

Example 12.8: Test.java - Java program to illustrate `strictfp` modifier

```
01  package ch12;
02  public class Test
03  {
04      public strictfp double sum()
05      {
06          double num1 = 5e+10;
07          double num2 = 2e+03;
08          return(num1 + num2);
09      }
10      public static strictfp void main(String[] args)
11      {
12          Test t = new Test();
13          System.out.println(t.sum());
14      }
15  }
```

Output
```
5.0000002E10
```

NOTES
- `Strictfp` non access modifier cannot be applied on a variable.
- `strictfp` cannot be used with abstract methods.
- `strictfp` can be used with abstract classes and interfaces.
- `strictfp` cannot be used with any method inside an interface (methods of an interface are implicitly abstract).
- When a class or an interface is declared with `strictfp` modifier, then all methods declared in the class or interface, and all nested types declared in the class, are implicitly `strictfp`.

Cheat sheet (non-access modifiers)

- Non access modifiers available in Java are `static, final, abstract, synchronized & volatile`
- `static` keyword can be applied to variables and methods.
- static variables are those variables which are not associated to any instance but it is associated to class means all instances will access the same single copy of variable.
- Local variables can not be declared as `static`.

- `static` keyword can also be applied to methods. They will work for all the instances and they will not be dependent on instances created.
- `final` modifier can be applied to method and variables.
- `final` is the only modifier which will be available to local variable.
- Once declared as final value of the variable can not be changed.
- `final` variable don't get default value opposed to instance variable because value can't be changed once assigned.
- `final` method can not be overridden.

Summary

- The term access modifiers refer to the keywords which are used to control accessibility to interfaces, classes, methods, constructors and fields.
- There are two types of access modifiers: top-level access modifiers - these access modifiers apply to types only (classes, interfaces, enums and annotations), and member-level access modifiers - these access modifiers apply to fields, constructors and methods.
- Classes in Java can use only `public` and `default` access modifiers.
- Variables are eligible for all of the following modifiers: `default`, `public`, `protected and private`.
- Methods are eligible for all of the following modifiers: `default`, `public`, `protected and private`.
- A method will be accessible only from within the class in which it is defined. Such methods are not accessible from outside the defined class, not even its subclass.
- No access modifiers can be applied to local variables.
- The non access modifiers available in Java: `final`, `abstract`, `static`, `strictfp`, `native`, `synchronized`, and `transient`.

Chapter 13

Static Class Members

Introduction

Each instance of a class has its own set of fields which are know as instance fields. So you can create several instances of a class and store different values in each instance's fields. A Static class member belongs to the class, not objects instantiated from the class.

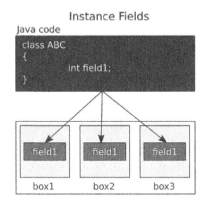

Figure 13.1 | Instance Fields

Static Fields

A `static` field does not belong to any instance of a class. When a value is stored in a `static` field, it is not stored in an instance of the class. So, `static` fields are belonging to the class instead of an instance of the class.

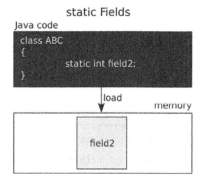

Figure 13.2 | Static field

A single copy of a class's `static` field is shared by all instances of the class. There will be only one copy of the field in memory, regardless of the number of instances of the class that might exist. Let's see an example for this.

Example 13.1: VarDemo.java

```
01  package ch13;
02  class VarDemo
03  {
04      static int count=0;
05      public void increment()
06      {
07          count++;
08      }
09      public static void main(String args[])
10      {
11          VarDemo obj1=new VarDemo();
12          VarDemo obj2=new VarDemo();
13          obj1.increment();
14          obj2.increment();
15          System.out.println("Obj1: count is= "+obj1.count);
16          System.out.println("Obj2: count is= "+obj2.count);
17      }
18  }
```

Output
```
    Obj1: count is= 2
```

```
Obj2: count is= 2
```

In the above example, both the objects of class are sharing a same copy of static variable that's why they displayed the same value of count.

Static variable initialization
› Static variables are initialized when class is loaded.
› Static variables in a class are initialized before any object of that class can be created.
› Static variables in a class are initialized before any static method of the class.

Here is a simple example to use static variable.

Example 13.2: Count.java

```
01  public class Count
02  {
03      private static int count = 0;
04      public Count()
05      {
06          count++;
07      }
08      public int getCount()
09      {
10          return count;
11      }
12  }
```

Explanation

Uses a `static` field to keep count of the number of instances of the class that are created.

```
private static int count = 0;
```

› Is the declaration of the `static` field named `count`.
› Explicitly initialized the `count` field with the value **0**.
› This initialization only takes place once, regardless of the number of instances of the class that are created.
› Java automatically stores **0** in all uninitialized `static` member variables. The `count` field in this class is explicitly initialized so it is clear to anyone reading the code that the field starts with the value 0.

```
public Count() { ... }
```

› The constructor uses the `++` operator to increment the `count` field.
› Each time an instance of the `Count` class is created, the constructor will be called and the `count` field will be incremented.
› As a result, the `count` field will contain the number of instances of the `Count` class that have been created.

```
public int getCount() {…}
```

› Returns the value in `count` field.

Example 13.3: StaticDemo.java - same package as Count.java file

```
01  package ch13;
02  public class StaticDemo
03  {
04      public static void main(String[] args){
05
06          int objectCount;
07
08          // Create three instances of the Count class.
09          Count object1 = new Count();
10          Count object2 = new Count();
11          Count object3 = new Count();
12
13          // Get the number of instances from the class's static field.
14          objectCount = object1.getCount();
15          System.out.println(objectCount + " instances of the class were created.");
16      }
17  }
```

Output
```
3 instances of the class were created.
```

A program creates three instances of the `Count` class, referenced by the variables `object1`, `object2`, & `object3`. There are three instances of the class, there's only one copy of the static field.

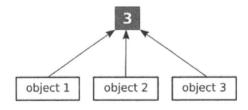

Figure 13.3 | All instances of the class share the static field

The program calls the `getCount` method to retrieve the number of instances that have been created.

```
objectCount = object1.getInstanceCount( );
```

The program calls the `getCount` method from `object1`, the same value would be returned from any of the objects.

Static Methods

A `static` method is a method that does not belong to any instance of a class. An instance of the class doesn't even have to exist in order for values to be stored in the class's `static` fields.

Also, static methods do not operate on the fields that belong to any instance of the class. Instead, they can operate only on static fields. So static methods are belonging to the class instead of an instance of the class.

So when a class contains a `static` method, it isn't necessary for an instance of the class to be created in order to execute the method. The following example shows the use of static method.

Example 13.4: Converter.java

```
class Converter{
    public static double metersToCentimeters(double m){
        return m * 100;
    }
    public static double centimetersToMeters(double c){
        return c / 100;
    }
}
```

The Converter class has two static methods: `metersToCentimeters` & `centimetersToMeters`. Because they are declared as `static`, they belong to the class and may be called without any instances of the class being in existence.

Calling Static Methods. You simply write the name of the class before the dot operator in the method call.

```
meters = Converter.metersToCentimeters(30.0);
```

This statement calls the `metersToCentimeters` method, passing the value `10.0` as an argument.

Notice: The method is not called from an instance of the class, but is called directly from the `Converter` class.

So, here is an example that uses the `Converter` class.

Example 13.5: ConverterTest.java - A program that uses the `Converter` class

```
package ch13;
import java.text.DecimalFormat;
import java.util.Scanner;
04
```

```java
public class ConverterTest{
    public static void main(String[] args) {
        String input;              // To hold input
        double centimeters;        // A distance in centimeters
        double meters;             // A distance in meters

        // Create a DecimalFormat object
        DecimalFormat dml = new DecimalFormat("0.00");

        // Get a distance in centimeters
        Scanner sc = new Scanner(System.in);
        System.out.println("Enter a distance in centimeters");
        input = sc.nextLine();
        centimeters = Double.parseDouble(input);

        // Convert the distance from centimeters to meters
        meters = Converter.centimetersToMeters(centimeters);
        System.out.println(dml.format(centimeters)+ " centimeters equals " +
                dml.format(meters) + " meters.");

        meters = Double.parseDouble(input);

        // Get a distance in Meters
        Scanner sc1 = new Scanner(System.in);
        System.out.println("Enter a distance in meters");
        input = sc1.nextLine();
        meters = Double.parseDouble(input);

        // Convert the distance from meters to centimeters
        centimeters = Converter.metersToCentimeters(meters);
        System.out.println(dml.format(meters) + " meters equals " +
                dml.format(centimeters) + " centimeters");
    }
}
```

Output
```
Enter a distance in centimeters
250
250.00 centimeters equals 2.50 meters.
Enter a distance in meters
2.5
2.50 meters equals 250.00 centimeters
```

IMPORTANT

☐ `static` methods are convenient for many tasks because they can be called directly from the class, as needed.

☐ They are most often used to create utility classes that perform operations on data, but have no need to collect and store data.

☐ For example, `Converter` class is used as a container to hold methods that convert centimeters to meters and vice verse, but is not intended to store any data.

Limitations

`static` methods cannot refer to non-static members of the class. This means that:

> Any method called from a `static` method must also be static.
> If the method uses any of the class's field, they must be static as well.

Passing Objects as Arguments to Methods

To pass an object as a method argument, you pass an object reference. For example, you can pass primitive data types, references to `String` objects, and references to other types of objects as arguments to methods.

Passing primitive data type as arguments to method

Primitive arguments, such as an `int` or a `float`, are passed into methods by value. This means that any changes to the values of the parameters exist only inside the method. When the method returns, the parameters are gone and any changes to them are lost, however this will not effect an instance variables. Here is a simple example.

Example 13.6: PassPrimitiveByValue.java - passing primitive data type as arguments to methods

```
01  public class PassPrimitiveByValue {
02      public static void main(String[] args){
03          int x = 3;
04
05          // invoke passMethod() with x as argument
06          passMethod(x);
07
08          // print x to see if its value has changed
09          System.out.println("After invoking passMethod, x = " + x);
10      }
11      // change parameter in passMethod()
12      public static void passMethod(int p){
13          p = 10;
14      }
15  }
```

Output
```
After invoking passMethod, x = 3
```

Explanation

- The purpose of this method is to show that changing a method parameter doesn't change the caller.
- Line 03: **x** becomes 3. It stays 3 for the whole program.
- Line 06: Call the `passMethod()` method. The value 3 is passed as an argument to `passMethod()`.
- Line 13: There `(int p)` is the parameter and it is a local variable to the `passMethod()`. When the statement `p = 10` is executed, the value of (p) is changed to 10 only inside the `passMethod()`. This will not effect the instance variable **x** inside the object. Any change to the value of the parameter (p), exists only within the scope of the `passMethod()` method.
- However **x** and **p** are different because the values are being passed.

NOTE: When a method is defined with parameters, then we can't call that method without passing the corresponding arguments to the corresponding parameter of the method.

Passing references to string objects as arguments to methods

As we can define methods to accept primitive data types as arguments, we can define methods to accept object of a class (or reference data type parameters, such as objects) by value as an argument. This means that when the method returns, the passed-in reference still references the same object as before.

Here is a simple example.

Example 13.7: Record.java and Test.java Classes

Record.java Class

```
01  package ch13;
02  public class Record { // Define the Record class
03      int num;
04      String city;
05  }
```

`Test.java` Class

```
01  package ch13;
02  public class Test { // Define the Test class
03
04      // Pass a Record class as a parameter to the tryObj method
05      public static void tryObj(Record r){
```

```
            r.num = 100;
            r.city = "Omdurman";
        }
        public static void main(String[] args){
            // Create an object of our new class Record,
            // set its fields, and call the method tryObj
            Record id = new Record();
            id.num = 2;
            id.city = "Khartoum";
            tryObj(id);
            System.out.println(id.city + " " + id.num);
        }
    }
```

Output

    Omdurman 100

Explanation

> The `print` statement prints out `Omdurman 100` the object has been changed in this case. Why?

> The reference to `id` is the parameter to the method, so the method cannot be used to change that reference; i.e., it can't make `id` reference a different `Record`.

> But the method can use the reference to perform any allowed operation on the `Record` that it already references.

NOTES
☐ It is often not good programming style to change the values of instance variables outside an object.
☐ Normally, the object would have a method to set the values of its instance variables.
☐ The values of the object's fields CAN BE CHANGED in the method, if they have the proper access level.

We cannot however make the object parameter or reference refer to a different object by reassigning the reference or calling `new` on the reference. For example 13.8, the following method would not work as expected:

```
    public void createRecord(Record r, int n, String name)
    {
        r = new Record();
        r.num = n;
        r.name = name;
    }
```

We can still encapsulate the initialization of the `Record` in a method, but we need to return the reference.

```
    public Record createRecord(int n, String name)
```

```
02  {
03      Record r = new Record();
04      r.num = n;
05      r.name = name;
06      return r;
07  }
```

Passing references to other objects as arguments to methods

When a variable is passed as an argument to a method, it is said to be passed by value. This means that a copy of the variable's value is passed into the method's parameter. When the method changes the contents of the parameter variable, it does not affect the contents of the original value that was passed as an argument.

When a reference variable is passed as an argument to a method, however, the method has access to the object that the variable references. Recall that a reference variable holds the memory address of an object. Here is a simple example Square.java.

Here is a simple example.

Example 13.9: Square.java Class

```
01  package ch13;
02  public class Square {
03      private double length;
04      private double width;
05
06      public Square(double len, double w) {
07          length = len;
08          width = w;
09      }
10
11      public void setLength(double len) {
12          length = len;
13      }
14
15      public void setWidth(double w) {
16          width = w;
17      }
18
19      public double getLength() {
20          return length;
21      }
22
23      public double getWidth() {
24          return width;
25      }
```

```
26
27      public double getArea() {
28          return length * width;
29      }
30 }
```

Example 13.10: SquareDemo.java

```
01 package ch13;
02 public class SquareDemo{
03      public static void main(String[] args){
04      // Create a Square object.
05      Square box = new Square(16.0, 10.0);
06
07          // Pass a reference to the object to
08          // the displaySquare method.
09          displaySquare(box);
10      }
11
12      public static void displaySquare(Square s) {
13          // Display the length and width.
14          System.out.println("Length :" + s.getLength() +
15                  " width: " + s.getWidth());
16      }
17 }
```

Output

```
Length :16.0 width: 10.0
```

Explanation

› The `box` variable is Square reference variable. Its value is passed as an argument to the `displaySquare` method.

› A parameter variable (**s**) is also Square reference variable, that receives the argument.

› When `displaySquare` method is called, the address that is stored in box is passed into the **s** parameter variable.

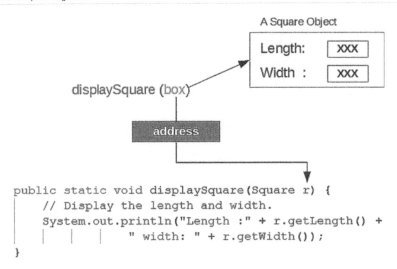

Figure 13.4 | Passing a reference as an argument

Both `box` and **(s)** reference the same object.

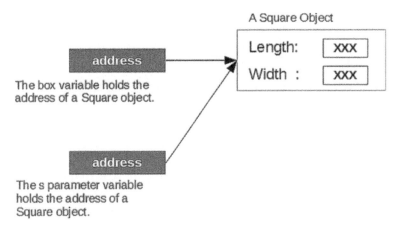

Figure 13.5 | Both box and r reference the same object

Reference data type parameters, such as objects, are also passed into methods by value. This means you can also pass references to other types of objects as arguments to methods. The **SquareDemo2** program demonstrates that.

Example 13.11: SquareDemo2.java
```
01  public class SquareDemo2
02  {
03      public static void main(String[] args)
04      {
05          // Create a Square object.
06          Square box = new Square(12.0, 5.0);
07
```

```
            // Display the object's contents.
            System.out.println("Contents of the box object:");
            System.out.println("Length : " + box.getLength() +
                        " Width : " + box.getWidth());
12
            // Pass a reference to the object to the
            // changeSquare method.
            changeSquare(box);
16
            // Display the object's contents again.
            System.out.println("\nNow the contents of the " +
                        "box object are:");
            System.out.println("Length : " + box.getLength() +
                        " Width : " + box.getWidth());
        }
        public static void changeSquare(Square s)
        {
            s.setLength(0.0);
            s.setWidth(0.0);
        }
    }
```

Output

```
Contents of the box object:
Length : 12.0 Width : 5.0

Now the contents of the box object are:
Length : 0.0 Width : 0.0
```

NOTE: When writing a method that receives the value of a reference variable as an argument, you must take care not to accidentally modify the contents of the object that is referenced by the variable.

Returning Objects from Methods

In Java Programming a method can return any type of data, including class types that you create. A method can return:

› An `int`, `double`, `float`, or other primitive data type.
› A reference to an object.

In the following example we have `ReOb` class and it returns an object when we make a call to its method.

Example 13.12: ReOb.java - returning the object from method

```
package ch13;
```

```
02    static class Square {
03        int length;
04        int breadth;
05
06        Square(int x, int y) {
07            length = x;
08            breadth = y;
09        }
10
11        Square getSquareObj(){
12            Square squ = new Square(15, 30);
13            return squ;
14        }
15    }
```

ReObDemo.java

```
01  package ch13;
02  import ch13.ReOb.Square;
03
04  class ReObDemo{
05      public static void main(String args[]) {
06          // Square ob1 = ReOb.Square(70, 90);
07          Square ob1 = new Square(70, 90);
08          Square ob2;
09
10          ob2 = ob1.getSquareObj();
11          System.out.println("ob1.length : " + ob1.length);
12          System.out.println("ob1.breadth: " + ob1.breadth);
13
14          System.out.println("ob2.length : " + ob2.length);
15          System.out.println("ob2.breadth: " + ob2.breadth);
16      }
17  }
```

Output

```
ob1.length : 70
ob1.breadth: 90
ob2.length : 15
ob2.breadth: 30
```

Explanation

> We have called a method `getSquareObj()` and the method creates object of class from which it has been called.
> All objects are dynamically allocated using `new`, you don't need to worry about an object going out-of-scope because the method in which it was created terminates.
> The object will continue to exist as long as there is a reference to it somewhere in your program. When there are no references to it, the object will be reclaimed the next time garbage collection takes place.

The `toString` Method

The `toString` method returns a String that represents the **state** of an object. An objects **state** is the data that is stored in the object's fields at any given moment.

Syntax
```
String toString()
static String toString(int i)
```

Parameters

> i - An `int` for which string representation would be returned.

Return Value

> `toString()` – This returns a `String` object representing the value of this Integer.
> `toString(int i)` – This returns a `String` object representing the specified Integer.

The following example shows the usage of `toString()` method.

Example 13.13: ToString.java - Using the toString method
```
01  package ch13;
02  public class TestString{
03      public static void main(String[] args){
04          Double d = 12.5;
05
06          System.out.println(d.toString());
07          System.out.println(Double.toString(15.6));
08
09          System.out.println(d.getClass().getSimpleName());
10          System.out.println(d.getClass().getName());
11      }
12  }
```

Output
```
12.5
15.6
Double
java.lang.Double
```

Note that I'm overriding the method `toString` that exists in the `class` Object.

Summary

› Each instance of a class has its own set of fields which are known as **instance fields**. So you can create several instances of a class and store different values in each instance's fields.
› A Static class member belongs to the class, not objects instantiated from the class.
› A **static field** does not belong to any instance of a class. When a value is stored in a static field, it is not stored in an instance of the class. So, static fields are belonging to the class instead of an instance of the class.
› A single copy of a class's static field is shared by all instances of the class. There will be only one copy of the field in memory, regardless of the number of instances of the class that might exist.
› A static method is a method that does not belong to any instance of a class. An instance of the class doesn't even have to exist in order for values to be stored in the class's static fields.
› Static methods cannot refer to non-static members of the class.
› Static methods are convenient for many tasks because they can be called directly from the class, as needed. They are most often used to create utility classes that perform operations on data, but have no need to collect and store data.

Chapter 14

ArrayList in Java

Introduction

`ArrayList` is similar to an array and allows you to store objects. Unlike an array, an `ArrayList` object's size is automatically adjusted to accommodate the number of items being stored in it. The `ArrayList` class is used for storing and retrieving objects. Once you create an `ArrayList` object, you can thing of it as a container for holding other objects.

`ArrayList's` Advantages
› An `ArrayList` object automatically expands as items are added to it.
› In addition to adding items to an `ArrayList`, you can remove items as well.
› An `ArrayList` object automatically shrinks as items are removed from it.
› `ArrayList` class enables us to use predefined methods of it which makes our task easy.

Initialize and Use an ArrayList

The `ArrayList` class has a no-arg constructor, so creating an `ArrayList` object is simple and straight forward. There are multiple ways to initialize an `ArrayList`.

Syntax (ArrayList Initialization)
```
ArrayList<T> obj = new ArrayList<T>();
obj.add("Object One");
obj.add("Object Two");
```

```
    obj.add("Object Three");
```

The T is replaced by the type of element such as String, Employee, and so on. Here we create an `ArrayList` object that stores a particular object type. For example, if we want to create an ArrayList `String` object type, we may write:

```
    ArrayList<String> strList = new ArrayList<>();
```

Example 14.1: ArrayListEx.java - ArrayList Initialization
```
01  import java.util.ArrayList;
02
03  public class ArrayListEx{
04      public static void main(String[] args){
05          ArrayList<String> books = new ArrayList<String>();
06          books.add("Java Book");
07          books.add("C++ Book");
08          books.add("C Book");
09          System.out.println("Books Stored in Array List are: " + books);
10      }
11  }
```

Output
```
    Books Stored in Array List are: [Java Book, C++ Book, C Book]
```

Explanation
- Line 05: Create a new `ArrayList` object of type `String`, and stores its address in the `books` variable.
- Line 06: Add a `String` object ("Java Book") to the `ArrayList` object using add method. After execution, `books` will hold reference to String object ("Java Book"). "Java Book" is stored at index 0.
- Line 07: Add a String object ("C++ Book") to the `ArrayList` object using add method. After execution, `books` will hold reference to String object ("C++ Book"). "C++ Book" is stored at index 1.
- Line 08: Add a String object ("C Book") to the `ArrayList` object using add method. After execution, `books` will hold reference to String object ("C Book"). "C Book" is stored at index 2.

ArrayList Add/Remove

Add element to ArrayList

The `add` method is used for adding an element to the `ArrayList`. Let's see an example.

Example 14.2: `Languages.java` - Add items to the `ArrayList` Object

```
01  import java.util.ArrayList;
02
03  public class Languages {
04      public static void main(String[] args){
05          ArrayList<String> languages = new ArrayList<String>();
06          languages.add("Arabic");
07          languages.add("English");
08          languages.add("Hindi");
09          languages.add("French");
10          System.out.println("List of Languages: " + languages);
11
12          ArrayList<Integer> years = new ArrayList<Integer>();
13          years.add(2011);
14          years.add(2012);
15          years.add(2013);
16          years.add(2014);
17          years.add(2015);
18          years.add(2016);
19          years.add(2017);
20          years.add(2018);
21          System.out.println("List of Years: " + years);
22      }
23  }
```

Output
```
List of Languages: [Arabic, English, Hindi, French]
List of Years: [2011, 2012, 2013, 2014, 2015, 2016, 2017, 2018]
```

Explanation

> Line 05: Create a new ArrayList object and stores its address in the `languages` variable.
> Lines 06-09: Add a series of String objects to `Languages`. (Arabic, English, Hindi and French)
> Line 12: Create a new `ArrayList` object and stores its address in the `years` variable.
> Lines 13-20: Add a series of Integer objects to `years`. (2011, 2012, 2013, 2014, 2015, 2016, 2017, 2018)

Add element at particular index of ArrayList

The `add` method, as previously shown, adds an item at the last position or at the end of the list in an `ArrayList` object. The `ArrayList` class has an overloaded version of the `add` method that allows you to add an item at a specific index. This causes the item to be inserted into the `ArrayList` object at a specific position.

Syntax

```
public void add(int index, Object element)
```

Example 14.3: AddMethodEx.java

```java
01  package ch14;
02  import java.util.ArrayList;
03  public class AddMethodEx {
04      public static void main(String[] args){
05          // ArrayList of String type
06          ArrayList<String> country = new ArrayList<String>();
07          // Simple add() method for adding elements at the end
08          country.add("India");
09          country.add("Egypt");
10          country.add("Canada");
11          country.add("China");
12
13          // adding element to the 3rd position
14          // 3rd position = 2 index as index starts with 0
15          country.add(2, "USA");
16          System.out.println("Elements after adding string USA: " + country);
17
18          // Adding string to 1st position
19          country.add(0, "Sudan");
20          System.out.println("Elements after adding string Sudan: " + country);
21      }
22  }
```

Output

```
Elements after adding string USA:    [India, Egypt, USA, Canada, China]
Elements after adding string Sudan:  [Sudan, India, Egypt, USA, Canada, China]
```

When a new item was added to index 2, the item that was previously stored at index 2 was shifted in position to index 3. And when an item is added at a specific index, the items that come after it are shifted upward in position to accommodate the new item. This means that the index of each item after the new item will be increased by one.

NOTE: An error will occur if you call the `add` method with an invalid index.

Append collection elements to ArrayList

In this part we will see the usage of `addAll()` method. This method is used for adding all the elements of an `ArrayList` to the another `ArrayList`. The elements will be added at the end of the list.

Syntax
```
public boolean addAll(Collection c)
```

It adds all the elements of specified `Collection c` to the current list.

Example 14.4: AddAllEx.java
```
01  import java.util.ArrayList;
02
03  public class AddAllEx {
04      public static void main(String[] args){
05          // Arraylist1 of String type
06          ArrayList<String> numbers1 = new ArrayList<String>();
07          numbers1.add("One");
08          numbers1.add("Three");
09          numbers1.add("Five");
10          System.out.println("ArrayList1 before addAll: " + numbers1);
11
12          // ArrayList2 of String type
13          ArrayList<String> numbers2 = new ArrayList<String>();
14          numbers2.add("Two");
15          numbers2.add("Four");
16
17          // Adding ArrayList2 into ArrayList1
18          numbers1.addAll(numbers2);
19          System.out.println("ArrayList1 after addAll: " + numbers1);
20      }
21  }
```

Output
```
ArrayList1 before addAll: [One, Three, Five]
ArrayList1 after addALl: [One, Three, Five, Two, Four]
```

Copy all list elements to ArrayList

Here we will see another variant of `add` method which adds all the elements of `(c)` at the specified index of a list.

Syntax

```
public boolean addAll(int index, Collection c )
```

Example 14.5: CopyAll.java

In this example we have two `ArrayList` of `String` type and we are adding the element of second `ArrayList` at the 3rd position (index =2) of first `ArrayList`.

```
01  import java.util.ArrayList;
02
03  public class CopyAll {
04      public static void main(String[] args){
05          // Arraylist1 of String type
06          ArrayList<String> numbers1 = new ArrayList<String>();
07          numbers1.add("One");
08          numbers1.add("Four");
09          numbers1.add("Five");
10          System.out.println("ArrayList1 before addAll: " + numbers1);
11
12          // ArrayList2 of String type
13          ArrayList<String> numbers2 = new ArrayList<String>();
14          numbers2.add("Two");
15          numbers2.add("Three");
16
17          // Adding ArrayList2 in ArrayList1 at 2rd position (index = 1)
18          numbers1.addAll(1, numbers2);
19          System.out.println("ArrayList1 after adding ArrayList2 at 3rd Pos: " +
20                              numbers1);
21      }
22  }
```

Output

```
ArrayList1 before addAll: [One, Four, Five]
ArrayList1 after adding ArrayList2 at 3rd Pos: [One, Two, Three, Four, Five]
```

Loop ArrayList

Earlier we shared ArrayList example and how to initialize ArrayList in Java. In this section we are sharing how to iterate (loop) ArrayList in Java.

There are four ways to loop ArrayList -

1. For Loop
2. Advanced for loop
3. While Loop
4. Iterator

Lets have a look at the below example – I have used all of the mentioned methods for iterating list.

Example 14.6: AllLoopEx.java

```
01  import java.util.ArrayList;
02  import java.util.Iterator;
03
04  public class AllLoopEx {
05      public static void main(String[] args){
06          ArrayList<Integer> arrlist = new ArrayList<Integer>();
07          arrlist.add(10);
08          arrlist.add(20);
09          arrlist.add(30);
10
11          // For loop for iterating Araylist
12          System.out.println("For loop");
13          for (Integer num: arrlist){
14              System.out.println(num);
15          }
16
17          // While loop for iterating ArrayList
18          System.out.println("While loop");
19          int count = 0;
20          while (arrlist.size() > count){
21              System.out.println(arrlist.get(count));
22              count++;
23          }
24
25          // Looping ArrayList usign Iterator
26          System.out.println("Iterator");
27          Iterator iter = arrlist.iterator();
28          while (iter.hasNext()){
29              System.out.println(iter.next());
30          }
31
32      }
33  }
```

Output

```
For loop
10
20
30
While loop
10
20
30
Iterator
10
20
30
```

Find length of ArrayList (`size()` method)

The `ArrayList` class has a `size` method that determines the number of items stored in an `ArrayList`. It returns the number of elements as an `int`.

Syntax
```
public int size()
```

The following example display the number of items stored in `num` variable.

Example 14.7: SizeEx.java - display the number of items stored in num.

```
01  import java.util.ArrayList;
02
03  public class SizeEx {
04      public static void main(String[] args){
05          ArrayList<Integer> num = new ArrayList<Integer>();
06          System.out.println("Initial Size: " + num.size());
07
08          num.add(2010);
09          num.add(2011);
10          num.add(2012);
11          num.add(2013);
12          num.add(2014);
13          num.add(2015);
14          System.out.println("Size after few additions: " +
15                              num.size());
16
17          num.add(2016);
18          num.add(2017);
19          num.add(2018);
20          System.out.println("Size after another few additions: " +
21                              num.size());
22
23          num.remove(0); // remove 2010
24          num.remove(1); // remove 2012
25          System.out.println("Size after remove operations: " + num.size());
26          System.out.println("Final ArrayList");
27          for (int number: num){
28              System.out.println(number);
29          }
30      }
31  }
```

Output
```
Initial Size: 0
Size after few additions: 6
Size after another few additions: 9
Size after remove operations: 7
```

```
Final ArrayList
2011
2013
2014
2015
2016
2017
2018
```

Remove element from the specified index in `ArrayList`

Method `remove()` is used for removing an element of the specified index from a list. It removes an element and returns the same.

Syntax

```
public Object remove(int index)
```

Here is an example for that.

Example 14.8: RemoveEx.java

```
01  import java.util.ArrayList;
02
03  public class RemoveEx {
04      public static void main(String[] args){
05          // String ArrayList
06          ArrayList<String> letter = new ArrayList<String>();
07          letter.add("A");
08          letter.add("B");
09          letter.add("C");
10          letter.add("D");
11          System.out.println("ArrayList before remove: ");
12          for (String var: letter){
13              System.out.println(var);
14          }
15          // Remove 1st element (A)
16          letter.remove(0);
17
18          // Removing 2nd element from the remaining list (C)
19          letter.remove(1);
20          System.out.println("ArrayList after remove: ");
21          for (String var2: letter){
22              System.out.println(var2);
23          }
24      }
25  }
```

Output

```
ArrayList before remove:
A
B
C
```

```
D
ArayList after remove:
B
D
```

NOTES
☐ When the item at **index 0** was removed, the item that was previously stored as index 1 was shifted in position to index 0.
☐ When an item is removed from an `ArrayList,` the items that come after it are shifted downward in position to fill the empty space.
☐ This means that the index of each item after the removed item will be decreased by one.
☐ An error will occur if you call the `remove` method with an invalid index. It throws `IndexOutOfBoundsException` if the specified index is less than zero or greater than the size of the list (index size of `ArrayList`).

Remove specified element from `ArrayList`

The method `remove(Object obj)` removes the specified object from the list.

Syntax
```
public boolean remove(Object obj)
```

NOTE: It returns `false` if the specified element doesn't exist in the list. If there are duplicate elements present in the list it removes the first occurrence of the specified element from the list.

Example 14.9: RemoveEx2.java

In this example we have an ArrayList<String> and we are removing few strings from the list.

```
01  import java.util.ArrayList;
02
03  public class RemoveEx2 {
04      public static void main(String[] args){
05          // String ArrayList
06          ArrayList<String> letter = new ArrayList<String>();
07          letter.add("A");
08          letter.add("B");
09          letter.add("C");
10          letter.add("D");
11          System.out.println("ArrayList before remove: ");
12          for (String var: letter){
13              System.out.println(var);
```

```
            }
            // Remove element C from the ArrayList
            letter.remove("C");
17
            // Removing element A from the ArrayList
            letter.remove("A");
20
            // Removing element X from the ArrayList
            letter.remove("X");
            // This element is not present in the list so it should return false
            boolean b = letter.remove("X");
            System.out.println("Element X removed: " + b);
26
            System.out.println("ArrayList after remove: ");
            for (String var2: letter){
                System.out.println(var2);
            }
        }
    }
```

Output

```
ArrayList before remove:
A
B
C
D
Element X removed: false
ArrayList after remove:
B
D
```

Replacing an element

The `ArrayList` class's `set()` method can be used to replace or update an item at a specific index with another item. The `ArrayListDemo.java` demonstrates that.

Example 14.10: ArrayListDemo.java

```
01  import java.util.ArrayList; // Needed for ArrayList class
02  public class ArrayListDemo
03  {
04      public static void main(String[] args)
05      {
06          // Create an ArrayList to hold some names.
07          ArrayList nameList = new ArrayList();
08
09          // Add some names to the ArrayList.
10          nameList.add("Mohammed");
11          nameList.add("Mustafa");
12          nameList.add("Nuha");
```

```
13
14          // Display the items in nameList and their indices.
15          for (int index = 0; index < nameList.size(); index++)
16          {
17             System.out.println("Index: " + index + " Name: " +
18                         nameList.get(index));
19          }
20
21          // Now replace the item at index 1 with the string "Jasmine".
22          nameList.set(1, "Jasmine");
23
24          System.out.println("Mustafa was replaced with Jasmine. " +
25                         "Here are the items now.");
26
27          // Display the items in nameList and their indices.
28          for (int index = 0; index < nameList.size(); index++)
29          {
30             System.out.println("Index: " + index + " Name: " +
31                         nameList.get(index));
32          }
33     }
34 }
```

Output

```
Index: 0 Name: Mohammed
Index: 1 Name: Mustafa
Index: 2 Name: Nuha
Mustafa was replaced with Jasmine. Here are the items now.
Index: 0 Name: Mohammed
Index: 1 Name: Jasmine
Index: 2 Name: Nuha
```

Sorting of ArrayList

Sorting of `ArrayList<String>`

Here we are sorting the `ArrayList` of `String` type. We are doing it by simply calling the `Collections.sort(arraylist)` method. The output list will be sorted alphabetically.

Example 14.11: SortStringEx.java

```
01 import java.util.ArrayList;
02 import java.util.Collections;
03
04 public class SortStringEx {
05    public static void main(String[] args){
06       ArrayList<String> countries = new ArrayList<String>();
```

```
07          countries.add("Sudan");
08          countries.add("Palestine");
09          countries.add("India");
10          countries.add("Egypt");
11
12          // Unsorted List
13          System.out.println("Before Sorting: ");
14          for(String counter: countries){
15              System.out.println(counter);
16          }
17
18          // Sort statement
19          Collections.sort(countries);
20
21          // Sorted List
22          System.out.println("After Sorting: ");
23          for (String counter: countries){
24              System.out.println(counter);
25          }
26      }
27  }
```

Output

```
Before Sorting:
Sudan
Palestine
India
Egypt
After Sorting:
Egypt
India
Palestine
Sudan
```

Sorting of `ArrayList<Integer>`

The same `Collections.sort()` method can be used for sorting the `Integer` ArrayList as well.

Example 14.12: SortIntegerEx.java

```
01  import java.util.ArrayList;
02  import java.util.Collections;
03
04  public class SortIntegerEx{
05      public static void main(String[] args){
06          ArrayList<Integer> num = new ArrayList<Integer>();
07          num.add(  );
08          num.add(  );
09          num.add(  );
10
11          // ArrayList before the sorting
12          System.out.println("Before Sorting: ");
```

```
13            for (int counter: num) {
14                System.out.println(counter);
15            }
16
17            // Sorting of ArrayList using Collections.sort
18            Collections.sort(num);
19
20            // ArrayList after sorting
21            System.out.println("After Sorting: ");
22            for (int counter: num) {
23                System.out.println(counter);
24            }
25
26       }
27 }
```

Output
```
Before Sorting:
30
20
10
After Sorting:
10
20
30
```

Sort ArrayList in descending order

Here we will learn how to sort an ArrayList in descending (or decreasing) order. We are using `Collections.reverseOrder()` method along with `Collections.sort()` in order to sort the list in decreasing order. In the below example we have used the following statement for sorting in reverse order.

```
Collections.sort(arraylist,Collections.reverseOrder());
```

However the reverse order sorting can also be done as following - This way the list will be sorted in ascending order first and then it will be reversed.

```
Collections.sort(list);
Collections.reverse(list);
```

Example 14.13: SortArrayListEx.java
```
01 import java.util.ArrayList;
02 import java.util.Collections;
03
04 public class SortArrayListEx {
05     public static void main(String[] args) {
06         ArrayList<String> al = new ArrayList<String>();
07         al.add("A");
08         al.add("B");
09         al.add("C");
```

```
            al.add("D");
11
            // Unsorted List: ArrayList content before sorting
            System.out.println("Before Sorting: ");
            for (String str: al){
                System.out.println(str);
            }
17
            // Sorting in descending order
            Collections.sort(al,Collections.reverseOrder());
20
            // Sorted list in reverse order
            System.out.println("ArrayList in descending order: ");
            for (String str: al){
                System.out.println(str);
            }
26
        }
    }
```

Output

```
Before Sorting:
A
B
C
D
ArrayList in descending order:
D
C
B
A
```

Sort ArrayList objects using comparable and comparator interfaces

We generally use `Collections.sort()` method to sort a simple array list. In this section we will see how to sort an ArrayList of objects by properties or data members using comparable and comparator interfaces. Before going through the example of them, let's see what's the output when we try to sort ArrayList of objects without implementing any of these interfaces.

Example 14.14: Book.java

```
01  package ch14;
02
03  public class Book {
04      private String bookName;
05      private int pageNo;
06      private int pubYear;
07
08      public Book(String bookName, int pageNo, int pubYear){
```

```
            this.bookName = bookName;
            this.pageNo = pageNo;
            this.pubYear = pubYear;
        }
        public String getBookName(){
            return bookName;
        }
        public void setBookName(String bookName){
            this.bookName = bookName;
        }
        public int getPageNo(){
            return pageNo;
        }
        public void setPageNo(int pageNo){
            this.pageNo = pageNo;
        }
        public int getPubYear(){
            return pubYear;
        }
        public void setPubYear(int pubYear){
            this.pubYear = pubYear;
        }
    }
```

And I want to have an ArrayList of `Book` Object. We do it like this:

Example 14.15: BookDemo.java

```
01  package ch14;
02
03  import java.util.ArrayList;
04  import java.util.Collections;
05
06  public class BookDemo {
07      public static void main(String[] args) {
08          ArrayList<Book> list = new ArrayList<Book>();
09          list.add(new Book("C Programming", 552, 2007));
10          list.add(new Book("How to Design Classes", 666, 2012));
11          list.add(new Book("Modern C", 222, 2015));
12
13          Collections.sort(list);
14          for (Book str: list){
15              System.out.println(str);
16          }
17
18      }
19  }
```

So when I tried to run this, it throws the following error message-

```
Information:java: Errors occurred while compiling module 'Learn-
Java'
Information:javac 10.0.1 was used to compile java sources
Information:7/14/2019 9:04 AM - Build completed with 1 error and
0 warnings in 11 s 531 ms
```

```
C:\Users\MOHAMMED\Desktop\Full Book - Learn Java and
JavaFX\jearnjava_source\ch02_ch24\src\ch14\BookDemo.java
    Error:Error:line (13)java: no suitable method found for
sort(java.util.ArrayList<ch14.Book>)
    method java.util.Collections.<T>sort(java.util.List<T>) is
not applicable
        (inference variable T has incompatible bounds
            equality constraints: ch14.Book
            upper bounds: java.lang.Comparable<? super T>)
    method
java.util.Collections.<T>sort(java.util.List<T>,java.util.Compar
ator<? super T>) is not applicable
        (cannot infer type-variable(s) T
            (actual and formal argument lists differ in length))
```

I Just called the `sort` method on an ArrayList of objects which actually doesn't work until unless we use interfaces like Comparable and Comparator. Let's see how to use them to get the sorting done.

Sorting of `ArrayList<Object>` with Comparable

A comparable object is capable of comparing itself with another object. The class itself must implements the Comparable interface to compare its instance. This is how it can be done-

› 1st implement Comparable interface. A comparable object is used to comparing itself with other objects. The objects of classes that implement the Comparable interface can be ordered. In other words. classes that implement the Comparable interface contain an object that can be compared in some meaningful manner.

› 2nd Override the `compareTo()` method of Comparable interface. The `compareTo()` method is used to compare the current object with the specified object.

Let's say we need to sort the `ArrayList<Book>` based on year of publication property – first implement Comparable interface and then Override the `compareTo` method, as shown in the Book2.java file.

Example 14.16: Book2.java

```
01  package ch14;
02
03  public class Book2 implements Comparable<Book2>{
04      private String bookName;
05      private int pageNo;
06      private int pubYear;
07
08      public Book2(String bookName, int pageNo, int pubYear){
09          this.bookName = bookName;
10          this.pageNo = pageNo;
```

```
11              this.pubYear = pubYear;
12          }
13          public String getBookName(){
14              return bookName;
15          }
16          public void setBookName(String bookName){
17              this.bookName = bookName;
18          }
19          public int getPageNo(){
20              return pageNo;
21          }
22          public void setPageNo(int pageNo){
23              this.pageNo = pageNo;
24          }
25          public int getPubYear(){
26              return pubYear;
27          }
28          public void setPubYear(int pubYear){
29              this.pubYear = pubYear;
30          }
31
32          @Override
33          public String toString(){
34              return ("Book Name = " + bookName + ", Page No = " +
35                      pageNo + ", Publish Year = " + pubYear);
36          }
37          @Override
38          public int compareTo(Book2 compareto){
39              int comparepub;
40              comparepub = compareto.getPubYear();
41
42              // For Ascending order
43              return this.pubYear - comparepub;
44          }
45     }
```

Now we can very well call `Collections.sort` on ArrayList.

Example 14.17: BookDemo2.java

```
01  package ch14;
02
03  import java.util.*;
04
05  public class BookDemo2 {
06      public static void main(String[] args) {
07          ArrayList<Book2> list = new ArrayList<Book2>();
08          list.add(new Book2("C Programming", 552, 2007));
09          list.add(new Book2("How to Design Classes", 666,
2012));
10          list.add(new Book2("Modern C", 222, 2015));
11
12          Collections.sort(list);
13          for (Book2 str1: list) {
14              System.out.println(str1);
```

Output
```
Book Name = C Programming, Page No = 552, Publish Year = 2007
Book Name = How to Design Classes, Page No = 666, Publish Year = 2012
Book Name = Modern C, Page No = 222, Publish Year = 2015
```

As you can see that `Book2` array is sorted by publication year in ascending order. If we want sort books by name, we have to change `Book2` class to do that:

Example 14.18: Book2.java (revised version)

```
01  package ch14;
02
03  public class Book2 implements Comparable<Book2>{
04      private String bookName;
05      private int pageNo;
06      private int pubYear;
07
08      public Book2(String bookName, int pageNo, int pubYear){
09          this.bookName = bookName;
10          this.pageNo = pageNo;
11          this.pubYear = pubYear;
12      }
13      public String getBookName(){
14          return bookName;
15      }
16      public void setBookName(String bookName){
17          this.bookName = bookName;
18      }
19      public int getPageNo(){
20          return pageNo;
21      }
22      public void setPageNo(int pageNo){
23          this.pageNo = pageNo;
24      }
25      public int getPubYear(){
26          return pubYear;
27      }
28      public void setPubYear(int pubYear){
29          this.pubYear = pubYear;
30      }
31
32      @Override
33      public String toString(){
34          return ("Book Name = " + bookName + ", Page No = " +
35              pageNo + ", Publication Year = " + pubYear);
36      }
37  /*  @Override
38      // Comparison by publication year
39      public int compareTo(Book2 compareto){
40          int comparepub;
```

```
41            comparepub = compareto.getPubYear();
42
43        // For Ascending order
44        return this.pubYear-comparepub;
45    }*/
46
47    @Override
48    // Comparison by name
49    public int compareTo(Book2 compareto){
50        int comparepub;
51        comparepub = compareto.getBookName().compareTo(getBookName());
52        return comparepub;
53    }
54 }
```

Example 14.19: DemoBook2.java (revised version)

```
01  package ch14;
02
03  import java.util.*;
04
05  public class BookDemo2 {
06      public static void main(String[] args) {
07          ArrayList<Book2> list = new ArrayList<Book2>();
08          list.add(new Book2("C Programming", 552, 2007));
09          list.add(new Book2("How to Design Classes", 666, 2012));
10          list.add(new Book2("Modern C", 222, 2015));
11
12          // For Descending order
13          Collections.sort(list);
14          for (Book2 str1: list) {
15              System.out.println(str1);
16          }
17
18          // For Ascending order
19          Collections.reverse(list);
20          for (Book2 str1: list) {
21              System.out.println(str1);
22          }
23      }
24  }
```

Output

```
Book Name = Modern C, Page No = 222, Publication Year = 2015
Book Name = How to Design Classes, Page No = 666, Publication Year = 2012
Book Name = C Programming, Page No = 552, Publication Year = 2007
Book Name = C Programming, Page No = 552, Publication Year = 2007
Book Name = How to Design Classes, Page No = 666, Publication Year = 2012
Book Name = Modern C, Page No = 222, Publication Year = 2015
```

Now, suppose we want sorts Books by their publication year and page numbers also. In case you want to have more than way of sorting your class objects you should use Comparators.

Sorting `ArrayList<Object>` multiple properties with Comparator (Method 1)

The Comparator interface contains two methods called `compare` and `equals`. The `compare` method compares its two input arguments and imposes an order between them.

We are overriding `compare` method of Comparator for sorting, as shown below:

Example 14.20: Book3.java

```java
01  package ch14;
02
03  import java.util.Comparator;
04
05  public class Book3{
06      private String bookName;
07      private int pageNo;
08      private int pubYear;
09
10      public Book3(String bookName, int pageNo, int pubYear){
11          this.bookName = bookName;
12          this.pageNo = pageNo;
13          this.pubYear = pubYear;
14      }
15      public String getBookName(){
16          return bookName;
17      }
18      public void setBookName(String bookName){
19          this.bookName = bookName;
20      }
21      public int getPageNo(){
22          return pageNo;
23      }
24      public void setPageNo(int pageNo){
25          this.pageNo = pageNo;
26      }
27      public int getPubYear(){
28          return pubYear;
29      }
30      public void setPubYear(int pubYear){
31          this.pubYear = pubYear;
32      }
33
34      /* Comparator for sorting the list by publication year */
35      public static Comparator<Book3> PubYearComparator=new Comparator<Book3>(){
36          @Override
37          public int compare(Book3 o1, Book3 o2) {
38              int pubYear1 = o1.getPubYear();
39              int pubYear2 = o2.getPubYear();
```

```
40
41                //ascending order
42                return pubYear1-pubYear2;
43                //desending order
44                //return pubYear2-pubYear1;
45            }
46        };
47
48        /* Comparator for sorting the list by page no */
49        public static Comparator<Book3> PageNoComparator = new Comparator<Book3>(){
50            @Override
51            public int compare(Book3 o1, Book3 o2){
52                int pageNo1 = o1.getPageNo();
53                int pageNo2 = o2.getPageNo();
54
55                // ascendign order
56                return pageNo1-pageNo2;
57            }
58        };
59        @Override
60        public String toString(){
61            return ("Book Name = " + bookName + ", Page No = " +
62                    pageNo + ", Publish Year = " + pubYear);
63        }
64 }
```

Now we can very well call `Collections.sort` on ArrayList as shown on the `BookDemo3.java` program.

Example 14.21 `BookDemo3.java`

```
01 package ch14;
02
03 import java.util.ArrayList;
04 import java.util.Collections;
05
06 public class BookDemo3 {
07     public static void main(String[] args) {
08         ArrayList<Book3> list = new ArrayList<Book3>();
09         list.add(new Book3("C Programming", 552, 2007));
10         list.add(new Book3("How to Design Classes", 665, 2012));
11         list.add(new Book3("Modern C", 222, 2015));
12
13         /* Sorting based on Book's Published year */
14         System.out.println("Book Publish Year Sorting: ");
15         Collections.sort(list, Book3.PubYearComparator);
16         for (Book3 str1: list) {
17             System.out.println(str1);
18         }
19
20         /* Sorting based on Book's Pages Number */
21         System.out.println("PageNo Sorting: ");
22         Collections.sort(list, Book3.PageNoComparator);
```

```
            for (Book3 no: list){
                System.out.println(no);
            }
    26
        }
    }
```

Output
```
Book Publish Year Sorting:
Book Name = C Programming, Page No = 552, Publish Year = 2007
Book Name = How to Design Classes, Page No = 666, Publish Year = 2012
Book Name = Modern C, Page No = 222, Publish Year = 2015
PageNo Sorting:
Book Name = Modern C, Page No = 222, Publish Year = 2015
Book Name = C Programming, Page No = 552, Publish Year = 2007
Book Name = How to Design Classes, Page No = 666, Publish Year = 2012
```

Sorting `ArrayList<Object>` multiple properties with Comparator (Method 2 - recommended)

We Create one `Book4` class without change it, and we create a class for each comparison (by Publication year, by Page numbers) as shown below:

Example 14.22: Book4.java
```
01  package ch14;
02
03  import java.util.Comparator;
04
05  public class Book4 {
        private String bookName;
        private int pageNo;
        private int pubYear;
09
        public Book4(String bookName, int pageNo, int pubYear){
            this.bookName = bookName;
            this.pageNo = pageNo;
            this.pubYear = pubYear;
        }
        public String getBookName(){
            return bookName;
        }
        public void setBookName(String bookName){
            this.bookName = bookName;
        }
        public int getPageNo(){
            return pageNo;
        }
        public void setPageNo(int pageNo){
            this.pageNo = pageNo;
        }
        public int getPubYear(){
            return pubYear;
```

```
29      }
30      public void setPubYear(int pubYear){
31          this.pubYear = pubYear;
32      }
33
34      @Override
35      public String toString(){
36          return ("Book Name = " + bookName + ", Page No = " +
37              pageNo + ", Publish Year = " + pubYear);
38      }
39  }
```

Example 14.23: PubYearComparator.java
```
01  package ch14;
02
03  import java.util.*;
04
05  public class PubYearComparator implements Comparator<Book4> {
06      /* Comparator for sorting the list by publication year */
07
08      @Override
09      public int compare(Book4 o1, Book4 o2) {
10          int pubYear1 = o1.getPubYear();
11          int pubYear2 = o2.getPubYear();
12
13          //ascending order
14          return pubYear1-pubYear2;
15          //descending order
16          //return pubYear2-pubYear1;
17      }
18  }
```

Example 14.24: PageNoComparator.java
```
01  package ch14;
02
03  import java.util.Comparator;
04
05  public class PageNoComparator implements Comparator<Book4> {
06      /* Comparator for sorting the list by page numbers */
07
08      @Override
09      public int compare(Book4 o1, Book4 o2) {
10          int pageNo1 = o1.getPageNo();
11          int pageNo2 = o2.getPageNo();
12
13          // ascending order
14          return pageNo1-pageNo2;
15      }
16  }
```

Example 14.25: Test.java (Test class - main method)
```
01  package ch14;
02
03  import java.util.ArrayList;
```

```
04  import java.util.Collections;
05
06  public class Test {
07      public static void main(String[] args) {
08          ArrayList<Book4> list = new ArrayList<Book4>();
09          list.add(new Book4("C Programming", 552, 2007));
10          list.add(new Book4("How to Design Classes", 666, 2012));
11          list.add(new Book4("Modern C", 222, 2015));
12
13          // Sort by Publication Year
14          Collections.sort(list, new PubYearComparator());
15          for (Book4 ls: list){
16              System.out.println(ls);
17          }
18
19          // Sort by Page Numbers
20          Collections.sort(list, new PageNoComparator());
21          for (Book4 ls: list){
22              System.out.println(ls);
23          }
24      }
25  }
```

Output

```
Book Name = C Programming, Page No = 552, Publish Year = 2007
Book Name = How to Design Classes, Page No = 666, Publish Year = 2012
Book Name = Modern C, Page No = 222, Publish Year = 2015
Book Name = Modern C, Page No = 222, Publish Year = 2015
Book Name = C Programming, Page No = 552, Publish Year = 2007
Book Name = How to Design Classes, Page No = 666, Publish Year = 2012
```

Comparable vs Comparator

Comparable Interface	Comparator Interface
Used to provide single way of sorting. Logically compares **this** reference with the object specified.	Used to provide different ways of sorting. Logically compares two objects.
It contains only one method - `compareTo()`.	It contains two methods `compare()` and `equals()`.
`compareTo()` method is responsible to sort the elements.	`compare()` method is responsible to sort the elements.
For using Comparable, Class needs to implement it.	For using Comparator, we don't need to make any change in the class.
Is defined in `java.lang` package.	Is defined in `java.util` package.

Both Comparable interface and Comparator interface are used for sorting the data members or attributes of the objects. We can use any interface for sorting but it is preferable to choose comparator as it works simultaneously on many data members or attributes.

Get/Search

Get sub list of ArrayList

To get a `sublist` of an existing ArrayList we use `subList` method of ArrayList class.

Syntax

    List subList(int fromIndex, int toIndex)

Here `fromIndex` is inclusive and `toIndex` is exclusive.

Example 14.26: SublistEx.java - Getting sub-list from an ArrayList

The `subList` method returns a list therefore to store the sublist in another ArrayList we must need to type cast the returned value in same way as I did in the below example. On the other side if we are storing the returned sublist into a list then there is no need to type cast (Refer the example).

```
01  import java.util.ArrayList;
02  import java.util.List;
03
04  public class SublistEx {
05      public static void main(String args[]){
06          ArrayList<String> capitals = new ArrayList<String>();
07          // Addition of elements in ArrayList
08          capitals.add("CAIRO");
09          capitals.add("KHARTOUM");
10          capitals.add("ROME");
11          capitals.add("TOKYO");
12          capitals.add("NAIROBI");
13          capitals.add("NEW DELHI");
14          System.out.println("Original ArrayList Content: " + capitals);
15
16          // Sublist to ArrayList
17          ArrayList<String> capitals2 = new
18              ArrayList<String>(capitals.subList(1, 4));
19          System.out.println("Sublist stored in ArrayList: " + capitals2);
20      }
21  }
```

Output

```
Original ArrayList Content: [CAIRO, KHARTOUM, ROME, TOKYO,
NAIROBI, NEW DELHI]
Sublist stored in ArrayList: [KHARTOUM, ROME, TOKYO]
```

> **NOTE:** The `subList` method throws
> ☐ `IndexOutOfBoundsException` – if the specified indexes are out of the range of ArrayList (fromIndex < 0 || toIndex > size).
> ☐ `IllegalArgumentException` – if the starting index is greater than the end point index (fromIndex > toIndex).

Get the index of last occurrence of the element in the ArrayList

The method `lastIndexOf(Object obj)` returns the index of last occurrence of the specified element in the ArrayList. It returns **-1** if the specified element does not exist in the list.

Syntax

```
public int lastIndexOf(Object obj)
```

This would return the index of last Occurrence of element obj in the ArrayList.

Example 14.27: LastIndexOfEx.java

In the below example we have an Integer ArrayList which has few duplicate elements. We are fetching the last index of few elements using `lastIndexof` method.

```java
import java.util.ArrayList;
public class LastIndexOfEx {
    public static void main(String args[]){
        // ArrayList of Integer Type
        ArrayList<Integer> num1 = new ArrayList<Integer>();
        num1.add(100); // 0
        num1.add(200); // 1
        num1.add(300); // 2
        num1.add(400); // 3
        num1.add(500); // 4
        num1.add(100); // 5
        num1.add(600); // 6
        num1.add(700); // 7
        num1.add(300); // 8
        System.out.println("The last occurence of element 100: "
                + num1.lastIndexOf(100));
        System.out.println("The last occurence of element 300: "
                + num1.lastIndexOf(300));
    }
}
```

Output

```
The last occurrence of element 100: 5
The last occurrence of element 300: 8
```

Get element from ArrayList (`get()` method)

The `get(int index)` method is used to get an element of a specified position from the list.

Syntax

```
get(int index)
```

The `ArrayList` class's `get` method returns the item stored at a specific index. You pass the index as an argument to the method. This method throws `IndexOutOfBoundException` if the index is out of range (index < 0 || index >= size()).

Here is a simple example.

Example 14.28: `ArrayListEx2.java`

```java
import java.util.ArrayList; // Needed for ArrayList class
```

```
02
03  public class ArrayListEx2
04  {
05      public static void main(String[] args)
06      {
07          // Create an ArrayList to hold some names
08          ArrayList nameList = new ArrayList();
09
10          // Use add() method to add values (e.g. names) to the ArrayList
11          nameList.add("Mohammed");
12          nameList.add("Mustafa");
13          nameList.add("Nuha");
14
15          // Display the size of the ArrayList
16          System.out.println("The ArrayList has " +
17                             nameList.size() + " objects stored in it.");
18
19          // Now display the items in nameList
20          for (int index = 0; index < nameList.size(); index++){
21              System.out.println(nameList.get(index));
22          }
23      }
24  }
```

Output
```
The ArrayList has 3 objects stored in it.
Mohammed
Mustafa
Nuha
```

Explanation (line 20)

> For loop uses the value returned from **nameList**'s `size` method to control the number of times the loop iterates. This is to prevent a bounds checking error from occurring.

> The last item stored in an `ArrayList` will have an index that is one less than the size of the `ArrayList`.

> If you pass a value larger than this to the `get` method, an error will occur.

NOTES
☐ `ArrayListEx.java` uses unchecked or unsafe operations.
☐ Recompile with -Xlnt: unchecked for details.
☐ This warnings appears because an `ArrayList` can be used to store any type of object reference, and the compiler cannot assure you that the types of objects you are storing in an `ArrayList` are the type you intended to store.

Here is a simple example.

Example 14.29: AnotherGetMethodEx.java

```java
import java.util.ArrayList;
public class AnotherGetMethodEx {
    public static void main(String[] args){
        ArrayList<String> colors = new ArrayList<String>();
        colors.add("White");
        colors.add("Blue");
        colors.add("Black");
        colors.add("Brown");
        colors.add("Gray");
        colors.add("Red");
        colors.add("Green");
        System.out.println("First element of the ArrayList: "
                + colors.get(0));
        System.out.println("Third element of the ArrayList: "
                + colors.get(2));
        System.out.println("Fifth element of the ArrayList: "
                + colors.get(4));
        System.out.println("Seventh element of the ArrayList: "
                + colors.get(6));
    }
}
```

Output

```
First element of the ArrayList: White
Third element of the ArrayList: Black
Fifth element of the ArrayList: Gray
Seventh element of the ArrayList: Green
```

The toString() method

The `ArrayList` class has a `toString()` method that returns a string representing all of the items stored in an `ArrayList` object.

Example 14.30: ArrayListDemo2.java - Suppose we have set up the nameList object as previously shown, with the strings "Mohammed", " Mustafa", "Shereen" (Display all of the names)

```java
import java.util.ArrayList;    // Needed for ArrayList class

public class ArrayListDemo2
{
    public static void main(String[] args)
    {
        // Create a vector to hold some names.
        ArrayList<String> nameList = new ArrayList<String>();

        // Add some names to the ArrayList.
        nameList.add("Mohammed");
        nameList.add("Mustafa");
        nameList.add("Shereen");
```

```
            // Now display the items in nameList.
            System.out.println(nameList);
    }
}
```

Output

```
[Mohammed, Mustafa, Shereen]
```

When we are dealing with ArrayList of Objects then it is must to Override the `toString()` method in order to get the output in desired format. In the next example we will see how to override the `toString()` method for ArrayList in Java.

Example 14.31: Employee.java

```
01  package ch14;
02  public class Employee{
03      private String employeename;
04      private int employeeage;
05      Employee(String name, int age){
06          this.employeename = name;
07          this.employeeage = age;
08      }
09      @Override
10      public String toString() {
11          return "Name is: " + this.employeename
12                  + " and Age is: " + this.employeeage;
13      }
14  }
```

Another class (EmployeeDemo.java):

```
01  package ch14;
02  import java.util.ArrayList;
03  public class EmployeeDemo {
04      public static void main(String[] args){
05          ArrayList<Employee> emp = new ArrayList<Employee>();
06          emp.add(new Employee("Steve", 44));
07          emp.add(new Employee("Mary", 32));
08          emp.add(new Employee("Anthony", 70));
09          emp.add(new Employee("John", 18));
10
11          for (Employee temp: emp){
12              System.out.println(temp);
13          }
14      }
15  }
```

Output

```
Name is: Steve and Age is: 44
Name is: Mary and Age is: 32
Name is: Anthony and Age is: 70
Name is: John and Age is: 18
```

Get the index of first occurrence of the element in the ArrayList

The `indexOf(Object o)` method is used for finding out the index of a particular element in a list.

Syntax

```
public int indexOf(Object o)
```

This method return **s-1** if the specified element is not present in the list.

Example 14.32: IndexOfEx.java

```
01  import java.util.ArrayList;
02  public class IndexOfEx {
03      public static void main(String args[]) {
04          ArrayList<String> chars = new ArrayList<String>();
05          chars.add("A");
06          chars.add("B");
07          chars.add("C");
08          chars.add("D");
09          chars.add("E");
10          System.out.println("Index of 'A':" + chars.indexOf("A"));
11          System.out.println("Index of 'B':" + chars.indexOf("B"));
12          System.out.println("Index of 'C':" + chars.indexOf("C"));
13          System.out.println("Index of 'D':" + chars.indexOf("D"));
14          System.out.println("Index of 'E':" + chars.indexOf("E"));
15      }
16  }
```

Output

```
Index of 'A':0
Index of 'B':1
Index of 'C':2
Index of 'D':3
Index of 'E':4
```

Check whether element exists in ArrayList

ArrayList `contains()` method is used for checking the specified element existence in the given list.

```
public boolean contains(Object element)
```

It returns `true` if the specified element is found in the list else it gives `false`.

Example 14.33: ContainsEx.java

In this example we have two array lists (`ArrayList<String>` and `ArrayList<Integer>`) and we are checking the existence of few elements in both the lists.

```java
import java.util.ArrayList;
public class ContainsEx {
    public static void main(String[] args){
        ArrayList<String> colors = new ArrayList<String>();
        colors.add("White");
        colors.add("Blue");
        colors.add("Black");
        colors.add("Brown");
        colors.add("Gray");
        colors.add("Red");
        colors.add("Green");
        System.out.println("ArrayList contains the string 'White': "
                    + colors.contains("White"));
        System.out.println("ArrayList contains the string 'Brown': "
                    + colors.contains("Brown"));
        System.out.println("ArrayList contains the string 'Green': "
                    + colors.contains("Green"));
    }
}
```

Output

```
ArrayList contains the string 'White': true
ArrayList contains the string 'Brown': true
ArrayList contains the string 'Green': true
```

Capacity

Previously you learned that an `ArrayList` object's size is the number of item stored in the `ArrayList` object. When you add an item to the `ArrayList` object, its size increase by one, and when you remove an item from the `ArrayList` object, its size decreases by one.

An `ArrayList` object also has a **capacity**, which is the number of items it can store without having to increase its size. When an `ArrayList` object is first created, using the `no-arg` constructor, its has an initial capacity of 10 items. This means that it can hold up to 10 items without having to increase its size. When the eleventh item is added, the `ArrayList` object must increase its size to accommodate the new item. You can specify a different starting capacity, if you desire, by passing an int argument to the `ArrayList` constructor, as follow:

Example 14.34: Create an `ArrayList` object with an initial capacity of 100 items:
```
ArrayList list = new ArrayList(100);
```

Consider a scenario when there is a need to add huge number of elements to an already full ArrayList, in such case `ArrayList` has to be resized several number of times which would result in a poor performance. For such scenarios `ensureCapacity()` method is very useful as it increases the size of the ArrayList by a specified capacity.

Syntax
```
public void ensureCapacity(int minCapacity)
```

Example 14.35: EnsureCapacityEx.java
```java
01  import java.util.ArrayList;
02  public class EnsureCapacityEx {
03      public static void main(String args[]){
04          // ArrayList with Capacity 3
05          ArrayList<String> numbers = new ArrayList<String>(3);
06
07          // Add 3 elements
08          numbers.add("One");
09          numbers.add("Two");
10          numbers.add("Three");
11
12          // Increase capacity to 4
13          numbers.ensureCapacity(4);
14          numbers.add("Four");
15
16          // Print all the element available in list
17          for (String temp: numbers) {
18              System.out.println(temp);
19          }
20      }
21  }
```

Output
```
One
Two
Three
Four
```

Summary

> An `ArrayList` object automatically expands as items are added to it.

- An `ArrayList` object automatically shrinks as items are removed from it.
- The `ArrayList` class has a no-arg constructor.
- To add items to the `ArrayList` object, you use the `add` method.
- The items that are stored in `ArrayList` have a corresponding index.
- The `ArrayList` class has a `size` method that reports the number of items stored in an `ArrayList`.
- The `ArrayList` class's `get` method returns the item stored at a specific index.
- The `ArrayList` class has a `toString()` method that returns a string representing all of the items stored in an `ArrayList` object.
- The `ArrayList` class has a `remove()` method that removes an item at a specific index.
- The `ArrayList` class's `set()` method can be used to replace an item at a specific index with another item.
- When an `ArrayList` object is first created, using the no-arg constructor, its has an initial capacity of 10 items.
- `ArrayList` can be used to store objects of any type. In fact, you can store a mixture of objects of different types in the same `ArrayList`.
- With the release of Java5, however, the `ArrayList` class become "type-safe generic data types". This means that you can specify the type of object that an `ArrayList` will store, and Java will make sure that only objects of the specified type are stored in it. You can still use the `ArrayList` class, the traditional way (With no specified type), but in most cases you should specify the type in order to reduce the chances of errors.

Chapter 15

Overloading Methods and Constructors

Overloading Methods

Method is **Overloaded** means that two or more methods in the same class share the same name, but use different types of parameters (based on types and count).

The benefits:
> Sometimes you need several different ways to perform the same operation.
> We can write smaller, more direct methods and then call them as needed.

The `Overload.java` example shows the usage of Overloading methods.

Example 15.1: Overload.java - Suppose a class has the following two methods

```
01  public class OverloadingMethods {
02
03      static int add(int val1, int val2) {
04          int sum;
05          sum = val1 + val2;
06          return sum;
07      }
08
09      static String add(String s1, String s2) {
10          String name;
11          name = s1 + s2;
12          return name;
13      }
14
15      public static void main(String[] args) {
16          int total = add(  ,  );
```

```
17            System.out.println(total);
18
19            String fullName = add("Mohammed ", "Mansour");
20            System.out.println(fullName);
21        }
22 }
```

Both methods are named `add`. Both take two arguments which are added together. First method accepts `int` arguments and returns their `sum`. And the second method accepts two String references and return a reference to a String that is a concatenation of the two arguments.

When call an `add` method, the compiler must determine which one of the overloaded methods we intended to call.

Method's signature

Java uses a method's signature to distinguish it from other methods of the same name. A method's signature consists of:

› the method's name;
› the number of input parameters;
› the data types of the method's parameter; and
› the order of the parameters.

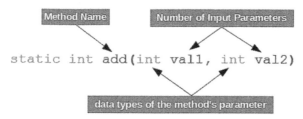

Figure 15.1 | The Components of a Method's Signature

Example 15.2: Method's Signature
```
public static int add(int, int);
public static String add(String, String);
```

NOTE: The method's return type is not part of the signature. For this reason, the following *add* method cannot be added to the same class with the previous ones:
```
01 public int add (String str1, String str2)
02 {
03     int num = Integer.parseInt(str1) +
04         Integer.parseInt(str2);
05     return sum;
06 }
```

For this reason, an error message will be issued when a class containing all of these methods is compiled.

NOTE: The process of matching a method call with the correct method is known as **binding**. When an overloaded method is being called, Java uses the method's name and parameters list to determine which method to bind the call to. If two **int** arguments are passed to the *add* method, the version of the method with two parameters is called. If two String arguments are passed to *add*, the version with two String parameters is called.

Overloading Constructors

Overloading constructor means that a class can have any number of constructors. The rules for overloading constructors are the same for overloading other methods. The compiler differentiates these constructors by taking into account the number of parameters and their type. Here is a simple example Add.java.

Example 15.3: Add.java - Constructor Overloading

```
class add {
    int id;
    String name;
    int age;

    add(int i, String n) {
        id = i;
        name = n;
    }
    add(int i, String n, int a) {
        id = i;
        name = n;
        age=a;
    }
    void display(){System.out.println(id+" "+name+" "+age);}

    public static void main(String args[]) {
        add s1 = new add(111,"Mohammed");
        add s2 = new add(222,"Mansour",25);
        s1.display();
        s2.display();
    }
}
```

Output
```
111 Mohammed 0
222 Mansour 25
```

How each constructor is called:

```
add s1 = new add(111,"Mohammed");
add s2 = new add(222,"Mansour",25);
```

The first statement creates an `add` object, referenced by the `s1` variable and executes the constructor. Its **id** and **name** fields will be set to `111` and "Mohammed". The second statement create another `add` object, referenced by the `s2` variable and executes the second constructor. Its **id, name** and **age** fields will be set to `222, "Mansour",` and `25` respectively.

Remember

Java provides a default constructor only when you do not write any constructor for a class. If a class has a constructor that accepts arguments, but it does not have a no-arg constructor, you cannot create an instance of the class without passing arguments to the constructor.

Therefore, anytime you write a constructor for a class and that constructor accepts arguments, you should also write a no-arg constructor if you want to be able to create instances of the class without passing arguments to the constructor.

Summary

- Method is overloaded means that two or more methods in the same class share the same name, but use different types of parameters (based on types and count).
- Java uses a method's signature to distinguish it from other methods of the same name. A method's signature consists of: the method's name, the number of input parameters, the data types of the method's parameter; and the order of the parameters.
- The process of matching a method call with the correct method is known as binding.
- Overloading constructor means that a class can have any number of constructors. The rules for overloading constructors are the same for overloading other methods.
- Java provides a default constructor only when you do not write any constructor for a class.

Chapter 16

Introduction to Aggregation

Introduction

In real life, objects are frequently made of other objects. For example, a school is made of door, window, wall objects. It is the combination of all these objects that makes a school object.

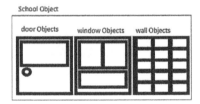

Figure 16.1 | A school object.

Aggregation is a special form of association. It is a relationship between two classes, however it is a one way association.

For example consider two classes, `Employee` class and `Address` class. Every employee has an address, but if you consider its vice versa it would not make any sense as an address doesn't need to have an employee necessarily. Lets write this examples.

Example 16.1: Address.java class
```
01  public class Address{
02      String city;
03      String state;
04      String country;
05      Address (String c, String st, String coun){
06          this.city=c;
```

```
07          this.state=st;
08          this.country=coun;
09      }
10  }
```

Example 16.2: Employee.java class

```
01  public class Employee {
02      int rollNum;
03      String EmployeeName;
04
05      // Create a one way relationship with Address class
06      Address EmployeeAddr;
07      Employee(int roll, String name, Address addr){
08          this.rollNum=roll;
09          this.EmployeeName=name;
10          this.EmployeeAddr=addr;
11      }
12      public static void main(String[] args){
13          Address ad = new Address("Omdurman", "Khartoum", "Sudan");
14          Employee obj = new Employee(123, "Mohammed", ad);
15          System.out.println(obj.rollNum);
16          System.out.println(obj.EmployeeName);
17          System.out.println(obj.EmployeeAddr.city);
18          System.out.println(obj.EmployeeAddr.state);
19          System.out.println(obj.EmployeeAddr.country);
20      }
21  }
```

Output (Employee.java)

```
123
Mohammed
Omdurman
Khartoum
Sudan
```

Explanation

› Aggregation occurs when an instance of a class is a field in another class. For example (Employee.java class):
```
06      Address EmployeeAddr;
```
You can see that in `Employee` class I have declared a field of type `Address` to obtain employee address. It's a typical example of Aggregation in Java.

› Aggregation represents a type of relationship between two classes in which one contain the other's reference.

Why we need aggregation?

To maintain code re-usability. To understand this lets take the same example again. Suppose there are two other classes Department and Client along with above two classes Employee and Address. In order to maintain Employee's address, Department Address and Client's address we don't need to use the same code again and again. We just have to use the reference of Address class while defining each of these classes. Hence we can improve code re-usability by using Aggregation relationship.

So if I have to write this in a program, I would do it like this:

Example 16.3: Address2.java class

```
01  package ch16;
02
03  public class Address2{
04      String city;
05      String state;
06      String country;
07      Address2(String c, String st, String coun){
08          this.city=c;
09          this.state=st;
10          this.country=coun;
11      }
12  }
```

Example 16.4: Department.java class

```
01  public class Department {
02      String DeparmentName;
03
04      // Creating a one direction relationship with address class
05      Address DepartmentAddr;
06
07      Department(String name, Address addr){
08          this.DeparmentName = name;
09          this.DepartmentAddr = addr;
10      }
11  }
```

Example 16.5: Client.java class

```
01  public class Client{
02      String clientName;
03
04      // Creating a one direction relationship with Address class
05      Address clientAddr;
06      Client(String name, Address addr){
07          this.clientName = name;
```

```
08            this.clientAddr = addr;
09        }
10  }
```

Example 16.6: Employee2.java class

```
01  package ch16;
02
03  public class Employee2{
04      int rollNum;
05      String EmployeeName;
06
07      // Create a one way relationship with Address2 class
08      Address2 EmployeeAddr;
09      Employee2(int roll, String name, Address2 addr){
10          this.rollNum=roll;
11          this.EmployeeName=name;
12          this.EmployeeAddr=addr;
13      }
14      public static void main(String[] args){
15          Address2 ad = new Address2("Omdurman", "Khartoum", "Sudan");
16          Employee2 obj = new Employee2(123, "Mohammed", ad);
17          System.out.println(obj.rollNum);
18          System.out.println(obj.EmployeeName);
19          System.out.println(obj.EmployeeAddr.city);
20          System.out.println(obj.EmployeeAddr.state);
21          System.out.println(obj.EmployeeAddr.country);
22      }
23  }
```

Output (Employee2.java)
```
123
Mohammed
Omdurman
Khartoum
Sudan
```

As you can see that we didn't write the `Address` code in any of the three classes, we simply created the relationship with the `Address` class to use the Address code. The dot dot (…) part in the above code can be replaced with the `public static void main` method, the code in it would be similar to what we have seen in the first example.

Example 2: An object to represent a course in college

> `Course` class - hold the course related data.
> `Teacher` class - hold the instructor related data.
> `NoteBook` class - hold the Text Book related data.

Instances of these classes could then be used as fields in the Course Class.

Example 16.7: Teacher.java class

```
01  public class Teacher
02  {
03      private String firstName;
04      private String lastName;
05
06      public Teacher(String lname, String fname)
07      {
08          lastName = lname;
09          firstName = fname;
10      }
11
12      public Teacher(Teacher object2)
13      {
14          lastName = object2.lastName;
15          firstName = object2.firstName;
16      }
17
18      public void set(String lname, String fname)
19      {
20          lastName = lname;
21          firstName = fname;
22      }
23
24      public String toString()
25      {
26          String str = "Last Name: " + lastName + "\nFirst Name: " + firstName;
27
28          return str;
29      }
30  }
```

Example 16.8: NoteBook.java class

```
01  public class NoteBook
02  {
03      private String title;
04      private String author;
05
06      public NoteBook(String textTitle, String auth)
07      {
08          title = textTitle;
09          author = auth;
10      }
11      public NoteBook(NoteBook object2)
12      {
13          title = object2.title;
14          author = object2.author;
15      }
16      public void set(String textTitle, String auth)
17      {
18          title = textTitle;
```

```
19         author = auth;
20      }
21      public String toString()
22      {
23         String str = "Title: " + title +
24                     "\nAuthor: " + author ;
25         return str;
26      }
27   }
```

POINTS:
☐ The `Course` class has a `Teacher` object and a `NoteBook` object as fields.
☐ Making an instance of once class a field in another class is called **OBJECT AGGREGATION**.
☐ The word aggregate means "a whole which is made of constituent parts."
☐ In this example, the `Course` class is an aggregate class because it is made of constituent objects.

Example 16.9: Course.java class

```
01   public class Course
02   {
03      private String courseName;
04      private Teacher teacher;
05      private NoteBook noteBook;
06
07      public Course(String name, Teacher teach, NoteBook note)
08      {
09         courseName = name;
10         teacher = new Teacher(teach);
11         noteBook = new NoteBook(note);
12      }
13
14      public String getName()
15      {
16         return courseName;
17      }
18
19      public Teacher getTeacher()
20      {
21         return new Teacher(teacher);
22      }
23
24      public NoteBook getNoteBook()
25      {
26         // Return a copy of the noteBook object.
27         return new NoteBook(noteBook);
28      }
29
30      public String toString()
31      {
32         String str = "Course name: " + courseName +
```

```
                        "\nTeacher Information:\n" + teacher +
                        "\nNotebook Information:\n"+ noteBook;
35
        return str;
    }
}
```

Example 16.10: CourseDemo.java class

```
01  public class CourseDemo
02  {
03      public static void main(String[] args)
04      {
05          Teacher myTeacher = new Teacher("Mohamed", "Mansour");
06          NoteBook myNoteBook = new NoteBook("Core Java", "Mohammed");
07
08          Course myCourse =
09              new Course("Core Java", myTeacher, myNoteBook);
10
11          System.out.println(myCourse);
12      }
13  }
```

Output (CourseDemo.java)

```
Course name: Core Java
Teacher Information:
Last Name: Mohamed
First Name: Mansour
Notebook Information:
Title: Core Java
Author: Mohammed
```

Summary

> Java aggregation indicates a special relationship between classes. This type of relationship is referred to as a HAS-A relationship. It's a one-way relationship.
> Aggregation occurs when an instance of a class is a field in another class.
> We need aggregation to maintain code re-usability. Code re-usability means using of already developed coded or classes without writing from the scratch.

Chapter 17

Enumerated Types

Introduction

An enumerated data type consists of a group of **named constants** by using a single name. For example the 7 days in a week (Sat, Sun ..etc) may be 7 enumerated types named **Day**. Enums are used when we know all possible values at compile time.

> "The main objective of enum is to define our own data types (Enumerated Data Types)."

You can use the data type to create variables that can hold only the values that belong to the enumerated data type. For example; A variable of the `int` data type can hold integer values within a certain range (from -2,147,483,648 to 2,147,483,647). You cannot assign floating point values to an `int` variable because only `int` values may be assigned to `int` variables.

A data type defines the values that are legal for any variable by that data type. Sometimes it is helpful to create your own data type that has a specific set of legal values.

For example suppose you want to create a data type named **Day**, and the legal values in that data type were the names of the days of the week (SUNDAY, MONDAY, and so forth). When you create a variable of the **Day** data type, you can only store the names of the days of the week in that variable. Any other values would be illegal.

Data Type	Legal values in that data type
Day	SUNDAY, MONDAY, TUESDAY, WEDNESDAY, THURSDAY, FRIDAY, SATURDAY.
MONTH	January, February, March, April, May, June, July, August, September, October, November, December.

In Java, such a type is known as an **"enumerated data type."**

Creating an enumerated data type

Syntax

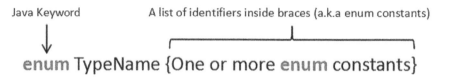

Figure 17.1 | Format of An enumerated data type

> TypeName: name of user defined data type.
> enum: Java keyword.
> enum constants: values of user defined data type.

You use the **enum** keyword to create your own data type and specify the values that belong to that type. The **enum** constants are not enclosed in quotation marks, therefore they are not strings, enum constant must be legal Java identifiers.

Once the enumeration is defined, programmers can create a variable of its type. However, even though enumeration define a class type, programmers do not initiate an enum using **new**. Instead, they can declare and use enumeration variable like that of primitive data types as used before.

Valid Enum Declarations

We can declare enum's as below:

> Inside a class
> Outside a class
> In its own file

Invalid Enum Declarations

> Inside a method.

› Inside a block

If you try to declare an enum inside a method or block then compile time error will show up.

Applicable modifiers

› enum is implicitly final so `final` is not allowed, and abstract is not applicable for final types hence "abstract" is not allowed.
› If enum declared outside of a class or within its own file then applicable modifiers are: public, default and strictfp.
› If enum declared inside a class then applicable modifiers are: public, default, strictfp + private, protected, static.

Enum Declaration

Method 1: Where enum is declared outside any class (*Enum1.java - Lines 01 - 04*)

```
01  enum Day
02  {
03      SUNDAY, MONDAY, TUESDAY, WEDNESDAY, THURSDAY, FRIDAY, SATURDAY;
04  }
05  public class Enum1 {
06      // Driver Method
07      public static void main(String[] args){
08          Day d1 = Day.MONDAY;
09          System.out.println(d1);
10      }
11  }
```

Output:

```
MONDAY
```

Method 2: Where enum is declared inside a class (*Enum2.java - Lines 02 - 05*)

```
01  public class Enum2 {
02      enum  Day
03      {
04          SUNDAY, MONDAY, TUESDAY, WEDNESDAY, THURSDAY, FRIDAY, SATURDAY;
05      }
06      // Driver Method
07      public static void main(String[] args){
08          Day d1 = Day.FRIDAY;
09          System.out.print(d1);
10      }
11  }
```

Output

```
FRIDAY
```

According to Java naming conventions, it is recommended that we name constant with all capital letters. The example declaration creates an enumerated data type named **Day**. The identifiers SUNDAY, MONDAY,...etc, which are listed inside the braces, are known as **enum constants**. They represent the values that belong to the **Day** data type.

Declare a variables of the enumerated data type

Once you have created an enumerated data type in your programs, you can declare variables of that type. For example, declares **workDay** as a variable of the **Day** data type:

```
Day workDay;
```

Because **workDay** is a **Day** variable, the only values that we legally assign to it are the enum constants (Day.SUNDAY, Day.MONDAY, Day.TUESDAY, Day.WEDNESDAY, Day.THURSDAY, Day.FRIDAY and Day.SATURDAY)

If you try to assign any value other than one of the Day type's enum constants, a compiler error will result. For example:

```
Day workDay = Day.FRIDAY;  // right
Day workDay = FRIDAY;      // wrong
```

Assigns the value Day.WEDNESDAY instead of just WEDNESDAY. Under most circumstances you must use the fully qualified name of an enum constant.

Example 17.1: Declaring a variable workDay of the enumerated data type Day inside a method (*Enum2.java - Line 08*)

```
01  public class Enum2 {
02      enum  Day
03      {
04          SUNDAY, MONDAY, TUESDAY, WEDNESDAY, THURSDAY, FRIDAY, SATURDAY;
05      }
06      // Driver Method
07      public static void main(String[] args){
08          Day workDay = Day.WEDNESDAY;
09          System.out.print(workDay);
10      }
11  }
```

Output

```
WEDNESDAY
```

Explanation

> Line 02: Creating an Enum data type named **Day** inside an *Enum2* class.

> Line 04: Defines the values for the **Day** data type.
> Line 08: Create a variable named **workdDay** of type **Day**, and assign it a value Day.WEDNESDAY.
> Line 09: Displaying the value of the **workdDay** variable on the screen by sending the **workdDay** variable to the `print(workDay)` method as an argument. When you send a variable name to the `println()` method, the variable's contents are displayed on the screen.

Enumerated Types are Specialized Classes

In Java, we can also add variables, methods and constructors to enumerated types. First line inside enum should be list of constants and then other things like methods, variables and constructor.

When you write an enumerated type declaration, you are actually creating a special kind of class. Every enum internally implemented by using class.

Enum simplifies developer job by simplifying the lengthy code, and follows below steps internally:

> Every enum constant is internally implemented using a class.
> Every enum constant is internally "public static final"
> Every enum constant is Enum (class) declaration represents an object of the Type Enum.

Consider below example and see how it will converted internally:

```
enum Day
{
    SUNDAY, MONDAY, TUESDAY, WEDNESDAY, THURSDAY, FRIDAY, SATURDAY;
}
```

Above Enum declaration will be internally converted as below:

```
/* Internally above enum Day is converted to class Day */
class Day
{
    public static final Day SUNDAY = new Day();
    public static final Day MONDAY = new Day();
    public static final Day TUESDAY = new Day();
    public static final Day WEDNESDAY = new Day();
    public static final Day THURSDAY = new Day();
    public static final Day FRIDAY = new Day();
    public static final Day SATURDAY = new Day();
}
```

In addition, the enum constants that you list inside the braces are actually objects of the class. In Previous example, `Day` is a class, and the enum constants `Day.SUNDAY`, `Day.MONDAY`,…etc are all instances of the `Day` class. When we assigned `Day.WEDNESDAY` to the **workDay** variable, we are assigning the address of the `Day.WEDNESDAY` object to the variable. The **workDay** variable holds the addresses of the `Day.WEDENSDAY` object.

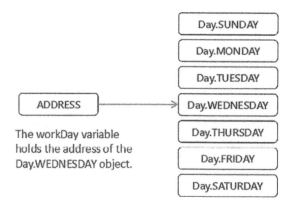

Figure 17.2 | The workDay variable holds the address of the Day.WEDNESDAY object

---

NOTE: Every enum constant is always implicitly `public static final`. Since it is static, we can access it by using enum name. Since it is final, we can't create child enums.

We can declare `main()` method inside enum. Hence, we can invoke enum directly from the command prompt.

Example 17.2: Enum3.java

```
01  package Enum;
02  /* A Java program to demonstrate that we can have main()
    inside enum class. */
03  enum Color
04  {
05      RED, GREEN, BLUE;
06      // Driver method
07      public static void main(String[] args)
08      {
09          Color c1 = Color.RED;
10          System.out.println(c1);
11      }
12  }
```

Output
```
RED
```

toString(), values(), ordinal() and valueOf() methods

The toString method

enum constants, which are actually objects, come automatically equipped with a few methods. One of them is the `toString` method. The `toString` method simply returns the name of the calling **enum** constant as a String.

Example 17.3: Assuming that the Day data type has been declared as previously shown, both of the following code segments display the string **WEDNESDAY**

Recall that the `toString` method is simplicity called when an object is passed to `System.out.println()`;

```
// This code displays WEDENSDAY
Day workDay = Day.WEDENSDAY;
System.out.println(workDay);
// This code also display WEDENSDAY
System.out.println(Day.WEDENSDAY);
```

The ordinal method

The `ordinal` method returns an integer value representing the constant's `ordinal` value. The constant's `ordinal` value is its position in the enum declaration, with the first constant being at position **0**.

Figure 17.3 | The Day enumerated data type and the ordinal positions of its enum constants

Example 17.4: Assuming that the Day data type has been declared as previously shown:
```
Day lastWorkDay = Day.FRIDAY;
System.out.println(lastWorkDay.ordinal());  // 5
System.out.println(Day.MONDAY.ordinal());   // 1
```

output
```
5
1
```

The values method

The `values` method returns an array that contains a list of all enumeration constants.

Example 17.5: EnumValues.java - Java program to demonstrate working of *values* method

```java
01  enum Day
02  {
03      SUNDAY, MONDAY, TUESDAY, WEDNESDAY, THURSDAY, FRIDAY, SATURDAY;
04  }
05  public class EnumValues {
06
07      public static void main(String[] args)
08      {
09          // Calling values() method
10          Day arr[] = Day.values();
11
12          // enum with loop
13          for (Day day: arr)
14          {
15              // Calling ordinal() to find index of Day
16              System.out.println(day + " at index " + day.ordinal());
17          }
18          // Using valueOf(). Returns an object of Day with given constant
19          System.out.println(Day.valueOf("MONDAY"));
20      }
21  }
```

Output

```
SUNDAY at index 0
MONDAY at index 1
TUESDAY at index 2
WEDNESDAY at index 3
THURSDAY at index 4
FRIDAY at index 5
SATURDAY at index 6
MONDAY
```

The last enumerated data type methods that we will discuss here are `equals` and `compareTo`.

The equals method

The `equals` method accepts an object as its argument and returns true if that object is equal to the calling enum constant.

Example 17.6: EnumEquals.java

Assuming that the **Day** data type has been declared as previously shown, the following code segment will display "SAME."

```
01  package ch17;
02
03  enum Day2
04  {
05      SUNDAY, MONDAY, TUESDAY, WEDNESDAY, THURSDAY, FRIDAY, SATURDAY;
06  }
07  public class EnumEquals {
08      public static void main(String[] args){
09          Day2 anyDay = Day2.TUESDAY;
10          if (anyDay.equals(Day2.TUESDAY)) {
11              System.out.println("SAME");
12          } else {
13              System.out.println("NOT SAME");
14          }
15      }
16  }
```

Output

    SAME

Explanation

> `equals` method accepts a `Day.TUESDAY` as its argument and return true. Why? Because the `Day.TUESDAY` object is equal to the **anyDay** variable's value, which is also `Day.TUESDAY`.

Example 17.7: EnumEquals2.java

```
01  enum Languages {
02      Arabic, English, Spanish, Hindi, Russian, French;
03  }
04
05  public class EnumEquals2 {
06      public static void main(String[] args){
07          Languages l1, l2, l3, l4, l5, l6;
08          l1 = Languages.Arabic;
09          l2 = Languages.English;
10          l3 = Languages.Spanish;
11          l4 = Languages.Hindi;
12          l5 = Languages.Russian;
13          l6 = Languages.French;
14
15          if (l1.equals(l2)){
16              System.out.println(l1 + " is equal to " + l2);
17          }else if (l2.equals(l3)){
18              System.out.println(l2 + " is equal to " + l3);
19          }else if (l3.equals(l4)){
20              System.out.println(l3 + " is equal to " + l4);
```

```
21              }else if (14.equals(15)){
22                  System.out.println(14 + " is equal to " + 15);
23              }else if (15.equals(16)){
24                  System.out.println(15 + " is equal to " + 16);
25              }else {
26                  System.out.println("All 6 languages are different");
27          }
28      }
29  }
```

Output

```
All 6 Languages are different
```

The compareTo() method

The `compareTo()` method is designed to compare **enum** constants of the same type. It accepts an object as its argument and returns the following:

› A negative integer value if the calling enum constant's ordinal value is less that the argument's ordinal value.
› Zero if the calling enum constant is the same as the argument.
› A positive integer value if the calling enum constant's ordinal value is greater than the argument's ordinal value.

Here is a simple example.

Example 17.8: EnumCompare.java - Assuming that the Day data type has been declared as previously shown, the following code segment will display **"FRIDAY is greater than SUNDAY"**.

```
01  package ch17;
02
03  enum Day3
04  {
05      SUNDAY, MONDAY, TUESDAY, WEDNESDAY, THURSDAY, FRIDAY, SATURDAY;
06  }
07  public class EnumCompare {
08      public static void main(String[] args){
09          Day3 anyDay = Day3.TUESDAY;
10          if (anyDay.compareTo(Day3.FRIDAY) > 0) {
11              System.out.println(anyDay + " is greater than " + Day3.FRIDAY);
12          } else {
13              System.out.println(anyDay + " is less than " + Day3.FRIDAY);
14          }
15      }
16  }
```

Output
```
TUESDAY is less than FRIDAY
```

Once place to declare an enumerated type inside a class. If you declare an enumerated type inside a class, it cannot be inside a method. The following example demonstrates that concept.

Example 17.9: EnumColors.java

```
01  public class EnumColors {
02      // Declare the Color enumerated type
03      enum Color
04      {
05          RED, ORANGE, PINK, YELLOW, BLUE, BROWN, GREEN ,PURPLE;
06      }
07      public static void main(String[] args){
08          // Declare a Color variable and assign it a value
09          Color color = Color.RED;
10
11          // The following statement displays RED
12          System.out.println(color);
13
14          // The following statement displays the ordinal value for
15          // Color.ORANGE, which is 1
16          System.out.println("The ordinal value for " +
17                      Color.ORANGE + " is " +
              Color.ORANGE.ordinal());
18
19          // The following statement displays the ordinal
20          // value for Color.PURPLE, which is 7
21          System.out.println("The ordinal value for "
22                      + Color.PURPLE + " is " +
              Color.PURPLE.ordinal());
23
24          // The following statement compares two enum constants
25          if (Color.ORANGE.compareTo(Color.PURPLE) > 0)
26          {
27              System.out.println(Color.ORANGE + " is greater than "
28                                  + Color.PURPLE);
29          }else {
30              System.out.println(Color.ORANGE + " is NOT greater than "
31                                  + Color.PURPLE);
32          }
33      }
34  }
```

Output
```
RED
The ordinal value for ORANGE is 1
The ordinal value for PURPLE is 7
ORANGE is NOT greater than PURPLE
```

Writing Enumerated Type Inside Its Own File

You can also write an enumerated type declaration inside its own file. If you do, the file name must match the name of the type. For example, if we stored the **Day** type in its own file, we must name the file `Day.java`. This make sense because enumerated data types are specialized classes.

The following example demonstrate that concept.

Example 17.10: Day4.java

```
01  package ch17;
02  enum Day4 {SUNDAY, MONDAY, TUESDAY, WEDNESDAY, THURSDAY,
    FRIDAY, SATURDAY;}
```

The `Day4.java` program contains the declaration of an enumerated data type named **Day4**. When it compiled, a byte code file name `Day4.class` will be generated.

Here, the `Day4Demo` program use the `Day4` enumerated data type.

Example 17.11: Day4Demo.java

Uses these enumerated types.

```
01  package ch17;
02
03  public class Day4Demo {
04      private Day4 d1;
05      // Driver Method
06      public static void main(String[] args){
07          Day4 d1 = Day4.MONDAY;
08          System.out.println(d1);
09      }
10  }
```

Output

```
MONDAY
```

Switching On an Enumerated Type

Java allows you to test an enum constant with a switch statement.

Example 17.12: EnumSwitch.java - Passing an enum type as an argument to switch statement

```
01  package ch17;
02
```

```java
enum Day5
{
    SUNDAY, MONDAY, TUESDAY, WEDNESDAY, THURSDAY, FRIDAY, SATURDAY;
}
// Driver class that contains an object of 'Day' and main()
public class EnumSwitch {
    private Day5 day;

    // Constructor
    public EnumSwitch(Day5 day){
        this.day = day;
    }

    // Prints a line about day using switch
    public void Day5IsLike()
    {
        switch (day)
        {
            case MONDAY:
                System.out.println("Mondays are bad");
                break;
            case FRIDAY:
                System.out.println("Fridays are better");
                break;
            case SATURDAY:
            case SUNDAY:
                System.out.println("Weekends are best.");
                break;
            default:
                System.out.println("Midweek days are so-so.");
                break;
        }
    }

    // Driver method
    public static void main(String[] args)
    {
        String str = "MONDAY";
        EnumSwitch enumSwitch = new EnumSwitch(Day5.valueOf(str));
        enumSwitch.Day5IsLike();
    }
}
```

Output

```
Mondays are bad
```

Explanation

› The switch statement tests the value of the **day** variable.
› Based upon the value of the **day**, the program then branches to the appropriate case statement.

Enum with Customized Value in Java

By default enums have their own string values, we can also assign some custom values to enums. Consider below example for that.

Example 17.13: EnumFruits.java
```
enum Fruits
{
    LIME("GREEN"), BANANA("YELLOW"), APPLE("RED");
}
```

In above example we can see that the `Fruits` enum have three members i.e LIME, BANANA and APPLE witch have their own different custom values GREEN, YELLOW and RED respectively. Now to use this enum in code, follow the below example:

Example 17.14: EnumFruits.java - Full Code
```
01  // Java Program to demonstrates how values can be assigned to enums
02  enum Fruits
03  {
04      // This will call enum constructor with one string argument
05      LIME("GREEN"), BANANA("YELLOW"), APPLE("RED");
06
07      // declaring private variable for getting values
08      private String fruitCode;
09
10      // getter method
11      public String getFruitCode()
12      {
13          return this.fruitCode;
14      }
15
16      // enum constructor- cannot be public or protected
17      private Fruits (String Code)
18      {
19          this.fruitCode = Code;
20      }
21  }
22  // Driver code
23  public class EnumFruits {
24
25      public static void main(String[] args){
26          Fruits fr = Fruits.APPLE;
27          System.out.println(fr.getFruitCode());
28
```

```
            Fruits fr2 = Fruits.BANANA;
            System.out.println(fr2.getFruitCode());
31
            Fruits fr3 = Fruits.LIME;
            System.out.println(fr3.getFruitCode());
        }
    }
```

Output
```
RED
YELLOW
GREEN
```

Explanation

> - As you can see in this example we have a field `fruitCode` for each of the constant (Line 08), along with a method `getFruitCode()` which is basically a getter method for this field (Line 11).
> - When we define a constant like this `APPLE("RED")`, it calls the enum constructor (Line 17 - `Fruits`) with the passed argument. This way the passed value is set as a value for the field of the corresponding enum's constant (RED, GREEN and YELLOW)
> - [APPLE("RED") => Would call constructor `Fruits("RED")`
>   => this.fruitCode = code
>   => this.fruitCode = "RED"
>   => fruitCode field of constant APPLE is set to "RED"].

IMPORTANT

☐ We have to create parameterized constructor for this enum class. Why? Because as we know that enum class's object can't be create explicitly, so for initializing we use parametermized constructor. And the constructor cannot be the `public` or `protected`, it must have `private` or `default` modifiers. Why? If we create public or protected, it will allow initializing more than one objects. This is totally against enum concept.

☐ We have to create one getter method to get the value of enums.

☐ While defining Enums, the constants should be declared first, prior to any fields or methods.

☐ When there are fields and methods declared inside Enum, the list of enum constants must end with a semicolon (;).

Where You Use Java Enums

Enums are usually used when using constants. They act as providing a type for the constant, instead of leaving them 'loose' as ints or strings like it was being done before they were introduced.

Instead of saying:

```
public static final int MALE = 1;
public static final int FEMALE = 2;
```

You can say:

```
public enum Gender
{
    MALE, FEMALE;
}
```

and refer to them as `Gender.MALE` and `Gender.FEMALE`. Enums provide a clear and easy way in such situations.

The finalize Method

> - If a class has a method named `finalize`, it is called automatically just before an instance of the class is destroyed by the garbage collector.
> - If you wish to execute code just before an object is destroyed, you can create a `finalize` method in the class and place the code there.
> - The `finalize` method accepts no arguments and has a `void` return type.
>
> **NOTE:** The garbage collector runs periodically, and you cannot predict exactly when it will execute. Therefore you cannot know exactly when an object's `finalize` method will execute.

Summary

> - An enumerated data type consists of a group of named constants.

- Enums are used when we know all possible values at compile time.
- The main objective of enum is to define our own data types (Enumerated Data Types).
- You can use the data type to create variables that can hold only the values that belong to the enumerated data type.
- The enum constants are not enclosed in quotation marks, therefore they are not strings, enum constant must be legal Java identifiers.
- In Java, we can also add variables, methods and constructors to the enumerated data type. First line inside enum should be list of constants and then other things like methods, variables and constructor.
- Every enum constant is always implicitly `public static final`. Since it is `static`, we can access it by using enum name. Since it is `final`, we can't create child enums.
- The `toString` method simply returns the name of the calling enum constant as a String.
- The `ordinal` method returns an integer value representing the constant's ordinal value. The constant's ordinal value is its position in the enum declaration, with the first constant being at position 0.
- `values` method can be used to return all values present inside enum.
- The `equals` method accepts an object as its argument and returns true if that object is equal to the calling enum constant.
- The `compareTo` method is designed to compare enum constants of the same type.
- You can also write an enumerated type declaration inside its own file. If you do, the file name must match the name of the type.
- Java allows you to test an enum constant with a `switch` statement.
- If a class has a method named `finalize`, it is called automatically just before an instance of the class is destroyed by the garbage collector.

Chapter 18

The **this** Reference Variable

Introduction

The `this` keyword is the name of a reference variable that an object can use to refer to itself. It is available to all non-static methods. You can refer to any member of the current object from within an instance method or a constructor by using **this**.[1]

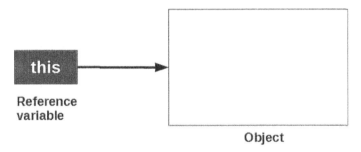

Figure 18.1 | this is a reference variable that refers to the current object.

Usage of java this keyword[2]

Here is given the 6 usage of java this keyword.

> `this` can be used to refer current class instance variable.
> `this` can be used to invoke current class method (implicitly)
> `this()` can be used to invoke current class constructor.
> `this` can be passed as an argument in the method call.
> `this` can be passed as argument in the constructor call.

---
[1] https://docs.oracle.com/javase/tutorial/java/javaOO/thiskey.html
[2] https://docs.oracle.com/javase/tutorial/java/javaOO/thiskey.html

> `this` can be used to return the current class instance from the method.

Suggestion: If you are beginner to java, lookup only three usage of this keyword.

Using this to Overcome Shadowing

Using `this` with a field

One common use of the `this` keyword is to overcome the shadowing of a field name by a parameter name. Remember, if a method's parameter has the same name as a field in the same class, then the parameter name shadows the field name. Let's see an example for that.

Example 18.1: Square.java Class - without `this`
```
01 public class Square {
02    public int x = 10;
03    public int y = 10;
04
05    //constructor
06    public Square(int a, int b) {
07       x = a;
08       y = b;
09    }
10 }
```

Example 18.2: Square2.java Class - with `this`
```
01 public class Square2 {
02    public int x = 0;
03    public int y = 0;
04
05    //constructor
06    public Square2(int x, int y) {
07       this.x = x;
08       this.y = y;
09    }
10 }
```

Each argument to the constructor shadows one of the object's fields — inside the constructor `x` is a local copy of the constructor's first argument. To refer to the Square field `x`, the constructor must use `this.x`.

Using `this` to Call an Overloaded Constructor from Another Constructor

Recall that a constructor is automatically called when an object is created. You cannot call a constructor explicitly, as you do with other methods.

There is one exception to this rule, you can use the `this` keyword to call one constructor from another constructor in the same class. Consider below example for that.

Example 18.3: Shape.java
```
01 public Shape(int l, int w)
02 {
03    length = l;
04    width = w;
05 }
```

This constructor accepts arguments that are assigned to the `length` and `width` fields.

Suppose we also want a constructor that only accepts an argument for the length field and assigns 0.0 to the width field. For example 18.4:

```
01 public Shape (int l)
02 {
03    this(l, 0.0);
04 }
```

This constructor uses the `this` variable to call the first constructor. It passes the value in l as the first argument and `0.0` as the second argument. The result is that the `length` field is assigned the value in l and the `width` field is assigned 0.0.

From within a constructor, you can also use the `this` keyword to call another constructor in the same class. Doing so is called an **Explicit Constructor Invocation**.[1]

Example 18.5: Square3.java
```
01 public class Square3 {
02    private int x, y;
03    private int width, height;
04
05    public Square3() {
06       this(0, 0, 1, 1);
```

---
[1] https://docs.oracle.com/javase/tutorial/java/javaOO/thiskey.html

```
07    }
08    public Square3(int width, int height) {
09      this(0, 0, width, height);
10    }
11    public Square3(int x, int y, int width, int height) {
12      this.x = x;
13      this.y = y;
14      this.width = width;
15      this.height = height;
16    }
17 }
```

This class contains a set of constructors. Each constructor initializes some or all of the `square3`'s member variables. The constructors provide a default value for any member variable whose initial value is not provided by an argument.

For example, the no-argument constructor creates a 1x1 Square at coordinates 0,0. The two-argument constructor calls the four-argument constructor, passing in the `width` and `height` but always using the 0,0 coordinates. As before, the compiler determines which constructor to call, based on the number and the type of arguments. If present, the invocation of another constructor must be the first line in the constructor.

Rules about using `this` to call a constructor

> `this` can only be used to call a constructor from another constructor in the same class.

> It must be the first statement in the constructor that is making the call. If it is not the first statement, a compiler error will result.

Chapter 19

Text Processing and Wrap Classes

Introduction to Wrap Classes

Recall that the primitive data types are called primitive because they are not created from classes, and variables do not have attributes or methods. They are designed simply to hold a single value in memory.

Java provides wrapper classes for all of the primitive data types. A wrapper class is a class that is **"wrapped around"** a primitive data type and allows you to create objects instead of variables.

The wrapper class for a given primitive type contains not only a value of that type, but also methods that perform operations related to the type. For example, you have already used the wrapper class "parse" methods to convert strings to primitive values.

Although these wrapper classes can be used to create objects instead of variables, few programmers use them that way. Why?

> Because the wrapper classes are immutable, which means that once you create an object, you cannot change the object's value.
> Because they are not as easy to use as variables for simple operations.

For example; to get the value stored in an object you must call a method, whereas variables can be used directly in assignment statements, mathematical operations, passed as arguments to methods, and so forth.

Although it is not normally useful to create objects from the wrapper classes, they do provide static methods that are very useful.

We begin by looking at the character class, which is the wrapper class for the char data type.

Character Testing and Conversion with the `Character` Class

The `Character` class is a wrapper class for the `char` data type. It provides numerous methods for testing and converting character data. The `Character` class is part of the `java.lang` package, so no import statement is necessary to use this class.

This class provides several static methods for testing the value of a `char` variable. Some of these methods are listed in next table. Each of the methods accepts a single `char` argument and returns a `boolean` value.

Table 19.1 | Some Static Character Class Methods for Testing Char Values

Method	Description
`boolean isDigit(char ch)`	Returns true if the argument passed into ch is a digit from 0 through 9. Otherwise returns false.
`boolean isLetter(char ch)`	Returns true if the argument passed into ch is an alphabetic letter. Otherwise returns false.
`boolean isLetterOrDigit(char ch)`	Returns true if the character passed into ch contains a digit (0 through 9) or an alphabetic letter. Otherwise returns false.
`boolean isLowerCase(char ch)`	Returns true if the argument passed into ch is a lowercase letter. Otherwise returns false.
`boolean isUpperCase(char ch)`	Returns true if the argument passed into ch is an uppercase letter. Otherwise returns false.
`boolean isSpaceChar(char ch)`	Returns true if the argument passed into ch is a space character. Otherwise returns false.
`boolean isWhiteSpace(char ch)`	Returns true if the argument passed into ch is a whitespace character (a space, tab, or newline character). Otherwise returns false.

Below is an example of a program that uses the `Character` class and the static method `isLetter()`.

Example 19.1: CharacterTest.java

```
01  package ch19;
02  import java.util.Scanner;
03
04  public class CharacterTest
05  {
06      public static void main(String[] args)
07      {
08          String input;   // To hold the user's input
09          char ch;        // To hold a single character
10
11          // Get a character from the user and store
12          // it in the ch variable.
13          Scanner sc = new Scanner(System.in);
14          System.out.println("Enter any single character");
15          input = sc.nextLine();
16          ch = input.charAt(0);
17
18          // Test the character.
19          if (Character.isLetter(ch))
20          {
21              System.out.println("That is a letter.");
22          }
23
24          if (Character.isDigit(ch))
25          {
26              System.out.println("That is a digit.");
27          }
28      }
29  }
```

Output
```
Enter any single character
r
That is a letter.
```

Below is an example of a program that tests a string to determine whether it is a 7 character customer number - in the proper format - or not.

Example 19.2: CustomerNumber.java

```
01  package ch19;
02
03  import java.util.Scanner;
04
05  public class CustomerNumber
06  {
07      public static void main(String[] args)
08      {
09          String input;   // To hold the user's input
10
11          // Get a customer number.
12          Scanner sc = new Scanner(System.in);
```

```java
13              System.out.println("Enter a customer number in the form LLLNNNN\n" +
14                      "(LLL = Letters and NNNN = numbers");
15              input = sc.nextLine();
16
17
18              // Validate the input.
19              if (isValid(input))
20              {
21                  System.out.println("That's a valid customer number.");
22              }
23              else
24              {
25                  System.out.println("That is not the proper format of a " +
26                          "customer number.\nHere is an example: ABC1234");
27              }
28          }
29
30          private static boolean isValid(String custNumber)
31          {
32              boolean goodSoFar = true;   // Flag
33              int i = 0;                  // Control variable
34
35              // Test the length.
36              if (custNumber.length() != 7)
37                  goodSoFar = false;
38
39              // Test the first three characters for letters.
40              while (goodSoFar && i < 3)
41              {
42                  if (!Character.isLetter(custNumber.charAt(i)))
43                      goodSoFar = false;
44                  i++;
45              }
46
47              // Test the last four characters for digits.
48              while (goodSoFar && i < 7)
49              {
50                  if (!Character.isDigit(custNumber.charAt(i)))
51                      goodSoFar = false;
52                  i++;
53              }
54              return goodSoFar;
55          }
56      }
```

Explanation

> It tests a string to determine whether it is a seven-character customer number in the proper format.

> The Customer number is expected to be 7 characters long and consist of 3 alphabetic letters followed by 4 numeric digits.
> The `isValid` method accepts a String argument, which will be tested.
> The method uses the following local variables, which are declared in Lines 32 and 33:
> ```
> boolean goodSoFar = true ; //flag
> int i=0; // control variable.
> ```
> The `goodFar` variable is a `flag` variable that is initialized with **true**, but will be set to **false** immediately when the method determines the customer number is not in a valid format. The (i) variable is a loop control variable.
> The first test is to determine whether the string is the correct length. In `Line 36` the method tests the length of the `CustNumber` argument. If the argument is not 7 characters long, it is not valid and the `goodSoFar` variable is set to false in `Line 37`.
> Next, the method uses the following loop in `Lines 40 to 45`, to variable the first 3 characters.
> Recall that the String class's `charAt` method returns a character at a specific position in a string (position numbering starts at 0). This code uses the `Character.isLetter` method to test the character at position 0, 1, and 2 in the `custNumber` String. If any of these characters are not letters, the `goodSoFar` variable is set to `false` and the loop terminates.
> Next, the method uses the following loop, in `Lines 48/53`, to validate the last 4 characters. This code uses the `character.isDigit` method to test the characters at position 3, 4, 5, & 6 in the `CustNumber` string. If any of these characters are not digits, the `goodSoFar` variable is set to `false`, and loop terminates. Last, the method returns the value of the `goodSoFar` method.

Character case conversion

The `character` class also provides the static methods.

Table 19.2 | Some Character Class Methods for Case Conversion (Each method accepts a char argument and return a char value)

Method	Description
`char toLowerCase(char ch)`	Returns the lowercase equivalent of the argument passed to ch.
`char toUpperCase(char ch)`	Returns the uppercase equivalent of the argument passed to ch.

If the `toLowerCase` method's argument is an uppercase character, the method returns the lowercase equivalent.

Example 19.3: Display the character "a" on the screen
```
System.out.println(Character.toLowerCase('A'));
```

If the argument is already lowercase, the `toLowerCase` method returns it unchanged.

Example 19.4: Display the character 'A' on the screen
```
System.out.println(Character.toUpperCase('a'));
```

Explanation

› If the `toUpperCase` method's argument is a lowercase character, the method returns the uppercase equivalent. Ex: Display the character A on the screen:
```
System.out.println(character.toUpperCase('a'));
```
› If the argument is already uppercase, the `toUpperCase` method returns it unchanged.

Any non-letter argument passed to `toLowerCase` or `toUpperCase` is returned as it is. Each of the following statements displays the method argument without any change:
```
System.out.println(Character.toLowerCase('*'));
System.out.println(Character.toLowerCase('$'));
System.out.println(Character.toLowerCase('&'));
System.out.println(Character.toLowerCase('%'));
```

The following example calculates and displays an area of a circle.

Example 19.5: CircleArea.java
```
01   import java.util.Scanner;
02   import java.text.DecimalFormat;
03
04   public class CircleArea
05   {
06      public static void main(String[] args)
07      {
08         double radius;   // The circle's radius
09         double area;     // The circle's area
10         String input;    // To hold a line of input
11         char choice;     // To hold a single character
12
13         // Create a Scanner object to read keyboard input.
14         Scanner keyboard = new Scanner(System.in);
15
16         // Create a DecimalFormat object.
17         DecimalFormat fmt = new DecimalFormat("0.00");
18
19         do
```

```
            {
                // Get the circle's radius.
                System.out.print("Enter the circle's " +
                                 "radius: ");
                radius = keyboard.nextDouble();

                // Consume the remaining newline character.
                keyboard.nextLine();
28
                // Calculate and display the area.
                area = Math.PI * radius * radius;
                System.out.println("The area is " +
                                   fmt.format(area));
33
                // Repeat this?
                System.out.print("Do you want to do this " +
                                 "again? (Y or N) ");
                input = keyboard.nextLine();
                choice = input.charAt(0);
39
            } while (Character.toUpperCase(choice) == 'Y');
        }
    }
```

Output
```
Enter the circle's radius: 12
The area is 452.39
Do you want to do this again? (Y or N) n
Process finished with exit code 0
```

Searching For SubStrings

The `String` class provides several methods for searching and working with String objects. The `String` class provides several methods that search for a sting inside of a string. The term "substring" commonly is used to refer to a string that is part of another string.

Table 19.3 | String methods that search for a substring

Method	Description
boolean startsWith(String str)	This method returns true if the calling string begins with the string passed into str.
boolean endsWith(String str)	The method returns true if the calling string ends with the string passed into str.
boolean regionMatches(int start, String str, int start2, int n)	This method returns true if a specified region of the calling string matches a specified region of the string passed into str. The start parameter indicates the starting position of the region within the calling string. The start2 parameter indicates the starting position of the region within str. The n parameter indicates the number of characters in both regions.
boolean regionMatches(Boolean ignoreCase, int start, String str, int start2, int n)	This overloaded version of the regionMatches method has an additional parameter, ignoreCase, If true is passed into this parameter, the method ignores the case of the calling string and str when comparing the regions. If false is passed into the ignoreCase parameter, the comparison is case-sensitive.

Each of the methods returns a boolean value indicating whether the string was found. Let's take a closer look at each of these methods.

The `startsWith` & `endsWith` Methods

The `startsWith` method determines whether the calling object's string begins with a specified substring.

Example 19.6: Determine whether the string "**Four Score and Sever Years Ago**" begins with "four". The method returns true if the string begins with the specified substring, or false otherwise

```
01  String str = "Four Score and Severn Year Ago.";
02  if (str.startsWith("Four"))
03      System.out.println("The string starts with four.");
04  else
05      System.out.println("The string does not start with four");
```

Explanation

> The method call `str.StartsWidth("four")` returns true because the string does begins with "Four".
> The `startsWidth` method performs a case-sensitive comparison, so the method call `str.startsWidth("Four")` would return false.

Example 19.7: Determine whether the string **"Four score and seven years ago"** ends with **"go"**. The method returns true if the string does end with the specified substring or false otherwise

```
01  String str = "Four Score and Severn Year Ago.";
02  if (str.endsWith("Ago"))
03      System.out.println("The string starts with Ago.");
04  else
05      System.out.println("The string does not start with Ago");
```

The `endsWith` method also performs a case-sensitive comparison, so the method `str.endsWith("Ago")` returns **true** because the string does end with **Ago**.

Example 19.8: PersonSearch.java - Display all of the names that begin with the string entered by the user

```
01  package ch19;
02
03  import java.util.Scanner;
04  public class PersonSearch
05  {
06      public static void main(String[] args)
07      {
08          String lookUp;   // To hold a lookup string
09
10          // Create an array of names
11          String[] people = {
12                          "Mohammed, Mansour",
13                          "Davis, George",
14                          "Osman, Ahmed",
15                          "Russert, Phil",
16                          "Russell, Cindy",
17                          "Setzer, Charles",
18                          "Smathers, Holly",
19                          "Smith, Chris",
20                          "Smith, Brad",
21                          "Williams, Jean"
22                      };
23
24          // Create a Scanner object for keyboard input.
25          Scanner keyboard = new Scanner(System.in);
26
27          // Get a partial name to search for.
28          System.out.print("Enter the first few characters of "
                    +
29                  "the last name to look up: ");
30          lookUp = keyboard.nextLine();
31
32          // Display all of the names that begin with the
```

```
33              // string entered by the user.
34              System.out.println("Here are the names that match:");
35              for (String person : people)
36              {
37                  if (person.startsWith(lookUp))
38                      System.out.println(person);
39              }
40          }
41      }
```

Output
```
Enter the first few characters of the last name to look up: M
Here are the names that match:
Mohammed, Mansour
```

The regionMatches() Methods

The String class provides overloaded versions of the `regionMatches`, which determines whether specified regions of two string match. Lets write this example.

Example 19.9: RegionEx.java
```
01  String str = "Four Score and Seven Years Ago.";
02  String str2 = "Those Seven Years Passed Quickly";
03  if (str.regionMatches(15, str2, 6, 11))
04      System.out.println("The regions match.");
05  else
06      System.out.println("The regions do not match.");
```

Output
```
The regions match.
```

Explanation

> The specified region of the **str** string begins at position 15, and the specified region of the **str2** string begins at position 6. Both regions consist of 11 characters.

> The specified region in the **str** string is "seven years" and the specified region in the **str2** string is also "seven years".

> Because the 2 regions match, the `regionMatches` method in this code returns true.

> This version of the `regionMatches` method performs a case-sensitive comparison.

An overloaded version accepts an additional argument indicting whether to perform a case insensitive comparison.

Example 19.10: RegionEx2.java

```
    String str = "Four Score and Seven Years Ago.";
    String str2 = "THOSE SEVEN YEARS PASSED QUICKLY";
    if (str.regionMatches (true, 15, str2, 6, 11))
       System.out.println("The regions match.");
    else
       System.out.println("The regions do not match.");
```

Explanation

Display `"The regions match."`

› The first argument passed to this version of the `regionMatches` method can be true or false, indicating whether a case-insensitive comparison should be performed.

› In this example, `true` is passed, so case will be ignored when the regions "seven years" and "SEVEN YEARS" are compared.

› Each of these methods indicates by a boolean return value whether a substring appears within a string.

› The `String` class also provides methods that not only search for items within a string, but also report the location of those items.

Table 19.4 | String methods for getting a character or substring's location (describes overloaded versions of the indexOf andlatIndexOf methods)

Method	Description
`int indexOf(char ch)`	Searches the calling String object for the character passed into ch. If the character is found, the position of its first occurrence is returned. Otherwise, -1 is returned.
`int indexOf(char ch, int start)`	Searches the calling String object for the character passed into ch, beginning at the position passed into start and going to the end of the string. If the character is found, the position of its first occurrence is returned. Otherwise, -1 is returned.
`int indexOf(String str)`	Searches the calling String object for the string passed into str. If the string is found, the beginning position of its first occurrence is returned. Otherwise, -1 is returned.

`int indexAOf(String str, int start)`	Searches the calling String object for the string passed into str. The search begins at the position passed into start and goes to the end of the string. If the string is found, the beginning position of its first concurrence is returned. Otherwise, -1 is returned.
`int lastIndexOf(char ch)`	Searches the calling String object for the character passed into ch. If the character is found, the position of its last concurrence is returned. Otherwise, -1 is returned.
`int lastIndexOf(char ch, int start)`	Searches the calling String object for the character passed into ch, beginning at the position passed into start. The search is conducted backward through the sting, to position 0. If the character is found, the position of its last occurrence is returned. Otherwise, -1 is returned.
`int lastIndexOf(String str)`	Searches the calling string object for the string passed into str. If the string is found, the beginning position of its last concurrence is returned. Otherwise, -1 is returned.
`int lastIndexOf(String str, int start)`	Searches the calling String object for the string passed into str, beginning at the position passed into start. The search is conducted backward through the string, to position 0. If the string is found, the beginning position of its last occurrence is returned. Otherwise, -1 is returned.

Finding Characters with the `indexOf` and `lastIndexOf` Methods

The `indexOf` and `lastIndexOf` methods can search for either a character or a substring within the calling string. If the item being searched for is found, its position is returned. Otherwise, -1 is returned.

Example 19.11: FindChar.java - Use two of the methods to search for a character

```
01  String str = "Four Score and Seven Year ago";
02  int first, last;
03  first = str.indexOf('r');
04  last = str.lastIndexOf('r');
05  System.out.println("The letter r first appears at " +
06      "position " + first);
07  System.out.println("The letter r last appears at " +
08      "position " + last);
```

Output
```
The letter r first appears at position 3
The letter r last appears at position 24
```

Example 19.12: FindChar2.java - Use a loop to show the positions of each letter 'r' in the string
```
01  String str = "Four Score and Seven Year ago";
02  int position;
03  System.out.println("The letter r appears at the following locations:");
04  position = str.indexOf('r');
05  while (position != -1)
06  {
07      System.out.println(position);
08      position = str.indexOf('r', position + 1);
09  }
```

Output
```
The letter r appears at the following locations:
3
8
24
```

Example 19.13: FindChar3.java - Use the `lastIndexOf` method and shows the position in reverse order
```
01  String str = "Four Score and Seven Year ago";
02  int position;
03  System.out.println("The letter r appears at the following locations:");
04  position = str.lastIndexOf('r');
05  while (position != -1)
06  {
07      System.out.println(position);
08      position = str.indexOf('r', position + 1);
09  }
```

Output
```
The letter r appears at the following locations:
24
```

Finding Substrings with the `indexOf` and `lastIndexOf` methods

The `indexOf` and `lastIndexOf` methods can also search for substrings within a string. Consider below examples for that.

Example 19.14: FindSubStr.java - Displays the starting positions of each occurrence of the word "and" within a string

```
01  String str = "and a one and a two and a three";
02  int position;
03  System.out.println("The word and appears at the following positions:");
04  position = str.indexOf("and");
05  while (position != -1)
06  {
07      System.out.println(position);
08      position = str.indexOf('r', position + 1);
09  }
```

Output
```
The word and appears at the following positions:
0
28
```

Example 19.15: FindSubStr2.java - Displays the same results, but in reverse order

```
01  String str = "and a one and a two and a three";
02  int position;
03  System.out.println("The word and appears at the following positions:");
04  position = str.lastIndexOf("and");
05  while (position != -1)
06  {
07      System.out.println(position);
08      position = str.indexOf('r', position + 1);
09  }
```

Output
```
The word and appears at the following positions:
20
28
```

Extracting SubStrings

The String class provides several methods that allow you to retrieve a substring from a string.

Table 19.5 | String methods for extracting substrings

Method	Description
`String substring(int start)`	This method returns a copy of the substring that begins at start and goes to the end of the calling object's string.
`String substring(int start, int end)`	This method returns a copy of a substring. The argument passed into start is the substring's starting position, and the argument passed into end is the substring's ending position. The character at the start position is included in the substring, but the character at the end position is not included.
`void getChars(int start, int end, char[ ] array, int arrayStart)`	This method extracts a substring from the calling object and stores it in a char array. The argument passed into start is the substring's starting position, and the argument passed into end is the substring's ending position. The character at the start position is included in the substring, but the character at the end position is not included. (The last character in the substring ends at end -1) The characters in the substring are stored as elements in the array that is passed into the array parameter. The arrayStart parameter specifies the starting subsdript withhe characters are to be stored.
`char[ ] toCharArray()`	This method returns all of the characters in the calling objects as a char array.

The substring method

The `substring` method returns a copy of a substring from the calling object. There are two overloaded versions of the method.

› The first version accepts an **int** argument that is the starting position of the substring.
› The method returns a reference to a `String` object containing all of the characters from the starting position to the end of the string.

> The character at the starting positing is part of the substring.

Consider the following example.

Example 19.16: FindSubStr3.java
```
01  String fullName = "Mohammed Abdelmoniem";
02  String lastName = fullName.substring(9);
03  System.out.println("The full name is " + fullName);
04  System.out.println("The last name is " + lastName);
```
Output
```
The full name is Mohammed Abdelmoniem
The full name is Abdelmoniem
```

Keep in mind that the substring method returns a new String object that holds a copy of the substring. When this code executes, the fullName and lastName variables will reference two different String objects.

The fullName and lastName variables reference separate objects.

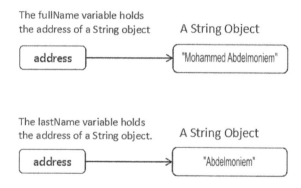

Figure 19.1 | The fullName and lastName variables references separate objects

The second version of the method accepts two int arguments. The first specifies the substring's starting position and the second specifies the substring's ending position. The character at the starting position is included in the substring, but the character at the ending position is not.

Consider the following example.

Example 19.17: FindSubStr4.java
```
01  String fullName = "Mohammed Abdelmoniem";
02  String middleName = fullName.substring(8, 20);
03  System.out.println("The full name is " + fullName);
04  System.out.println("The middle name is " + middleName);
```
Output
```
The full name is Mohammed Abdelmoniem
The middle name is Abdelmoniem
```

The getChars and toCharArray methods

The `getChars` and `toCharArray` methods convert the calling string object to a char array. The `getChars` method can be used to convert a substring, while the `toCharArray` method converts the entire string.

Here is a simple example.

Example 19.18: GetCharEx.java - How the getChars method works

```
   String fullName = "Mohamed Osman Ali";
   char[] nameArray = new char[ ];
   fullName.getChars( ,  , nameArray,  );
   System.out.println("The full name is " + fullName);
   System.out.println("The values in the array are: ");
   for (int i= ; i < nameArray.length ; i++)
       System.out.println(nameArray[i] + " " );
```

Output
```
The full name is Mohamed Osman Ali
The values in the array are:
O
S
M
A
N
```

This code stores the individual characters of the substring "osman" in the elements of the `nameArray` array, beginning at element 0. The `toCharArray` method returns a reference to a **char** array that contains all of the characters in the calling object.

Here is a simple example.

Example 19.19: ToCharEx.java

```
   String fullName = "Mohamed Osman Ali";
   char[] nameArray;
   nameArray = fullName.toCharArray();
   System.out.println("The full name is " + fullName);
   System.out.println("The values in the array are: ");
   for (int i =  ; i < nameArray.length; i++)
       System.out.println(nameArray[i] + " " );
```

Output
```
The full name is Mohamed Osman Ali
The values in the array are:
M
o
h
a
m
```

e
d

O
s
m
a
n

A
l
i

These methods can be used when you want to use an array processing algorithm on the contents of a String object. Consider blow example for that.

Example 19.20: StringAnalyzer.java

```java
01  package ch19;
02
03
04  import java.util.Scanner;
05
06  public class StringAnalyzer
07  {
08      public static void main(String [] args)
09      {
10          String input;           // To hold input
11          char[] array;           // Array for input
12          int letters = 0;        // Number of letters
13          int digits = 0;         // Number of digits
14          int whitespaces = 0;    // Number of whitespaces
15
16          // Get a string from the user.
17          Scanner sc = new Scanner(System.in);
18          System.out.println("Enter a string");
19          input = sc.nextLine();
20
21          // Convert the string to a char array.
22          array = input.toCharArray();
23
24          // Analyze the characters.
25          for (int i = 0; i < array.length; i++)
26          {
27              if (Character.isLetter(array[i]))
28                  letters++;
29              else if (Character.isDigit(array[i]))
30                  digits++;
31              else if (Character.isWhitespace(array[i]))
32                  whitespaces++;
33          }
34
35          // Display the results.
36          System.out.println("That string contains " +
37                  letters + " letters, " +
```

```
                    digits + " digits, and " +
                    whitespaces + " whitespace characters.");
        }
    }
```

Output
```
Enter a string
SUDAN 2019
That string contains 5 letters, 4 digits, and 1 whitespace
characters.
```

Methods That Returns a Modified String

The String class methods returns a modified copy of a String object.

Table 19.6 | Methods that return a modified copy of a String object

Method	Description
String concat(String str)	This method returns a copy of the calling String object with the contents of str concatenated to it.
String replace(char oldChar, char newChar)	This method returns a copy of the calling String object, in which all occurrences of the character passed into oldChar have been replaced by the character passed into newChar.
String trim()	This method returns a copy of the calling String object, in which all leading and trailing whitespace characters have been deleted.

The `concat` method performs the same operation as the `(+)` operator when used with strings.

Example 19.21: ConcatEx1.java - Code uses the + operator
```
01  package ch19;
02
03  public class ConcatEx1 {
04      public static void main(String[] args) {
05          String fullName;
06          String firstName = "Mustafa";
07          String lastName = " Mansour";
08          fullName = firstName + lastName;
09          System.out.println(fullName);
10      }
11  }
```

Output

Mustafa Mansour

Example 19.22: ConcatEx2.java - Equivalent code can also be written with the `concat` method
```
01  public class ConcatEx2 {
02      public static void main(String[] args) {
03          String fullName;
04          String firstName = "Mustafa";
05          String lastName = " Mansour";
06          fullName = firstName.concat(lastName);
07          System.out.println(fullName);
08      }
09  }
```

Output
Mustafa Mansour

The `replace` method returns a copy of a *String* object, where every occurrence of a specified character has been replaced with another character.

Example 19.23: ReplaceEx.java
```
01  public class ReplaceEx {
02      public static void main(String[] args) {
03          String fullName;
04          String firstName = "Mustafa";
05          String lastName = " Mansour";
06          fullName = firstName.concat(lastName);
07
08          // String str1 = "Tom Talbert Tried Trains.";
09          String str1 = "How";
10          String str2;
11          str2 = str1.replace('H', 'N');
12          System.out.println(str1);
13          System.out.println(str2);
14          // The replace method will return a copy of the
15          // 'H' replaced with the letter 'N'
16      }
17  }
```

Output
How
Now

REMEMBER: The `replace` method does not modify the contents of the calling `String` object, but returns a reference to a String that is a modified copy of it.

After execution, the **str1** and **str2** variables will reference different String objects.

The `trim` method returns a copy of a `String` object with all leading and trailing whitespace characters deleted. A leading whitespace character is one that appears at the beginning, left side, of a string. Example: The following string has 3 leading whitespace characters "   Hello".

A trailing whitespace character is one that appears at the end, or right side, of a string after the non-space characters. For example, the following String has three trailing whitespace characters: `"Hello   "`. Consider blow example.

Example 19.24: TrimEx.java

```
public class TrimEx {
    public static void main(String[] args) {
        String greeting1 = "   Hello   ";
        String greeting2;
        greeting2 = greeting1.trim();
        System.out.println("*" + greeting1 + "*");
        System.out.println("*" + greeting2 + "*");
    }
}
```

Output
```
*   Hello   *
*Hello*
```

The first statement assigns the string "   Hello   " (with three leading spaces and three trailing spaces) to the **greeting1** variable. The `trim` method is called, which returns a copy of the string with the leading and trailing spaces removed.

One common use of the `trim` method is to remove any leading or trailing spaces that the user might have entered while inputting data.

The static `valueOf` Methods

This method accepts a value of String type or any primitive data type as its argument and returns a string representation of the value.

Table 19.7 | Some of the String class's valueOf methods

Method	Description
`String valueOf(boolean b)`	Returns the string representation of the `boolean` argument
`String valueOf(char c)`	Returns the string representation of the `char` argument
`String valueOf(char[ ] array)`	Returns the string representation of the `char` array argument

`String valueOf(char[ ] array, int subscript, int count)`	Returns the string representation of a specific subarray of the char array argument
`String valueOf(double number)`	Returns the string representation of the `double` argument
`String valueOf(float number)`	Returns the string representation of the `float` argument
`String valueOf(int number)`	Returns the string representation of the `int` argument
`String valueOf(long number)`	Returns the string representation of the `long` argument

Example 19.25: ValueOf1.java - A `valueOf()` method with primitive type as argument

This form of `valueOf` method takes primitive data type as an argument and returns the string representation of the primitive data type.

```
01  public class ValueOf1 {
02      public static void main(String[] args){
03          int i = 46;
04          float f = 23.5f;
05          double d = 15.4981567;
06          boolean b = true;
07          char c = 'A';
08          char[] letters = {'a','b','c'};
09
10          System.out.println(String.valueOf(i));
11          System.out.println(String.valueOf(f));
12          System.out.println(String.valueOf(d));
13          System.out.println(String.valueOf(b));
14          System.out.println(String.valueOf(c));
15          System.out.println(String.valueOf(letters));
16      }
17  }
```

Output
```
46
23.5
15.4981567
true
A
abc
```

The `StringBuilder` Class

Introduction

› The `StringBuilder` class is similar to the `String` class, except that you may change the contents of `StringBuilder` objects, but you cannot change the contents of the String object.

› The `StringBuilder` class also provides several useful methods that the `String` class does not have.

› Recall that the `String` objects are immutable. This means that once you set the contents of a `String` object, you cannot change the string value that it holds.

Example 19.26:
```
01   String name;
02   name = "George";
03   name = "Sally";
```

Explanation

› The first argument creates the **name** variable.

› The second argument creates a `String` object containing the string `"George"` and assigns its address to the **name** variable.

› Although we can make the **name** variable reference a different `String` object. That's what the third statement does, it creates another `String` object containing the string `"sally"`, and assigns its address to name. The `String` object containing `"George"` is no layer referenced.

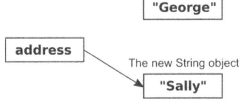

Figure 19.2 | The String object containing "George" is no layer referenced

› Unlike `String` objects, `StringBuilder` objects have methods that allow you to modify their contents without creating a new object in memory.

> You can change specific characters, insert characters, delete characters, and perform other operations.
> The `StringBuilder` object will grow or shrink in size, as needed, to accommodate the changes.
> The fact that `String` objects are immutable is rarely a problem, but you might consider using `StringBuilder` objects if your program needs to make a lot of changes to one or more strings.
> This will improve the program's efficiency by reducing the number of `String` objects the must be created and then removed by the garbage collector.

Now let's look at the `StringBuilder` class's constructor and method.

The `StringBuilder` Constructor

Table 19.8 | `StringBuilder` Constructors

Constructor	Description
`StringBuilder()`	This constructor accepts no arguments. It gives the object enough storage space to hold 16 characters, but no characters are stored in it.
`StringBuilder(int length)`	This constructor gives the object enough storage space to hold length characters, but no characters are stored in it.
`StringBuilder(String str)`	This constructor initializes the object with the string in **str**. The object's initial storage space will be the length of the string plus 16.

The first two constructors create empty `StringBuilder` objects of a specified size. The first constructor makes the `StringBuilder` object large enough to hold 16 characters, and the second constructor makes the object large enough to hold length characters. Remember, `StringBuilder` objects automatically resize themselves, it is not a problem if you later want to store a larger string in the object.

The third constructor accepts a `String` object as its argument and assigns the object's content to the `StringBuilder` object. Consider below exampl.

Example 19.27: StringB.java class
```
01  StringBuilder city = new StringBuilder("Cairo");
02  System.out.println(city);
```

Explanation

> Creates a `StringBuilder` object and assigns its address to the **city** variable.
> The object is initialized with the string "Cairo".
> Pass a `StringBuilder` object to `println` and `print` methods.

One limitation of the `StringBuilder` class is that you cannot use the assignment operator to assign strings to `StringBuilder` objects. For example:

```
StringBuilder city = "Cairo"; // Error! Will not work.
```

Instead of using the assignment operator (=), you must use the **new** keyword and a constructor, or use one of the `StringBuilder` methods, to store a string in a `StringBuilder` object.

Other `StringBuilder` Methods

The `StringBuilder` class provides many of the same methods as the String class. In addition, the `StringBuilder` class provides several methods that the `String` class does not have. Let's look at a few of them.

The `append` Methods

> The `StringBuilder` class has several overloaded versions of a method named `append`.
> These methods accept an argument, which may be of any primitive data type, a `char` array, or a `String` object.
> They append a string representation of their argument for the calling object's current contents.

Because there are so many overloaded versions of `append`, we will examine the general form of a typical call to the method as follows:

```
object.append(item);
```

After the method is called, a string representation of item will be appended to objects contents. Consider below example for that.

Example 19.28: AppendEx.java - Some of the `append` method being used

```
01  public class AppendEx {
02      public static void main(String[] args) {
03          StringBuilder str = new StringBuilder();
04
05          // Append values to the object
06          str.append("We Sold ");          // Append a String object
07          str.append(12);                   // Append an int.
08          str.append(" doubhnuts for $");   // Append another string
```

```
09          str.append(15.95);            // Append a double
10
11          // Display the object's contents
12          System.out.println(str);
13      }
14 }
```

Output
```
We Sold 12 doubhnuts for $15.95
```

The `insert` Methods

The `StringBuilder` class also has several overloaded versions of a method named `insert`, which inserts a value into the calling object's string. These methods accept two arguments:

› An `int` that specifies the position in the calling object's string where the insertion should begin &

› The `value` to be inserted. The value to be inserted may be of any primitive data type, a char array ,or a `String` object.

Because there are so many overloaded versions of `insert`, we will examine the general form of a typical call to the method as follows:

`object.insert(start, item);`

› `start` is the starting position of the insertion and
› `item` is the item to be inserted.

Here is a simple example.

Example 19.29: InsertEx.java - Some of the `insert` methods being used
```
01 public class InsertEx {
02     public static void main(String[] args) {
03         StringBuilder str = new StringBuilder("July sold cars.");
04         char[] array = {'w', 'e', ' '};
05
06         // Insert values to the object
07         str.insert(0 , "in ");        // insert a String object
08         str.insert(8, array);         // insert a char array
09         str.insert(16, 20);           // insert an int
10         str.insert(18, ' ');          // insert a char
11
12         // Display the object's contents
13         System.out.println(str);
14     }
15 }
```

Output
```
in July we sold 20 cars.
```

Here is another example.

Example 19.30: Telephone.java
```
01  public class Telephone
02  {
03      public static String format(String number)
04      {
05          StringBuilder str = new StringBuilder(number);
06
07          // Insert parentheses around the area code.
08          str.insert(0, '(');
09          str.insert(4, ')');
10
11          // Insert a hyphen after the prefix.
12          str.insert(8, '-');
13
14          // Return the formatted number as a string.
15          return str.toString();
16      }
17  }
```

The `Telephone` class has a static method named `format` that accepts a string containing an unformatted telephone number. The method inserts parentheses around the area code and inserts a hyphen after the prefix. The below example implements the Telelephone.java.

Example 19.31: TelephoneTester.java
```
01  public class TelephoneTester
02  {
03      public static void main(String[] args)
04      {
05          // Create an unformatted number.
06          String phone = "9195551212";
07
08          // Get a formatted version of it.
09          String properNum = Telephone.format(phone);
10
11          // Display the formatted number.
12          System.out.println(properNum);
13      }
14  }
```

Output (TelephoneTester.java)
    (919) 555-1212

The `replace` Methods
> The `StringBuilder` class has a `replace` method that differs slightly from the `String` class's `replace` method.

> While the `String` class's `replace` method replaces the occurrences of one character with another characters, the `StringBuilder` class's `replace` method replaces a specified substring with a string.

General form of a call to the `replace()` method:

```
object.replace(start, end, str);
```

> `start` is an `int` that specifies the starting position of a substring in the calling object.
> `end` is an `int` that specifies the ending position of the substring.
> The starting position is included in the substring, but the ending position is not.
> The **str** parameter is a String object.
> After the method executes, the substring will be replaced with **str**.

Example 19.32: ReplaceStringEx.java
```
01  public class ReplaceStringEx {
02      public static void main(String[] args) {
03          StringBuilder str =
04              new StringBuilder("We moved from Khartoum to Atlanta");
05          str.replace(14, 22, "New York");
06          System.out.println(str);
07      }
08  }
```

Output
```
We moved from New York to Atlanta
```

The `replace` method replaces the word `"Chicago"` with `"New York"`.

The **delete, deleteCharAt,** *and* **setCharAt** Methods

> The `delete` and `deleteCharAt` methods are used to delete a substring or a character from a `StringBuilder` object.
> The `setCharAll` method changes a specified character to another value.

The **StringBuilder** class's **delete, deleteCharAt,** and **setCharAt** methods

Example 19.33: StringBuilderDemo.java - Demonstrate all 3 of these methods
```
01  public class StringBuilderDemo {
02      public static void main(String[] args) {
03          StringBuilder str =
04              new StringBuilder("I ate 100 blueberries");
05          // Display the StringBuilder object
06          System.out.println(str);
07
```

```
            // Delete the 'o'
            str.deleteCharAt( );
10
            // Delete "blue"
            str.delete( ,   );
13
            // Display the StringBuilder object
            System.out.println(str);
16
            // Change the '1' to '5'
            str.setCharAt( , '5');
19
            // Display the object's contents
            System.out.println(str);
        }
    }
```

Output
```
    I ate 100 blueberries
    I ate 10 berries
    I ate 50 berries
```

NOTES:
☐ Java provides a class named `StringBuffer` which is essentially the same as the `StringBuilder` class, with the same constructors and the same methods. The difference is that the methods in the `StringBuffer` class are synchronized. This means that the `StringBuffer` class is safe to use in a multi-threaded application.

☐ A **Multi-threaded** application is that concurrently runs multiple threads of execution. In such an application, it is possible for more than one thread to access the same objects in memory at the same time. In Multi-threaded applications, it is important that the methods by synchronized, to prevent the possibility of data corruption.

☐ Because synchronization requires extra steps to be performed, the `StringBuffer` class is slower than the `StringBuilder` class.

☐ In an application where the object will not be accessed by multiple threads, you should use the `StringBuilder` class to get the best performance.

☐ In an application where multiple threads will be accessing the object, you should use the `StringBuffer` class to ensure that its data does not become corrupted.

Tokenizing Strings

Tokenizing a string is a process of breaking string down into its components, which are called **tokens**. The `StringTokenize` class and the `String` class's split method can be used to tokenize strings.

Sometimes a string will contains a series of words or other items of data separated by spaces or other characters. For example: `"peach raspberry strawberry vanilla"`. This String contains the following four items of data: `peach`, `raspberry`, `strawberry`, and `vanilla`. In programming terms, items such as these are known as "**tokens**". Notice that a space appears between the items. The character that separates tokens is known as a "**delimiter**".

Example 19.34: "17;92;81;12;46;5"
> This string contains the following tokens: 17, 92, 81, 12, 46, and 5.
> Notice that a semicolon appears between each item. In this example the semicolon is used as a delimiter.
> Some programming problems require you to read a string that contains a list of items, and then extract all of the tokens from the string for processing.

Example 19.35: "13-22-2005" - // String that contains a date
> The tokens in this string are 3, 22, and 2005.
> The delimiter is the hyphen character.
> Perhaps a program needs to extract the month, day, and year from such a string.

Example 19.36: An OS pathname: **/home/rsullivan/data**
> The tokens: `home`, `rsullivan`, and `data`.
> The delimiter: `/ character`.
> Perhaps a program needs to extract all of the directory names from such a pathname.

The process of breaking a string into tokens is known as **tokenizing**.

In this section we will discuss two of Java's tools for tokenizing strings: the `StringTokenizer` class and the String class's `split` method.

The `StringTokenizer` Class

Java provides a class, `StringTokenizer`, which allows you to tokenize a string. The class is part of the `java.util` package, so you need the following import statement in any program that uses it: `import java.util.StringTokenizer;`

When you create an instance of the `StringTokenizer` class, you pass a string as an argument to one of the constructors. The tokens will be extracted from this string.

Table 19.9 | The StringTokenizer constructors

Constructor	Description
`StringTokenizer(String str)`	The string to be tokenized is passed into str. Whitespace characters (space, tab, and newline) are used as delimiters.
`StringTokenizer(String str, String delimiters)`	The string to be tokenized is passed into str. The characters in delimiters will be used as delimiters.
`StringTokenizer(String str, String delimiters, Boolean returnDelimeters)`	The string to be tokenizd is passed into str. The characters in delimiters will be used as delimiters. If the returnDelimiters parameter is set to true, the delimiters will be included as tokens. If this parameter is set to false, the delimiters will not be included as tokens.

The first constructor uses whitespace characters as delimiters. Example:
`StringTokenizer strTokenizer = new StringTokenizer("2 4 5 6 8");`

The second constructor accepts a 2nd argument, which is a string containing one or more characters that are to be used as delimiters. For example:

Example 19.37: Creates an object using this constructor. It specifies that the `(-)` character is to be used as a delimiter

```
StringTokenizer strTokenizer = new StringTokenizer("10-14-
2005","-");
```

The third constructor accepts a 2nd argument, which is a string containing one or more characters that are to be used as delimiters, and a 3rd argument, which indicates whether the delimiters should be included as tokens. Example: Create an object using this constructor. It specifies that the `(-)` character is to be used as a delimiter and that the delimiters are to be included as tokens.

Example 19.38:
```
StringToknizer strTokenizer = new StringTokenizer("10-14-
2005","-", true);
```

NOTE: The first two constructors do not include the delimiter characters as tokens.

Extracting tokens

Once you have created a `StringTokenizer` object, you can use its methods to extract tokens from the string you passed to the constructor.

Table 19.10 | Some of the `StringTokenizer` methods

Method	Description
`int countTokens()`	This method returns the number of tokens left in the string.
`boolean baseMoreTokens()`	This method returns true if there are more tokens left in the string. Otherwise it returns false.
`String nextToken()`	This method returns the next token found in the string.

Example 19.39: StrTokenEx.java - Code demonstrates how all of the tokens can be extracted from a `StringTokenizer` object. The loop executes as long as there are tokens left to extract

```
01  import java.util.StringTokenizer;
02
03  public class StrTokenEx {
04      public static void main(String[] args) {
05          StringTokenizer strTokenizer = new StringTokenizer("One Two Three");
06          while (strTokenizer.hasMoreTokens())
07          {
08              System.out.println(strTokenizer.nextToken());
09          }
10      }
11  }
```

Output
```
One
Two
Three
```

Example 19.40: DateComponent.java

```
01  import java.util.StringTokenizer;
02  public class DateComponent
03  {
04      private String month;    // To hold the month
05      private String day;      // To hold the day
06      private String year;     // To hold the year
07      public DateComponent(String dateStr)
08      {
09          // Create a StringTokenizer object.
```

```
            StringTokenizer strTokenizer =
                new StringTokenizer(dateStr, "/");

            // Extract the tokens.
            month = strTokenizer.nextToken();
            day = strTokenizer.nextToken();
            year = strTokenizer.nextToken();
        }
        public String getMonth()
        {
            return month;
        }
        public String getDay()
        {
            return day;
        }
        public String getYear()
        {
            return year;
        }
    }
```

Use a `StringTokenizer` object. Its constructor accepts a string containing a date in the form MONTH/DAY/YEAR. It extracts the `month`, `day`, and `year` and stores these values in the `month`, `day`, and `year` fields. The methods `getMonth`, `getDay`, and `getYear` can then be used to retrieve the values.

The below example implements the `DateComponent.java`.

Example 19.41: DateTester.java

```
public class DateTester
{
    public static void main(String[] args)
    {
        String date = "10/23/2007";
        DateComponent dc =
                new DateComponent(date);

        System.out.println("Here's the date: " +
                        date);
        System.out.println("The month is " +
                        dc.getMonth());
        System.out.println("The day is " +
                        dc.getDay());
        System.out.println("The year is " +
                        dc.getYear());
    }
}
```

Output(DateTester.java)
```
Here's the date: 10/23/2007
The month is 10
The day is 23
```

```
The year is 2007
```

Using multiple delimiters

Some situations require that you use multiple characters as delimiters in the same string. For example:

Email Address: `ata4tech@gmail.com`

> This string uses two delimiters: `@` (the at symbol) `and` `.` (the period)
> To extract the tokens from this string we must specify both characters as delimiters to the constructor.

Consider below example or that.

Example 19.42: MultiDe.java

```
01  package ch19;
02
03  import java.util.StringTokenizer;
04
05  public class MultiDe {
06      public static void main(String[] args) {
07          StringTokenizer strTokenizer =
08              new StringTokenizer("ata4tech@gmail.com", "@.");
09          while (strTokenizer.hasMoreTokens())
10          {
11              System.out.println(strTokenizer.nextToken());
12          }
13      }
14  }
```

Output
```
ata4tech
gmail
com
```

Triming a string before tokenizing

When you are tokenizing a string that was entered by the user, and you are using characters other than whitespaces as delimiters, you will probably want to trim the string before tokenizing it.

Otherwise, if the user enters leading whitespace characters, they will become part of the first token. Likewise, if the user enters trailing whitespace characters, they will become part of the last token.

Example 19.43: TrimingEx.java - Create a string with leading and trailing whitespaces

```
01  package ch19;
02
03  import java.util.StringTokenizer;
04  public class TrimingEx {
05      public static void main(String[] args) {
06          String str = "   One;Two;Three   ";
07          // Tokenize the string using the semicolon as a delimiter
08          StringTokenizer strTokenizer =
09                  new StringTokenizer(str, ";");
10          // Display the tokens
11          while (strTokenizer.hasMoreTokens())
12          {
13              System.out.println("*" + strTokenizer.nextToken() + "*");
14          }
15      }
16  }
```

Output
```
*   One*
*Two*
*Three   *
```

To prevent leading and/or trailing whitespace characters from being included in the first and last tokens, use the *String* class's `trim` method to remove them.

Example 19.44: TrimingEx2.java - Some code, modified to use the `trim` method

```
01  package ch19;
02
03  import java.util.StringTokenizer;
04
05  public class TrimingEx2 {
06      public static void main(String[] args) {
07          String str = "   One;Two;Three   ";
08
09          StringTokenizer strTokenizer =
10                  new StringTokenizer(str.trim(), ";");
11          // Display the tokens
12          while (strTokenizer.hasMoreTokens())
13          {
14              System.out.println("*" + strTokenizer.nextToken() + "*");
15          }
16      }
17  }
```

Output
```
*One*
*Two*
*Three*
```

The string class's `Split` method

The String class has a method named `split`, which tokenizes a string and returns an array of `String` objects. Each element in the array is one of the tokens.

Example 19.45: SplitDemo1.java

```
01  public class SplitDemo1
02  {
03      public static void main(String[] args)
04      {
05          // Create a string to tokenize.
06          String str = "one two three four";
07
08          // Get the tokens, using a space delimiter.
09          String[] tokens = str.split(" ");
10
11          // Display the tokens.
12          for (String s : tokens)
13              System.out.println(s);
14      }
15  }
```

Output
```
one
two
three
four
```

Explanation

> The argument passed to the `split` method indicates the delimiter. In this example, a space is used as the delimiter.
> The argument that you pass to the `split` method is a **regular expression**.
> We passed a string containing a single space to the `split` method. This specifies that the space character was the delimiter.
> The `split` method also allows you to use multi-character delimiters. This means you are not limited to a single character as a delimiter.
> Your delimiters can be entire words, if you wish

NOTE: A regular expression is a string that specifies a pattern of characters. Regular expressions can be powerful tools, and are commonly used to search for patterns that exist in strings, files, or other collections of text.
(Regular expression and Multithreading outside of the scope of this book)

Example 19.46: SplitDemo2.java - Code token from the program

```
01  public class SplitDemo2
02  {
03      public static void main(String[] args)
04      {
05          // Create a string to tokenize.
06          String str = "one and two and three and four";
07
08          // Get the tokens, using " and " as the delimiter.
09          String[] tokens = str.split(" and ");
10
11          // Display the tokens.
12          for (String s : tokens)
13              System.out.println(s);
14      }
15  }
```

Output
```
one
two
three
four
```

The code demonstrates multi-character delimiters (delimiters containing multiple characters). You can also specify a series of characters where each individual characters is a delimiter. We must enclose delimiters in brackets inside our regular expression.

Wrapper Classes for The Numeric Data Types

Java provides wrapper classes for each of the numeric data types. These classes have methods that perform useful operations involving primitive numeric value.

Table 19.11 | Wrapper Classes for the numeric primitive data types

Wrapper Class	Primitive Type It Applies To
Byte	byte
Double	double
Float	float
Integer	int
Long	long
Short	short

Now we'll examine other methods and uses of the wrapper classes.

The static toString methods

Each of the numeric wrapper classes has a static toString method that converts a number to a string. The method accepts the number as its argument and returns a string representation of that number. Here is a simple example:

Example 19.47: ToStringEx.java
```
01  public class ToStringEx {
02      public static void main(String[] args) {
03          int i = 12;
04          double d = 14.95;
05          String str1 = Integer.toString(i);
06          String str2 = Double.toString(d);
07          System.out.println(str1);
08          System.out.println(str2);
09      }
10  }
```

Output
```
12
14.95
```

The toBinaryString, toHexString and toOctalString methods

The toBinaryString, toHexString and toOctalString methods are static members of the Integer and Long wrapper classes. These methods accepts an Integer as an argument and return a string representation of that number converted to binary, hexadecimal, or octal. For example;

Example 19.48: ToEx.java
```
01  public class ToEx {
02      public static void main(String[] args) {
03          int number = 14;
04          System.out.println(Integer.toBinaryString(number));
05          System.out.println(Integer.toHexString(number));
06          System.out.println(Integer.toOctalString(number));
07      }
08  }
```

Output
```
1110
e
16
```

The MIN_VALUE and MAX_VALUE constants

The numeric wrapper classes each have a set of static final variables named `MIN_VALUE` & `MAX_VALUE`. These variables hold the minimum and maximum values for a particular data type. Here is a simple example.

Example 19.49: MinMaxEx.java - Display the `min` and `max` values for an `int`

```
01  public class MinMaxEx {
02      public static void main(String[] args) {
03          System.out.println("The min value for an int is " +
04              Integer.MIN_VALUE);
05          System.out.println("The max value for an int is " +
06              Integer.MAX_VALUE);
07      }
08  }
```

Output
```
The min value for an int is -2147483648
The max value for an int is 2147483647
```

Autoboxing and unboxing

It is possible to create objects from the wrapper classes. One way is to pass initial value to the constructor:

```
Integer number = new Integer(7);
```

This creates an Integer object initialization with the value 7, referenced by the variable number. Another way is to simply declare a wrapper class variable, and then assign a primitive value to it. For example:

```
Integer number;
number = 7;
```

Explanation

> The first statement declares an Integer variable named `number`. It does not create an Integer object, just a variable.
> The second statement is a simple assignment statement. It assigns the primitive value 7 to the variable.
> You might suspect that this will cause an error. After all, `number` is a reference variable, not a primitive variable.
> However, because `number` is a wrapper class variable, Java performs an Autoboxing operation.

Autoboxing is Java's process of automatically **boxing up** a value inside an object. When this assignment statement executes, the boxes up the value 7 inside an integer object, and then assigns the address of that object to the number variable.

Unboxing is the opposite of boxing. It is the process of converting a wrapper class object to a primitive type.

Example 19.50: UnBoxEx.java - An Unboxing Operation
```
01  public class UnBoxEx {
02      public static void main(String[] args) {
03          Integer myInt = 5;         // Autoboxes the value 5
04          int primitiveNumber;
05          primitiveNumber = myInt;   // Unboxes the object
06      }
07  }
```

Explanation
> Line 03: declares `myInt` as an Integer reference variable.
> The primitive value 5 is autoboxes, and the address of the resulting object is assigned to the `myInt` variable.
> Line 04: declares `primitiveNumber` as an `int` variable.
> Line 05: assigns the `myInt` object to `primitiveNumber`.
> When this statement executes, Java automatically unboxes the `myInt` wrapper class object and stores the resulting value, which is 5, in `primitiveNumber`.

Although you rarely need to create an instance of a wrapper class, Java's autoboxing and unboxing features make some operations more convenient.

Occasionally, you will find yourself in a situation where you want to perform an operation using a primitive variable, but the operation can only be used with an object.

Recall from the ArrayList class
> An ArrayList is an array-like object that can be used to store other objects.
> You cannot, however, store primitive values in an ArrayList.
> It is intended for objects only.
> If you try to compile the following statement, an error will occur:
```
ArrayList<int> list = new ArrayList<int>( );  // Error
```

However, you can store wrapper class objects in an ArrayList. If we need to store `int` values in an ArrayList, we have to specify that the ArrayList will hold Integer objects. For example:
```
ArrayList<Integer> list = new ArrayList<Integer>( );  // Okay
```

This statement declares that list reference an ArrayList that can hold Integer objects.

One way to store an int value in the ArrayList is to instantiate an Integer object, initialize it with the desired int value, and then pass the Integer object to the ArrayList's add method. For example:

```
ArrayList<Integer> list = new ArrayList<Integer>();
Integer myInt = 5;
list.add(myInt);
```

However, Java's autoboxing and unboxing features make it unnecessary to create the Integer object. If you add an `int` value to the ArrayList, Java will autobox the value. For example:

```
ArrayList<Integer> list = new ArrayList<Integer>();
list.add(myInt);
```

When the value 5 is passed to the `add` method, Java boxes the value up in an Integer object. When necessary, Java also unboxes values that are retrieved from the ArrayList. For example:

```
ArrayList<Integer> list = new ArrayList<Integer>();
list.add(myInt);
int primitiveNumber = list.get(0);
```

The last statement retrieves the item at index `0`. Because the item is being assigned to an int variable, Java unboxes it and stores the primitive value in the `int` variable.

Summary

> Java provides wrapper classes for all of the primitive data types. A wrapper class is a class that is **"wrapped around"** a primitive data type and allows you to create objects instead of variables.

> The wrapper class for a given primitive type contains not only a value of that type, but also methods that perform operations related to the type.

> Although these wrapper classes can be used to create objects instead of variables, few programmers use them that way.

> Because the wrapper classes are immutable, which means that once you create an object, you cannot change the objective's value. Because they are not as easy to use as variables for simple operations.

- The `Character` class is a wrapper class for the `char` data type. It provides numerous methods for testing and converting character data. The `Character` class is part of the `java.lang` package.
- The `startsWith` method determines whether the calling object's string begins with a specified substring.
- The String class provides overloaded versions of the `regionMatches`, which determines whether specified regions of two string match.
- The `indexOf` and `lastIndexOf` methods can search for either a character or a substring within the calling string. If the item being searched for is found, its position is returned. Otherwise, -1 is returned.
- The `indexOf` and `lastIndexOf` methods can also search for substrings within a string.
- The `substring` method returns a copy of a substring from the calling object.
- The `getChars` and `toCharArray` methods convert the calling string object to a char array. The `getChars` method can be used to convert a substring, while the `toCharArray` method converts the entire string.
- The `concat` method performs the same operation as the `(+)` operator when used with strings.
- The `replace` method returns a copy of a `String` object, where every occurrence of a specified character has been replaced with another character.
- The `replace` method does not modify the contents of the calling `String` object, but returns a reference to a String that is a modified copy of it.
- The `trim` method returns a copy of a `String` object with all leading and trailing whitespace characters deleted. A leading whitespace character is one that appears at the beginning, left side, of a string.
- The `StringBuilder` class is similar to the `String` class, except that you may change the contents of `StringBuilder` objects, but you cannot change the contents of the String object. The `StringBuilder` class also provides several useful methods that the `String` class does not have.
- Unlike `String` objects, `StringBuilder` objects have methods that allow you to modify their contents without creating a new object in memory.
- The `StringBuilder` object will grow or shrink in size, as needed, to accommodate the changes.
- The fact that `String` objects are immutable is rarely a problem, but you might consider using `StringBuilder` objects if your program needs to make a lot of changes to one or more strings. This will improve the program's

efficiency by reducing the number of `String` objects that must be created and then removed by the garbage collector.
› The `StringBuilder` class also has several overloaded versions of a method named `insert`, which inserts a value into the calling object's string.
› The `delete` and `deleteCharAt` methods are used to delete a substring or a character from a `StringBuilder` object.
› The `setCharAll` method changes a specified character to another value.
› Java provides a class named `StringBuffer` which is essentially the same as the `StringBuilder` class, with the same constructors and the same methods. The difference is that the methods in the `StringBuffer` class are synchronized. This means that the `StringBuffer` class is safe to use in a multi-threaded application.
› Tokenizing a string is a process of breaking string down into its components, which are called **tokens**. The `StringTokenize` class and the `String` class's split method can be used to tokenize strings. The process of breaking a string into tokens is known as **tokenizing.**
› Java provides a class, `StringTokenizer,` which allows you to tokenize a string.
› The `toBinaryString`, `toHexString` and `toOctalString` methods accepts an Integer as an argument and return a string representation of that number converted to `binary`, `hexadecimal`, or `octal`.
› The numeric wrapper classes each have a set of `static final` variables named `MIN_VALUE` & `MAX_VALUE`. These variables hold the minimum and maximum values for a particular data type.
› Autoboxing is the process of automatically **boxing up** a value inside an object.
› Unboxing is the process of converting a wrapper class object to a primitive type.

Chapter 20

Inheritance

What is Inheritance?

Inheritance allows a new class to extend an existing class. The new class inherits the members of the class it extends. In the real world you can find many objects that are specialized versions of other more general objects. For example:

General Objects	Special Objects
Dog	Poodle
Vehicle	Car
Shape	Rectangle
Plant	Flower

The specialized objects has all of the characteristics of the general object, plus additional characteristics that make it special.

In Object Oriented Programming, inheritance involves a **superclass** and a **subclass**. The superclass is the general class and the subclass is the specialized class. Subclass is an extended version of the superclass. The subclass inherits fields and methods from the superclass without any of them having to be rewritten.

New fields and methods may added to the subclass, and that is what makes it a specialized version of the superclass. Superclasses are also called "**base classes**" and subclasses are also called "**derived classes**". Consider below example for that.

Example 20.1: Vechicle.java

```
01  class Vehicle
02  {
03      // member declarations
04  }
05  class Car extends Vehicle
06  {
07      // inherit accessible members from Vehicle
08      // provide own member declarations
09  }
10  class Bus extends Vehicle
11  {
12      // inherit accessible members from Vehicle
13      // provide own member declarations
14  }
```

The `extends` keyword is specified after the class name and before another class name. The class name before extends identifies the child and the class name after extends identifies the parent.

The `Superclass's` constructor

In an inheritance relationship, the superclass constructor always executes before the subclass constructor. Consider below examples.

Example 20.2: SuperClass .java

```
01  public class SuperClass
02  {
03      public SuperClass()
04      {
05          System.out.println("This is the " +
06                  "superclass constructor.");
07      }
08  }
```

A class, `SuperClass`, that has a `no-arg` constructor. The constructor displays the message `"This is the superclass constructor"`.

Example 20.3: SubClass.java

```
01  public class SubClass extends SuperClass
02  {
03      public SubClass()
04      {
05          System.out.println("This is the " +
06                  "subclass constructor.");
07      }
08  }
```

`SubClass` extends `SuperClass`. This is also has a `no-arg` constructor, which displays the message `"This is the subclass constructor"`.

Example 20.4: ConstructorDemo.java

```
01  public class ConstructorDemo
02  {
03      public static void main(String[] args)
04      {
05          SubClass obj = new SubClass();
06      }
07  }
```

Output
```
This is the subclass constructor.
```

Create a `SubClass` object. The `superclass` constructor executes first, followed by the `SubClass` constructor. If a `superclass` has either (a) a default constructor or (b) a no-arg constructor that was written into the class, then that constructor will be automatically called just before a `subclass` constructor executes.

Inheritance does not work in reverse

In an inheritance relationship, the subclass inherits members from the superclass, not the other way around. This means it is not possible for a superclass to call a subclass's method.

Calling the `superclass` Constructor

Introduction

Recall that, a superclass's default constructor or no-arg constructor is automatically called just before the subclass's constructor executes. But what if the superclass does not have a default constructor or a no-arg constructor? Or, what if the superclass has multiple overloaded constructors and you want to make sure a specific one is called? Solution: Use the `super` keyword to call a superclass constructor explicitly.

The `super` keyword refers to object's superclass and can be used to access members of the superclass.

Example 20.5: SuperClass1.java

```
01  public class SuperClass1
02  {
03      public SuperClass1()
04      {
```

```
05         System.out.println("This is the superclass " +
06                    "no-arg constructor.");
07     }
08     public SuperClass1(int arg)
09     {
10         System.out.println("The following argument " +
11                    "was passed to the superclass " +
12                    "constructor: " + arg);
13     }
14 }
```

`SuperClass` class has `no-arg` constructor and a constructor that accepts an int argument.

Example 20.6: SubClass1.java
```
01 public class SubClass1 extends SuperClass1
02 {
03     public SubClass1()
04     {
05         super(10);
06         System.out.println("This is the " +
07                    "subclass constructor.");
08     }
09 }
```

`SubClass` extends `SuperClass`. This class's constructor uses the `super` keyword to call the superclass's constructor and pass an argument to it. Line 05, call the superclass constructor and passes the argument 10 to it.

Three Guide Lines you should remember about calling a superclass constructor:

> The `super` statement that calls the `superclass` constructor may be written only in the subclass's constructor. You cannot call the superclass constructor from any other method.

> The `super` statement that calls the superclass constructor must be the first statement in the subclass's constructor. This is because the superclass's constructor must execute before the code in the subclass's constructor executes.

> If a subclass constructor does not explicitly call a superclass constructor, Java will automatically call the superclass's default constructor, or no-arg constructor, just before the code in the subclass's constructor executes. This is equivalent to placing the following statement at the beginning of a subclass constructor:
super( );

When the superclass has no default or `No-Arg` constructor

- Java provides a default constructor for a class only when you provide no constructor for the class.
- This makes it possible to have a class with no default constructor.
- The `SuperClass1` class has a constructor that accepts one argument. Because we have provided this constructor, the `SuperClass1` class does not have a default constructor.
- In addition, we have not written a `no-arg` constructor for the class.
- If a `SuperClass1` does not have a default constructor and does not have a `no-arg` constructor, then a class that inherits form it must call one of the constructors that the superclass does have. If it does not, an error will result when the subclass is compiled.

Summary of constructor issues in inheritance

Important issues that you should remember about constructors in inheritance relationship. The following list summarize them:

- The `Superclass` constructor always executes before the subclass constructor.
- You can write a super statement that calls a superclass constructor, but only in the subclass's constructor. You cannot call the superclass constructor from any other method.
- If a super statement that calls a superclass constructor appears in a subclass constructor, it must be the first statement.
- If a subclass constructor does not explicitly call a superclass constructor, Java will automatically call `super()` just before the code in the subclass's constructor executes.
- If a superclass does not have a default constructor and does not have a `no-arg` constructor, then a class that inherits from it must call one of the constructors that the superclass does have.

The `Object` Class

When a class does not use the `extends` keyword to inherits from another class, java automatically extends it from the object class. Every class in java directly or indirectly inherits from a class named `Object`, which is part of the `java.lang` package. For example:

```
// Class Declaration
public class MyClass
{
    (Member Declaration ...)
}
```

This class does not explicitly extend any other class, so Java treats It as through it were written as follow:

```
// Class Declaration
public class MyClass extends Object
{
    (Member Declarations ...)
}
```

Ultimately, every class extends the `Object` class. So every class inherits the `Object` class's members. Two of the most useful are the `toString` and `equal` methods.

Overriding Superclass Methods

A subclass may have a method with the same signature as a superclass method. In such a case, the `subclass` method overrides the superclass method. Sometimes a subclass inherits a method from its superclass, but the method is inadequate for the subclass's purpose.

Because the subclass is more specialized than the superclass, it is sometimes necessary for the subclass to replace inadequate superclass methods with more suitable ones. This is known as **Method Overriding**. We can understand it more clearly using this code snippet:

Example 20.7: Abc.java - Method Overriding

```
01  package ch20;
02  public class Abc {
```

```
        public static void main(String args[]){
            Company a = new Company();
            Company b = new Xyz();
            a.address();
            b.address();
        }
    }
    class Company{
        public void address() {
            System.out.println("This is address of Abc company..."
);
        }
    }
    class Xyz extends Company{
        public void address(){
            super.address();
            System.out.println("This is Xyz's address..." );
        }
    }
```

Output
```
This is address of Abc company...
This is address of Abc company...
This is Xyz's address...
```

Explanation

› In order for a **subclass** method to override a **superclass** method, it must have the same signature.
› When an object of the subclass invokes the method, it invokes the subclass's version of the method, not the super class's.
› As you know, the `super` keyword refers to the object's superclass.
› A subclass may call an overridden superclass method by prefixing its name with the `super` keyword and a dot `(.)`

Rules for method overriding

› In java, a method can only be written in Subclass, not in same class.
› The argument list should be exactly the same as that of the overridden method.
› The return type should be the same or a subtype of the return type declared in the original overridden method in the super class.
› The access level cannot be more restrictive than the overridden method's access level. For example, if the super class method is declared public then the overriding method in the subclass cannot be either private or protected.
› Instance methods can be overridden only if they are inherited by the subclass.

- A method declared `final` cannot be overridden.
- A method declared `static` cannot be overridden but can be re-declared.
- If a method cannot be inherited then it cannot be overridden.
- A subclass within the same package as the instance's superclass can override any superclass method that is not declared `private or final`.
- A subclass in a different package can only override the non-final methods declared `public or protected`.
- An overriding method can throw any uncheck exceptions, regardless of whether the overridden method throws exceptions or not. However the overriding method should not throw checked exceptions that are new or broader than the ones declared by the overridden method. The overriding method can throw narrower or fewer exceptions than the overridden method.
- Constructors cannot be overridden.

Overloading versus overriding

- **Overloading: i**s when a method has the same name as one or more other methods, but a different parameter list or different signature.
- **Overriding:** is when a method overrides another method, however, they both have the same signature.
- Both overloading and overriding can take place in an inheritance relationship.
- You already know that overloaded methods can appear within the same class. A method in a subclass can overload a method in the superclass. If a class **A** is the superclass and class **B** is the subclass, a method in class **B** may overload a method in class **A**, or another method in class **B**.
- **Overriding**, on the other hand, can only take place in an inheritance relationship. If class **A** is the superclass and class **B** is the subclass, a method in class **B** may override a method n class **A**. However, a method cannot override another method in the same class.

The distinction between overloading and overriding

The distinction between overloading and overriding is important because it can affect the accessibility of superclass methods in a subclass.

- If two methods have the same name but different signatures, they are overloaded. This is true when the methods are in the same class or when one method is in the superclass and the other method is in the subclass.

- If a method in a subclass has the same signature as a method in the superclass, the subclass method overrides the superclass method.
- When a subclass overloads a superclass method, both methods may be called with a subclass object.
- However, when a subclass overrides a superclass method, only the subclass's version of the method can be called with a subclass object.

Following is the code snippet to explain the above concept:

Example 20.8: SuperClass2.java - Overloading

```java
01  public class SuperClass
02  {
03     public void showValue(int x)
04     {
05        System.out.println("SUPERCLASS: " +
06           "The int argument was " + x);
07     }
08     public void showValue(String s)
09     {
10        System.out.println("SUPERCLASS: " +
11           "The String argument was " + s);
12     }
13  }
```

Two overloaded methods named `showValue`. One of the methods accepts an `int` argument and the other accepts a `String` argument.

Example 20.9: SubClass2.java - Overriding

```java
01  public class SubClass2 extends SuperClass2
02  {
03     public void showValue(int x)
04     {
05        System.out.println("SUBCLASS: The int argument was " + x);
06     }
07     public void showValue(double s)
08     {
09        System.out.println("SUBCLASS: The double argument was " + s);
10     }
11  }
```

Two methods named `showValue`. The first one (L3-L6), accepts an `int` argument. This method overrides one of the superclass methods because they have the same signature. The second `showValue` method (L7-L10), accepts a double argument. This method overloads the other `showValue` methods because none of the other have the same signature. Although there is a total of four `showValues` methods in these classes, only three of them may be called from a `SubClass3` object. This is demonstrated in next example.

Example 20.10: ShowValueDemo.java
```
01  public class ShowValueDemo
02  {
03      public static void main(String[] args)
04      {
05          // Create a SubClass object.
06          SubClass2 myObject = new SubClass2();
07
08          myObject.showValue(10);          // Pass an int.
09          myObject.showValue(1.2);         // Pass a double.
10          myObject.showValue("Hello");     // Pass a String.
11      }
12  }
```

Output
```
SUBCLASS: The int argument was 10
SUBCLASS: The double argument was 1.2
SUPERCLASS: The String argument was Hello
```

When an `int` argument is passed to `showValue`, the `subClass`'s method is called because it overrides the superclass method. In order to call the overridden superclass method. we would have to use the `super` keyword in the subclass method.

Example 20.11: Using the super keyword in the subclass method
```
01  public class SubClass2 extends SuperClass2
02  {
03      public void showValue(int x)
04      {
05          super.showValue(x);
06          System.out.println("SUBCLASS: The int argument was " + x);
07      }
08      public void showValue(double s)
09      {
10          System.out.println("SUBCLASS: The double argument was " + s);
11      }
12  }
```

Preventing a method from being overridden

When a method is declared with the `final` modifier, it cannot be overridden in a subclass. The following method header is an example that uses the final modifier:
```
public final void message( );
```

If a subclass attempts to override a `final` method, the compiler generates an error. This technique can be used to make sure that a particular superclass method is used by subclasses and not a modified version of it.

Protected Members

Java access modifiers

A Java access modifier specifies which classes can access a given class and its fields, constructors and methods.

Java provides a number of access modifiers to set access levels for classes, variables, methods, and constructors. The four access levels are:

> `default` (visible to the package). No modifiers are needed.
> `private` (visible to the class only).
> `public` (visible to the world).
> `protected` (visible to the package and all subclasses).

Protected members

A protected members of a class may be:

> accessed by methods in a subclass, and by methods in the same package as the class.
> accessed by methods of the same class or methods of a subclass.
> accessed by methods of any class that are in the same package as the protected member's class.

A protected members are not quite public either because access to them is restricted to methods in the same class, subclasses, and classes in the same package as the member's class. A protected member's access is somewhere between private and public. We can understand it more clearly using these examples.

Example 20.12: Shape.java - Protected Members
```
01  package ch20;
02
03  public class Shape
04  {
05      protected int sides;
```

```
06
07      public Shape()
08      {
09          sides = 2;
10      }
11      public int getSides()
12      {
13          return sides;
14      }
15      public void printSides()
16      {
17          System.out.println("This object has " + sides + " sides." );
18      }
19  }
```

Example 20.13: Square.java

```
01  package ch20;
02
03  public class Square extends Shape
04  {
05      public Square(int nSides)
06      {
07          sides = nSides;
08      }
09  }
```

Example 20.14: ProtectedVariable.java

```
01  package ch20;
02
03  class ProtectedVariableDemo
04  {
05      public static void main(String args[])
06      {
07          Square Obj = new Square(10);
08          Obj.printSides();
09      }
10  }
```

Output(ProtectedVariable.java)
```
This object has 10 sides.
```

Although making a class member protected instead of private might make some tasks easier, you should avoid this practice when possible because any class that inherits from the class, or is in the same package, has unrestricted access to the protected member. It is always better to make all of fields private and then provide public methods for accessing those fields.

Package Access

If you do not provide an access specifier for a class member, the class member is given `package` access by default. This means that any method in the same package may access the member. Here is a simple example.

Example 20.15: AA.java - package access

```
// AA.java
package A;
class AA {
    void messsage() {
        System.out.println("Welcome");
    }
}

// BB.java
package B;
import A.*;
class BB {
    public static void main(String args[]) {
        AA obj = new AA();     // compile time error
        obj.message();          // compile time error
    }
}
```

Explanation

› We have created two packages **A** and **B**.
› We are accessing the `AA` class from outside its package, since `AA` class is not public, so it cannot be accessed from outside the package.
› In the above example, the scope of class `AA` and its method `message()` is default so it cannot be accessed from outside the package.

There is a subtle difference between protected access and package access.

› Protected access members may be accessed by methods in the same package, or in a subclass. This is true if the subclass is in a different package (through inheritance only).
› Members with package access, however, cannot be accessed by subclasses that are in a different packages.

NOTES
☐ It is more likely that you will give package access to class members by accident than by design, because it is easy to forget the access specifier.

- Although there are circumstances under which package access can be helpful, you should normally avoid it.
- Be careful always to specify an access specifier for class members.

The following table summarizes the above concepts.

Table 20.1 | Accessibility from within the class's package

Access Specifier	Accessible to a subclass inside the same package?	Accessible to all other classes in the same package
default (no modifier)	Yes	Yes
public	Yes	Yes
protected	Yes	Yes
private	No	No

Table 20.2 | Accessibility from outside the class's package

Access Specifier	Accessible to a subclass outside the same package?	Accessible to all other classes outside the same package
default (no modifier)	No	No
public	Yes	Yes
protected	Yes	No
private	No	No

Summary

> - Inheritance allows a new class to extend an existing class. The new class inherits the members of the class it extends.
> - In Object Oriented Programming, inheritance involves a **superclass** and a **subclass**. The superclass is the general class and the subclass is the specialized class.
> - Subclass is an extended version of the superclass. The subclass inherits fields and methods from the superclass without any of them having to be rewritten. Superclasses are also called "**base classes**" and subclasses are also called "**derived classes**".

- In an inheritance relationship, the superclass constructor always executes before the subclass constructor.
- In an inheritance relationship, the subclass inherits members from the superclass, not the other way around. This means it is not possible for a superclass to call a subclass's method.
- The `super` keyword refers to object's superclass and can be used to access members of the superclass.
- The `super` statement that calls the superclass constructor must be the first statement in the subclass's constructor. This is because the superclass's constructor must execute before the code in the subclass's constructor executes.
- If a subclass constructor does not explicitly call a superclass constructor, Java will automatically call the superclass's default constructor, or `no-arg` constructor, just before the code in the subclass's constructor executes. This is equivalent to placing the following statement at the beginning of a subclass constructor: `super();`
- Java provides a default constructor for a class only when you provide no constructor for the class. This makes it possible to have a class with no default constructor.
- If a superclass does not have a default constructor and does not have a `no-arg` constructor, then a class that inherits form it must call one of the constructors that the superclass does have.
- The Superclass constructor always executes before the subclass constructor.
- You can write a super statement that calls a superclass constructor, but only in the subclass's constructor. You cannot call the superclass constructor from any other method.
- When a class does not use the `extends` keyword to inherits from another class, java automatically extends it from the object class. Every class in java directly or indirectly inherits from a class named `Object`, which is part of the `java.lang` package.
- The `return` type in the subclass's method should be the same of a subtype of the `return` type declared in the original overridden method in the super class.
- The access level cannot be more restrictive than the overridden method's access level. For example, if the super class method is declared public then the overriding method in the subclass cannot be either private or protected.
- Instance methods can be overridden only if they are inherited by the subclass.
- A method declared `final` cannot be overridden.

- A method declared `static` cannot be overridden but can be re-declared.
- If a method cannot be inherited then it cannot be overridden.
- A subclass within the same package as the instance's superclass can override any superclass method that is not declared `private or final`.
- A subclass in a different package can only override the non-final methods declared `public or protected`.
- An overriding method can throw any uncheck exceptions, regardless of whether the overridden method throws exceptions or not. However the overriding method should not throw checked exceptions that are new or broader than the ones declared by the overridden method. The overriding method can throw narrower or fewer exceptions than the overridden method.
- Constructors cannot be overridden.
- **Overloading is** when a method has the same name as one or more other methods, but a different parameter list or different signature.
- **Overriding** is when a method overrides another method, however, they both have the same signature.
- Both overloading and overriding can take place in an inheritance relationship.
- You already know that overloaded methods can appear within the same class. A method in a subclass can overload a method in the superclass. If a class **A** is the superclass and class **B** is the subclass, a method in class **B** may overload a method in class **A**, or another method in class **B**.
- **Overriding** can only take place in an inheritance relationship. If class **A** is the superclass and class **B** is the subclass, a method in class **B** may override a method in class **A**. However, a method cannot override another method in the same class.
- If two methods have the same name but different signatures, they are overloaded. This is true when the methods are in the same class or when one method is in the superclass and the other method is in the subclass.
- If a method in a subclass has the same signature as a method in the superclass, the subclass method overrides the superclass method.
- When a subclass overloads a superclass method, both methods may be called with a subclass object.
- However, when a subclass overrides a superclass method, only the subclass's version of the method can be called with a subclass object.
- A Java access modifier specifies which classes can access a given class and its fields, constructors and methods.

> Java provides a number of access modifiers to set access levels for classes, variables, methods, and constructors. The four access levels are – `default` (visible to the package), `private` (visible to the class only), `public` (visible to the world), `protected` (visible to the package and all subclasses).

Chapter 21

Polymorphism

Introduction

A superclass reference variable can reference objects of a subclass. As we know that in order to declare a variable that references an object, we use the following syntax.

```
ClassName variableName;
```

Here, `variableName` is the name of the reference variable and `ClassName` is the name of its class. Thus, `variablename` can reference any object of class `ClassName`. However, it can also reference any object whose class is a subclass of `ClassName`.

For example: If a class **A** is a superclass of class **B** and class **B** is a superclass of class **C** then in that case, variable of class **A** can reference any object derived from that class (i.e. object of class **B** and class **c**). This is possible because each subclass object is an object of its superclass but not vice versa.

Example 21.1: Abc.java - To illustrate how a superclass reference variable can refer the derive class object, let us consider the following example in which the class SubClass1 and SubClass2 are derived from common superclass SuperClass. All these classes have methods with the same name and we are accessing these methods using superclass reference variable.

```
01  package ch21;
02
03  class SuperClass {
04      public void display() {
05          System.out.println("SuperClass class display method is called");
06      }
```

```
07  }
08  class SubClass1 extends SuperClass {
09      public void display() {
10          System.out.println("SubClass1 class display method is called");
11      }
12  }
13  class SubClass2 extends SuperClass {
14      public void display(){
15          System.out.println("SubClass2 class display method is called");
16      }
17  }
18  class polymorphism {
19      public static void main(String[] args){
20          SuperClass ptr; //SuperClass class reference variable
21          SubClass1 d1 = new SubClass1();
22          SubClass2 d2 = new SubClass2();
23          ptr = d1; // ptr contain reference of SubClass1 object
24          ptr.display();
25          ptr = d2; // ptr contain reference of SubClass2 object
26          ptr.display();
27      }
28  }
```

Output
```
SubClass1 class display method is called
SubClass2 class display method is called
```

The output of the program reveals that the method `display()` of the subclasses are invoked. If the reference variable `ptr` of the superclass `SuperClass` contains a reference to `SubClass1` object, the `display()` method for that object will be called. Similarly, if the reference variable `ptr` contains a reference to `SubClass2` object, the method for that object will be called. This means that one method call,

```
ptr().display;
```

can call different methods depending on the momentary contents of `ptr`. This is how polymorphism is achieved. Notice that which overridden method will called is always determined by the type of the object referenced by the variable, not the type of the object reference variable. This task of determining which implementation of method will be used is performed by the JVM dynamically at run time. This is known as Dynamic Binding.

The polymorphic behavior can only be achieved if the following requirements are fulfilled:

› The method call for a subclass object must be through a superclass reference variable.

- The method called must be declared in the superclass and defined in the subclass.
- The method in the superclass and subclass must have the same name and parameter list with the same number of parameters where corresponding parameters must be of the same type.
- The method return type must either be the same in the superclass and subclasses or must be covariant. Return types are said to be covariant if the return type of the method in the derived class is a subclass of the return type of the base class.
- The method access specifier must be no more restrictive in the subclass than in the superclass.

Example 21.2: Consider `Square` and `Circle` be the subclasses of class `Shape`. Suppose we want to calculate area of any shape so we will define an `area()` method in the `Shape` class and override it in the `Square` and `Circle` subclass to calculate area of rectangle and circle.

```
01  class Shape
02  {
03      public void area()
04      {
05          System.out.println("Super class area method is called");
06      }
07  }
08  class Square extends Shape
09  {
10      private double length, breadth;
11      Square(double x, double y)
12      {
13          length = x ;
14          breadth = y ;
15      }
16      public void area()
17      {
18          System.out.println("Area of Square is = " + (length * breadth));
19      }
20  }
21  class Circle extends Shape
22  {
23      private double radius;
24      Circle(double r)
25      {
26          radius = r;
27      }
28      public void area()
29      {
30          System.out.println("Area of Circle is = " + (Math.PI*radius));
31      }
```

```
32  }
33  class ShapeEx
34  {
35      public static void main(String[] args)
36      {
37      Shape s;
38      Square r = new Square(10,20);
39      s = r;
40      s.area();
41      Circle c = new Circle(5);
42      s = c;
43      s.area();
44      }
45  }
```

Output
```
Area of Square is = 200.0
Area of Circle is = 15.707963267948966
```

Example 21.3: SuperClass3.java
```
01  package ch21;
02
03  class SuperClass3
04  {
05      void Message1()
06      {
07          System.out.print("Hello");
08      }
09  }
10
11  class SubClass extends SuperClass3
12  {
13      public void Message1()
14      {
15          System.out.print("Welcome");
16      }
17  }
18
19  class SubClass3 extends SuperClass3
20  {
21      public void Message1()
22      {
23          System.out.print("Hi");
24      }
25
26  }
27  class Demo
28  {
29      public static void main(String args[])
30      {
31          SuperClass3 ref; //Declares a reference variable named SuperClass3
32          SubClass3 obj = new SubClass3();
33          ref = obj;
34          ref.Message1();
```

```
35      }
36  }
```

Result
```
Hi
```

Explanation

> A `SuperClass3` class reference variable can refer to a `SubClass3` class object!
> `SuperClass3 ref` Tells us that the `ref` variable's data type is `SuperClass3`. Therefore, we can use the `ref` variable to reference a `SuperClass3` object, as shown:
> `obj = new SubClass3();`
> The `SuperClass3` class is also used as the `SuperClass3` for the `SubClass3` class.

Polymorphism & Dynamic Binding

Runtime Polymorphism is a process in which a call to an overridden method is resolved at runtime rather than compile-time. In this process, an overridden method is called through the reference variable of a superclass. When reference variable of parent class refers to the object of Child class, it is known as **UpCasting**.

Example 21.4
```
01      class X{}
02      class Y extends X{}
03
04  //upcasting
05      X x = new Y();
```

Illustration

When a superclass variable reference a subclass object, a potential problem exists. What if the subclass has overridden a method in the superclass and the variable makes a call to that method? Does the variable call the superclass's version of the method, or the subclass's version?

The process of matching a method call with the correct method definition is know as **binding**. Java performs dynamic binding or late binding when a variable contains a Polymorphism reference. This means that the Java Virtual Machine determines at runtime which method to call, depending on the type of object that the variable reference. So, it is the object's type that determines which method is called, not the variable's type. Consider below example for that.

Example 21.5: Polymorphic.java
```
01  package ch21;
02
03  class Car{
04      void run()
05      {
06          System.out.println("running");
07      }
08  }
09  class Splender extends Car
10  {
11      void run()
12      {
13          System.out.println("Running safely with 60km" );
14      }
15
16      public static void main(String args[])
17      {
18          Car b = new Splender();//upcasting
19          b.run();
20      }
21  }
```

Output
```
Running safely with 60km
```

The `Instanceof` Operator

There is an operator in Java named `instanceof` that you can use to determine whether an object is an instance of a particular class.

General Form of Expression that uses the `instanceof` operator
```
refVar instanceof ClassName
```

Explanation

> `refVar` - Is a reference variable.
> `ClassName` - Is the name of a class.

This is the form of a boolean expression that will return `true` if the object referenced by `refVar` is an instance of `ClassName`. Otherwise, the expression returns `false`.

Example 21.6: The if statement in the following code determines whether the reference variable `one` references a `ClassOne` object.

```
01  ClassOne one = new ClassOne();
02  if (one instanceof ClassOne)
03  {
04      System.out.println("Yes, one is a ClassOne" );
05  }
06  else
07  {
08      System.out.println("No, one is not a ClassOne" );
09  }
```

Example 21.7

```
01  ClassTwo two = new ClassTwo( , );
02  if (two instanceof ClassTwo)
03      System.out.println("Yes, two is a ClassTwo" );
04  else
05      System.out.println("No, two is not a ClassTwo" );
```

Even through the object referenced by two is a `ClassTwo` object, this code will display "Yes, two is a ClassTwo.". This `instanceof` operator returns true because `ClassTwo` is a subclass of `ClassTwo`.

Summary

> A superclass reference variable can reference objects of a subclass.
> **Runtime Polymorphism** is a process in which a call to an overridden method is resolved at runtime rather than compile-time.
> When reference variable of parent class refers to the object of Child class, it is known as **UpCasting**.
> The process of matching a method call with the correct method definition is know as **binding**.
> Java performs dynamic binding or late binding when a variable contains a polymorphism reference. This means that the Java Virtual Machine determines at Runtime which method to call, depending on the type of object that the variable reference.
> `instanceof` operator is use to determine whether an object is an instance of a particular class.

Chapter 22

Abstract Classes and Interfaces

Abstract Classes & Abstract Methods

An abstract class is not instantiated, but other classes extend it. An abstract method has no body and must be overridden in a subclass. An abstract method is a method that appears in a superclass, but expects to be overridden in a subclass. As abstract method has only a header and no body.

Syntax (Abstract Method)
```
AccessSpecifier abstract ReturnType MethodName (ParameterList);
```

Syntax (Abstract Class)
```
AccessSpecifier abstract class ClassName
```

NOTES
- When an abstract method appears in a class, the method must be overridden in a subclass.
- If a subclass fails to override the method, an error will result. Abstract methods are used to ensure that a subclass implements the method.
- When a class contains an abstract method, you cannot create an instance of the class.
- Abstract methods are commonly used in abstract classes.
- An abstract class is not instantiated itself, but serves as a superclass for other classes.
- The abstract class represents the generic or abstract form of all of the classes that inherit from it.

Example 22.1: Student.java

```
01  package ch22;
02
03  public abstract class Student
04  {
05      private String name;          // Student name
06      private String idNo;          // Student ID
07      public Student(String n, String id)
08      {
09          name = n;
10          idNo = id;
11      }
12      public String toString()
13      {
14          String str;
15
16          str = "Name: " + name +
17              "\nID Number: " + idNo ;
18          return str;
19      }
20      public abstract int getRemainingHours();
21  }
```

Explanation

› An Abstract Class `student` holds data common to all students, but does not hold all the data needed for students of specific majors.
› The `students` class contains fields for sorting a student's name, id number, and year admitted. It also has a constructor, a `toString` method, and an abstract method named `getRemainingHours`.
› This abstract method must be overridden in classes that inherit from the `Student` class. The idea behind this method is that it returns the number of hours remaining for a Student to take in his or her major. It was made abstract because this class is intended to be the base for other classes that represent students of specific majors.

For example, a `CompStudent` class might hold data for a computer science student and a Biology Student Class might hold the data for a biology student.

Example 22.2: CompStudent.java

```
01  package ch22;
02
03  public class CompStudent extends Student
04  {
05      // Required hours
06      private final int OS_HOURS = 40; // Operating System hours
07      private final int DB_HOURS = 60; // Database hours
08
09      // Hours taken
10      private int osHours;     // Operating System hours taken
11      private int dbHours;     // Database hours taken
12      public CompStudent(String n, String id)
```

```
13      {
14          super(n, id);
15      }
16      public void setOsHours(int os)
17      {
18          osHours = os;
19      }
20      public void setDbHours(int db)
21      {
22          dbHours = db;
23      }
24      public int getRemainingHours()
25      {
26          int reqHours,          // Total required hours
27              remainingHours;    // Remaining hours
28
29          // Calculate the required hours.
30          reqHours = OS_HOURS + DB_HOURS; // 100
31
32          // Calculate the remaining hours.
33          remainingHours = reqHours - (osHours + dbHours);
34
35          return remainingHours;
36      }
37      public String toString()
38      {
39          String str;
40
41          str = super.toString() +
42              "\nMajor: Computer Science" +
43              "\nOperating System Hours Taken: " + osHours +
44              "\nDatabase Hours Taken: " + dbHours;
45
46          return str;
47      }
48  }
```

Explanation

› Computer science students must take courses in different disciplines than those taken by biology students.
› It stands to reason that the `CompStudnet` class will calculate the number of hours remaining to be taken differently than the `BilogyStudent` class.
› The `CompStudent` class, which extends the `Student` class, declares the following final integer fields: `OS_HOURS`, & `DB_HOURS`. These fields hold the required number of operating system, and database hours for a computer science student.
› It also declares the following fields: `osHours`, `dbHours`. These fields hold the number of operating system, and database hours taken by the student.
› Mutator methods are provided to store values in these fields.

> In addition, the class overrides the `toString` method, and the abstract `getRamainningHours` method.

The `CompStudentDemo` implements the `CompStudent.java`.

Example 22.3: CompStudentDemo.java

```
01  package ch22;
02
03  public class CompStudentDemo
04  {
05      public static void main(String[] args)
06      {
07          // Create a CompStudent object.
08          CompStudent csStudent =
09              new CompStudent("Mohammed Mansour",
10                  "92500000");
11
12          // Store values for OS, and DB hours.
13          csStudent.setOsHours(20);
14          csStudent.setDbHours(35);
15
16          // Display the student's data.
17          System.out.println(csStudent);
18
19          // Display the number of remaining hours.
20          System.out.println("Hours remaining: " +
21              csStudent.getRemainingHours());
22      }
23  }
```

Output(CompStudentDemo.java)
```
Name: Mohammed Mansour
ID Number: 92500000
Year Admitted: 2005
Major: Computer Science
Operating System Hours Taken: 20
Database Hours Taken: 35
Hours remaining: 45
```

Remember the following points about abstract methods and classes:

> Abstract methods and abstract classes are defined with the `abstract` keyword.
> Abstract methods have no body, and their header must end with a semicolon.
> An Abstract method must be overridden in a subclass.
> When a class contains an abstract method, it cannot be instantiated. It must serve as a superclass.

Interfaces

An interface specifies behavior for a class. An Interface is similar to an abstract class that has all abstract methods. It cannot be instantiated, and all of the methods listed in an interface must be written else where. The purpose for an interface is to specify behavior for a class.

Syntax
```
public interface InterfaceName
{
    (Methods headers...)
}
```

An interface looks similar to a class except, the keyword `interface` is used instead of the keyword `class`, and the methods that are specified in an interface have no bodies, only header that are terminated by semicolons. Also no access specifier is used with the method headers, because all methods specified by an interface are **public**.

In order for a class to use an interface, it must implement the interface. This is accomplished with the `implements` keywords. For example (MyClass.java)

```
01  public class MyClass implements MyInterface
02  {
    . . .
07  }
```

A class that implements an interface must provide all of the methods that are listed in the interface, with the exact signatures specified and with the same return type.

"The interface only specifies the headers for these methods, not what the methods should do."

Fields in interfaces

An interface can contain field declaration, but all fields in an interface are treated as `final` and `static`. Because they automatically become `final`, you must provide an initialization value.

Example 22.5: Interface Definition

```
public interface Double
{
    int FIELD1 = 1;
    int FIELD2 = 2;
    (Method headers...)
}
```

`FIELD1`, and `FIELD2` are `final static int` variables. Any class that implements this interface has access to these variables.

Implementing multiple interfaces

Why we need both abstract classes and interfaces, since they are so similar to each other.

> The reason is that a class can extend only one superclass, but Java allows a class to implement multiple interfaces.
> When a class implements multiple interfaces, it must provide the methods specified by all of them.
> To specify multiple interfaces in a class definitions, simply list the names of the interfaces, separated by commas, after the implements keyword.

Example: First line of an example of a class that implements multiple interfaces
```
public class MyClass implements interface1, interface2, interface3
```
This class implements three interfaces: `Interface1`, `Interface2`, `Interface3`.

Polymorphism and Interfaces

Just as you create reference variables of a class type, Java allows you to create reference variables of an interface type. An interface reference variable can reference any object that implements that interface, regardless of its class type.

Example 22.6: RetailItems.java - Another example of Polymorphism
```
01  public interface RetailItem
02  {
03      public double getRetailPrice();
04  }
```

This interface specifies only one method: `getRetailPrice`. The `Book` class, implements this interface.

Example 22.7: Book.java
```
01  public class Book implements RetailItem
```

```
02  {
03      private String title;         // The Book's title
04      private String author;        // The Book's author
05      private double retailPrice;   // The Book's retail price
06      public Book(String bookTitle, String bookAuthor, double bookPrice)
07      {
08          title = bookTitle;
09          author = bookAuthor;
10          retailPrice = bookPrice;
11      }
12      public String getTitle()
13      {
14          return title;
15      }
16      public String getAuthor()
17      {
18          return author;
19      }
20      public double getRetailPrice()
21      {
22          return retailPrice;
23      }
24  }
```

The `MainDemo` implements the `RetailItems` interface.

Example 22.9: MainDemo.java

```
01  package ch22;
02
03  import java.text.DecimalFormat;
04  public class MainDemo
05  {
06      public static void main(String[] args)
07      {
08          // Create a book object.
09          Book bo = new Book("Learn Java", "Mohammed Abdelmoniem", 19.95);
10
11          RetailItem bo = new Book("Learn Java", "Mohammed Abdelmoniem", 19.95);
12
13          // Display the book's author
14          System.out.println("Author: " + bo.getAuthor());
15
16          // Display the Book's title.
17          System.out.println("Item #1: " + bo.getTitle());
18
19          // Display the book's price.
20          System.out.println("Price: $" + bo.getRetailPrice());
21      }
22  }
```

Output (MainDemo.java)

```
Author: Mohammed Abdelmoniem
Item #1: Learn Java
Price: $19.95
```

Because the `Book` class implements the `RetailItem` interface, object of this class may be referenced by a `RetailItem` reference variable. For example

```
RetailItem bo = new Book ("Learn Java" ," Mohammed Abdelmoniem",
19.95);
```

Explanation

> `RetailItem` reference variables `bo` is declared.
> The `bo` variable references a `book's` object. This is possible because the `Book` class implement the `RetailItem` interface.
> When a class implements an interface, an inheritance relationship known as interface inheritance is established.

Because of this inheritance relationship, a `Book` object is a `RetailItem`. Therefore, we can create `RetailItem` reference variables and have them reference `Book` object.

There are some limitations to using interface reference variables

> You cannot create an instance of an interface.

When an interface variable references an object, you can use the interface variable to call only the methods that are specified in the interface.

Here is a simple example.

Example 22.10: MainDemo.java - Reference an `Book` object with a `RetailItem` variable

```
Book bo = new Book("Learn Java", "Mohammed Abdelmoniem", 19.95);

RetailItem item = new Book("Learn Java", "Mohammed Abdelmoniem",
19.95);
// Call the getRetailPrice method
System.out.println(item.getRetailPrice()); // Ok, this works

// Attempts to call the getTitle method
System.out.print(item.getTitle()); // ERROR! will not compile
```

The last line of code will not compile because the `RetailItem` interface specifies only one method: `getRetailPrice`. So, we cannot use a `RetailItem` reference variable to call any other method.

TIPS: It is possible to cast an interface reference variable to the type of the object it references, and then call methods that are members of that type. The syntax is somewhat awkward, however. The statement that causes the compiler error in the

example code could be rewritten as:
```
System.out.println(((Book)item).getTitle());
```

Summary

- An abstract class is not instantiated, but other classes extend it.
- An abstract method has no body and must be overridden in a subclass.
- An abstract method is a method that appears in a superclass, but expects to be overridden in a subclass.
- As abstract method has only a header and no body.
- When an abstract method appears in a class, the method must be overridden in a subclass. If a subclass fails to override the method, an error will result. Abstract methods are used to ensure that a subclass implements the method.
- When a class contains an abstract method, you cannot create an instance of the class.
- Abstract methods are commonly used in abstract classes.
- An abstract class is not instantiated itself, but serves as a superclass for other classes.
- The abstract class represents the generic or abstract form of all of the classes that inherit from it.
- Abstract methods and abstract classes are defined with the abstract keyword.
- Abstract methods have no body, and their header must end with a semicolon.
- An Interface is similar to an abstract class that has all abstract methods. It cannot be instantiated, and all of the methods listed in an interface must be written else where. The purpose for an interface is to specify behavior for a class.
- An interface can contain field declaration, but all fields in an interface are treated as final and static. Because they automatically become final, you must provide an initialization value.
- Java allows you to create reference variables of an interface type. An interface reference variable can reference any object that implements that interface, regardless of its class type.
- An interface looks similar to a class except, the keyword `interface` is used instead of the keyword `class`, and the methods that are specified in an interface have no bodies, only header that are terminated by semicolons.

- A class that implements an interface must provide all of the methods that are listed in the interface, with the exact signatures specified and with the same return type.
- The interface only specifies the headers for these methods, not what the methods should do.

Chapter 23

Exceptions

Introduction

What Is an exception?

An exception is unexpected event, which occurs during the execution of a program. When an exception occurs, it interrupts the normal flow of the program.

To prevent exceptions from crashing your program, you must write code that detects and handles them. When an exception is generated, it is said to have been "**thrown**". Unless an exception is detected by the application and dealt with, it causes the application to halt.

An **exception handler** is a section of code that responds to exception when they are **thrown**. The process of interpreting and responding to exception is called **exception handling**. To detect that an exception has been thrown and prevent it from halting your application, Java allows you to create exception handlers.

If your code does not handle an exception when it is thrown, the default exception handlers deals with it. The default exception handler prints an error message and crashes the program. Here is a simple example-

Example 23.1: ArrayErro.java

```
01  public class ArrayError
02  {
03      public static void main(String[] args)
04      {
05          // Create an array with 5 elements.
06          int[] numbers = { 1, 2, 3, 4, 5 };
07
```

```
08          // Attempt to read beyond the bounds
09          // of the array.
10          for (int i = 0; i <= 5; i++)
11              System.out.println(numbers[i]);
12      }
13  }
```

Output

```
1
2
3
4
5
Exception in thread "main"
java.lang.ArrayIndexOutOfBoundsException: 4
    at ch23.ArrayError.main(ArrayError.java:13)
```

Explanation

> This program attempts to read beyond the bounds of an array. The `numbers` array has only five elements, with the subscripts 0 through 4.

> The program crashes when it tries to read the element at `numbers[5]`, and displays an error message similar to that shown at the end of the program output.

> This message indicates that an exception occurred, and it gives some information about it.

The developer must check for exceptions and write code to process them.

Handling Exception

Before you can catch an exception, some code somewhere must raise (throw) one. Any code can throw an exception: your code, code from a package written by someone else. Regardless of what throws the exception, it's always thrown with the `throw` statement.

The code that might throw certain exceptions must be enclosed by either of the following:

> Using the `try-catch`.
> Using the `throws` keyword.

Catching and handling exceptions using `try` statement

This lesson describes how to use the three exception handler components — the `try`, `catch`, and `finally` blocks — to write an exception handler.

`Try` and `catch` means it is like if you try a bit of code and if you have an error, instead of shutting down your program you're going to catch that error and do something with it.

Syntax
```
01  try
02  {
03      (try block statements...)
04  }
05  catch (ExceptionType parameterName)
06  {
07      (catch block statements...)
08  }
```

Explanation

> Line 01: The keyword `try` appears.
> Lines 02 - 04: A block of code appears insides braces, which are required. This block of code is known as a **try block**. A `try` block is one or more statements that are executed and can potentially throw an exception. You can think of code in the `try` block as being "protected" because the application will not halt if the try block throws an exception.
> Line 05: A `catch` clause appears. A `catch` clause begins with the keyword `catch`, followed by the code (`ExceptionType parameterName`). This is a parameter variable declaration, where `ExceptionType` is the name of an exception class and `parameterName` is a variable name. If code in the `try` block throws an exception of the `ExceptionType` class, then the parameter variable will reference the exception object. In addition, the code that immediately follows the `catch` clause is executed.
> Lines 06 - 08: The code that immediately follows the `catch` clause is known as a "**catch block**". Once again, the braces are required.

Let's try to understand the problem if we don't use a try-catch block.

Example 23.2: WithoutTry.java - without **try** statement
```
01  import java.util.*;
02
03  public class WitoutTry{
04      public static void main(String[] args){
05          Scanner input = new Scanner(System.in);
```

```
            System.out.println("Enter Your First NO: ");
            int number1 = input.nextInt();

            System.out.println("Enter Your Second NO: ");
            int number2 = input.nextInt();

            int sum = number1/number2;
            System.out.println(sum);
        }
    }
```

Output

```
Enter Your First NO:
12
Enter Your Second NO:
0
Exception in thread "main" java.lang.ArithmeticException: / by
zero
    at Ex1.ex1.main(ex1.java:14)
C:\Users\HP\AppData\Local\NetBeans\Cache\8.2\executor-
snippets\run.xml:53: Java returned: 1
BUILD FAILED (total time: 7 seconds)
```

Divide by zero it gives you an exception, so this shuts down the whole program. Let's see the solution of the above problem by using a Java try-catch block.

Example 23.3: WithTry.java - use `try-catch` statement

```
import java.util.*;

public class WithTry {
    public static void main(String[] args){
        Scanner input = new Scanner(System.in);

        try {
            System.out.println("Enter Your First NO: ");
            int number1 = input.nextInt();

            System.out.println("Enter Your Second NO: ");
            int number2 = input.nextInt();

            int sum = number1/number2;
            System.out.println(sum);
        }
        catch (Exception e){
            System.out.println("Error!");
        }
        System.out.println("Out of Try catch statement");
    }
}
```

Output

```
Enter Your First NO:
12
```

```
Enter Your Second NO:
0
Error!
Out of Try catch statement
```

Remember there always needs to be a `catch` after a `try`. And we're going to catch all errors (exceptions). The parameter `Exception` means to catch all the exceptions. It is means if the user do anything wrong at all.

Catching and handling exceptions using `throws` clause

Java `throws` keyword is used to declare a list of exceptions that may occur during the METHOD EXECUTION. The CALLER to this method has to handle the exception using a `try-catch` block.

Syntax
```
<return type> method_name (parameters if any) throws
type_of_exception_list;
```

(type_of_exception_list is a comma separated list of all the exceptions which a method might throw)

Syntax
```
public static void method() throws FileNotFoundException ,
ConnectException
{
    // Code
}
```

In a program, if there is a chance of rising an exception then compiler always warn us about it and compulsorily we should handle that exception, otherwise we will get compile time error.

To understand what an exception is, consider the following code.

Example 23.4: ThrowEx1.java - error in case of unhandled exception
```
01  public class ThrowEx1{
02      public static void main(String[] args){
03          Thread.sleep(10000);
04          System.out.println("Welcome");
05      }
06  }
```

Output
```
Error:Error:line (5)java: unreported exception
java.lang.InterruptedException; must be caught or declared to be
thrown
```

Explanation

In the previous example, we are getting compile time error because there is a chance of exception if the `main` method is going to sleep, other threads get the chance to execute `main()` method which will cause `InterruptedException`.

Let's see the solution of the previous example by using a Java `throws` keyword.

Example 23.5: ThrowEx2.java -using `throws`

```
01  package ch23;
02
03  public class ThrowEx2 {
04      public static void main(String[] args)
05      {
06          try {
07              // Thread.sleep(10000);
08              method();
09              System.out.println("Welcome");
10          }catch (InterruptedException e){
11              // code
12          }
13      }
14      public static void method() throws InterruptedException {
15          Thread.sleep(10000);
16      }
17  }
```

Output

```
Welcome
```

Explanation

> In the above program, by using `throws` keyword we handled the `InterruptedException` and we will get the output as `Welcome`.
> Java `throws` keyword is used to declare a list of exceptions that may occur during the `method` method execution (in our case `InterruptedException` exception)
> The caller (`main` method) to the `method` method has to handle the exception using a `try-catch` block.

Exception Propagation

An exception propagates from method to method, up the call stack, until it's caught. So if `main()` calls `method()`, and if `method()` throws an exception, the exception will propagate from `method()` method to `main()` method, unless one of these methods catches the exception - in our case the `main` method.

Suppose, if `one()` calls `two()`, which calls `three()`, which calls `four()`, and if `four()` throws and exception, the exception will propagate from `four()` to `three()` to `two()` to `one`, unless are of these methods catches the exception.

When an appropriate handler (catch block) is found (in our case the `main` method), the runtime system passes the exception to the handler. If no exception handler is found then exception reaches to JVM's default exception handler which prints the exception details to logs and terminate the application.

Important points to remember about throws keyword

› `throws` keyword is required only to convince compiler and usage of `throws` keyword doesn't prevent termination of program.

› By the help of `throws` keyword we can provide information to the caller of the method about the exception.

NOTE: Don't confuse the `throw` statement with the `throws` clause. The `throw` statement causes an exception to be thrown. The `throws` clause informs the compiler that a method throws one or more exceptions.

NOTE: We can declare checked and unchecked exceptions using throws clause. But the method calling the given method must handle only checked exception.

Throwing exceptions using `throw` statement

In Java exception handling, `throw` keyword is used to throw an exception from a method, or constructor.

Syntax of throw statement

```
throw new ExceptionType (MessageString);
```

Syntax 2

```
public void method()
{
    // throwing an exception
    throw new SomeException("Message");
}
```

Explanation

If we throw an exception using `throw` statement, we MUST either handle the exception in catch block or method must explicitly declare it using `throws` declaration.

> The `throw` statement causes an exception object to be created and thrown.
> `ExceptionType` is an exception clause name and
> `MessageString` is an optional String argument passed to the exception object's constructor.
> The `MessageString` argument contains a custom error message that can be retrieved from the exception object's `getMessage` method.
> If you do not pass a message to the constructor, the exception will have a null message.

Here is a simple example that demonstrates the use of throw.

Example 23.6: ThrowExcep.java

```
01  public class ThrowExcep {
02      static void test()
03      {
04          try{
05              throw new NumberFormatException("demo");
06          } catch (NumberFormatException e){
07              System.out.println("Caught inside test().");
08              throw e; // rethrowing the exception
09          }
10      }
11      public static void main(String[] args)
12      {
13          try {
14              test();
15          }catch (NumberFormatException e){
16              System.out.println("Caught in main");
17          }
18      }
19  }
```

Output
```
Caught inside test().
Caught in main
```

Explanation

> The flow of execution of the program stops immediately after the `throw` statement is executed (Line 05) and the nearest enclosing `try` block is checked to see if it has a `catch` statement (Line 06) that matches the type of exception (`NumberFormatException`).
> If it finds a match, control is transferred to that statement, otherwise next enclosing `try` block is checked and so on.

> If no matching catch is found then default exception handler will halt the program.

Difference between throw and throws in Java

Table 23.1 | Difference between throw and throws in Java[1]

throw keyword	throws keyword
Is used to throw a single exception explicitly from any method or constructor.	Is used in method and constructor declaration, denoted which exception can possible by thrown by this method.
Is followed by an instance of exception class.	Is followed by exception class name.
Is used within the method and constructor.	Is used with the method and constructor signature.
We can throw only single exception using throw.	We can declare multiple exceptions using throws one of which may or may not throw by method.
Using throw keyword we can also break a switch statement or a loop without using break keyword which cannot be performed using throws.	

Finding Details of the Exception

In java there are three ways to find the details of the exception. They are:
> Using an object of `java.lang.Exception` class.
> Using `public void printStrackTrack` method.
> Using `public string getMessage` method.

Using an object of `java.lang.Exception`

An object of Exception class prints the name of the exception and nature of the message.

Example 23.7: Try1.java

---

[1] https://howtodoinjava.com/java/exception-handling/throw-vs-throws/

```
01  public class Try1 {
02      public static void main(String[] args){
03          try {
04              double x = Double.parseDouble("100.00y");
05          } catch (Exception e) {
06              System.out.println(e);
07          }
08      }
09  }
```

Output

```
java.lang.NumberFormatException: For input string: "100.00y"
```

Explanation

> `java.lang.NumberFormatException`: **Name of the exception**
> For input String `100.00y` : **Nature of the message**

Using `printStackTrace` method

This is the method which is defined in `java.lang.Throwable` class and it is inherited into `java.lang.Error` class and `java.lang.Exception` class. This method will display name of the exception, nature of the message and line number where the exception has taken place. Here is a simple example.

Example 23.8: Try2.java

```
01  public class Try2 {
02      public static void main(String[] args){
03          try {
04              double x = Double.parseDouble("100.00y");
05          } catch (Exception e) {
06              e.printStackTrace();
07          }
08      }
09  }
```

Output

```
java.lang.NumberFormatException: For input string: "100.00y"
    at
java.base/jdk.internal.math.FloatingDecimal.readJavaFormatString
(FloatingDecimal.java:2054)
    at
java.base/jdk.internal.math.FloatingDecimal.parseDouble(Floating
Decimal.java:110)
    at java.base/java.lang.Double.parseDouble(Double.java:543)
    at ch23.Try2.main(Try2.java:6)
```

Explanation

> `java.lang.NumberFormatException`: **Name of the exception**

> For input String `100.00y`: Nature of the message

Using `getMessage` method

This is a method which is defined in `java.lang.Throwable` class and it is inherited into both `Error` and `Exception` classes. This method will display only nature of the message. Here is a simple example.

Example 23.9: Try3.java

```
01  public class Try3 {
02      public static void main(String[] args) {
03          try {
04              double x = Double.parseDouble("100.00y");
05          } catch (Exception e) {
06              System.out.println(e.getMessage());
07          }
08      }
09  }
```

Output

```
For input string: "100.00y"
```

Polymorphic References to Exceptions

Recall from previous lessons that, a reference variable of a superclass type can reference subclass objects. This is called Polymorphism.

When handling exceptions, you can use a polymorphic reference as a parameter in the `catch` clause. For example: all of the exceptions that we have dealt with inherit from the `Exception` class. So, a `catch` clause that uses a parameter variable of the `Exception` type is capable of catching any exception that inherits from the `Exception` class. Consider below example for that.

Example 23.10. ParseIntError.java

```
01  package ch23;
02
03  import java.util.Scanner;
04
05  public class ParseIntError {
06      public static void main(String[] args) {
07          Scanner sc = new Scanner(System.in);
08          System.out.println("Enter Yor Number");
09          String input = sc.nextLine();
10          try
11          {
```

```
12                  Integer number = Integer.parseInt(input);
13                  System.out.println("The Result is " + number/0);
14              }
15          catch (Exception e)
16          {
17                  System.out.println("Conversion error: " + e.getMessage());
18          }
19      }
20  }
```

Output
```
Enter Yor Number
8
Conversion error: / by zero
```

The Integer class's `parseInt` method throws a `NumberFormatException` object, this code still works because the `NumberFormatException` class inherits from the `Exception` class.

Handling Multiple Exception

The programs we have studied so far test only for a single type of exception. In many cases, however, the code in the `try` block will be capable of throwing more than one type of exception. In such a case, you need to write a `catch` clause for each type of exception that could potentially be thrown. Here is a simple example.

Example 23.11: MultiExcp.java
```
01  public class MultiExcp {
02      public static void main(String[] args){
03          try{
04              int arr[] = new int[10];
05              arr[3] = 10/0;
06              System.out.println("Try Block Statement");
07          } catch (ArithmeticException e) {
08              System.out.println("Divide By Zero Error Encoun-
tered");
09          } catch (ArrayIndexOutOfBoundsException e){
10              System.out.println("Access Array Beyond the Limit");
11          } catch (Exception e) {
12              System.out.println("Other Exception");
13          }
14          System.out.println("Out of the try-catch");
15      }
16  }
```

Output

```
Divide By Zero Error Encountered
Out of the try-catch
```

In the above example, the first `catch` block got executed because the code we have written in `try` block throws `ArithmeticException` (because we divided the number by zero).

Now lets change the code a little bit and see the change in output.

Example 23.12: MultiExcp2.java

```
01  public class MultiExcp2 {
02      public static void main(String[] args){
03          try{
04              int arr[] = new int[10];
05              arr[12] = 10/2;
06              System.out.println("Try Block Statement");
07          } catch (ArithmeticException e) {
08              System.out.println("Divide By Zero Error Encountered");
09          } catch (ArrayIndexOutOfBoundsException e){
10              System.out.println("Access Array Beyond the Limit");
11          } catch (Exception e) {
12              System.out.println("Other Exception");
13          }
14          System.out.println("Out of the try-catch");
15      }
16  }
```

Output

```
Access Array Beyond the Limit
Out of the try-catch
```

In this case, the second `catch` block got executed because the code throws `ArrayIndexOutOfBoundsException`. We are trying to access the 12th element of array in above program but the array size is only 10. When an exception occurs, the specific `catch` block (that declares that exception) executes.

If an exception occurs in the above code which is not Arithmetic and Array IndexOutOfBounds then the `generic catch` handler would execute. You should always place this block at the end of all other specific exception catch blocks. A generic `catch` block can handle all the exceptions. Whether it is `ArrayIndexOutOfBoundsException` or `ArithmeticException` or `NullPointerException` or any other type of exception, this handles all of them.

The `finally` Clauses

A `finally` block contains all the crucial statements that must be executed whether exception occurs or not. The statements present in this block will always execute regardless of whether exception occurs in `try` block or not.

The `try` statement may have an optional `finally` clause, which must appear after all of the catch clauses.

General Syntax (try statement with a finally clause)
```
01  try
02  {
03      (try block statement...)
04  }
05  catch (ExceptionType ParameterName)
06  {
07      (catch block statement....)
08  }
09  finally
10  {   }
```

The `finally` block is one or more statements that are always executed after the `try` block has executed and after any `catch` blocks have executed if an exception was thrown. The statements in the `finally` block execute whether an exception occurs or not.

Example 23.13: Fin.java A Simple Example of finally block

Here you can see that the exception occurred in `try` block which has been handled in `catch` block, after that `finally` block got executed.

```
01  public class Fin {
02      public static void main(String[] args){
03          try{
04              int arr[] = new int[10];
05              arr[12] = 10/2;
06              System.out.println("Try Block Statement");
07          } catch (ArithmeticException e) {
08              System.out.println("Divide By Zero Error Encountered");
09          } catch (ArrayIndexOutOfBoundsException e){
10              System.out.println("Access Array Beyond the Limit");
11          } catch (Exception e) {
12              System.out.println("Other Exception");
13          }finally {
14              System.out.println("This is finally block ");
```

```
15        }
16            System.out.println("Out of the try-catch");
17    }
18 }
```

Output

```
Access Array Beyond the Limit
This is finally block
Out of the try-catch
```

Points about finally block:
☐ A `finally` block must be associated with a `try` block.
☐ `finally` block is optional.

The only case where the finally block will not execute is when it encounters `System.exit()`. For example:

Example 23.14: Fin2.java

```
01 public class Fin2 {
02     public static void main(String[] args){
03         try{
04             int arr[] = new int[10];
05             arr[12] = 10/2;
06             System.out.println("Try Block Statement");
07         } catch (ArithmeticException e) {
08             System.out.println("Divide By Zero Error Encountered");
09         } catch (ArrayIndexOutOfBoundsException e){
10             System.out.println("Access Array Beyond the Limit");
11             System.exit(0);
12         } catch (Exception e) {
13             System.out.println("Other Exception");
14         }finally {
15             System.out.println("This is finally block ");
16         }
17         System.out.println("Out of the try-catch");
18     }
19 }
```

Output

```
Access Array Beyond the Limit
```

The finally block overrides the value returned by try and `catch` blocks

Example 23.15: MyFinal.java - Lets take an example to understand this:

```
01 public class MyFinal {
02     public static int myTestingMethod(){
03         try{
04             // code goes here
```

```
05              return 9;
06          }finally {
07              // code goes here
08              return 20;
09          }
10      }
11      public static void main(String[] args){
12          MyFinal my = new MyFinal();
13          int i = my.myTestingMethod();
14          System.out.println(i);
15      }
16  }
```

Output
```
20
```

This program would return value `20` since the value returned by try has been overridden by `finally`.

The Stack Trace

Quite often, a method will call another method, which will call yet another method. For example, method **A** calls method **B**, which calls method **C**.

What is the Call Stack?

› The call stack is an internal list of all of the methods that are currently executing.
› When an exception is thrown by a method that is executing under several layers of method calls, it is sometimes helpful to know which methods were responsible for the method being called.
› A Stack trace is a list of all the methods in the call stack. It indicates the method that was executing when an exception occurred and all of the methods that were called in order to execute that method.

Consider the following example.

Example 23.16: StackTrace.java
```
01  public class StackTrace
02  {
03      public static void main(String[] args)
04      {
05          System.out.println("Calling myMethod...");
06          myMethod();
07          System.out.println("Method main is done.");
08      }
09      public static void myMethod()
```

```
10      {
11          System.out.println("Calling produceError...");
12          produceError();
13          System.out.println("myMethod is done.");
14      }
15      public static void produceError()
16      {
17          String str = "abc";
18
19          // The following statement will cause an error.
20          System.out.println(str.charAt(3));
21          System.out.println("peoduceError is done.");
22      }
23  }
```

Output
```
Calling myMethod...
Calling produceError...
Exception in thread "main"
java.lang.StringIndexOutOfBoundsException: String index out of
range: 3
    at
java.base/java.lang.StringLatin1.charAt(StringLatin1.java:44)
    at java.base/java.lang.String.charAt(String.java:692)
    at ch23.StackTrace.produceError(StackTrace.java:22)
    at ch23.StackTrace.myMethod(StackTrace.java:14)
    at ch23.StackTrace.main(StackTrace.java:8)
```

Explanation

> The program has three methods: `main`, `myMethod`, and `produceError`.
> The `main` method calls `myMethod`, which calls `produceError`.
> The `produceError` position number to the String class's `charAt` method.
> The exception is not handled by the program, but is dealt with by the default exception handler.
> When the exception occurs, the error message shows as stack trace listing the methods that were called in order to produce the exception.
> The first method that is listed in the stack trace, `charAt`, is the method that is responsible for the exception.
> The next method, `produceError`, is the method that called `charAt`.
> The next method, `myMethod`, is the method that called `produceError`.
> The last method, `main` is the method that called `myMethod`.
> The stack trace shows the chain of method's that were called when the exception was thrown.

NOTE: All exception objects has a `printStackTrace` method, inherited from the `Throwable` class, which can be used to print a stack trace.

When an Exception Is Not Caught

› When an exception is thrown, it cannot be ignored. It must be handled by the program, or by default exception handler.
› When the code in a method throws an exception, the normal execution of that method stops and JVM searches for a compatible exception handler inside the method.
› If there is no code the method to handle the previous method in the call stack (that is, the method that called the offending method)
› If that method cannot handle the exception, then control is passed again, up the call stack, to the previous method.
› This continues until control reaches the `main` method. The `main` method does not handle the exception, then the program is halted and the default exception handler handles the exception.
› This was the case for the program in `StackTrace.java`. Because the `produceError` method did not handle the exception, control was passed back to `myMethod`.
› It didn't handle the exception either, so control was passed back to `main`. Because `main` didn't handle the exception, the program halted and the default exception handler displayed the error messages.

Exception Classes

An exception is an object. Exception objects are created from classes in Java. The Java has an extensive hierarchy of exception classes. A small part of the hierarchy is shown in next figure.

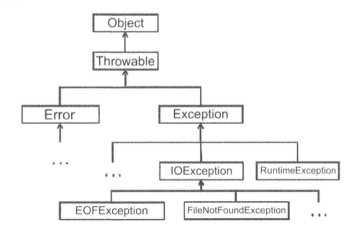

Figure 23.1 | Part of the Exception Class Hierarchy

All of the classes inherit from the `Throwable` class. Just below the `Throwable` class are the classes `Error` and `Exception`.

Classes that inherit from `Error` are for exceptions that are thrown when a critical error occurs, such as an internal error in the Java Virtual Machine or running out of memory. Your application should not try to handle these errors because they are the result of a serious condition. All of the exception that you will handle are instances of classes that inherit from *Exception*.

Part of the exception class hierarchy: Shows two of these classes: `IOException` & `RuntimeException`. These classes also serve as superclasses.

> `IOException` serves as a superclass for exceptions that are related to input and output operations.
> `RuntimeException` serves as a superclass for exceptions that result from programming errors, such as an out-of-bounds array subscript.

Part of the exception class hierarchy **shows two of the classes that inherit from the IOException class:** `EOFException` and `FileNotFoundException`. These are examples of classes that exception objects are created from.

An `EOFException` object is thrown when an application attempts to read beyond the end of a file, and a `FileNotFoundException` object is thrown when an application tries to open a file that does not exist.

Checked and Unchecked Exceptions

In Java, there are two categories of exceptions: unchecked and checked.

Unchecked exception

Unchecked exceptions are those that inherit from the `Error` class or the `RuntimeException` class. Recall that the exceptions that inherit from Error are thrown when a critical error occurs, such as running out of memory. You should not handle these exceptions because the conditions that cause them can rarely be dealt with in the program.

Recall that the `RuntimeException` serves as a superclass for exceptions that result from programming errors, such as an out-of-bounds array subscript. It is best no to handle these exceptions either, because they can be avoided with properly written code. So you should not handle unchecked exceptions.

Checked exceptions

All of the remaining exceptions (that is, those that do not inherit from `ErrorRuntimeException`) are **checked** exceptions. These are the exceptions that you should handle in your program.

If the code in a method can potentially throw a checked exceptions, then that method must meet one of the following requirements:

> It must handle the exception - or
> It must have a `throws` clause listed in the method `handler`. The `throws` clause informs the compiler of the exceptions that could get thrown from a method.

Here is a simple example.

Example 23.17

```
01  // This method, will not compile
02  public void displayFile(String name)
03  {
04      // Open the file
05      File file = new File(name);
06      Scanner inputFile = new Scanner(file);
07
08      // Read and display the file's contents
```

```
        while (inputFile.hasNext())
        {
            System.out.println(inputFile.nextLine());
        }

        // Close the file
        inputFile.close();
    }
```

Explanation

> The code in this method is capable of throwing a `FileNotFoundException`, which is a checked exception.
> Because the method does not handle this exception, it must have a `throws` clause in its header or it will not compile.
> The keyword `throws` is written at the end of the method header, followed by a list of the types of exceptions that the method can throw.

Revised method header
```
public void displayFile(String name) throws FileNotFoundException
```

The `throws` clause tells the compiler that this method can throw a `FileNotFoundException` (if there is more than one type of exception, you separate them with commas.)

Now you know why you wrote a throws clause on methods in the previous chapters. We had to inform the compiler that our methods might pass them up the call stack.

Summary

> An exception is unexpected event, which occurs during the execution of a program. When an exception occurs, it interrupts the normal flow of the program.
> To prevent exceptions from crashing your program, you must write code that detects and handles them. When an exception is generated, it is said to have been "thrown". Unless an exception is detected by the application and dealt with, it causes the application to halt.
> An **exception handler** is a section of code that responds to exception when they are **thrown**. The process of interpreting and responding to exception is called **exception handling**. To detect that an exception has been thrown

› and prevent it from halting your application, Java allows you to create exception handlers.
› If your code does not handle an exception when it is thrown, the default exception handlers deals with it. The default exception handler prints an error message and crashes the program.
› The code that might throw certain exceptions must be enclosed by using the **try-catch** or using the **throws** keyword.
› Try and catch means it is like if you try a bit of code and if you have an error, instead of shutting down your program you're going to catch that error and do something with it.
› **throws** is a keyword in Java which is used in the signature of method to indicate that this method might throw one of the listed type exceptions. The caller to these methods has to handle the exception using a try-catch block. The **throw** keyword in Java is used to explicitly throw an exception from a method or any block of code. The **throw** keyword is mainly used to throw custom exceptions.
› You can write code that throws one of the standard Java exceptions, or an instance of a custom exception class that you have designed. You can use the **throw** statement to throw an exception manually.
› In java there are three ways to find the details of the exception. They are using : an object of `java.lang.Exception` class, `public void printStrackTrack` method and `public string getMessage` method.
› When handling exceptions, you can use a polymorphic reference as a parameter in the `catch` clause. For example: all of the exceptions that we have dealt with inherit from the `Exception` class. So, a `catch` clause that uses a parameter variable of the Exception type is capable of catching any exception that inherits from the Exception class.
› A reference variable of a superclass type can reference subclass objects. This is called Polymorphism. When handling exceptions, you can use a polymorphic reference as a parameter in the catch clause.
› In many cases, however, the code in the `try` block will be capable of throwing more than one type of exception. In such a case, you need to write a catch clause for each type of exception that could potentially be thrown.
› A `finally` block contains all the crucial statements that must be executed whether exception occurs or not.
› All exception objects has a `printStackTrace` method, inherited from the `Throwable` class, which can be used to print a stack trace.

- An exception is an object. Exception objects are created from classes in Java. The Java has an extensive hierarchy of exception classes. All of the classes inherit from the `Throwable` class. Just below the `Throwable` class are the classes `Error` and `Exception`.
- Classes that inherit from `Error` are for exceptions that are thrown when a critical error occurs, such as an internal error in the Java Virtual Machine or running out of memory. Your application should not try to handle these errors because they are the result of a serious condition. All of the exception that you will handle are instances of classes that inherit from `Exception`. Part of the exception class hierarchy: Shows two of these classes: `IOException` & `RuntimeException`. These classes also serve as superclasses. `IOException` serves as a superclass for exceptions that are related to input and output operations. `RuntimeException` serves as a superclass for exceptions that result from programming errors, such as an out-of-bounds array subscript.
- In Java, there are two categories of exceptions: unchecked and checked. **Unchecked** exceptions are those that inherit from the `Error` class or the `RuntimeException` class. All of the remaining exceptions (that is, those that do not inherit from `ErrorRuntimeException`) are **checked** exceptions. These are the exceptions that you should handle in your program.
- `Main` method should not throw any exception since the main method is called by **JVM** and **JVM** cannot provide user friendly message.

Chapter 24

Java File I/O

Introduction

Storage of data in variables and arrays is temporary and disappears once the program stops running or the power is switched off. For permanent storage, we use files, which are collections of data stored in computer's secondary memory, such as hard disk, CD-ROM, DVD-ROM, and USB memory stick.

Files are organized into directories (sometimes called folders). A directory can hold other directories, as well as files. With Java we can read data from existing files, create new files, write data to files, and so on.

In Java, the main I/O are called **streams**. **Input stream** represents a source of input, and **output stream** represents a destination to which output can be sent. There are many predefined classes that represent streams of each type. Java has two main categories of streams -

- **byte-streams**: deals with machine-formatted data (string of zeros and ones)
  - For reading machine-formatted data, the main class is the class **InputStream**.
  - For writing machine-formatted data, the main class is the class **OutputStream**.
  - If you write numbers to an **OutputStream**, you won't be able to read the resulting data yourself. But the data can be read back into the computer with an **InputStream**
- **character-streams**: deals with human-readable data (characters such as 12.5, ABC, etc)

- For reading human-readable character data, the main class is the class **Reader**
- For writing human-readable character data, the main class is the class **Writer**

The standard stream classes discussed in this section are defined in the package `java.io`, along with several supporting classes. The basic I/O classes `Reader`, `Writer`, `InputStream`, and `OutputStream` provide only very primitive I/O methods or operations as shows in the following Table 24.1

Table 24.1 Primitive I/O Classes and their methods

Class	Method	Description
InputStream	read()	Read one byte of data from input stream.
OutputStream	write()	Write one byte of data to an output stream
Reader	read()	Read one character of data from input stream
Writer	write()	Write one character of data to an output stream.

This is not a problem, because instead, you'll use subclasses of InputStream/OutputStream and Reader/Writer that add more convenient input/output methods rather than primitive capabilities.

The File Class

The `File` only gives you access to the file and file system meta data. Using the `File` class you can create a file, delete a file, rename or move a file, create a directory and so on. So let's start.

Instantiating a `File` object

Before you can do anything with the file system or `File` class, you must create a `File` instance. Here is how that is done:

```
import java.io.File;
. . .
File f = new File("c:\\dir\\file.txt");
```

Explanation

> 1st Line: The **java.io** package provides a class library for reading and writing any type of data (text, numbers, images) in streams from any type of location (disk, network, memory).
> 2nd Line: Create a `File` object, and define the path of a file - in this case (`c:\dir\file.txt`)

What we're going to be doing is testing whether a file exists on our computer.

Check if file exists

Once you have instantiated a `File` object you can check if the corresponding file actually exists already. To check if the file exits, we call the `exists()` method. Here is a simple example.

Example 24.1: CheckFile.java - check if file exists

```
01  import java.io.File;
02  public class File1 {
03      public static void main(String[] args){
04          File f = new File("D:\\Documents\\lang2.txt");
05          if(f.exists())
06              System.out.println("The " + f.getName() + " file is exists.");
07          else
08              System.out.println("The " + f.getName() + " file doesn't exists.");
09      }
10  }
```

Output(If the lang2.txt file exist)
```
The lang2.txt file is exists.
```

Output(if the lang2.txt file doesn't exists)
```
The lang2.txt file doesn't exists.
```

Create a file if it does not exist

The following example shows the usage of `createNewFile()` method using `try.. catch` statement.

Example 24.2: CreateEmptyFile.java - create a file if it doesn't exist using try.. catch statement

```
01  import java.io.File;
02  import java.io.IOException;
03
04  public class CreateEmptyFile
05  {
06      public static void main( String[] args )
```

```
07    {
08        try {
09
10            File f = new File("d:\\newfile.txt");
11
12            if (f.createNewFile()){
13              System.out.println("File is created!");
14            }else{
15              System.out.println("File already exists.");
16            }
17
18        } catch (IOException e){
19            e.printStackTrace();
20        }
21      }
22  }
```

Output (if the newFile.text doesn't exist)
```
File is created!
```

Output (if the newFile.text already exist)
```
File already exists.
```

Explanation
> Line 10: Create a **File** object and define the path of a file.
> Line 12: Return true if the file was created and false if the file already exists.
> Line 13: Executed if the expression on Line 12 is true.
> Line 15: Executed if the expression on Line 12 is false

Create a directory if it does not exist

You can use the `File` class to create directories if they don't already exists. The `File` class contains the `mkdir()` and `mkdirs()` methods for that purpose. The following two examples explains both methods.

Example 24.3: CreateSingleDir.java - create a single directory if it does not exist using `mkdir()` method

```
01  package ch24;
02
03  import java.io.File;
04  import java.io.IOException;
05
06  public class CreateSingleDir{
07      public static void main(String[] args){
08          try{
09              File f = new File("D:\\Documents\\MyFiles\\newDir");
10              if (f.mkdir()){
11                  System.out.println("Directory is created!");
12              }else{
```

```
                    System.out.println("Directory already exists.");
                }
            } catch(Exception e) {
                e.printStackTrace();
            }
        }
    }
```

Output (if directory does not exist)
```
Directory is created!
```

Output (if directory already exist)
```
Directory already exists.
```

Explanation

> Provided that the directory `D:\Documents\MyFiles` already exists, the above code will create a subdirectory of `MyFiles` named `newdir`.

> The `mkdir()` returns `true` if the directory was created, and `false` if the directory already exists..

Example 24.4: CreateAllDirs.java - create all directories that are missing in the path the **File** object represent using **mkdirs()** method

```
01  package ch24;
02
03  import java.io.File;
04  import java.io.IOException;
05
06  public class CreateSingleDir {
07      public static void main(String[] args) {
08          try{
09              File f = new File("D:\\Documents\\MyFiles\\newDir");
10              if (f.mkdirs()){
11                  System.out.println("Directory is created!");
12              }else{
13                  System.out.println("Directory already exists.");
14              }
15          } catch(Exception e) {
16              e.printStackTrace();
17          }
18      }
19  }
```

Output (if directory does not exist)
```
Directory is created!
```

Output (if directory already exist)
```
Directory already exists.
```

Explanation

> Provided that the D drive exists, this example will create all the directories in the path, which are Documents, MyFiles, and newdir (D:\Documents\MyFiles\newdir)
> The `mkdirs()` method will return `true` if all the directories were created, and `false` if all directories already exists.

Rename or move file

To rename (or move) a file, call the method `renameTo()` on the `File` class. Here is a simple example.

Example 24.5: RenameFile.java
```
01  package ch24;
02
03  import java.io.File;
04  import java.io.IOException;
05
06  public class RenameFile {
07      public static void main(String[] args) throws IOException
    {
08          try {
09              // Create a directory
10              File dir = new File("D:\\Documents\\dir1");
11              if (dir.mkdirs()) {
12                  System.out.println("Directory is created!");
13              } else {
14                  System.out.println("Directory already exists.");
15              }
16
17              // Create the file1.txt file.
18              File file1 = new File("D:\\Documents\\dir1\\file1.txt");
19              if (file1.createNewFile()) {
20                  System.out.println("File is created!");
21              } else {
22                  System.out.println("File already exists.");
23              }
24
25              // Rename the file1.txt to file2.txt
26              boolean file2 = file1.renameTo(new File("D:\\Documents\\dir1\\file2.txt"));
27              if (file2) {
28                  System.out.println("File is renamed!");
29              } else {
30                  System.out.println("File already exists.");
31              }
32          } catch (IOException e) {
33              e.getStackTrace();
34          }
35      }
```

Explanation
› Line 26: The `renameTo()` method returns `true` if the file is renamed, and `false` if the file name is already exists.

The new file name passed to the `renameTo()` method does not have to be in the same directory as the file was already residing in, as shown in the following example.

Example 24.6: MoveFile.java

```
01  package ch24;
02
03  import java.io.File;
04  import java.io.IOException;
05
06  public class MoveFile{
07      public static void main(String[] args) throws IOException {
08          try {
09              // Create a directory
10              File dir = new File("D:\\Documents\\dir2");
11              if (dir.mkdirs()) {
12                  System.out.println("Directory is created!");
13              } else {
14                  System.out.println("Directory already exists.");
15              }
16
17              // Create the file2019.txt file.
18              File file1 = new File("D:\\Documents\\dir2\\file2019.txt");
19              if (file1.createNewFile()) {
20                  System.out.println("File is created!");
21              } else {
22                  System.out.println("File already exists.");
23              }
24
25              // Rename the file2019.txt to file2020.txt
26              // and move the file2020.txt to d: drive
27              boolean file2 = file1.renameTo(new File("D:\\file2020.txt"));
28              if (file2) {
29                  System.out.println("File is renamed and moved to d drive!");
30              } else {
31                  System.out.println("File already exists.");
32              }
33          } catch (IOException e) {
34              e.getStackTrace();
35          }
36      }
37  }
```

Output
```
Directory is created!
File is created!
File is renamed and moved to D drive!
```

Delete file

To delete a file call the `delete()` method.

Example 24.7: DeleteFile.java
```
File f = new File("D:\\Documents\\dir2\\file2019.txt");
boolean success = f.delete();
```

The `delete()` method returns `true` if the file was deleted successful, and `false` if not.

Check if path is file or directory

A `File` object can point to both a file or a directory. By calling `isDirectory()` method, you can check if a File object points to a file or directory. This method returns `true` if the `File` points to a directory, and `false` if the `File` points to a file. Here is how that is done.

Example 24.8: CheckDir.java
```
01  package ch24;
02
03  import java.io.File;
04
05  public class CheckDir {
06      public static void main(String[] args) {
07          File f = new File("D:\\Documents");
08          boolean isDir = f.isDirectory();
09          if (isDir){
10              System.out.println("Directory is exists.");
11          }else{
12              System.out.println("Directory doesn't exists.");
13          }
14      }
15  }
```

Output (if directory is already exists)
```
Directory is exist.
```

Explanation
› Line 08: The `isDirectory()` method returns true if the File points to a directory, and false if the File points to a file.

Read list of files in directory

You can obtain a list of all the files in a directory by calling either the `list()` method or the `listFiles()` method. The following example explains both methods.

Example 24.9: ReadListFiles.java

```
01  package ch24;
02
03  import java.io.File;
04  import java.io.IOException;
05
06  public class ReadListFiles {
07      public static void main(String[] args) throws IOException
    {
08          File f = new File("D:\\Documents");
09          String[] fileNames = f.list();
10          File[] files = f.listFiles();
11
12          for (int i = 0; i < fileNames.length; i++){
13              System.out.println(fileNames[i]);
14          }
15
16          for (int j = 0; j < files.length; j++){
17              System.out.println(files[j]);
18          }
19      }
20  }
```

Output
```
dir1
New Text Document - Copy (2).txt
New Text Document - Copy (3).txt
New Text Document - Copy.txt
New Text Document.txt
D:\Documents\dir1
D:\Documents\New Text Document - Copy (2).txt
D:\Documents\New Text Document - Copy (3).txt
D:\Documents\New Text Document - Copy.txt
D:\Documents\New Text Document.txt
```

Explanation
› The `list()` method returns an array of String's with the file and / or directory names of directory the **File** object points to.
› The `listFiles()` method returns an array of **File** objects representing the files and / or directory in the directory the File points to.

Text Files

Writing data to a text file using `PrintWriter` class

The `PrintWriter` class provides convenient methods for outputting human-readable character representation. Here is how that is done.

Example 24.10: DataToFile.java - write data to the text file

```
01  package ch24;
02
03  import java.io.File;
04  import java.io.PrintWriter;
05
06  public class DataToFile {
07      public static void main(String[] args) {
08          try{
09              PrintWriter outputFile = new PrintWriter("d:\\Number.txt");
10              int x = 1297;
11              // Writes the contents of the variable x to the d:\\Number.txt file
12              outputFile.print(x);
13              outputFile.flush();
14              // When the number is written, however,
15              // it is stored as the characters
16              // '1','2','9', and '7
17          }catch (Exception e){
18              System.out.println("Error" + e.getMessage());
19          }
20      }
21  }
```

The number 1297 expressed as characters:

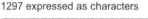

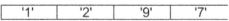

Figure 24.1 | The number 1297 expressed as character

Binary Files

A file that contains raw binary data is known as a **binary file**. The content of a binary file is not formatted as text, and not meant to be opened in a text editor.

Storing data in its binary format is more efficient than storing it as text because there are fewer conversions to take place. In addition, there are some types of data that should only be stored in their raw binary format. Images are an example. However, when data is stored in a binary file, you cannot open the file in a text editor such as Notepad.

Writing data to a binary file

To write data to a binary file you must create objects from the following classes:

Class	Description
`FileOutputStream`	This class allows you to open a file for writing binary data and establish a connection with it. It provides only basic functionality for writing bytes to the file.
`DataOutputStream`	This class allows you to write data of any primitive type or String objects to a binary file.

The `DataOutputStream` class by default cannot directly access a file. However, the `DataOutputStream` class is used in conjunction with a `FileOutputStream` object that has a connection to a file. You wrap `DataOutputStream` object around a `FileOutputStream` object to write data to a binary file. The following example shows how a file named `MyInfo.dat` can be opened for binary output.

Example 24.11: MyInfo.java

```
01  package ch24;
02
03  import java.io.DataOutputStream;
04  import java.io.FileOutputStream;
05  import java.io.IOException;
06
07  public class MyInfo {
08      public static void main(String[] args) throws IOException
        {
09          FileOutputStream fstream = new FileOutputStream("MyInfo.dat");
```

```
10          DataOutputStream outputFile = new
DataOutputStream(fstream);
11      }
12  }
```

Explanation

> Line 09: Creates an instance of the `FileOutputStream` class, which has the ability to open a file for binary output and establish a connection with it. You pass the name of the file that you wish open, as a String, to the constructor.

> Line 10: Creates an instance of the `DataOutputStream` object that is connected to the `FileOutputStream` referenced by `fstream`. The result of the statement in that the `outputFile` variable will reference an object that is able to write binary data to the `MyInfo.dat` file.

> Warning: If the file that you are opening with the `FileOutputStream` object already exists, it will be erased and an empty file by the same name will be created.

NOTES

☐ The `FileOutputStream` constructor throws an `IOException` if an error occurs when it attempts to open the file.

☐ If there is no reason to reference the `FileOutputStream` object, then these statements can be combined into one, as follow:
   DataOutputStream outputFile = new DataOutputStream(new
            FileOutputStream("MyInfo.dat");

Once the `DataOutputStream` object has been created, you can use it to write binary data to the file.

Here is a simple example.

Example 24.12: WriteBinaryFile.java

An array of `int` values is written to the file `Numbers.dat`

```
01  import java.io.*;
02  public class WriteBinaryFile
03  {
04      public static void main(String[] args)
05                  throws IOException
06      {
07          // An array to write to the file
08          int[] numbers = { 2, 4, 6, 8, 10, 12, 14 };
09
10          // Create the binary output objects.
11          FileOutputStream fstream =
12                  new FileOutputStream("D:\\Numbers.dat");
```

```
            DataOutputStream outputFile =
                new DataOutputStream(fstream);

            System.out.println("Writing the numbers to the
file...");
17
            // Write the array elements to the file.
            for (int i = 0; i < numbers.length; i++)
                outputFile.writeInt(numbers[i]);

            System.out.println("Done.");

            // Close the file.
            outputFile.close();
        }
    }
```

Output
```
Writing the numbers to the file...
Done.
```

Explanation
> Line 20: Writes the array elements to the Numbers.dat file.

Table 24.2 | Some of the DataOutputStream methods (note: Each of the methods listed in the table throws an IOException if an error occurs)

Method	Description
void close()	Close the file.
void writeChar(int c)	This method accepts an int, which is assumed to be a character code. The character it represents is written to the file as a two-byte Unicode character.
void writeInt(int i)	Writes the int value passed to (i) to the file
void writeUTF(String str)	Writes the String object passed to str to the file using the Unicode Text Format.

Reading data from a binary file

The `DataInputStream` class by default can't directly access a file. However, the `DataInputStream` class is used in conjunction with a `FileInputStream` object that has a connection to a file. You wrap `DataInputStream` around a `FileInputStream` object to write data to a binary file. The following example shows how a file named **Numbers.dat** can be opened for binary reading.

Example 24.13: ReadBinaryFile.java
```
    package ch24;
```

```java
02
03  import java.io.*;
04  public class ReadBinaryFile
05  {
06      public static void main(String[] args)
07              throws IOException
08      {
09          int number; // A number read from the file
10          boolean endOfFile = false;    // EOF flag
11
12          // Create the binary file input objects.
13          FileInputStream fstream =
14                  new FileInputStream("d:\\Numbers.dat");
15          DataInputStream inputFile =
16                  new DataInputStream(fstream);
17
18          System.out.println("Reading numbers from the file:");
19
20          // Read the contents of the file.
21          while (!endOfFile)
22          {
23              try
24              {
25                  number = inputFile.readInt();
26                  System.out.print(number + " ");
27              }
28              catch (EOFException e)
29              {
30                  endOfFile = true;
31              }
32          }
33
34          System.out.println("\nDone.");
35
36          // Close the file.
37          inputFile.close();
38      }
39  }
```

Output
```
Reading numbers from the file:
2 4 6 8 10 12 14
Done.
```

Explanation

> `close()`: Close the file.
> `readInt()`: Reads an `int` value from the file and returns it.
> `readUTF()`: Reads a `string` from the file and returns it as a String object. The string must have been written with the `DataOutputStream` class's `writeUFT` method.

> `readChar()`: Reads a `char` value from the file and returns it. The character is expected to be stored as a two-byte stored as a two-byte Unicode character, as written by the `DataOutputStream` classes `writeChar` method.

Writing and reading strings

To write a String to a binary file you should use the `DataOutputStream` class's `writeUFT` method. This method writes its String argument in a format known as UTF-8 encoding. UTF stands for Unicode Text Format.

Consider below example for that.

Example 24.14: WriteUTF.java

```
01  package ch24;
02
03  import java.io.*;
04
05  public class WriteUTF
06  {
07      public static void main(String[] args) throws IOException
08      {
09          String names[] = { "Mohammed", "Mustafa", "Shereen",
10              "Mansour", "Abd-Elrahman", "Nuha"};
11
12          // Create the output objects.
13          FileOutputStream fstream =
14              new FileOutputStream("d:\\UTFnames.dat");
15          DataOutputStream outputFile =
16              new DataOutputStream(fstream);
17
18          System.out.println("Writing the names to the file...");
19
20          // Write the array elements to the file.
21          for (int i = 0; i < names.length; i++)
22              outputFile.writeUTF(names[i]);
23
24          System.out.println("Done.");
25
26          // Close the file.
27          outputFile.close();
28      }
29  }
```

Output
```
Writing the names to the file...
Done.
```

Explanation

> Assuming that `outputFile` references a `DataOutputStream` object, the following code uses the `writeUTF` method to write a string:

```
String name = "Chloe";
outputFile.writeUTF(name);
```

To Read a string from a binary file you should use the writeUTF method. This method is used to read a UTF encoded string from the file. Here is an example.

Example 24.15: ReadUTF.java

```
01  package ch24;
02
03  import java.io.*;
04
05  public class ReadUTF
06  {
07      public static void main(String[] args)
08              throws IOException
09      {
10          String name;
11          boolean endOfFile = false;
12
13          // Create the input objects.
14          FileInputStream fstream =
15                  new FileInputStream("d:\\UTFnames.dat");
16          DataInputStream inputFile =
17                  new DataInputStream(fstream);
18
19          System.out.println("Reading the names from the file:");
20
21          // Read the contents of the file.
22          while (!endOfFile)
23          {
24              try
25              {
26                  name = inputFile.readUTF();
27                  System.out.print(name + " ");
28              }
29              catch (EOFException e)
30              {
31                  endOfFile = true;
32              }
33          }
34
35          System.out.println("\nDone.");
36
37          // Close the file.
38          inputFile.close();
39      }
40  }
```

Output

```
Reading the names from the file:
```

```
Mohammed Mustafa Shereen Mansour Abd-Elrahman Nuha
Done.
```

Explanation
> Assuming that `inputFile` references a `DataInputStream` object, the following statement uses the `readUTF` method to read a UTF-8 encoded string from the file:
> ```
> String name = inputFile.readUTF();
> ```

Remember: The `readUTF` method will correctly read a string only when the string is written with the `writeUTF` method.

Appending data to an existing binary file

If you pass the name of an existing file to the `FileOutputStream` constructor, it will be erased and a new empty file with the same name will be created.

The `FileOuputStream` constructor takes an optional second argument, which must be a boolean value (true or false).

> `TRUE`: The file will not be erased if it already exists and new data will be written to the end of the file.
> `FALSE`: The file will be erased if it already exists.

Example 24.16: Open the file **MyInfo.dat** for output. If the file exists, it will not be deleted, and any data written to the file will be appended to the existing data:
```
FileOutputStream fstream = new FileOutputStream("MyInfo.dat",
true);
DataOutputStream outputFile = new DataOutputStream(fstream);
```

Random Access Files

All of the programs that you have created to access files so far have performed **sequential file access**. With sequential access, when a file is opened for input, its read position at the very beginning of the file.

Java allows a program to perform **random file access**. In random file access, a program may immediately jump to any location in the file without first reading the preceding bytes.

A file that is opened or created with the `RandomAccessFile` class is treated as a binary file.

General Format:
```
RandomAccessFile (String filename, String mode)
```

Explanation

› First argument: The name of the file.
› Second argument: A String indicating the mode in which you wish to use the file. The two modes are `(r)` for reading, and `(rw)` for reading and writing.

To open a file for random reading you should use `RandomAccessFile` class. Here is a simple example.

Example 24.17: OpenRanFile.java - Open files using the Random Access File class:
```
01  package ch24;
02
03  import java.io.IOException;
04  import java.io.RandomAccessFile;
05
06  public class OpenRanFile {
07  public static void main(String[] args) throws IOException {
08
09  // Open a file for random reading
10  RandomAccessFile randomFile = new RandomAccessFile("d:\\MyData.dat", "r");
11
12  // Open a file for random reading and writing
13  RandomAccessFile randomFile2 = new RandomAccessFile("d:\\MyData.dat", "rw");
14  }
15  }
```

Output (if MyData.dat file exists)
```
nothing
```

Output (if MyData.dat file doesn't exists)
```
Exception in thread "main" java.io.FileNotFoundException:
d:\MyData.dat (The system cannot find the file specified)
```

Points to remember about the two modes

› If you open a file in `(r)` mode and the file does not exist, a `FileNotFoundException` will be thrown.
› If you open a file in `(r)` mode and try to write to it, an `IOException` will be thrown
› If you open an existing file in `(rw)` mode, it will not be deleted. The file's existing contents will be preserved.

> If you open a file in (rw) mode and the file does not exist, it will be created.

Reading and writing with the RandomAccessFile class

Use the RandomAccessFile class to process a binary file sequentially. In the following example, we used the RandomAccessFile class to open the **Letters.dat** file for reading and writing data. Then we used the writeChar() method to write the data of the array letters to **Letters.dat** the file.

Example 24.18: WriteLetters.java

```java
import java.io.*;
public class WriteLetters
{
    public static void main(String[] args)
                throws IOException
    {
        char[] letters = {'a', 'b', 'c', 'd'};

        System.out.println("Opening the file.");

        // Open a file for reading and writing.
        RandomAccessFile randFile =
            new RandomAccessFile("Letters.dat", "rw");

        System.out.println("Writing data to the file...");

        // Sequentially write the letters array to the file.
        for (int i = 0; i < letters.length; i++)
            randFile.writeChar(letters[i]);

        // Close the file.
        randFile.close();

        System.out.println("Done.");
    }
}
```

Output
```
Opening the file.
Writing data to the file
Done.
```

Explanation
> Line 12: Opens a file named Letters.dat in read and write (**rw**) mode.
> Line 19: Writes all of the letters of the alphabet to the Letters.dat file using writeChar() method.

The file pointer

Not only does the `RandomAccessFile` class let you read and write data, but also it allows you to move the file pointer. This means that you can:

› Read data from any byte location in the file.
› Write data to any location in the file, over existing data.

The `RandomAccessFile` class treats a file as a stream of bytes. The bytes are numbered, with the first byte being byte 0. The last byte's number is one less than the number of bytes in the file.

Internally, the `RandomAccessFile` class keeps a long integer value known as the file pointer. The file pointer holds the byte number of a location in the file. When a file is first opened, the file pointer is set to 0. This causes it to 'point' to the first byte in the file.

When an item is read from the file:

› It is read from the byte that the file pointer points to.
› It causes the file pointer to advance to the byte just beyond the item that was read.

Writing also takes place at the location pointed to by the file pointer.

To move the file pointer, you use the `seek()` method.

Format
```
void seek (long position)
```

The argument is the number of the byte that you want to move the file pointer to. Consider below example for that.

Example 24.19: SeekEx.java
```
01  package ch24;
02
03  import java.io.IOException;
04  import java.io.RandomAccessFile;
05
06  public class SeekEx {
07      public static void main(String[] args) throws IOException{
08          try {
09              RandomAccessFile f = new RandomAccessFile("d:\\MyInfo.dat", "r");
10              f.seek(99);
11              byte b = f.readByte();
12          }catch (IOException e) {
13              System.out.println(e.getMessage());
```

Output (if the file already exists)
```
null (means the file is empty)
```
Output (if the file does not exists)
```
MyInfo.dat (The system cannot find the file specified)
```
Explanation

› Line 09: The code opens the file `MyInfo.dat` for reading.
› Line 10: The `seek` method is called to move the file pointer to byte number 99 (which is the 100th byte in the file).
› Line 11: The `readByte` method reads byte number 99 from the file.

Statement executes, the file pointer will be advanced by one byte, so it will point to byte 100.

Example 24.20: Suppose, we continue processing the same file with the following code
```
RandomAccessFile f = new RandomAccessFile ("MyInfo.dat", "r");
f.seek(49);
int i = f.readInt();
```

Explanation

› 1st Line: The code opens the file `MyInfo.dat` for reading.
› 2nd Line The seek method moves the file pointer to byte number 49.
› 3rd Line: The `readInt` method reads an `int` from the file. An int is 4 bytes in size, so this statement reads 4 bytes, beginning at byte number 49.

The statement executes, the file pointer will be advanced by 4 bytes, so it will point to byte 53.

Although a file might contain `chars, ints, doubles, strings,` and so forth, the RandomAccessFile class sees it only as a Stream of bytes.

Let's see an example

Example 24.21: FilePtr.java
```
01  package ch24;
02
03  import java.io.IOException;
04  import java.io.RandomAccessFile;
05
06  public class FilePtr {
07      public static void main(String[] args) throws IOException
        {
08          // Open the file for reading.
```

```
09            RandomAccessFile randFile = new RandomAccessFile("d:\\UTFnames.dat", "r");
10            // Move the file pointer to byte 5, which is the 6th byte
11            randFile.seek( );
12            // Read the character
13            Character ch = randFile.readChar();
14            // What will this display?
15            System.out.println(" The 6th letter is " + ch);
16        }
17  }
```

Output

```
The 6th letter is  愁
```

The `writeChar` method writes a character as 2 bytes because each character occupies two bytes in the file, the 6th character begins at byte 10, not byte 5.

In fact, if we try to read a character starting at byte 5, we will read garbage because byte 5 is not at the beginning of a character.

To determine the position of a character in the file, we must take each character's size into account.

NOTES
☐ If the file pointer refers to a byte number that is beyond the end of the file, **EOFException** is thrown when a read operation is performed.
☐ If the file pointer points to the end of the file when a write operation is performed, then the data will be written to the end of the file.
☐ If the file pointer holds the number of a byte within the file, at a location where data is already stored, then a write operation will cause data to be written over the existing data at that location.

Example 24.22: FilePtr2.java - correctly read and display the 6th character.(size of a character X the number of the character we want to locate).

```
01  package ch24;
02  import java.io.FileNotFoundException;
03  import java.io.IOException;
04  import java.io.RandomAccessFile;
05  public class FilePtr2 {
06      public static void main(String[] args) throws IOException
    {
07          final int CHAR_SIZE = 2; // Each char uses 2 bytes
08
09          // Open the file for reading.
10          RandomAccessFile randFile = new RandomAccessFile("d:\\UTFnames.dat", "r");
11          // Move the file pointer to character 10
```

```
            randFile.seek(CHAR_SIZE + 10);
            // Read the character
14
            char ch = randFile.readChar();
            // This will display the correct character
            System.out.println("The 10th character is " + ch);
        }
    }
```

Output

```
The 10th character is 聖
```

Summary

› The `File` class gives you access to the underlying file system.
› Before you can do anything with the file system or `File` class, you must obtain a `File` instance.
› Once you have instantiated a `File` object you can check if the corresponding file actually exists already.
› You can use the `File` class to create directories if they don't already exists. The `File` class contains the method `mkdir()` and `mkdirs()` for that purpose.
› The `mkdirs()` will create all directories that are missing in the path the `File` object represents.
› The `mkdirs()` method will return `true` if all the directories were created, and `false` if not.
› To rename (or move) a file, call the method `renameTo()` on the `File` class.
› As briefly mentioned earlier, the `renameTo()` method can also be used to move a file to a different directory. The new file name passed to the `renameTo()` method does not have to be in the same directory as the file was already residing in.
› The `renameTo()` method returns `true` or `false`, indicating whether the renaming was successful.
› To delete a file call the `delete()` method.
› You can obtain a list of all the files in a directory by calling either the `list()` method or the `listFiles()` method. The `list()` method returns an array of String's with the file and/or directory names of directory the `File` object points to. The `listFiles()` returns an array of `File` objects representing the files and/or directories in the directory the `File` points to.

> To write a String to a binary file you should use the `DataOutputStream` class's `writeUFT` method.
> If you pass the name of an existing file to the `FileOutputStream` constructor, it will be erased and a new empty file with the same name will be created. The `FileOuputStream` constructor takes an optional second argument, which must be a boolean value.

Part 3

Building Graphical User Interface (GUI) Applications

"User interface is the process of shifting from chaotic complexity to elegant simplicity." – Akshat Paul, React Native for iOS Development

Chapter 25

JavaFX Layouts

Introduction

Java applications can have Graphical User Interfaces (GUIs) that contain things such as buttons, lists, menus, checkboxes, and many other controls that allows users to interact with applications. Now JavaFX is what we're going to be using in this book to build interfaces in Java. So what is JavaFX?

JavaFX is a set of Java packages that enable developers to design, create, test, debug, and deploy GUI applications that operate consistently across diverse platforms, such as Windows, Linux, and Mac.

JavaFX is the successor to the Swing, which was Java's User Interface (UI) toolkit recommended for many years, but now Oracle's direction is to use JavaFX. JavaFX is used to develop user interfaces for Desktop applications, Internet applications, and Mobile applications.

There are two VERY different methods to writing a JavaFX application:
- Method 1 - Using FXML code.(recommended and used in this book).
- Method 2 - Using Pure Java Code.

Now let's look at the first way you can get a new program started in JavaFX

Creating your first JavaFX application

IntelliJ IDEA has got a plug-in that supports JavaFX application and it installed and enabled by default with IntelliJ IDEA. So to create your first JavaFX application, do the following steps:

› Click **Create New Project** on the Welcome screen. Otherwise select **File** > **New** > **Project**. The New Project wizard opens.
› In the left-hand pane, select **JavaFX** category. In the right-hand part of the page select **JavaFX application**.

› You can also specify the JDK to be used in your project (the Project SDK field). Select the JDK from the list, or click **New** > select **JDK** and select the installation folder of the desired JDK.
Click on **Next**.
› In the **Project name** field, type a name for your new project (such as **JavaFXProject**). You can change the default file system location that is displayed in the Location field.

› Click **Finish**.

Wait while IntelliJ IDEA is creating the project. When this process is complete, the structure of your new project is shown in the **Project tool** window. When you do, you will get back some starting files for your JavaFX application.

Exploring project files

Project files are designed with the Module-View-Controller (MVC) pattern in mind. The MVC is dividing the application into three kinds of components, the *Model*, *View* and *Controller* design.

› A **View** can be any output representation of information, such as a diagram.
› The **Model** is the central component of the pattern. It directly manages the data, logic and rules of the application.
› The **Controller**, is the code that determines what happens when a user interacts with the user interface.

Let's take a quick look at what we've got in the IntelliJ IDEA Project Pane:

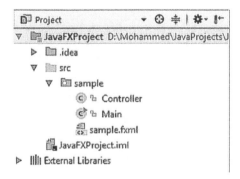

The folder **src** is for your source code. In this folder, there is already a package called **sample** containing three files:

› **sample.fxml**. This is the FXML file for defining the user interface (the *View*).
› **Main.java** (startup class). This is the main application class for starting the application. This class will load up a SCENE from the FXML document - in this case *sample.fxml* - and put it on the STAGE or WINDOW. All FXML documents need an opening 'Scene" and a "Stage" to put it on. This document does just that (the *Model*).
› **Controller.java**. This documents contains the code needed to run when the user interacts with the program or user interface (the *Controller*).

For the simple application there obviously isn't any data and also the code generated by IntelliJ doesn't create any Java UI controls by default.

Running the sample application

To make sure that everything is fine with the project, let's run the sample application straight away:

> Click **Run** > **Run 'Main'** or click ▶ on the toolbar.

  IntelliJ IDEA compiles the source code and then starts the application. The application window appears which, at the moment, is empty.

> Close the application window.

A JavaFX application skeleton

Regardless of which technique you use to write your JavaFX program, all JavaFX applications share the same basic skeleton. Therefore, before looking at any more JavaFX features, it will be useful to see what that skeleton looks like. The complete skeleton is shown here:

The Controller.java Class

```
package sample;
public class Controller {
}
```

You can see that it's actually empty at this stage because we haven't added any controls, such as button, menus, and labels. Controllers are often used to implement event handlers for user interface defined in FXML file.

The Main.java Class

```
01 package sample;
02 import javafx.application.Application;
03 import javafx.fxml.FXMLLoader;
04 import javafx.scene.Parent;
05 import javafx.scene.Scene;
06 import javafx.stage.Stage;
07
08 public class Main extends Application {
09
10     @Override
11     public void start(Stage primaryStage) throws Exception{
12         Parent root =
13 FXMLLoader.load(getClass().getResource("sample.fxml"));
14         primaryStage.setTitle("Hello World");
15         primaryStage.setScene(new Scene(root, 300, 275));
16         primaryStage.show();
17     }
18
19     public static void main(String[] args) {
20         launch(args); // or Application.launch(args)
21     }
22 }
```

Explanation

> **Line 01**: Add the `Main` class to the sample package using the `package` keyword.
> **Line 02-06**: Import the classes which are required to run the `Main` application.
> **Line 08**: The `Main` class is a primary launch class that created by you (required by JavaFX application). This class will be the entry point for the JavaFX applications. `Main` class contains two method the `main()` and the `start()` methods.
> **Line 11**: The `start()` method is called or executed when the JavaFX application is started. It takes a single parameter of type `Stage`. A stage is a top level JavaFX container that extends the `window` class. So think of it as a main window. And the JavaFX runtime constructs the initial stage and passes it as a parameter into the `start` method itself, that's happening automatically with JavaFX. The `Stage` object is created for you by the JavaFX runtime. The initial scene is created and set to the primary stage (Stage primaryStage).
> **Line 13**: Is loading the UI from the *sample.fxml* file.

> **Line 14**: Set the title of the stage by calling the `setTitle()` method. The **title** becomes the name of the main application window.
> **Line 15**: Load the FXML file, and assign it to a variable of type `parent` with a name `root`. A root node for a scene is created. In this case a Grid Pane is used for the root node (look inside *sample.fxml* file). The root node is the only node in a scene graph that doesn't have a parent. Then create a scene and set the scene on the stage. So every stage requires a scene and **every scene is a scene graph** and that's a tree in which each node corresponding to a UI control or an area of the scene, such as a rectangle. Nodes that descend from parent can have children in the scene graph. So the grid pane node will be the root of the scene graph or scene and as a result that's what was referred from the `FXMLLoader.load` method which were used on line 13. When we construct a scene we have to pass in the root of that scene graph back to the scene and will do that on line 15. We also set the width and height of the scene, which in turn becomes the width and height of the main window.

NOTE: The width and height are **double** values. This lets you pass fractional values.

> **Line 16**: A `show()` method displays the window (a.k.a. stage) and its scene.
> **Lines 19-21**: The `main()` method is used to launch the application via a call to `launch()` method. The static `launch()` method located in the application class. It launches the JavaFX runtime and your JavaFX application.

Notes that the args parameter to `main()` is passed to the `launch()` method. You can pass a different set of parameters to `launch()`, or none at all.

NOTES: The `start()` method is the starting point for a JavaFX application. The `main()` and `start()` methods are provided by Application class.

The sample.fxml file

```
01  <?import javafx.geometry.Insets?>
02  <?import javafx.scene.layout.GridPane?>
03
04  <?import javafx.scene.control.Button?>
05  <?import javafx.scene.control.Label?>
06  <GridPane fx:controller="sample.Controller"
07    xmlns:fx="http://javafx.com/fxml" alignment="center"
hgap="10" vgap="10">
08  </GridPane>
```

Explanation

FXML is an XML-based language designed to build user interface for JavaFX applications.

Lines 01, 02, 04 & 05: Import the classes which are required to run the application.

Line 06-08: Create a GridPane layout.

> The GridPane layout is a root element of the FXML document and as such as two attributes.
> The `fx:controller` attribute allows a caller to associate a "Controller" class with an FXML document.
> The `xmlns:fx` attribute is required and it specifies the **fx** name space.
> The `alignment` property changes the default position of the grid from the top left of the scene to the center.
> The `gap` properties manage the spacing between the rows and columns.

NOTE: We don't have to construct a new stage object. In practice, we load a different fxml file into a new scene and then just call it.

The three files in the JavaFX application

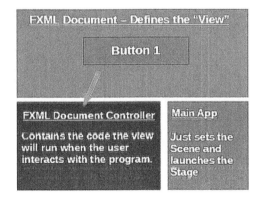

The three main objects that get the program on the screen are *(from outer to inner)*

First: THE STAGE – This is the top level containers of the application. Each application has a stage which is responsible for displaying a scene. In JavaFX language the entire window is called the **stage**. This entire window right here including the closes, maximize, minimize is called the **stage**.

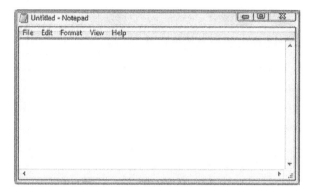

Figure 25.1 | The Stage

Second: THE SCENE – The object directly contained by the **stage**. A scene contains all the elements of the GUI. It is possible to design several scenes and switch between them using the Stage. The content inside your window or inside your stage that's the scene. On the scene is where we're going to be putting all the cool stuff like binds widget stuff like that.

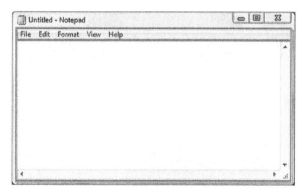

Figure 25.2 | The Scene

So just remember they don't call it a window. Stuff inside your window they call it a **stage** in the scene.

Third: THE ROOT Pane/Container – This object holds all the parts of the application, like buttons, labels, textfields, etc. The root container can be represented by a number of JavaFX containers such as the StackPane, GridPane and BorderPane.

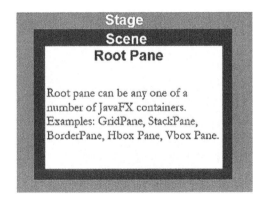

JavaFX Layout

JavaFX layout is a layout container class (also called *pane*) that is used to easily manage the user interface components or controls for JavaFX application. The JavaFX provides the following built-in layouts (a.k.a. *root panes*):

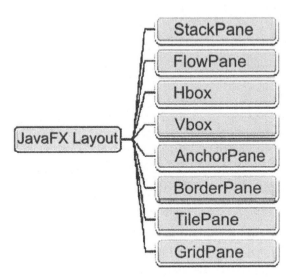

Figure 25.3 | JavaFX Built-in Layouts

But before we get into layouts, I just want to discuss the preferred size for JavaFX controls.

Preferred size[1]

The preferred size means the preferred width and height of the control. By default every user interface (UI) controls computes its default value for their preferred size based on its contents. For example, the computed size of a button is determined by the length and size of the text. The Figure 1.4 shows the default size of several buttons in a grid pane.

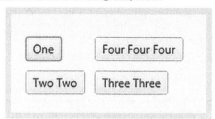

Figure 25.4 | Preferred Sizes

UI controls also provide default minimum and maximum sizes that are based on the typical usage of the control. For example, the maximum size of a Button object defaults to its preferred size because you don't usually want buttons to grow arbitrarily large. However, the maximum size of a **ScrollPane** object is unbounded because typically you do want them to grow to fill their spaces.

The GridPane layout

A JavaFX GridPane is a layout component which lays out its child components in a grid. Each position in a grid is called a **cell**. The size of the cells in the grid depends on the components displayed in the GridPane, but there are some rules.

› All cells in the same row will have the same height. A row can be a tall as a tallest controller it contains.
› All cells in the same column will have the same width. A column will be as wide as the widest controller it contains.
› Different rows can have different heights.
› Different columns can have different widths.
› A child may span multiple rows or columns.
› Children may freely overlap within rows or columns and their stacking order will be defined by the order of the grid pane's children list (first node in back, last node in front).

---
[1] https://docs.oracle.com/javafx/2/layout/size_align.htm

NOTE: When you add a component to a GridPane you tell in what cell (row, column) the component should be inserted, and how many rows and columns the component should span.

Creating a GridPane

› Create a new JavaFX project named **GridPane**.
› Set the Stage's `title` property to **GridPane Layout**. Go to *Main.java* class file and change the following code:
```
primaryStage.setTitle("GridPane Layout");
```
› Create GridPane using FXML. Go to the *sample.fxml* file, on line 2, we got an import for grid pane and obviously line 6 you can see the word GridPane so that's basically a grid pane layout that has been configured.
```
<GridPane fx:controller="sample.Controller"
          xmlns:fx="http://javafx.com/fxml"
          alignment="center" hgap="10" vgap="10">
</GridPane>
```

Adding children to the GridPane layout

› Add four buttons to this grid pane using `<Button>` element in JavaFX. Click inside the `<GridPane>` element and type the following:
```
01  <?import javafx.geometry.Insets?>
02  <?import javafx.scene.layout.GridPane?>
03
04  <?import javafx.scene.control.Button?>
05  <?import javafx.scene.control.Label?>
06  <GridPane fx:controller="sample.Controller"
07      xmlns:fx="http://javafx.com/fxml" alignment="center" hgap="10" vgap="10">
08      <Button text="One"/>
09      <Button text="One Two"/>
10      <Button text="One Two Three"/>
11      <Button text="One Two Three Four"/>
12
13  </GridPane>
```

› Run the application. Right click the *Main.java* file and select **Run 'Main'**. The screen will be like this:

The buttons are stacked on top of each other, and that's because we didn't specify a row and column for each button. By not specifying a row and column for each button the grid pane is adding all the buttons in the default position, row 0, and column 0. That's why the buttons overlapping.

Explanation

> **alignment** property: The alignment of the grid within the GridPane's width and height. The alignment is set to center of the window, so the grid pane is occupying the entire window and the gird is centered within that window.

> **hgap** property: The width of the horizontal gaps between columns. There is actually a 10 pixels gap between the rows as specified by hgap.

> **vgap** property: The height of the vertical gaps between rows. There is also a 10 pixels gap between the columns as specified by vgap.

Changing the position of each children (e.g. button)

A child's placement within the grid is defined by it's layout CONSTRAINTS

```
<Button text="One" GridPane.rowIndex="0"
GridPane.columnIndex="0"/>
<Button text="One Two" GridPane.rowIndex="1"
GridPane.columnIndex="0"/>
<Button text="One Two Three" GridPane.rowIndex="0"
GridPane.columnIndex="1"/>
<Button text="One Two Three Four" GridPane.rowIndex="1"
GridPane.columnIndex="1"/>
Here is the Illustration:
```

	0	1
0	(0,0)	(0,1)
1	(1,0)	(1,1)

1st button (row:0, column:0),   2nd button (row:1, column:0),
3rd button (row:0, column:1),   4th button (row:1, column: 1).

> Run the application. Now we can see all the buttons.

Explanation

> To use the GridPane, an application needs to set the layout constraints on the children and add those children to the GridPane instance.
> If the row/column indices are not explicitly set, then the child will be placed in the first row/column.
> `columnIndex` column where child's layout area starts (e.g. 0 means first column, 1 means second column and so on).
> `rowIndex` row where child's layout areas starts (e.g. 0 means first row, 1 means second row and so on).
> If row/column spans are not set, they will default to 1.
> `columnSpan` the number of columns the child's layout area spans horizontally.
> `rowSpan`   the number of rows the child's layout area spans vertically.

Setting the gridLineVisible property

The `gridLineVisible` property controls whether lines are displayed to show the GridPane's rows and columns. It help us to debug that grid pane (for debug purpose only).

Example: Set the grid lines visible property to true

> Open the *sample.fxml* file and add the `gridLineVisible` property to GridPane layout as follow:
> ```
> <GridPane fx:controller="sample.Controller"
>     xmlns:fx="http://javafx.com/fxml" alignment="center"
> hgap="10" vgap="10"
>     gridLinesVisible="true">
> ```

> Run your application. The grid lines and the 10 pixels gap between the rows and columns buttons have stretched to fill the width of their cells.

See any time you've got difficulties and things that aren't aligning the way you think they should be make sure you added `gridLinesVisible="true"`.

Resizing the window containing the GridPane

When we resizing the window containing the GridPane, the grid remains in the center.

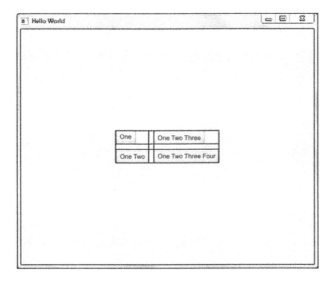

And if we go smaller or larger it is still centering itself automatically. And it doesn't resize because it is already large enough to accommodate the children in all its cells.

> So let's add some more text to another button to make it really long and see what actually happens. So go to *sample.fxml* file and add the following text to the `4th` button:

```
<Button text="One Two Three Four Four Four Four Four Four Four
Four "
    GridPane.rowIndex="1" GridPane.columnIndex="1"/>
```

› Run the application. The text have been cut off. Three dots means it is not feting.

› Resize the window larger. The grid pane will resize until it's large enough to accommodate all its children:

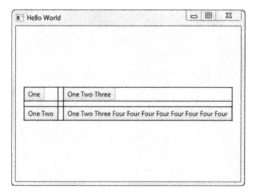

So once it is resized to that level it doesn't try resizing any more.

Specifying the width of GridPane using `percentWidth` attribute

To give each column 50% of the grid panes width, do the following steps:

› After the <GridPane> element, and before our first button press enter and then type the following:

```
. . .
<?import javafx.scene.layout.ColumnConstraints?>
<GridPane fx:controller="sample.Controller"
    xmlns:fx="http://javafx.com/fxml" alignment="center" hgap="10"
vgap="10"
    gridLinesVisible="true">
    <columnConstraints>
```

```
            <ColumnConstraints percentWidth="50.0"/>
            <ColumnConstraints percentWidth="50.0"/>
        </columnConstraints>
```
. . .

> Run the application. The screen will be like this:

Explanation

> Each column occupies 50% of the width. And the grid occupies the full width of the window.
> We told the grid pane that we want each column to be 50% of its width rather than being only large enough to accommodate the widest controls preferred width.
> The ordering is important. The first column constraint element will apply to the first column, the second column constraint element will apply to the second column and so on.

So `ColumnConstraints` class are used to set the initial width of each column, and we can use pixels or percentage.

Change the alignment of the GridPane

> To change the alignment of a grid pane we use the `alignment` property as follow:

```
<GridPane fx:controller="sample.Controller"
          xmlns:fx="http://javafx.com/fxml"
          alignment="TOP_CENTER">
```

> Run your application. The screen will be like this:

Notice that there is no gap between, where the title ends, the top of the window, and where the actual columns start or where the actual row starts.

Adding some padding at top

› Add a pad element to the grid pane and within that we add an inset child element to the `padding` element to the padding element: So inside the GridPane elements type:

```
<GridPane fx:controller="sample.Controller"
    xmlns:fx="http://javafx.com/fxml" alignment="TOP_CENTER"
hgap="10" vgap="10"
        gridLinesVisible="true">
<columnConstraints>
    <ColumnConstraints percentWidth="50.0"/>
    <ColumnConstraints percentWidth="50.0"/>
</columnConstraints>
<padding>
    <Insets top="10"/>
</padding>
<Button text="One" GridPane.rowIndex="0"
GridPane.columnIndex="0"/>
```

› Run your application. The screen will be like this:

Span across multiple rows using `columnSpan` attribute

First: Move the fourth button to the fourth row. Change the GridPane `rowIndex` to 2

```
<Button text="One Two Three Four" GridPane.rowIndex="2"
GridPane.columnIndex="0"/>
```

Second: Span The fourth button across multiple rows

```
<Button text="One Two Three Four" GridPane.rowIndex="2"
GridPane.columnIndex="0" GridPane.columnSpan="2"/>
```

`columnSpan` enables you to span more than one column.

`columnIndex=0` to start from the first column.

Change the horizontal alignment of Button 1

All buttons are left aligned in their cell. To change the horizontal alignment of button One we use the `halignment` property.

```
<Button text="One" GridPane.rowIndex="0"
GridPane.columnIndex="0"
    GridPane.halignment="RIGHT"/>
```

The HBoxPane layout

HBox is a container which position all its components horizontally in a single row, and sizes its components to their preferred widths. If there is any horizontal space left, the HBox is going to stretch to fill the excess rather than stretching its components.

If there is any extra height space left, this will depend on the fill height property. When fill height is true (default), the HBox is going to stretch itself to fill any height and if it is false, its going to try to resize its component to fill that extra height. Some components (children) can't be sized that way, and in that case the extra height going to remain empty.

Creating a HBoxPane Layout
› Create a new JavaFX project named **HBox**.
› Open *sample.fxml* file and change the `<GridPane>` to `<Hbox>`, then remove `hgap` and `vgap` properties because they aren't applicable for this layout as shown in the following code:
```
<?import javafx.scene.layout.HBox?>
<HBox fx:controller="sample.Controller"
    xmlns:fx="http://javafx.com/fxml" alignment="center">
```

Adding buttons to the HBox layout (*OK, Cancel, and About*)
```
<?import javafx.scene.layout.HBox?>
<HBox fx:controller="sample.Controller"
    xmlns:fx="http://javafx.com/fxml" alignment="center">
    <Button text="OK"/>
    <Button text="Cancel"/>
    <Button text="About"/>
</HBox>
```

› Run Your Application. Right click *Main.java* file and select **Run 'Main'**. The screen will be like this:

Our three buttons laid out horizontally at the center of the window. There's no space between the three buttons. And because the HBox's fill height property is set to `true` which is by default it would have herself to take up any extra height. In this case the extra height is actually below and above the buttons. So the HBox has stretch itself to fill any excess width and height.

Make all the buttons have the same width

To make all the buttons have the same width, set the preferred width to the same value (e.g., 70) for every button.

```
<Button text="OK" prefWidth="70"/>
<Button text="Cancel" prefWidth="70"/>
<Button text="About" prefWidth="70"/>
```

Add border style to HBox

› Open the *sample.fxml* file.
› After the alignment property of the HBox layout, start in a new line and type:
```
<HBox fx:controller="sample.Controller"
      xmlns:fx="http://javafx.com/fxml" alignment="center"
      style="-fx-border-color:red; -fx-border-width:3; -fx-border-style:dashed;">
```
› Run Your Application. Right click *Main.java* file and select **Run 'Main'**. The screen will be like this:

The HBox is occupying the entire width and height of its parent. So adding border around layouts and their children is a great way to visualize how much space is being given to the child.

› Change the alignment to `BOTTOM_CENTER`. HBox has stretched itself above the buttons.

Adjust the space between components

› To adjust the space between two buttons, type:
```
<HBox fx:controller="sample.Controller"
     xmlns:fx="http://javafx.com/fxml"
alignment="BOTTOM_CENTER"
         style="-fx-border-color:red; -fx-border-width:3; -fx-
border-           style:dashed; " spacing="10">
    <Button text="OK"/>
    <Button text="Cancel"/>
    <Button text="About"/>
</Hbox>
```

› Run Your Application. Right click *Main.java* file and select **Run 'Main'**. Now the buttons will be like this:

Adjust the space around components

Adjust the padding and insets of the GridPane

› After the HBox element, type the following highlighted code:
```
<HBox fx:controller="sample.Controller"
    xmlns:fx="http://javafx.com/fxml" alignment="BOTTOM_RIGHT"
    style="-fx-border-color:red; -fx-border-width:3; -fx-border-
    styled:dashed;"     spacing="10">
    <padding>
        <Insets bottom="20" right="20"/>
    </padding>
    <Button text="OK"/>
    <Button text="Cancel"/>
    <Button text="About"/>
</HBox>
```

› Run Your Application. Right click *Main.java* file and select **Run 'Main'**. The screen will be like this:

At the bottom we have a 20 gap. Also on the right hand side we also got a 20 gap. That should stay the same no matter how small or how big we make it.

The VBoxPane layout

VBoxPane is a container, which arranges sub-components on the single column.

Creating a VBox Layout
- Create a new JavaFX project named **VBox**
- Open *sample.fxml* file and change the GridPane to VBox. Then remove `hgap` and `vgap` properties because they aren't applicable for this layout.

Add three buttons to the VBox layout (*OK, Cancel, and About*).
```
<?import javafx.scene.layout.VBox?>
<VBox fx:controller="sample.Controller"
      xmlns:fx="http://javafx.com/fxml" alignment="center">
    <Button text="OK"/>
    <Button text="Cancel"/>
    <Button text="About"/>
</VBox>
```
- Run Your Application. Right click *Main.java* file and select **Run 'Main'**. The screen will be like this:

Our three buttons laid out vertically at the center of the window. There's no space between the three buttons. And because the VBox's fill height property is set to true, the extra height is actually below and above the buttons. So the VBox has stretch itself to fill any excess width and height.

The BorderPane Layout

A **BorderPane** divides its layout into five areas: Top, Bottom, Right, Left & Center. The following figure shows the five regions of the BorderPane:

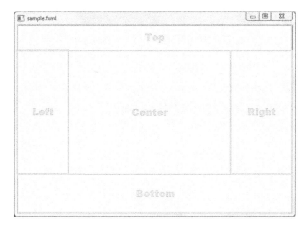

Figure 25.5 | The Areas of BorderPane

One Node Per Area

You can place only one node per area. And you can place anything you want in each region – either a single control or another container like an HBox or VBox (if you want to insert multiple controls such as buttons).

SIZE

A BorderPane uses the following resizing policies for its children:

› Top and bottom can take all full available width. The children in the top and bottom areas are resized to their preferred heights. Their widths are extended to fill the available extra horizontal space, provided the maximum widths of the children allow extending their widths beyond their preferred widths.

› Left and right can take full height. The children in the right and left areas are resized to their preferred widths. Their heights are extended to fill the extra vertical space, provided the maximum heights of the children allow extending their heights beyond their preferred heights.

› The center region takes up most of the room in the BorderPane layout. The child node in the center will fill the rest of the available space in both directions.

› If a region does not have a child node then no space is set aside for it.

> In between the top and bottom regions is a row containing the other three regions in the order of left, center and right.

Building a BorderPane Layout
> Create a new JavaFX project named **BorderPane**
> Open *sample.fxml* file and change the GridPane to BorderPane. Then remove `hgap`, `vgap` and `alignment` properties because they aren't applicable for this layout.

Add HBox pane at the bottom area of the BorderPane layout. Then add the following three buttons inside the HBox pane.

```xml
<?import javafx.scene.control.Button?>
<?import javafx.scene.layout.BorderPane?>
<?import javafx.scene.layout.HBox?>
<BorderPane fx:controller="sample.Controller"
            xmlns:fx="http://javafx.com/fxml">
    <bottom>
        <HBox alignment="TOP_LEFT">
            <Button text="OK" prefWidth="70"/>
            <Button text="Cancel" prefWidth="70"/>
            <Button text="About" prefWidth="70"/>
        </HBox>
    </bottom>
</BorderPane>
```

Add the alignment, spacing, and padding properties to the HBox Pane layout.

```xml
<BorderPane fx:controller="sample.Controller"
            xmlns:fx="http://javafx.com/fxml">
    <bottom>
        <HBox alignment="TOP_LEFT" spacing="10">
            <padding>
                <Insets bottom="20" right="20"/>
            </padding>
            <Button text="OK" prefWidth="70"/>
            <Button text="Cancel" prefWidth="70"/>
            <Button text="About" prefWidth="70"/>
        </HBox>
    </bottom>
</BorderPane>
```

> Run Your Application. Right click *Main.java* file and select **Run 'Main'**. The screen will be like this:

Adding a Label at the Top position of the BorderPane

After the <BorderPane ...> type the following code:

```
<BorderPane fx:controller="sample.Controller"
            xmlns:fx="http://javafx.com/fxml">
    <top>
        <Label text="The Top Position"/>
    </top>
```

› Align the label. We need to center the label itself within the top position rather than set its text. So to align a label we use the `BorderPane.alignment` attribute:

```
<top>
    <Label text="The Top Position"
BorderPane.alignment="CENTER"/>
</top>
```

› Run Your Application. Right click *Main.java* file and select **Run 'Main'**. The screen will be like this:

Adding left, right and center areas, and add text for each of them

After the <BorderPane> type the following code:

```
<top>
    <Label text="The Top Position"
BorderPane.alignment="CENTER"/>
</top>
<left>
    <Label text="The Left Area"/>
</left>
<right>
    <Label text="The Right Area"/>
</right>
<center>
    <Label text="The Cennnnnnnnnnnnnnnnter Area"/>
</center>
```

> Run Your Application. Right click *Main.java* file and select **Run 'Main'**. The screen will be like this:

The StackPane layout

The **StackPane** layout is a container which can contain different interface components, sub-components within a single stack with each new component added on top of the previous component. You can only see the sub-component lying on the top of stack. The StackPane layout provides an easy way to overlay text on a shape or image or overlap common shapes to create a complex shape.

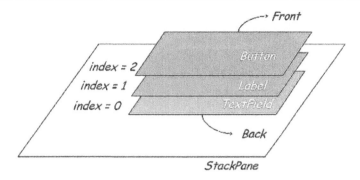

Building a StackPane Layout

› Create a new JavaFX project named **StackPane**
› Open *sample.fxml* file and change the *GridPane* to *StackPane*. And Remove `hgap` and `vgap` properties because they aren't applicable for this layout.
```
<?import javafx.scene.layout.StackPane?>
<StackPane fx:controller="sample.Controller"
           xmlns:fx="http://javafx.com/fxml" alignment="center">
</StackPane>
```

Add a button with a red background, and a label with a blue background.
```
<?import javafx.scene.control.Button?>
<?import javafx.scene.control.Label?>
<?import javafx.scene.layout.StackPane?>
<StackPane fx:controller="sample.Controller"
           xmlns:fx="http://javafx.com/fxml" alignment="center">
    <Button text="Button One" style="-fx-background-color:red"/>
    <Label text="Label One" style="-fx-background-color:blue"/>
</StackPane>
```

› Run Your Application. Right click *Main.java* file and select **Run 'Main'**. The screen will be like this:

Notice. The Button component disappear. Why? because sub-components stacked up to others, and at a certain moment, you can only see the sub-component lying on the top of Stack. The Label sub-components which are newly added will lie on the top of Stack.

Changing the Position of the Label
› Cut and paste it above the Button control and under the StackPane layout control.
```
<StackPane fx:controller="sample.Controller"
        xmlns:fx="http://javafx.com/fxml" alignment="center">
    <Label text="Label One" style="-fx-background-color:blue"/>
    <Button text="Button One" style="-fx-background-color:red"/>
</StackPane>
```
› Run your program. Right click *Main.java* file and select **Run 'Main'**. The screen will be like this:

› Save your project.

The FlowPane layout

A **FlowPane** arranges the consecutive sub-components on a row, and automatically pushes the sub-components down to next line if the current row is filled up.

Creating a FlowPane Layout
› Create a new JavaFX project named **FlowPane**

› Open *sample.fxml* file and change the *GridPane* to *FlowPane*. The `hgap` and `vgap` properties are applicable for this layout.

```
<?import javafx.scene.control.Button?>
<?import javafx.scene.layout.FlowPane?>
<FlowPane fx:controller="sample.Controller"
    xmlns:fx="http://javafx.com/fxml" alignment="center"
hgap="10" vgap="10">
</FlowPane>
```

Add buttons to the FlowPane layout.

```
<?import javafx.scene.control.Button?>
<?import javafx.scene.layout.FlowPane?>
<FlowPane fx:controller="sample.Controller"
          xmlns:fx="http://javafx.com/fxml"
alignment="center">
    <Button text="Button One"/>
    <Button text="Button Two"/>
    <Button text="Button Three"/>
    <Button text="Button Four"/>
    <Button text="Button Five"/>
    <Button text="Button Six"/>
    <Button text="Button Seven"/>
</FlowPane>
```

› Run your application. Right click *Main.java* file and select **Run 'Main'**. The screen will be like this:

› Resize the window. The screen will be like this:

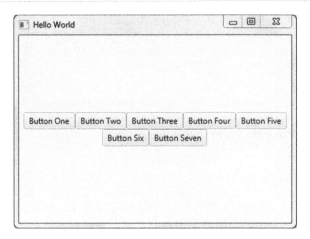

The TilePane layout

TilePane arranges its sub-components on a row, and automatically pushes the sub-components down to next line if the current line is filled up. However, it differs from FlowPane because the sub-components lie on the same size cell.

Creating a TilePane Layout
> Create a new JavaFX project, and name it **TilePane**
> Open *sample.fxml* file and change the GridPane to TilePane:
```
<?import javafx.scene.layout.TilePane?>
<TilePane fx:controller="sample.Controller"
          xmlns:fx="http://javafx.com/fxml" alignment="center"
          hgap="10" vgap="10">
</TilePane>
```

Add seven buttons to the TilePane Layout.
```
<?import javafx.scene.control.Button?>
<?import javafx.scene.layout.TilePane?>
<TilePane fx:controller="sample.Controller"
          xmlns:fx="http://javafx.com/fxml" alignment="center"
          hgap="10" vgap="10">
    <Button text="Button One"/>
    <Button text="Button Two"/>
    <Button text="Button Three"/>
    <Button text="Button Four"/>
    <Button text="Button Five"/>
    <Button text="Button Six"/>
    <Button text="Button Seven"/>
</TilePane>
```
> Run Your Application. Right click *Main.java* file and select **Run 'Main'**. The screen will be like this:

> Resize the window. The screen will be like this:

> The sub-components lie on the same size grid cells:

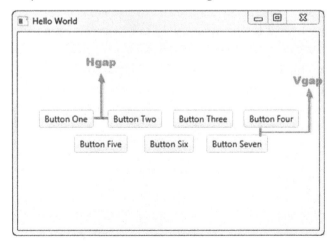

Summary

> Java applications can have Graphical User Interfaces (GUIs) that contain things such as buttons, lists, menus, checkboxes, and many other controls that allows users to interact with applications.
> JavaFX is a set of Java packages that enable developers to design GUI applications that operate consistently across diverse platforms, such as Windows, Linux, and Mac.
> JavaFX is the successor to the Swing, which was Java's User Interface (UI) toolkit recommended for many years, but now Oracle's direction is to use JavaFX.
> Project files In JavaFX are designed with the Module-View-Controller (MVC) pattern in mind. The MVC is dividing the application into three kinds of components, the *Model, View* and *Controller* design.
> The three main objects that get the program on the screen are (from outer to inner): the **stage** (the top level containers of the application), which is responsible for displaying a scene, the **scene** (the object directly contained by the stage) contains all the elements of the GUI, the **root pane/container**, holds all the parts of the application, like buttons, labels, textfields, etc. The root container can be represented by a number of JavaFX containers such as the StackPane, GridPane and BorderPane.
> JavaFX layout is a layout container class (also called *pane*) that is used to easily manage the user interface components or controls for JavaFX application. The JavaFX provides the following built-in layouts (a.k.a. *root panes*): GridPane, HBoxPane, VBoxPane, BorderPane, StackPane.
> The preferred size means the preferred width and height of the control. By default every user interface (UI) controls computes its default value for their preferred size based on its contents.

Chapter 26

JavaFX Controls

JavaFX controls

Java controls are reusable components you can use anywhere within your application. You can use built-in controls provided with Java, or you can create your own. So let's start with JavaFX Button control.

JavaFX Button

A control in a graphical user interface is an element of interaction, such as a button. The JavaFX Button control enables an application to perform some action when the user clicks the button. The Button control can display text, an image, or both.

Creating a JavaFX Button control
- Create a new JavaFX project named **Controls**.
- Open the *sample.fxml* file and create a button with a label **Click Me**, and add it to the grid column 0, row 0. The Button is added as a child of the GridPane layout.

```
<?import javafx.scene.layout.GridPane?>
<?import javafx.scene.control.Button?>
<?import javafx.scene.control.Label?>
<GridPane fx:controller="sample.Controller"
          xmlns:fx="http://javafx.com/fxml" alignment="center"
          hgap="10" vgap="10">
    <Button GridPane.rowIndex="0" GridPane.columnIndex="0"
    text="Click Me"/>
</GridPane>
```

› Run your application. Right click *Main.java* file and select **Run 'Main'**. The screen will be like this:

Add an image to a Button control

› Create a new package named **images**.
› Copy and paste the image you want to use to the **images** package.
› Open the *sample.fxml* file.
› To add a graphic to the button, type the following code inside the button element:

```
<GridPane fx:controller="sample.Controller"
xmlns:fx="http://javafx.com/fxml" alignment="center" hgap="10"
vgap="10">
    <Button GridPane.rowIndex="0" GridPane.columnIndex="0"
text="_Click Me">
        <graphic>
            <ImageView>
                <Image url="@/images/32_003.png"/>
            </ImageView>
        </graphic>
    </Button>
</GridPane>
```

› Run your application. Right click *Main.java* file and select **Run 'Main'**. The screen will be like this:

The image appearing to the left of the text.

JavaFX Label

A Label is useful for displaying text or image that is required to fit within a specific space.

Build a Label control
› Create a new JavaFX project named **Label**.
› Open the *sample.fxml* file and create a label control with a text **"This is a Note"**, and add it to the grid column 1, row 0. The Label is added as a child of the GridPane layout.
```
<Label GridPane.rowIndex="0" GridPane.columnIndex="1" text="This is a Note">
</Label>
```

Add an image to a Label control
› Create a new package named **images**.
› Copy and paste the image you want to use to the **images** package.
› To add an icon to a label type the following code inside the Label control:
```
<?import javafx.scene.control.Label?>
<?import javafx.scene.image.ImageView?>
<?import javafx.scene.image.Image?>
. . .
<Label GridPane.rowIndex="0" GridPane.columnIndex="1"
       text="This is a Note This is a Note This is a Note"
       textFill="blue" wrapText="true">
    <graphic>
```

```
        <ImageView>
            <Image url="@/images/note1.png"/>
        </ImageView>
    </graphic>
. . .
```

> Run your application. Right click *Main.java* file and select **Run 'Main'**. The screen will be like this:

Change the Color of the Label control

To change the color of the label use the **textFill** attribute:

```
<Label GridPane.rowIndex="0" GridPane.columnIndex="1"
       text="This is a Note" textFill="blue">
```

Change the font, style and size of the Label

To change the font name, size and style of the **Label**, add the following code to the *sample.fxml* file:

```
<?import javafx.scene.text.Font?>
. . .
<Label GridPane.rowIndex="0" GridPane.columnIndex="1"
       text="This is a Note" textFill="blue">
    <font>
        <Font name="Arial bold" size="14"/>
    </font>
    <graphic>
        <ImageView>
            <Image url="@/images/note1.png"/>
        </ImageView>
    </graphic>
</Label>
```

Wrapping Text

When you create a label, sometimes you must fit it within a space that is smaller than you need to render. To break up (wrap) the text so that is can fit into the layout area, do the following:

› Make the text of the label longer (ex; `text="This is a Note This is a Note This is a Note"`)

› Add the **wrapText** attribute as follow:
```
<Label GridPane.rowIndex="0" GridPane.columnIndex="1"
            text="This is a Note This is a Note This is a Note"
                                textFill="blue"
wrapText="true">
```

› Run your application. Right click *Main.java* file and select **Run 'Main'**. The screen will be like this:

JavaFX Radio Button

A **RadioButton** control can be either selected or deselected. Typically radio buttons are combined into a group (a.k.a. Toggle Group) where only one item can be selected.

Creating a Radio Button Control

› Create a new JavaFX project named **RadioButton**.
› Create a group of radio buttons.
```
<?import javafx.scene.layout.GridPane?>
<?import javafx.scene.control.RadioButton?>
<?import javafx.scene.control.ToggleGroup?>
<GridPane fx:controller="sample.Controller"
```

```
            xmlns:fx="http://javafx.com/fxml" alignment="center"
    hgap="10" vgap="10">
        <RadioButton GridPane.rowIndex="0" GridPane.columnIndex="0"
                            text="Banana"/>
        <RadioButton GridPane.rowIndex="0" GridPane.columnIndex="1"
                            text="Orange"/>
        <RadioButton GridPane.rowIndex="0" GridPane.columnIndex="2"
                            text="Apple"/>
</GridPane>
```

Adding Radio Buttons to ToggleGroup

The **ToggleGroup** provides references to all radio buttons that are associated with it and manages them so that only one of the radio buttons can be selected at a time. The following example creates a toggle group, creates three radio buttons, adds each radio button to the toggle group, and specifies which button should be selected when the application starts.

› Create a Toggle Group named **fruitTG**. The Toggle Group is added as a child of the GridPane layout.

```
<?import javafx.scene.control.ToggleGroup?>
<GridPane fx:controller="sample.Controller"
        xmlns:fx="http://javafx.com/fxml" alignment="center"
    hgap="10" vgap="10">
        <fx:define>
        <ToggleGroup fx:id="fruitTG"/>
        </fx:define>
        <RadioButton GridPane.rowIndex="0" GridPane.columnIndex="0"
                            text="Banana"/>
```

› Add Radio buttons to the **fruitTG** Toggle group.

```
        <RadioButton GridPane.rowIndex="0" GridPane.columnIndex="0"
                            text="Banana"
    toggleGroup="$fruitTG"/>
        <RadioButton GridPane.rowIndex="0" GridPane.columnIndex="1"
                            text="Orange"
    toggleGroup="$fruitTG"/>
        <RadioButton GridPane.rowIndex="0" GridPane.columnIndex="2"
                            text="Apple"
    toggleGroup="$fruitTG"/>
```

› Run your application. Right click *Main.java* file and select **Run 'Main'**, the screen will be like this:

Put Radio Buttons in a VBox layout
```
<?import javafx.scene.layout.VBox?>
. . .
<fx:define>
    <ToggleGroup fx:id="colorTG"/>
</fx:define>
<VBox GridPane.rowIndex="0" GridPane.columnIndex="1">
<RadioButton GridPane.rowIndex="0" GridPane.columnIndex="0"
        text="Banana" toggleGroup="$fruitTG"/>
<RadioButton GridPane.rowIndex="0" GridPane.columnIndex="1"
        text="Orange" toggleGroup="$fruitTG"/>
<RadioButton GridPane.rowIndex="0" GridPane.columnIndex="2"
        text="Apple" toggleGroup="$fruitTG"/>
</Vbox>
```

Set default selection to first radio button
```
<RadioButton GridPane.rowIndex="0" GridPane.columnIndex="0"
text="Banana"         toggleGroup="$fruitTG" selected="true"/>
```

› Run your application. Right click *Main.java* file and select **Run 'Main'**, the screen will be like this:

JavaFX CheckBox

A JavaFX CheckBox is a button which can be one of three states: Selected, not selected and unknown (indeterminate).

› **Checked**: A checkbox is in this state if selected is true and indeterminate is false.
› **Unchecked**: A checkbox is in this state if selected is false and indeterminate is false.
› **Undefined**: A checkbox is in this state if indeterminate is true, regardless of the state of selected. A typical rendering would by with a minus or dash, to indicate an undefined or indeterminate state of the checkbox.

Creating a CheckBox Control

› Create a new JavaFX project named **CheckBox**
› Open the *sample.fxml* file and create a new CheckBox control with a label **Orange**, and add it to the grid column 1, row 1. The CheckBox is added as a child of the GridPane layout:

```
<?import javafx.scene.control.CheckBox?>
<GridPane fx:controller="sample.Controller"
          xmlns:fx="http://javafx.com/fxml" alignment="center"
hgap="10"            vgap="10">
    <CheckBox GridPane.rowIndex="1" GridPane.columnIndex="1"
                        text="Orange"/>
</GridPane>
```

Make the checkbox selected

```
<CheckBox GridPane.columnIndex="0" GridPane.rowIndex="0"
selected="true"
         text="Orange"/>
```

Run your application. Right click *Main.java* file and select **Run 'Main'** the screen will be like:

Add a group of check boxes to a VBox layout

```
<?import javafx.geometry.Insets?>
<?import javafx.scene.layout.GridPane?>
<?import javafx.scene.control.CheckBox?>
<?import javafx.scene.layout.VBox?>
<GridPane fx:controller="sample.Controller"
          xmlns:fx="http://javafx.com/fxml" alignment="center"
hgap="10"              vgap="10">
    <VBox GridPane.rowIndex="0" GridPane.columnIndex="0">
        <CheckBox text="Orange" selected="true"/>
        <CheckBox text="Apple"/>
        <CheckBox text="Banana"/>
    </VBox>
</GridPane>
```

› Run your application. Right click *Main.java* file and select **Run 'Main'**. The screen will be like this:

JavaFX Toggle Buttons

The Toggle buttons are another type of buttons available through the JavaFX. Two or more toggle buttons can be combined into a group where only one button at a time can be selected, or where no selection is required.

Creating a Toggle Button
> Create a new JavaFX project named **ToggleButton**
> Open the *sample.fxml* file and add a new three toggle buttons, and add it to the HBox layout. The HBox layout is added as a child of the GridPane layout.
```
<?import javafx.scene.layout.GridPane?>
<?import javafx.scene.layout.HBox?>
<?import javafx.scene.control.ToggleButton?>
<?import javafx.scene.control.TextField?>
<GridPane fx:controller="sample.Controller"
          xmlns:fx="http://javafx.com/fxml" alignment="center"
hgap="10"              vgap="10">
    <HBox GridPane.rowIndex="0" GridPane.columnIndex="0">
           <ToggleButton text="New Delhi"/>
           <ToggleButton text="Khartoum"/>
           <ToggleButton text="Tokyo"/>
    </Hbox>
</GridPane>
```

Adding Toggle buttons to a Group
The implementation of the Toggle button is very similar to the implementation of the Radio button. However, unlike radio buttons, toggle buttons in a toggle group do not attempt to force the selection at least one button in the group. That

is, clicking the selected toggle button causes it to become deselected, clicking the selected radio button in the group has no effect.[1]

> Open the previous project **ToggleButton**
> Open the *sample.fxml* file and add a Toggle group named **cityTG**. The Toggle group is added as a child of the GridPane layout.
> Add the Toggle buttons to the Toggle group **cityTG**.

```
<?import javafx.scene.layout.GridPane?>
<?import javafx.scene.control.ToggleGroup?>
<?import javafx.scene.control.ToggleButton?>
<?import javafx.scene.layout.HBox?>
<GridPane fx:controller="sample.Controller"
          xmlns:fx="http://javafx.com/fxml"
          alignment="center" hgap="10" vgap="10">
    <fx:define>
        <ToggleGroup fx:id="cityTG"/>
    </fx:define>
    <HBox GridPane.rowIndex="0" GridPane.columnIndex="0">
        <ToggleButton text="New Delhi" toggleGroup="$cityTG"/>
        <ToggleButton text="Khartoum" toggleGroup="$cityTG"/>
        <ToggleButton text="Tokyo" toggleGroup="$cityTG"/>
    </HBox>
</GridPane>
```

> Run your application. Right click *Main.java* file and select **Run 'Main'**. The screen will be like this:

---
[1] https://docs.oracle.com/javafx/2/ui_controls/toggle-button.htm

JavaFX TextField

A Text Field is a text input component that enables a user to enter a single line of text.

Creating a Text Field control
- Create a new JavaFX project named **TextField**
- Open the *sample.fxml* file and add a text filed and add it to the grid column 0, row 0. The Text Field is added as a child of the GridPane layout.
    ```
    <?import javafx.scene.layout.GridPane?>
    <?import javafx.scene.control.TextField?>
    <GridPane fx:controller="sample.Controller"
              xmlns:fx="http://javafx.com/fxml" alignment="center"
    hgap="10"                 vgap="10">
        <TextField GridPane.rowIndex="0" GridPane.columnIndex="0"/>
    </GridPane>
    ```
- Run your application. Right click *Main.java* file and select **Run 'Main'**. The screen will be like this:

Set the Size of the Text Field

You can apply the *prefColumnCount* property to set the size of the text field. The size of the text field is defined as the maximum number of characters it can display at one time.
- To set the size of the text filed, type the following highlighted code:
    ```
    <?import javafx.scene.layout.GridPane?>
    <?import javafx.scene.control.TextField?>
    <GridPane fx:controller="sample.Controller"
    ```

```
                xmlns:fx="http://javafx.com/fxml" alignment="center"
hgap="10" vgap="10">
    <TextField GridPane.rowIndex="0" GridPane.columnIndex="0"
                        prefColumnCount="20"/>
</GridPane>
```

> Run your application. Right click *Main.java* file and select **Run 'Main'**. The screen will be like this:

JavaFX PasswordField

Password filed is an input field like Text Field but it is used for taking password as input. The characters typed by a user are hidden by displaying a circle for each character entered.

Creating a Password Field control

I will use the same project which I have created in the last lesson - JavaFX TextField

> Open the *sample.fxml* file and add a password field and add it to the grid column 0, row 1. The Password Field is added as a child of the GridPane layout as shown below:

```
<?import javafx.scene.layout.GridPane?>
<?import javafx.scene.control.TextField?>
<?import javafx.scene.control.PasswordField?>
<GridPane fx:controller="sample.Controller"
            xmlns:fx="http://javafx.com/fxml" alignment="center"
hgap="10"           vgap="10">
    <TextField GridPane.rowIndex="1" GridPane.columnIndex="0"/>
    <PasswordField GridPane.rowIndex="1"
GridPane.columnIndex="0"/>
</GridPane>
```

› Run your application. Right click *Main.java* file and select **Run 'Main'**. The screen will be like this:

JavaFX ComboBox

A combo box enables users to choose an item from a drop-down list of items.

Creating a ComboBox control

› Create a new JavaFX project named **ComboBox**
› Open the *sample.fxml* file and create a ComboBox and add it to the grid column 0, row 0. The ComboBox is added as a child of the GridPane layout.

```xml
<?import javafx.scene.layout.GridPane?>
<?import javafx.scene.control.ComboBox?>
<?import javafx.collections.FXCollections?>
<?import java.lang.String?>
<GridPane fx:controller="sample.Controller"
          xmlns:fx="http://javafx.com/fxml" alignment="center"
hgap="10"            vgap="10">
    <ComboBox GridPane.columnIndex="0" GridPane.rowIndex="0"
                    GridPane.columnSpan="2">
        <items>
            <FXCollections fx:factory="observableArrayList">
                <String fx:value="Item 1"/>
                <String fx:value="Item 2"/>
                <String fx:value="Item 3"/>
                <String fx:value="Item 4"/>
                <String fx:value="Item 5"/>
            </FXCollections>
        </items>
    </ComboBox>
</GridPane>
```

› Run your application. Right click *Main.java* file and select **Run 'Main'**. The screen will be like this:

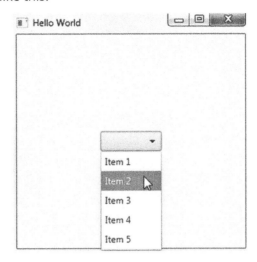

Set the Default Selection to ComboBox

› After the </items> element, type the following:
```
<value>
    <String fx:value="Item 2"/>
</value>
```

› Run your application. Right click *Main.java* file and select **Run 'Main'**. The screen will be like this:

Making the ComboBox Editable

> A ComboBox is not editable by default. But once the ComboBox is editable, the user can type in values into the ComboBox. To make the ComboBox editable type the following:
> ```
> <ComboBox GridPane.columnIndex="0" GridPane.rowIndex="0"
>         GridPane.columnSpan="2" editable="true">
> ```
> Run your application. Right click *Main.java* file and select **Run 'Main'**. The screen will be like this:

JavaFX ChoiceBox

The ChoiceBox enables users to choose an item from a list of items.

Creating a ChoiceBox control

> Create a new JavaFX project named **ChoiceBox**
> Open the *sample.fxml* file and create a choice box with an items (Item 1, Item 2, Item 3, Item 4, Item 5), and add it to the grid column 0, row 0. The ChoiceBox is added as a child of the GridPane layout.
> ```
> <?import javafx.scene.layout.GridPane?>
> <?import javafx.collections.FXCollections?>
> <?import java.lang.String?>
> <?import javafx.scene.control.ChoiceBox?>
> <GridPane fx:controller="sample.Controller"
>         xmlns:fx="http://javafx.com/fxml" alignment="center"
> hgap="10"             vgap="10">
>     <ChoiceBox GridPane.columnIndex="0" GridPane.rowIndex="1">
>         <items>
>             <FXCollections fx:factory="observableArrayList">
>                 <String fx:value="Item 1"/>
>                 <String fx:value="Item 2"/>
> ```

```xml
            <String fx:value="Item 3"/>
            <String fx:value="Item 4"/>
            <String fx:value="Item 5"/>
        </FXCollections>
    </items>
    <value>
        <String fx:value="Item 3"/>
    </value>
</ChoiceBox>
</GridPane>
```

› Run your application. Right click *Main.java* file and select **Run 'Main'**. The screen will be like this:

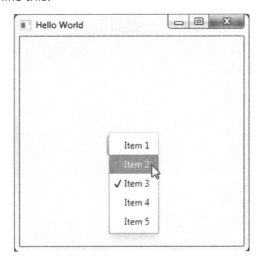

Differences between ComboBox and ChoiceBox
› ChoiceBox used for small set of list less than 10, for more ComboBox
› ComboBox used for small, medium, long set of list. Also ComboBox supports a `cellFactory` which allows essentially an arbitrary UI for displaying the item in each cell (discussed later).

If the number of items does not exceed a certain limit, developers can decide whether a combo box or a choice box better suits their needs.

JavaFX ListView

The JavaFX List View control allows you to choose one or more options from a predefined list of items.

Creating a List View control
› Create a new JavaFX project named **ListView**

- Open the *sample.fxml* file and create a List View control and add it to the grid column 0, row 0. The List View is added as a child of the GridPane layout.

  ```
  <?import javafx.scene.layout.GridPane?>
  <?import javafx.scene.control.ListView?>
  <GridPane fx:controller="sample.Controller"
          xmlns:fx="http://javafx.com/fxml"
          alignment="center" hgap="10" vgap="10">
      <ListView GridPane.columnIndex="0" GridPane.rowIndex="0"/>
  </GridPane>
  ```

- Run the application. Right click the *Main.java* file and select **Run 'Main'**. The screen will be like this:

Change the width and height of the ListView

To alter the width and height of the list view control, use the *prefWidth* and *prefHeight* attributes as follow:

```
<ListView GridPane.columnIndex="0" GridPane.rowIndex="0"
prefWidth="100" prefHeight="100">
```

Adding items to the ListView

- Create the items (Banana, Orange, Apple, Apricots, Plums, Kiwis, Peaches) and add it to the ListView control.

  ```
  <?xml version="1.0" encoding="UTF-8"?>
  <?import javafx.scene.control.ListView?>
  <?import javafx.scene.layout.GridPane?>
  <?import javafx.collections.FXCollections?>
  <?import java.lang.String?>
  <GridPane alignment="center" hgap="10" vgap="10"
          xmlns:fx="http://javafx.com/fxml/1"
          xmlns="http://javafx.com/javafx/8.0.102"
          fx:controller="sample.Controller">
      <ListView GridPane.columnIndex="0" GridPane.rowIndex="0"
  ```

```
            prefWidth="100" prefHeight="100">
        <items>
            <FXCollections fx:factory="observableArrayList">
                <String fx:value="Banana"/>
                <String fx:value="Orange"/>
                <String fx:value="Apple"/>
                <String fx:value="Apricots"/>
                <String fx:value="Plums"/>
                <String fx:value="Kiwis"/>
                <String fx:value="Peaches"/>
            </FXCollections>
        </items>
    </ListView>
</GridPane>
```

> Run the application. Right click *Main.java* file and select **Run 'Main'**. The screen will be like this:

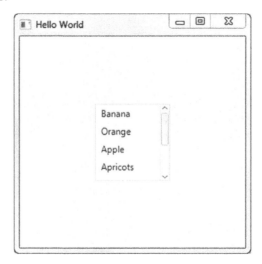

You can scroll through the list, selecting any of its items.

Orient a ListView object horizontally

You can orient a ListView object horizontally by setting the orientation property to HORIZONTAL. This can be done as follows:

> Change the `prefWidth` attribute to 250 and the `prefHeight` attribute to 100.

> Use the `orientation` property and assign it `"HORIZONTAL"` value.
```
<ListView orientation="HORIZONTAL" GridPane.columnIndex="0"
                     GridPane.rowIndex="0" prefWidth="250"
prefHeight="100"                   orientation="HORIZONTAL">
```

> Run the application. Right click *Main.java* file and select **Run 'Main'**. The screen will be like this:

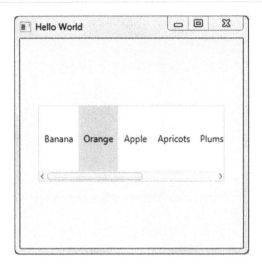

JavaFX TextArea

JavaFX TextArea is a component allowing users to enter multiple lines of text, which can then be read by the application.

Creating a TextArea control
› Create a new JavaFX project named **TextArea**
› Open the *sample.fxml* file and create a TextArea control and add it to the grid column 0, row 0. The TextArea added as a child of the GridPane layout.
```
<?import javafx.scene.layout.GridPane?>
<?import javafx.scene.control.TextArea?>
<GridPane fx:controller="sample.Controller"
          xmlns:fx="http://javafx.com/fxml"
          alignment="center" hgap="10" vgap="10">
    <TextArea GridPane.columnIndex="0" GridPane.rowIndex="0"/>
</GridPane>
```
› Run the application. Right click the *Main.java* file and select **Run 'Main'**. The screen will be like this:

Change the width and height of the TextArea control

To alter the width and height of the Text Area control, use the *preRowCount* and *preColumnCount* attributes as follow:

```
<TextArea GridPane.columnIndex="0" GridPane.rowIndex="0"
prefRowCount="10"          prefColumnCount="10">
```

`preColumnCount`: The preferred number of text columns (preferred width).

`preRowCount`: The preferred number of text rows (preferred height).

› Run the application. Right click the *Main.java* file and select **Run 'Main'**. The screen will be like this:

JavaFX Spinner

A Spinner is a single line text field that lets the user select a number or an object value from an ordered sequence of such values. To cycle through the elements of the sequence, you can use:

> A pair of tiny arrow buttons.
> The keyboard up/down arrow keys.
> Type a (legal) value directly into the Spinner. By default the spinner is non-editable, but input can be accepted if the editable property is set to true.

Creating a Spinner control
> Create a new JavaFX project named **Spinner**.
> Open the *sample.fxml* file and create a spinner with the following properties. And add it to the grid column 0, row 0. The Spinner is added as a child of the GridPane layout.
```
<?import javafx.scene.layout.GridPane?>
<?import javafx.scene.control.Spinner?>
<GridPane fx:controller="sample.Controller"
          xmlns:fx="http://javafx.com/fxml" alignment="center"
          hgap="10" vgap="10">
    <Spinner GridPane.columnIndex="0" GridPane.rowIndex="0"
             min="0" max="100" editable="true"
initialValue="50"/>
</GridPane>
```
> Run your application. Right click *Main.java* file and select **Run 'Main'**. The screen will be like this:

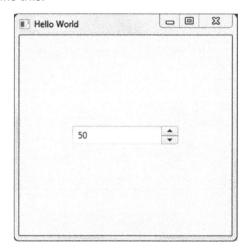

Explanation

> `min:` The minimum value for the spinner.
> `max:` The maximum value for the spinner.
> `editable:` To specify whether user is able to type into the spinner editor.
> `initial value:` The value of the Spinner when first instantiated. It must be within the bounds of min and max arguments, or else the max value will be used.

JavaFX ColorPicker

The color picker allows the user to select a particular color from the available range, or set their own custom color.

Creating a Color Picker control

> Create a new JavaFX project named **ColorPicker**
> Open the *sample.fxml* file and create a ColorPicker control, and add it to the grid column 0, row 0. The ColorPicker is added as a child of the GridPane layout.

```
<?import javafx.scene.layout.GridPane?>
<?import javafx.scene.control.ColorPicker?>
<GridPane fx:controller="sample.Controller"
          xmlns:fx="http://javafx.com/fxml" alignment="center"
          hgap="10" vgap="10">
    <ColorPicker GridPane.rowIndex="0"
GridPane.columnIndex="0"/>
</GridPane>
```

> Run your application. Right click *Main.java* file and select **Run 'Main'**. The screen will be like this:

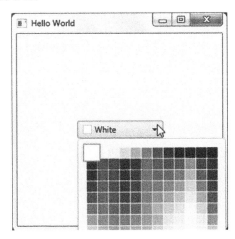

JavaFX DatePicker

The DatePicker control enables the user to enter a date or to select a date from a calendar. The calendar is based on either the standard ISO-8601 chronology or any of the other chronology classes defined in the java.time.chrono package.

Creating a DatePicker control
> Create a new JavaFX project named **DatePicker**
> Open the *sample.fxml* file and create a Date Picker control and add it to the grid column 0, row 0. The DatePicker is added as a child of the GridPane layout.

```
<?import javafx.scene.layout.GridPane?>
<?import javafx.scene.control.DatePicker?>
<GridPane fx:controller="sample.Controller"
          xmlns:fx="http://javafx.com/fxml" alignment="center"
          hgap="10" vgap="10">
    <DatePicker GridPane.columnIndex="0" GridPane.rowIndex="0"/>
</GridPane>
```

> Run your application. Right click *Main.java* file and select **Run 'Main'**. The screen will be like this:

JavaFX TitledPane

A titled pane is a panel with a title that can be expanded and collapsed. The panel in a TitledPane can be UI controls or groups of nodes added to a layout container.

Creating Titled Pane control

> - Create a new JavaFX project named **TitledPane**
> - Open the *sample.fxml* file and create a TitledPane with a label "**Titled Pane**", and add a Label to it with a text "**Label in titled Pane 1**". And add the TitledPane to the grid column 0, row 0. The TitledPane is added as a child of the GridPane layout.
> ```
> <?import javafx.scene.layout.GridPane?>
> <?import javafx.scene.control.Label?>
> <?import javafx.scene.control.TitledPane?>
> <GridPane fx:controller="sample.Controller"
>           xmlns:fx="http://javafx.com/fxml" alignment="center"
> hgap="10"           vgap="10">
>     <TitledPane text="Titled Pane" GridPane.rowIndex="0"
>                                    GridPane.columnIndex="0">
>         <Label text="Label in Titled Pane 1"/>
>     </TitledPane>
> </GridPane>
> ```
> - Run your application. Right click *Main.java* file and select **Run 'Main'**. The screen will be like this:

Adding Titled Panes to an Accordion

Titled panes can be grouped by using the accordion control.

> - Add Titled panes to an accordion:
> ```
> <?import javafx.scene.layout.GridPane?>
> <?import javafx.scene.control.Label?>
> <?import javafx.scene.control.TitledPane?>
> <?import javafx.scene.control.Accordion?>
> <GridPane fx:controller="sample.Controller"
>           xmlns:fx="http://javafx.com/fxml" alignment="center"
> hgap="10" vgap="10">
> ```

```
<Accordion GridPane.columnIndex="0" GridPane.rowIndex="0"
                    GridPane.columnSpan="2">
    <panes>
        <TitledPane text="Titled Pane 1">
            <Label text="Label in Titled Pane 1"/>
        </TitledPane>
        <TitledPane text="Titled Pane 2">
            <Label text="Label in Titled Pane 2"/>
        </TitledPane>
        <TitledPane text="Titled Pane 3">
            <Label text="Label in Titled Pane 3"/>
        </TitledPane>
        <TitledPane text="Titled Pane 4">
            <Label text="Label in Titled Pane 4"/>
        </TitledPane>
    </panes>
</Accordion>
</GridPane>
```

› Run your application. Right click *Main.java* file and select **Run 'Main'**. The screen will be like this:

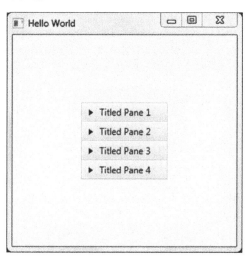

Set a Default TitledPane that will be Open in Your Accordion

› Add an `fx:id` tag into your selected TitledPane:
```
<TitledPane fx:id="tp3" text="Titled Pane 3">
```

› Add an expandedPane property into the Accordion element code that reference your selected TitledPane:
```
<Accordion GridPane.columnIndex="0" GridPane.rowIndex="0"
            GridPane.columnSpan="2" expandedPane="$tp3">
```

› Run your application. Right click *Main.java* file and select **Run 'Main'**. The screen will be like this:

JavaFX Menu

Menus are a standard way for desktop applications to select options. Menus are actually made up of:

> **Menu Bar**: is a container that holds individual menus, such as the File menu, and the Help menu.
> **At least one Menu:** The menus in turn hold menu items, for example some menu items in the Edit menu are often Cut, Copy, and Paste.
> **Several Menu Items**.

So Menu Bars contain Menus which in turn contain Menu items. So you must create a menu bar object (javafx.scene.control.MenuBar) to hold menu objects (javafx.scene.control.Menu). Menu objects can contain Menu and MenuItem objects (javafx.scene.control.MenuItem). A menu may contain other menus as sub-menus. MenuItems are child options within a Menu object.

Creating a Menu control
> Create a new JavaFX project named **Menu**
> Open *sample.fxml* file and change the GridPane to BorderPane.
> In BorderPane, remove the `alignment,` `hgap,` and `vgap` attributes because they aren't applicable for this layout.
> Create MenuBar control inside the BorderPane layout and specify the position of the MenuBar inside the BorderPane, for example top.

```
<?xml version="1.0" encoding="UTF-8"?>
<?import javafx.scene.control.MenuBar?>
```

```
<?import javafx.scene.layout.BorderPane?>
<BorderPane prefHeight="228.0" prefWidth="190.0"
            xmlns="http://javafx.com/javafx/8.0.102"
            xmlns:fx="http://javafx.com/fxml/1"
            fx:controller="sample.Controller">
    <top>
        <MenuBar>
        </MenuBar>
    </top>
</BorderPane>
```

› Then create a File Menu to the Menu Bar and add Menu Items Open and Close to the File Menu.

```
<?import javafx.scene.control.Menu?>
<?import javafx.scene.control.MenuItem?>
. . .
<top>
  <MenuBar>
      <Menu text="File">
          <MenuItem text="Open"/>
          <MenuItem text="Close"/>
      </Menu>
  </MenuBar>
</top>
```

› Run your application. Right click `Main.java` file and select Run `"Main.java"`. The screen will be like this:

NOTE: A menu bar can be placed elsewhere in the user interface, typically it is located at the top of the UI and it contains one or more menus. The menu bar automatically resizes to fit the width of the application window.

JavaFX Tooltip

The Tooltip can be set on any control. The Tooltip has two different states:

› **Activated**: when the mouse moves over a control.
› **Showing**: when the tooltip actually appears. A shown tooltip is also activated.

Creating a Tooltip (*Adding a Tooltip to the Password Field*)

Create a new JavaFX project named Password

```xml
<?xml version="1.0" encoding="UTF-8"?>
<?import javafx.scene.control.Tooltip?>
<?import javafx.scene.layout.GridPane?>
<?import javafx.scene.control.PasswordField?>
<GridPane alignment="center" hgap="10" prefHeight="400.0" prefWidth="600.0"
          vgap="10" xmlns:fx="http://javafx.com/fxml/1"
          xmlns="http://javafx.com/javafx/9.0.1"
          fx:controller="sample.Controller">
    <PasswordField>
        <tooltip>
            <Tooltip text="Your password must be at least 8 characters in length"/>
        </tooltip>
    </PasswordField>
</GridPane>
```

JavaFX Separator

The `Separator` class represents a horizontal or vertical separator line. It serves to divide elements of the application user interface and does not produce any action. By default, the separator is horizontal. You can change its orientation by using the *setOrientation* method.

Create a vertical separator

```xml
<Separator orientation="VERTICAL" prefHeight="200.0"
 GridPane.columnIndex="1"/>
```

Create a horizontal separator

```
<Separator orientation="HORIZONTAL" prefWidth="200.0" />
```
Typically, separators are used to divide groups of the UI controls.

Events and Event Handlers

In JavaFX applications. **events** are notifications that something has happened. As a user clicks a button, presses a key, moves a mouse, or performs other actions, events are dispatched. Registered event handlers within the application receive the event and provide a response.[1]

JavaFX Button Events

The primary function of each button is to produce an action when it is clicked. Use the `onAction` property of the Button control to define what will happen when a user clicks the button.

Assigning an event handler to a button control
> Create a new JavaFX project named **ButtonEvent**
> Open the *sample.fxml* file and create a button with a label **Click Me**, and add it to the grid column 0, row 0. The Button is added as a child of the GridPane layout.

Create an event handler named `onButtonClicked()`
> Open the *Controller.java* file and add the `onButtonClicked()` event handler as follow:
```
package sample;
public class Controller {
    public void onButtonClicked(){
        System.out.println("Hello");
    }
}
```
> Assign the Button control to the `onButtonClicked()` event handler . Open the *sample.fxml* file and assign the **#onButtonClicked** value to the `onAction` property:
```
<Button text="Click Me" GridPane.columnIndex="0"
GridPane.rowIndex="0"
    onAction="#onButtonClicked"/>
```

---
[1] http://docs.oracle.com/

› Run your application. Click on **Click Me** button many times. The screen will be like this:

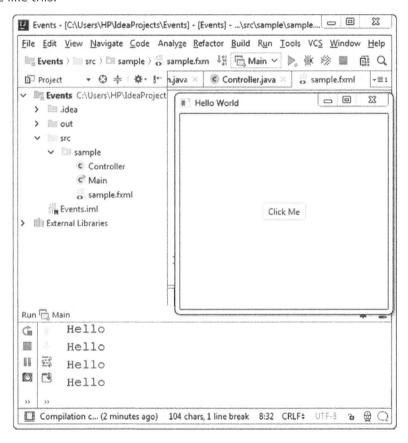

The button's action, which is invoked whenever the button is clicked, touched or key pressed.

JavaFX TextField Events

Let's add a TextField to a Button. And when a button is pressed, hello, followed by whether was typed in the fields is going to be written to the console.

› Open the *sample.fxml* file and add a text filed to a grid pane and place it into the second row.
```
<?import javafx.scene.control.TextField?>
. . .
<TextField GridPane.rowIndex="1" GridPane.columnIndex="0"/>
```

› Reference the TextField control in *sample.fxml* file in *Controller.java* file code. So go to *sample.fxml* file and assign `fx:id` to the TextField control:

```xml
<TextField fx:id="nameField" GridPane.rowIndex="1"
                    GridPane.columnIndex="0"/>
```

> Go to *Controller.java* file and create an instance field for the TextField control. We want to retrieves the data out of it. Then put comma after "Hello, " + and `getText()` method to get data from the Text Field.

```java
package sample;
import javafx.fxml.FXML;
import javafx.scene.control.TextField;
public class Controller {
    @FXML
    private TextField nameField;

    public void onButtonClicked(){
        System.out.println("Hello, " + nameField.getText());
    }
}
```

`getText()` method reads the text entered into a Text field.

> Run your application. Type any name in the field and click the **Click Me** button. The screen will be like this:

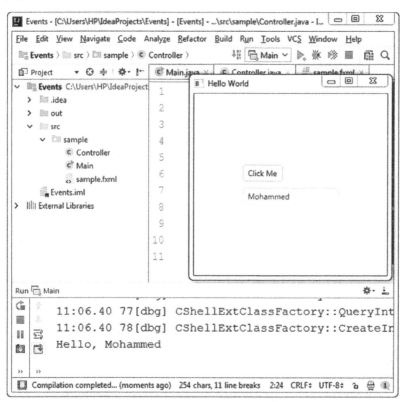

› It is a good idea to annotate event handler - but it is not required. Why? To be able to see at glance the method is an even handler associated with Controller and the FXML. So add @FXML annotation to `onButtonClicked()` method:

```
package sample;
import javafx.fxml.FXML;
import javafx.scene.control.TextField;
public class Controller {
    @FXML
    private TextField nameField;

    @FXML
    public void onButtonClicked(){
        System.out.println("Hello, " + nameField.getText());
    }
}
```

NOTES

☐ Makes sure that the variable - **nameField** - has the exact name as the **fx:id** value (*sample.fxml* file).

☐ The @FXML annotation enables an FXMLLoader to inject values defined in an FXML file into references in the `Controller` class. In other words, if you annotate your `nameField` with @FXML, it will be initialized by the FXMLLoader when the `load()` method is called by an element in the FXML file with `fx:id="nameField"`. When the FXMLLoader loads the FXML file, it will attempt to inject any elements that have are `fx:id` attribute into the controller. It will look for:

  ▪ Any public field with a variable name matching `fx:id` attribute or
  ▪ Any field (public or not) with a variable name matching the `fx:id` attribute that is annotated with @FXML.

☐ The `getText()` method is used to obtain the value of a text field.

Event Handler - Parameters

Some event handlers can take parameters. So if we want to do that we can actually add an action event parameter to our an existing event handler method. So let's do that and so how that work.

Example: Add ActionEvent parameter to an Event Handler method

› Go to *Controller.java* file and add the following code to the `onButtonClicked()` event handler method:

```
@FXML
```

```
public void onButtonClicked(ActionEvent e){
    System.out.println("Hello, " + nameField.getText());
}
```

So why we use **ActionEvent** parameter? Because if we want to use the same event / event handler for more than one control we need to know which control we used to interact with. So no need to create an event handler for each control, all we have to do is add this parameter to our method and then call the `getSource()` method which figure out which control was actually used. So add the following code to the `onButtonClick()` method:

Example: Create two button controls and add them to `onButtonClicked` method

› Open the *sample.fxml* and add two buttons.
```
<GridPane fx:controller="sample.Controller"
          xmlns:fx="http://javafx.com/fxml" alignment="center"
          hgap="10"              vgap="10">
    <TextField fx:id="nameField" GridPane.rowIndex="0"
                                 GridPane.columnIndex="0"/>
    <Button fx:id="byeButton" text="Bye"
GridPane.columnIndex="0"                  GridPane.rowIndex="1"
onAction="#onButtonClicked"/>
    <Button fx:id="helloButton" text="Hello"
GridPane.rowIndex="1"                     GridPane.columnIndex="1"
onAction="#onButtonClicked"/>
</GridPane>
```

› Go back to *Controller.java* file and add two private fields for two buttons:
```
import javafx.fxml.FXML;
import javafx.scene.control.Button;
import javafx.scene.control.TextField;
import javafx.event.ActionEvent;
. . .
@FXML
private TextField nameField;
@FXML
private Button helloButton;
@FXML
private Button byeButton;
```

› Then change the code of the `onButtonClicked(ActionEvent e)` method as follow (one event handler method that handling the events of two buttons):
```
@FXML
public void onButtonClicked(ActionEvent e){
    if (e.getSource().equals(helloButton)){
        System.out.println("Hello, " + nameField.getText());
    }else if (e.getSource().equals(byeButton)){
        System.out.println("Bye, " + nameField.getText());
    }
}
```

› Run your application. Right click *Main.java* file and select **Run 'Main'**. The screen will be like this:

Disable the button when the Text Field is empty

To Disable the Buttons when the Text field is empty, do the following:

› Go to *Controller.java* file and after the `onButtonClicked()` method, create a new method and name it `handleKeyReleased()`.

```
@FXML
public void handleKeyReleased(){
    String text = nameField.getText();
    boolean disableButtons = text.isEmpty() ||
text.trim().isEmpty();
    helloButton.setDisable(disableButtons);
    byeButton.setDisable(disableButtons);
}
```

Disable the buttons when the application first run

› To disable the Buttons when the application first run, we have to add an initialize method to our controller. JavaFX runtime call this method when it is initializing UI. The method can't have any parameter and must be public and we must add it to @FXML .So before `onButtonClicked()` method add the following code:

```
@FXML
public void initialize(){
    helloButton.setDisable(true);
    byeButton.setDisable(true);
}
```

› Associate the event handler we just wrote to our text field. Open the *sample.fxml* file and add the **onKeyReleased** property to TextField:

```
<TextField fx:id="nameField" GridPane.rowIndex="0"
        GridPane.columnIndex="0"
onKeyReleased="#handleKeyReleased"/>
```

> Run your application. Right click *Main.java* file and select **Run 'Main'**. The screen will be like this:

When you type something, the buttons are enabled.

JavaFX PasswordField Events

The PasswordField is for password input. The characters typed by a user are hidden by displaying an echo string. So in this lesson we'll create a password field component and set prompt message text to it.

Create a password field and then set the prompt message text
> Create a new JavaFX project named **PasswordEvents**.
> Open the *sample.fxml* file and add a password field and add it to the grid column 0, row 0. The Password Field is added as a child of the GridPane layout.

```
<?import javafx.scene.layout.GridPane?>
<?import javafx.scene.control.TextField?>
<?import javafx.scene.control.PasswordField?>
<GridPane fx:controller="sample.Controller"
        xmlns:fx="http://javafx.com/fxml" alignment="center"
hgap="10"              vgap="10">
    <PasswordField GridPane.rowIndex="0"
GridPane.columnIndex="0"/>
</GridPane>
```

› Set the the prompt message text. The prompt message is displayed as the grayed out text in the field and provides users a hint for what is the field is for without using the label control.
```
<PasswordField GridPane.rowIndex="0" GridPane.columnIndex="0" promptText="Enter Password"/>
```
› Run your application. Right click *Main.java* file and select **Run 'Main'**. The screen will be like this:

For the password field the string specified is hidden by the echo characters. By default, the echo character is a dot. The value in the password field can be obtained through the *getText* method.

› Create a `label` control, and add it to the grid column 0, row 1. The label is added as a child of GridPane layout.
```
<Label text="Label" GridPane.rowIndex="1" GridPane.columnIndex="0" />
```
› Use `fx:id` attribute to inject objects to the controller (*Controller.java* class) as follow:
```
<PasswordField fx:id="pwd" promptText="Enter Password" GridPane.rowIndex="0" GridPane.columnIndex="0" promptText="Enter Password"/>
<Label fx:id="message" text="Label" GridPane.rowIndex="1" />
```
› Set your `CheckPassword()` method to check the text in the Password Field. Your *Controller.java* code will look similar to the following:
```
01 package sample;
02
03 import javafx.fxml.FXML;
04 import javafx.scene.control.Label;
05 import javafx.scene.control.PasswordField;
06 import javafx.scene.paint.Color;
07
08 public class Controller {
09     @FXML
10     private PasswordField pwd;
11
12     @FXML
13     private Label message;
14
15     @FXML
16     public void initialize(){
17         message.setText("");
18     }
19
```

```
20        @FXML
21        public void CheckPassword(){
22            if (!pwd.getText().equals("abc")){
23                message.setText("Your password is incorrect!");
24                message.setTextFill(Color.rgb(210, 39, 84));
25            }else {
26                message.setText("Your password has been con-
firmed");
27                message.setTextFill(Color.web("black"));
28            }
29            pwd.clear();
30        }
31   }
```

› Use the `OnAction` attribute to connect the `CheckPassword()` method to PasswordField
```
<PasswordField fx:id="pwd" onAction="#CheckPassword"
promptText="Enter Password" />
```

Explanation

› If the typed value is different from the required password, the corresponding message appears in red.

› If the typed value satisfies the predefined criteria, the confirmation message appears.

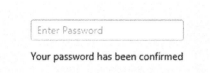

For security reasons, it is good practice to clear the password field after the value is typed.

JavaFX Menu Event Handler

Menu are actually made up of a:
› MenuBar
› At least one Menu &

- Several Menu Items.

The MenuBar is the container that holds individual menus, such as the File menu, the Edit menu, and the Help menu. The menus in turn hold menu items that you see when you click on the menus. Some Menu items in the File menu are often Save, Open and Quit. So let's start!

Building Menus in JavaFX Applications

The menus in a menu bar are typically grouped into categories. The coding pattern is to declare a menu bar, define the category menus, and populate the category menus with menu items. Let's build a new menu project.

- Create a new JavaFX project named **MenuPro**
- Set the Stage's **title** property to **JavaFX Menu**. Go to *Main.java* class and change the following code:
  ```
  primaryStage.setTitle("JavaFX Menu");
  ```
- Open *sample.fxml* file and add a MenuBar inside the GridPane layout as shown in the following code:
  ```
  01  <GridPane alignment="center" hgap="10" vgap="10"
  02      xmlns:fx="http://javafx.com/fxml/1"
  xmlns="http://javafx.com/javafx/9.0.1"
  03      fx:controller="sample.Controller">
  04      <children>
  05          <MenuBar>
  06              <menus>
  07                  <Menu mnemonicParsing="false" text="File">
  08                      <items>
  09                          <MenuItem mnemonicParsing="false" text="Close" />
  10                      </items>
  11                  </Menu>
  12                  <Menu mnemonicParsing="false" text="Help">
  13                      <items>
  14                          <MenuItem mnemonicParsing="false" text="About" />
  15                      </items>
  16                  </Menu>
  17              </menus>
  18          </MenuBar>
  19      </children>
  20  </GridPane>
  ```
- Change the size of GridPane layout to 200 X 400, using the `prefWidth` and `PrefHeight` attributes:
  ```
  <GridPane alignment="center" hgap="10" vgap="10"
  xmlns="http://javafx.com/javafx/9.0.1"
  xmlns:fx="http://javafx.com/fxml/1"
  fx:controller="sample.Controller" prefWidth="200"
  prefHeight="400">
  ```
- Set the alignment attribute of the GridPane layout to TOP_LEFT as follow:

```
01  <GridPane alignment="TOP_LEFT" hgap="10" vgap="10"
02      xmlns:fx="http://javafx.com/fxml/1"
xmlns="http://javafx.com/javafx/9.0.1"
03      fx:controller="sample.Controller">
```

> Set the `hgrow` attribute of the MenuBar control to STRETCH:

   `<MenuBar GridPane.hgrow="ALWAYS">`

   The menu bar automatically resizes to fit the width of the application window. By default, each menu added to the menu bar is represented by a button with the text value.

> Once the MenuBar is created, you can add Menu to it . A Menu represents a single vertical menu with nested menu items. Here is an example of adding a Menu to a MenuBar:
```
<MenuBar>
    <menus>
        <Menu mnemonicParsing="false" text="File">
        </Menu>
    </menus>
</MenuBar>
```
   As you can see, there is only a single menu in the MenuBar titled "File".

> Adding a menu items to a menu using <MenuItem> element.
```
<MenuBar>
    <menus>
        <Menu mnemonicParsing="false" text="File">
            <items>
                <MenuItem mnemonicParsing="false" text="Close" />
            </items>
        </Menu>
    </menus>
</MenuBar>
```

As you can see, there is only a single menu item in the "File" menu titled "Close".

> Run the application. Right click the *Main.java* file and select **Run 'Main'**. The screen will be like this:

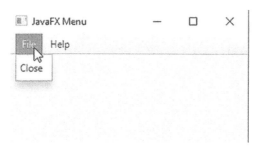

MenuItem Events

The **MenuBar** created in the previous examples do not react if you select any of the menu items. In order to respond to the selection of a MenuItem you must set an event on the MenuItem. Let's do that.

> Create an event handler named `onCloseClicked()`. Open the *Controller.java* file and add the `onCloseClicked()` event handler as follow:
> ```
> package sample;
>
> import javafx.application.Platform;
> import javafx.fxml.FXML;
> import javafx.scene.control.MenuItem;
>
> public class Controller {
>     @FXML
>     private MenuItem close;
>
>     @FXML
>     public void onCloseClicked(){
>         Platform.exit();
>     }
> }
> ```

> Assign the Menu item to the `onCloseClicked()` event handler. Open the *sample.fxml* file and assign the `#onCloseClicked` value to the `onAction` property:
> ```
> <MenuItem fx:id="close" mnemonicParsing="false"
> onAction="#onCloseClicked" text="Close"/>
> ```

> Run your application. Right click *Main.java* file and select Run '*Main.java*'. Select File > Close. The application will be closed.

Key Mnemonics

The mnemonic is when underscored letter of a menu of a **menubar**. When you press `Alt+<the letter>` the menu will be opened. It gives you a quick access to the menu.

In order to define a mnemonic, in the text of your menu, place the character '_' and set the `mnemonicParsingProperty()` to `true` either in your FXML or either in your backing code. And automatically, JavaFX will compute and set the mnemonic for your menu.

Example: Add key mnemonics to the `File` menu

Create a File menu that uses the letter "F" as the mnemonic.

> To add key mnemonics to the "File" menu, we place the character '_' before the F letter as shown below, and set the mnemonicParsing to `true` in FXML code:
> ```
> <Menu mnemonicParsing="true" text="_File">
> ```

> Run your application. Right click *Main.java* file and select **Run 'Main.java'**. Press `Alt + F`, the File menu will be opened.

Key Combinations

A key combination is a combination of keystrokes to select a menu option. The key combinations are referred as **keyboard shortcuts**.

A keyboard shortcut is called an accelerator. An accelerator is composed of a combination of keys:

> a main key: A, B, C, ...
> a modifier: Ctrl, Command, Meta, Shift, Alt

A keyboard shortcut is usually something like Ctrl + <a key> on Windows and Meta + <a key> on Mac. For example, on the Windows platform the key combination of (Ctrl + S) can save a file. On the Mac OS platform, the key combination would be (Command + S). Usually the modifiers are pressed in combination with a single letter.

Way 1: Create a key combination

We will be learning how to use the keys `Ctrl + C` to call a MenuItem accelerator which will exit the application.

```
<MenuItem fx:id="close" onAction="#onCloseClicked" text="Close"
    accelerator="shift+C">
```

OR

```
<MenuItem fx:id="close" onAction="#onCloseClicked" text="Close"
    accelerator="alt+C">
```

OR

```
<MenuItem fx:id="close" onAction="#onCloseClicked" text="Close"
    accelerator="meta+C">
```

OR

```
<MenuItem fx:id="close" onAction="#onCloseClicked" text="Close"
    accelerator="shortcut+C">
```

where Shortcut means Ctrl on Windows or Linux and Meta on Mac.

NOTES
☐ The code uses the KeyCombination.SHORTCUT_DOWN value as the key modifier instead of CONTROL_DOWN or META_DOWN. The value of SHORTCUT_DOWN will enable the application to be cross-platform.
☐ The values CONTROL_DOWN and META_DOWN are system dependent on the Windows and Mac OS platforms respectively, but SHORTCUT_DOWN works on all platforms.

JavaFX Context Menu and Events (Respond to a Mouse Right-Click)

A context menu is a pop-up window that appears in response to a mouse click. A context menu can contain one or more menu items. Note that the ContextMenu is quite similar to a Menu, you can add items with types of MenuItem, CheckMenuItem, RadioMenuItem, SeparatorMenuItem to ContextMenu.

Building ContextMenu in JavaFX Applications

The menus in a menu bar are typically grouped into categories. The coding pattern is to declare a menu bar, define the category menus, and populate the category menus with menu items.

> Create a new JavaFX project named **ContextMenu**.
> Set the Stage's **title** property to **JavaFX ContextMenu**. Go to *Main.java* class and change the following code:
> ```
> primaryStage.setTitle("JavaFX Context Menu");
> ```
> Go to the *sample.fxml* file and change the size of GridPane layout to 300 X 400, using the `prefWidth` and `PrefHeight` attributes:
> `<GridPane alignment="center" hgap="10" vgap="10" xmlns="http://javafx.com/javafx/9.0.1" xmlns:fx="http://javafx.com/fxml/1" fx:controller="sample.Controller" prefWidth="300" prefHeight="400">`
> Go to the *Main.java* file and change the size of GridPane layout to 300 X 400 as follows:
> `primaryStage.setScene(new Scene(root, 300, 400));`
> Open *sample.fxml* file and create `MenuBar` control inside the `GridPane` layout. Then add a `ContextMenu` control inside the MenuBar control. Then add the Menu item `"Close"` as follows:
> `01 <?xml version="1.0" encoding="UTF-8"?>`

```
02
03 <?import javafx.scene.control.ContextMenu?>
04 <?import javafx.scene.control.MenuBar?>
05 <?import javafx.scene.control.MenuItem?>
06 <?import javafx.scene.layout.GridPane?>
07
08 <GridPane alignment="center" hgap="10" prefHeight="400.0" prefWidth="300.0" vgap="10"
09           xmlns="http://javafx.com/javafx/9.0.1" xmlns:fx="http://javafx.com/fxml/1"
10           fx:controller="sample.Controller">
11     <children>
12         <MenuBar>
13             <contextMenu>
14                 <ContextMenu>
15                     <items>
16                         <MenuItem mnemonicParsing="false" text="Close" />
17                     </items>
18                 </ContextMenu>
19             </contextMenu>
20         </MenuBar>
21     </children>
22 </GridPane>
```

> Change the size of the MenuBar to `300 x 400`, using the `prefWidth` and `PrefHeight` attributes as follow:

```
<MenuBar prefHeight="400.0" prefWidth="300.0">
```

> Create an event handler named `onCloseClicked()`. Open the *Controller.java* file and add the `onCloseClicked()` event handler as follow:

```
package sample;

import javafx.application.Platform;
import javafx.fxml.FXML;
import javafx.scene.control.MenuItem;

public class Controller {
    @FXML
    private MenuItem close;

    @FXML
    public void onCloseClicked(){
        Platform.exit();
    }
}
```

> To respond to a mouse right-click, add an event handler to listen for a right-click event and call the context menu's `onCloseClickec()` method. Assign the Menu item to the `onCloseClicked()` event handler. Open the *sample.fxml* file and assign the `#onCloseClicked` value to the `onAction` property as follow:

```
<MenuItem fx:id="close" mnemonicParsing="false" text="Close"
    onAction="#onCloseClicked" />
```

> Run your application. Right click *Main.java* file and select **Run 'Main.java'**. Right click inside the window and select close.

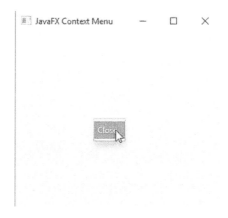

Summary

> Java Controls are reusable components you can use anywhere within your application. You can use built-in controls provided with Java, or you can create your own. So let's start with JavaFX Button control.
> A control in a graphical user interface is an element of interaction, such as a button, label, radio button, check box and text field.
> In JavaFX applications, **events** are notifications that something has happened. As a user clicks a button, presses a key, moves a mouse, or performs other actions, events are dispatched.

Chapter 27

JavaFX and Scene Builder

JavaFX and Scene Builder

Introduction

Up to this point, you've learned how to code and style UI elements programmatically. Now, in this chapter, you will learn how to build a simple UI using Scene Builder.

JavaFX Scene Builder is a visual layout tool that lets users quickly design JavaFX application user interfaces, without coding. Users can drag and drop UI components to a work area, modify their properties, apply style sheets, and the FXML code for the layout that they are creating is automatically generated in the background. The result is an FXML file that can then be combined with a Java project by binding the UI to the application's logic.[1]

Features

- **UI Layout Tool.** Scene Builder allows you to easily layout JavaFX UI controls, charts, shapes, and containers.
- **FXML Visual Editor.** Scene Builder generates FXML, an XML-based markup language that enables users to define an application's user interface.
- **Integrated Developer Workflow.** Scene Builder can be used in combination with any Java IDE, such as IntelliJ IDEA, NetBeans IDE and Eclipse IDE.
- **Preview Your Work.** At any time during the creation of your project, you can preview what the user interface will really look like when deployed.

---

[1] http://www.oracle.com/technetwork/java/javase/downloads/javafxscenebuilder-info-2157684.html

> **Cross Platform**. Scene Builder is written as a JavaFX application, supported on Windows, Mac OS X and Linux.
> **Self Contained**. Scene Builder is packaged as a self contained application, which means it comes bundled with its own private copy of the JRE.
> CSS Support. You can apply the look and feel of your choice to your GUI layout by using style sheets.

Installing Scene Builder

Installing Scene Builder is like installing most software. Here's how you do it:

> Visit Scene Builder (*http://gluonhq.com/products/scene-builder*)
> Click the **Download** button.
> Click the button corresponding to your computer's operating system (Windows, Mac, or Linux).
> On a Windows computer, you get an **.exe** file. Double-click the file to begin the installation.
> Follow the installation routine's instructions.

Specifying the path to the JavaFX Scene Builder executable

To be able to open your FXML files in JavaFX Scene Builder right in IntelliJ IDEA, you should specify where the Scene Builder executable file is located. You can do that separately, the way described in this section. You can also do that at a later time, the first time you open an FXML file in the Scene Builder from within IntelliJ IDEA.

To specify the path to the JavaFX Scene Builder executable file

> Choose **File** > **Settings** from the main menu, and then go to **Languages and Frameworks** > **JavaFX**.
> In the right-hand part of the dialog, on the JavaFX page, click **browse** Button to the right of the **Path to Scene Builder** field.
> In the dialog that opens, select the **Scene Builder executable** file and click **OK** (e.g. `C:\Users\<UserName>\AppData\Local\SceneBuilder\SceneBuilder.exe`).
> Click **OK** In the Settings/Preferences dialog.

Now, let's get started!

Create a new JavaFX project

To create a project for JavaFX application development from scratch:

> If no project is currently open in IntelliJ IDEA, click **Create New Project** on the Welcome screen. Otherwise, select **File > New > Project**.
> As a result, the **New Project** wizard opens. On the first page of the wizard, in the left-hand pane, select **JavaFX**.
> In the right-hand part of the page, specify the **SDK (JDK)** to be used in your project. Select the JDK from the list, or click **New**, select JDK and select the installation folder of the desired JDK. Click **Next**.
> Specify the project name (e.g., **SBProject**) and location, and click **Finish**.
> **Right-click** on sample.fxml and choose **Open In Scene Builder**. Now you should see the Scene Builder with just an AncherPane (visible under **Hierarchy** on the left).

The interface of the Scene Builder

After starting the Scene Builder, you get the following GUI:

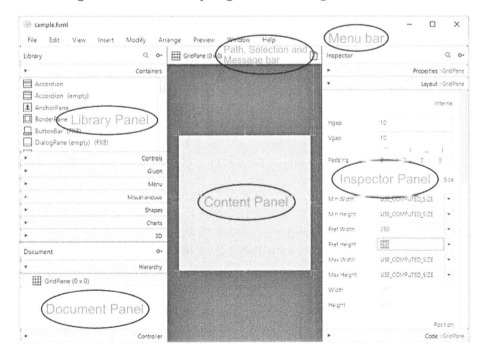

By default, the main window of JavaFX Scene Builder includes the following sections:

› **Menu Bar.** The Menu Bar provides access to the menu of commands available in JavaFX Scene Builder.

› **Path, Selection and Message Bar.** The Path, Selection and Message Bar displays the path to a selected element and allows you to select an element to put into focus. It also displays any error or status messages.

› **Content Panel.** The Content Panel represents the scene container for the GUI elements that make up your FXML layout. By default, a new empty FXML file is opened in JavaFX Scene Builder.

› **Library Panel.** The Library Panel lists the available JavaFX GUI elements or controls, including custom controls, that you can use to build your FXML layout. You select the GUI elements from this panel and add them to the Content panel or the Hierarchy panel.

› **Document Panel.** The Document Panel contains the Hierarchy and Controller sections. The Hierarchy section displays a tree view representation of the FXML layout that you are building in the Content panel. Elements that are not visible in the Content panel can be placed into focus by selecting it in the Hierarchy panel. The Controller section enables you to manage the controller source information and gives information about assigned fx:id values.

› **Inspector Panel.** The Inspector Panel contains the Properties, Layout, and Code sections. The Properties and Layout sections help you manage the properties of the currently selected GUI element in the Content panel or in the Hierarchy panel. The Code section enables you to manage the event handling actions to use for the selected GUI element. The Inspector panel also contains a Search text field that enables you to isolate specific properties that you want to modify.

Design with Scene Builder

Now, let´s create a simple interface using the JavaFX Scene Builder. We will create a **VBox** which contains a Label, a Button, a TextField and a TextArea.

› **Adding UI Elements.** The root element of the FXML document is the top-level object in the object-graph. Our top-level object is a **GridPane**. At first we add the VBox to the GridPane. This can be done via Drag a VBox from the list on the **Library** panel and drop it onto the **Content** panel or the **Hierarchy** panel from the **Containers,** as shown below:

› Setting Properties to the VBox layout
  • **Set the Style Properties to the VBox.** In the **Hierarchy** panel, select the **VBox** element and click the **Properties** section of the **Inspector** panel. In our example the following properties were inserted into the Style Text Field.

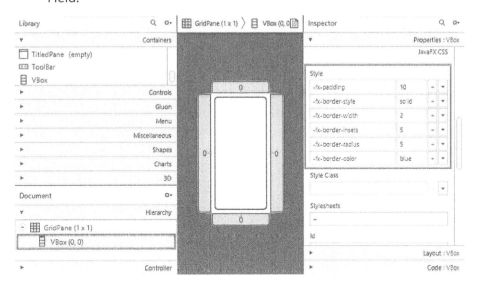

```
-fx-padding: 10;
-fx-border-style: solid;
-fx-border-width: 2;
-fx-border-insets: 5;
-fx-border-radius: 5;
-fx-border-color: blue;
```

  • **Set the Width and Height Properties to the VBox.** In the **Hierarchy** panel, select the **VBox** element and click the **Layout** section of the **Inspector** panel. In this example, the **Preferred Width** and the **Preferred Height** was set to **300px**.

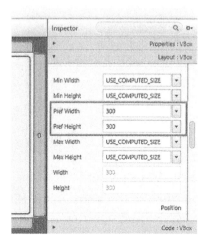

- **Assign an Identifier to the VBox**. An object created in FXML can be referred to somewhere else in the same document. It is common to get the reference of UI objects created in FXML inside the JavaFX code. You can achieve this by first identifying the objects in FXML with an `fx:id` attribute. The value of the `fx:id` attribute is the identifier for the object. In the **Hierarchy** panel, select the **VBox** element and click the **Code** section of the **Inspector** panel. In this example, the Identifier was set to **vbox1**.

› **Add the other UI Elements**. Now we have to add the other necessary elements to the VBox to finish our project. At first we add a Label.
  - Add a **Label**. Drag a **Label** control from the list on the **Library** panel onto the **Content** panel or the **Hierarchy** panel from the **Controls** section.

From the **Properties** section of the **Inspector** panel, set the **Text** to **Enter Your Name,** and set **Font size** to **14px**.

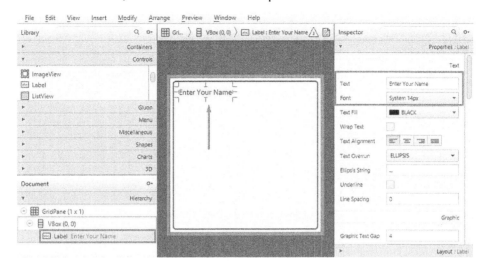

- **Add a TextField for the Input.** Drag a **TextField** control from the list on the **Library** panel onto the **Content** panel or the **Hierarchy** panel from the **Controls** section. From the **Code** section of the **Inspector** panel, set the `fx:id` to **inputText**.

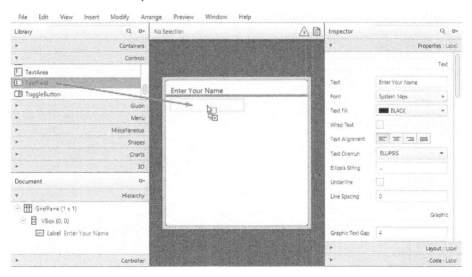

› **Add a Button which handles the necessary ActionEvent.** Drag a **Button** control from the list on the **Library** panel onto the **Content** panel or the **Hierarchy** panel from the **Controls** section. From the **Code** section of the **Inspector** panel, set the `fx:id` to **okBtn,** and from the **Properties** section, set the `Text` to **OK**.

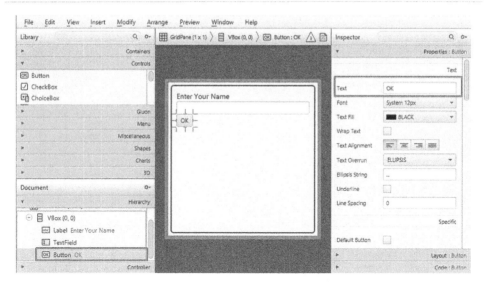

- **And finally, we have to add a TextArea**, which contains and display our input. Drag a **TextArea** control from the list on the **Library** panel onto the **Content** panel or the **Hierarchy** panel from the **Controls** section. From the **Code** section of the **Inspector** panel, set the `fx:id` to **outputText**.

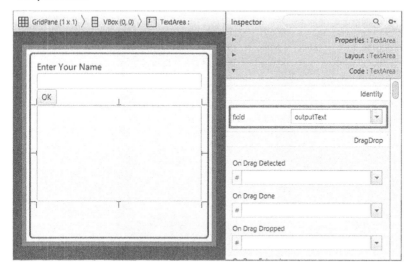

- Let´s save the project by selecting **File > Save**.
  › Preview of your Design. You can always make a Preview in the Scene Builder about your current design under usage of the **"Show Preview in Window"** Menu Entry in the **"Preview"** Menu.

After starting the Application, you can insert Text in the **Input Field** and press the **OK** Button. But at this time, it does not have any effect. The reason is the fact, that we don't have added an Event Handler to the Button. This will be discussed in the next part of this lesson.

Adding event handlers

FIRST: Bind the FXML layout to the source controller file

The controller source file, *Controller.java*, manages the events and actions taken on each element you add to the FXML GUI layout that you are building. Setting the controller class file name enables Scene Builder to provide you with the names of the event handlers and instance variables that are declared in the controller source file.[1]

Note that only ONE controller is allowed per FXML document, and if specified, it must be specified on the root element (e.g. *GridPane element*).

In Scene Builder you can set this in the **Controller** pane which is in the bottom left of the screen. Steps:

› Select the **GridPane** (root element) in your **Hierarchy** panel.

---

[1] https://docs.oracle.com/javase/8/scene-builder-2/get-started-tutorial/bind-ui-to-logic.htm

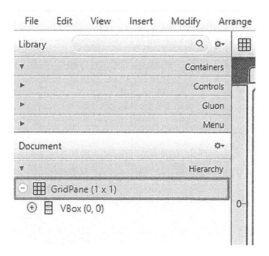

> In the **Document** panel, select the **Controller** section. Set the value in the Controller class text field to *sample.Controller* by selecting it from the drop-down list of available values.

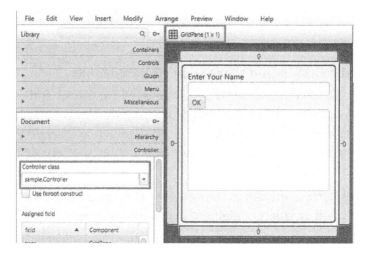

Second: Write a controller (e.g. *Controller.java*) for your root element. In our case the root element is the GridPane

```
01  package sample;
02
03  import javafx.fxml.FXML;
04  import javafx.scene.control.TextField;
05  import java.net.URL;
06  import java.util.ResourceBundle;
07
08
09  public class Controller {
10      @FXML
```

```
11      private TextField inputText;
12
13      @FXML
14      private TextField outputText;
15
16      // Add a public no-args constructor
17      public Controller() {
18
19      }
20
21      @FXML
22      private void initialize()
23      {
24
25      }
26
27      @FXML
28      private void printOutput() {
29          outputText.setText(inputText.getText());
30      }
31  }
```

The controller class uses a @FXML annotation on some members. The @FXML annotation can be used on fields and methods. It cannot be used on classes and constructors. By using a @FXML annotation on a member, you are declaring that the FXML loader can access the member even if it is private. A **public** member used by the FXML loader does not need to be annotated with @FXML. However, annotating a **public** member with @FXML is not an error. It is better to annotate all members, public and private, used by the FXML loader with @FXML annotation. This tells the reader of your code how the members are being used.

A controller needs to conform to some rules

> The controller must have a public **no-args** constructor. If it does not exist, the FXML loader will not be able to instantiate it, which will throw an exception at the load time.

```
17      // Add a public no-args constructor
18      public Controller() {
19
20      }
```

> The controller can have accessible methods, which can be specified as event handlers in FXML.

```
27      @FXML
28      private void printOutput() {
29          outputText.setText(inputText.getText());
30      }
```

> The FXML loader will automatically look for accessible instance variables of the controller. If the name of an accessible instance variable matches the

`fx:id` attribute of an element, the object reference from FXML is automatically copied into the controller instance variable. This feature makes the references of UI elements in FXML available to the controller. The controller can use them later, such as binding them to model.

```
13  <GridPane fx:id="pane" alignment="center"
14  hgap="10" vgap="10" xmlns="http://javafx.com/javafx/9.0.1"
15  xmlns:fx="http://javafx.com/fxml/1"
    fx:controller="sample.Controller">
```

› The controller can have an accessible `initialize()` method, which should take no arguments and have a return type of `void`. The FXML loader will call the `initialize()` method after the loading of the FXML document is complete.

```
21      @FXML
22      private void initialize()
23      {
24
25      }
```

Third: Set an Event Handlers for Nodes

You can set event handlers for nodes in FXML. Setting an event handler is similar to setting any other properties. For example, the Button class contains an `onAction` property to set an `ActionEvent` handler. Additionally you have to define the Java Method `printOutput` to the Button as follow:

› Select the **Button** (node) in your **Hierarchy** panel
› In the **Inspector** panel, select the **Code** section. Set the value in the **On Action** text field to `printOutput` by selecting it from the drop-down list of available values.

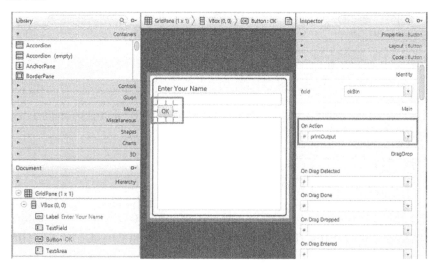

The FXML Code (sample.fxml)

Thereafter you get the following FXML Code:

```
01  <?xml version="1.0" encoding="UTF-8"?>
02
03  <?import javafx.scene.control.Button?>
04  <?import javafx.scene.control.Label?>
05  <?import javafx.scene.control.TextArea?>
06  <?import javafx.scene.control.TextField?>
07  <?import javafx.scene.layout.ColumnConstraints?>
08  <?import javafx.scene.layout.GridPane?>
09  <?import javafx.scene.layout.RowConstraints?>
10  <?import javafx.scene.layout.VBox?>
11  <?import javafx.scene.text.Font?>
12
13  <GridPane fx:id="pane" alignment="center"
14      hgap="10" vgap="10" xmlns="http://javafx.com/javafx/9.0.1"
15      xmlns:fx="http://javafx.com/fxml/1" fx:controller="sample.Controller">
16  <children>
17  <VBox fx:id="vbox1" prefHeight="300.0" prefWidth="300.0"
18  style="-fx-padding: 10; -fx-border-style: solid; -fx-border-width: 2;
19  -fx-border-insets: 5; -fx-border-radius: 5; -fx-border-color: blue;">
20  <children>
21  <Label text="Enter Your Name">
22          <font>
23              <Font size="14.0" />
24          </font>
25  </Label>
26  <TextField fx:id="inputText" />
27  <Button fx:id="okBtn" mnemonicParsing="false" onAction="#printOutput" text="OK" />
28  <TextArea fx:id="outputText" prefHeight="150.0" prefWidth="266.0" />
29  </children>
30  </VBox>
31     </children>
32     <columnConstraints>
33        <ColumnConstraints />
34     </columnConstraints>
35     <rowConstraints>
36        <RowConstraints />
37     </rowConstraints>
38  </GridPane>
```

The Java Code (*Controller.java*)

```
package sample;

import javafx.fxml.FXML;
import javafx.scene.control.TextArea;
import javafx.scene.control.TextField;
```

```
public class Controller {
    @FXML
    private TextField inputText;

    @FXML
    private TextArea outputText;

    // Add a public no-args constructor
    public Controller(){ }
    @FXML
    private void initialize(){ }
    @FXML
    private void printOutput(){
        outputText.setText(inputText.getText());
    }
}
```

The GUI

After starting the Application, we can insert a Text in the TextField, press the **OK** Button, and the Message appears in the TextArea.

Summary

> › JavaFX Scene Builder is a visual layout tool that lets users quickly design JavaFX application user interfaces, without coding.

- By default, the main window of JavaFX Scene Builder includes Menu bar, Path/Selection/Message bar, Content panel, Library panel, Document panel and Inspector panel.
- The controller source file, *Controller.java*, manages the events and actions taken on each element you add to the FXML GUI layout that you are building.
- The controller class uses a @FXML annotation on some members. The @FXML annotation can be used on fields and methods. It cannot be used on classes and constructors.

Chapter 28

Login Form Application Using Scene Builder

Introduction

In this chapter, we'll create a Login Form where users can enter their username and password then submit the form. When the user submits the wright user name and password, we'll greet him by showing an alert box.

Here is a screenshot of the application that we are going to build in this chapter.

What will you learn?

In this chapter, you will learn -

› How to create the layout of a JavaFX application window.
› How to add UI controls like Text Field, Password Field, and Button.
› How to respond to input events.

Cool! Let's get started.

Create the Main Application Class

The first thing you need to do is to create the Main class for your JavaFX application which extends `javafx.application.Applicaiton`, and override it's `start()` method.

> Open the IntelliJ IDEA IDE and create a new JavaFX project named **Login**.
> Rename the following files as follow:

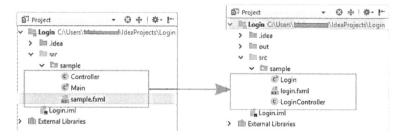

> Set the Stage's **title** property to **Login Form**. Go to the *Login.java* class and change the following code:
> ```
> primaryStage.setTitle("Login Form");
> ```

> Create a scene with the login form GridPane as the root node, and set the scene in primary stage
> ```
> primaryStage.setScene(new Scene(root, 450, 250));
> ```

If you run the application now, you'll get an empty window of width 450 and height 250. Let's add UI controls to the application.

Add User Interface (UI) Controls to the Layout

JavaFX provides several built-in GUI controls like TextField, PasswordField, Button etc. Let's add these UI controls to our Login Form pane.

Create the Layout of your Application

We will use a **GridPane** layout for designing our Login Form. GridPane layout enables you to create a flexible grid of rows and columns in which UI nodes can be laid out.

› So go to the Projects tab, right-click the **login.fxml** file and select **Open In Scene Builder**.
› Set the GridPane's width and height. In the **Hierarchy** panel, select the **GridPane** element. Locate the GridPane's **PrefWidth** and **PrefHeight** properties in the **Layout** section of the **Inspector** panel. Type **450** for the **PrefWidth** property value, and press Enter. Type **250** for the **PrefHeight** property value and press Enter.

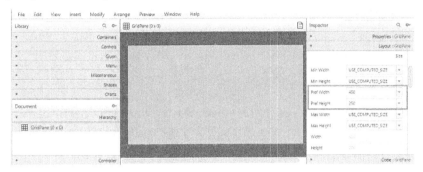

› Add a Label to the GridPane. Click the **Controls** section in the **Library** panel. If the Library panel is not visible, select **View > Show Library**. Double-click the **Label** control in the **Control** section. A Label will appear in the center of the GridPane, as show in the following figure. You will use this label control to display the **Login Form** text. The Label displays the text **Label** by default. Notes that the Label's background color is the White color.

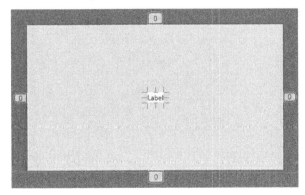

› Set the Label's **Text** property. Click the **Label** to select it. Type **Login Form** for the Label's **Text** property value under **Property** section and press Enter.

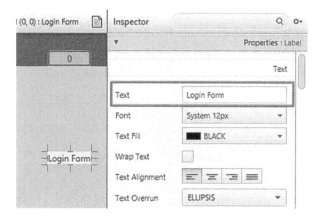

› Set the Label's font. Click the value of the **Font** property under **Properties** section. In this dialog you can select the Font/Family name (Arial, Tahoma, etc.), font style (Bold, italic, etc) and font size (12, 14, etc) in points (one point equals 1/72 of an inch). Under the **Size** category, select **24** points. Under the **Font** category, select **Times New Roman.**

› Add a column constraint to the GridPane. Click the **GridPane** to select it. Click the first column constraint to select it. Right-click the selected column constraint and select **Add Column After** to add another column constraint.

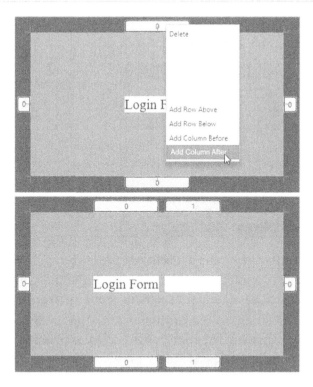

› Click the first column constraint to select it. Click the **Layout** section of the **Inspector** panel and set `MinWidth, PrefWidth` and `Halignment` properties as shown in the following figure:

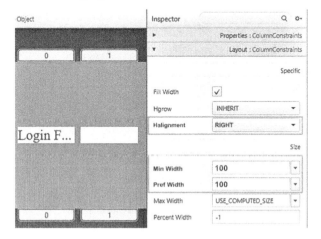

› Click the second **column constraint** to select it. Click the **Layout** section of the **Inspector** panel and set `MinWidth` and `PrefWidth` properties as shown in the following figure:

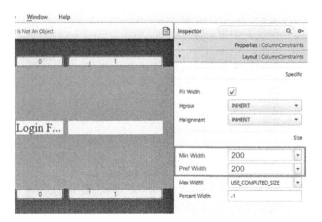

> Click the **GridPane** to select it. Click the **Layout** section of the **Inspector** panel and set a `padding` of `20px` on left and right side. Then click the **Code** section of the **Inspector** panel and set the **fx:id** property to **gridpane**.
> Add a row constraint to the **GridPane**. Click the **GridPane** to select it. Click the first row constraint to select it. Right-click the selected row constraint and select **Add Row Below** to add another row constraint below the selected one.

> Add another three row constraints to the GridPane as shown to the following figure:

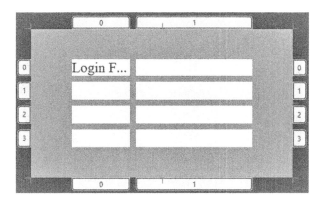

> Click the **Login Form** Label to select it. Click the **Layout** section of the **Inspector** panel and set a `colspan` to 2, `Halignment` to CENTER, `Margin top` to **10** and `Margin bottom` to **30** as shown to the following figure:

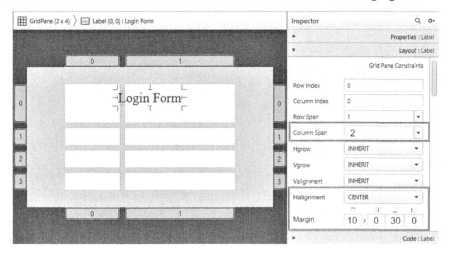

> Add two label controls (User Name and Password) and then add the following properties to it as shown in the following table:

Section / Property	Label 2	Label 3
Properties > Text	User Name	Password
Properties > Font > Family	Arial	Arial
Properties > Font > Size	14	14
Layout > rowIndex	1	2
Layout > columnIndex	0	0
Layout > Margin > right	5	5

The output:

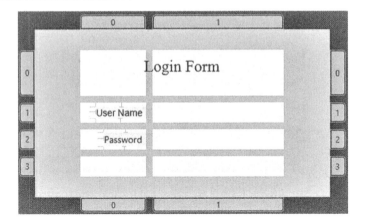

› Add a Text Field and a PasswordField controls as follows:

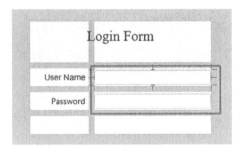

› Now, specify the following values for the `promptText`, `prefHeight` and `fx:id` properties of the **TextField** and **PasswordField** controls, according to the following table:

	TextField	PasswordField
Properties > promptText	Enter Your User Name	Enter Your Password
Layout > prefHeight	40	40
Layout > columnIndex	1	1
Layout > rowIndex	1	2
Code > fx:Id	txtUsername	txtPassword

› After specifying these values, the **Login Form** will appear as shown in the following figure:

> Now, add a button to the GridPane as shown in the following figure:

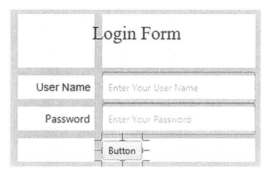

> Now, specify the following values for the `Text`, `PreWidth and PreHeight` properties of the **Button** control in the Properties, Layout and Code sections, according to the following table:

	Button
Properties > Text	OK
Code > fx:id	btnOK
Layout > prefHeight	40
Layout > preWidth	150

A button is left aligned in its cell. To change the horizontal alignment of a button, we use the halignment property to CENTER.

› set **Hgrow** property to **ALWAYS** in `columnTwoConstraints` (Under Layout Pane1.)

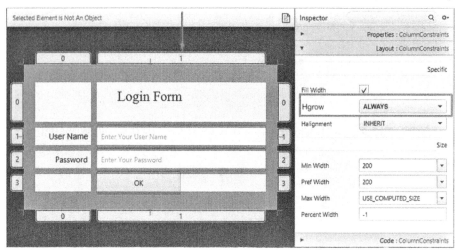

We're specifying that if the screen resizes, then column two should grow horizontally and fill in the extra space.

› Saving the project. Select **File > Save** to save your modified project.
› Close the Scene Builder. Select **File > Quit**.

Summary

› We first instantiate a new GridPane, and then set the alignment and padding properties.
› We have also applied some column constraints to the grid pane. The ColumnConstraints constructor takes the min width, preferred width, and max width values.
› All the nodes in column one will have a `min-width` of 100, `pref-width` of 100 and `max-width` of `Double.MAX_VALUE`.
› Similarly, all the nodes in column two will have a `min-width` of 200, `pref-width` of 200 and `max-width` of `Double.MAX_VALUE`.
› Also, we have set the `Halignment` property to `RIGHT` in `columnOneConstraints` so that all the nodes in column one are right aligned.
› Moreover, by setting `Hgrow` property to **ALWAYS** in `columnTwoConstraints`, we're specifying that if the screen resizes, then column 2 should grow horizontally and fill in the extra space.

Add the Handler Code that is Executed on Form Submit (*LoginController.java file*)

First Step: Create an event handler named `onButtonClicked()`

First Let's now add our handler code to the `OK` button. This handler is invoked wherever you click `OK` button, or press `Enter` key -

```
01  package sample;
02  import javafx.fxml.FXML;
03  import javafx.scene.control.Alert;
04  import javafx.scene.control.Button;
05  import javafx.scene.control.TextField;
06  import javafx.scene.layout.GridPane;
07  import javafx.stage.Window;
08
09  public class LoginController {
10      @FXML
11      private Button btnOK;
12
13      @FXML
14      private TextField txtUsername;
15
16      @FXML
17      private TextField txtPassword;
18
19      @FXML
20      private GridPane gridpane;
21
22      @FXML
23      public void onButtonClicked(){
24          if(txtUsername.getText().isEmpty()){
25              showAlert(Alert.AlertType.ERROR, gridpane.getScene().getWindow(),
26                      "Form Error!", "Please enter your name");
27              return;
28          }
29          if(txtPassword.getText().isEmpty()){
30              showAlert(Alert.AlertType.ERROR, gridpane.getScene().getWindow(),
31                      "Form Error!", "Please enter a password");
32              return;
33          }
34          showAlert(Alert.AlertType.CONFIRMATION, gridpane.getScene().getWindow(),
35                  "Registration Successful!", "Welcome " + txtUsername.getText());
```

```
36      }
37
38      private void showAlert(Alert.AlertType alertType,
                    Window owner, String title, String message){
39          Alert alert = new Alert(alertType);
40          alert.setTitle(title);
41          alert.setHeaderText(null);
42          alert.setContentText(message);
43          alert.initOwner(owner);
44          alert.show();
45      }
46  }
```

In the above code, we show an error alert if any of the form fields are missing, otherwise, we show a confirmation alert to the user. We use JavaFX's built-in `Alert` class to show the alert boxes to the user.

Second Step: Register an `onButtonClicked` event handler to a btnOK control

> Right click **login.fxml** file and select **Open In Scene Builder**.
> Click the **OK** Button to select it. Click the **Code** section of the **Inspector** panel and set a **On Action** property to **onButtonClicked**, which is used to register an event handler to the **Button** control.

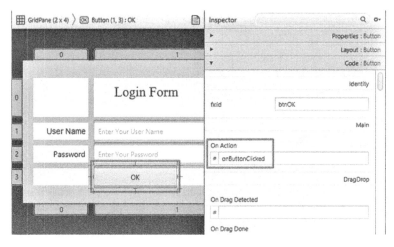

> Saving the project. Select **File > Save** to save your modified project.
> Close the Scene Builder. Select **File > Quit**.
> Run your application. Right click *Main.java* file and select **Run 'Main'**. The Login form will be shown. Enter any username and password. This gives a message tab showing welcome message:

> If any of the username or the password entered is empty, the screen shown below appears.

I hope that this tutorial has helped you in understanding the basics in creating a Login Form.

Chapter 29

Calculator Application

Introduction

A software calculator allows users to enter data, and they have a built-in formula that is automatically applied to this data. A calculator is capable of performing mathematical calculations such as addition, multiplication, subtraction or division.

In this project, we create a calculator that shares many features with Windows calculator. Here is a screenshot of the application that we are going to build in this chapter.

What will you learn?

In this chapter, you will learn how to -

> Design a GUI using a VBox, and GridPane layouts.
> Use Button, and TextField GUI components.
> Use Java object-oriented programming capabilities, including classes, objects, and inheritance.
> Programmatically interact with GUI components to respond to input events.

Cool! Let's get started.

Create the Main Application Class

The first thing you need to do is to create the Main class for your JavaFX application which extends javafx.application.Applicaiton, and override it's `start()` method.

> Open the IntelliJ IDEA IDE and create a new JavaFX project named **Calculator.**
> Rename the following files as follow:

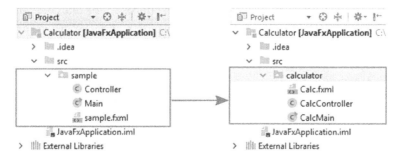

> Set the Stage's **title** property to **Calculator App**. Go to the `CalcMain.java` class and change the following code:
> ```
> primaryStage.setTitle("Calculator App");
> ```

4. Create a scene with the login form gridpane as the root node, and set the scene in primary stage
    ```
    primaryStage.setScene(new Scene(root, 300, 250));
    ```

If you run the application now, you'll get an empty window of width 300 and height 250.

Let's add UI controls to the application.

Add UI Controls to the Layout

JavaFX provides several built-in GUI controls like TextField, Button etc. Let's add these UI controls to our Calculator Form pane -

› Create the Layout of Your Application. We will use a **VBoxPane** layout for designing our Calculator application. Open the `Calc.fxml` file with Scene Builder. So go to the Project tab, right-click the `Calc.fxml` file and select **Open In SceneBuilder**.

› Delete the **GridPane** layout. In the **Hierarchy** section, select the **GridPane** element and hit the **Delete** key (or Right Click **GridPane** element > Select **Delete**).

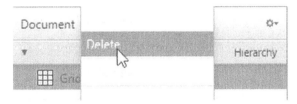

› Create the layout of Your Application. Click the **Containers** section in the **Library** panel. If the Library panel is not visible, select **View > Show Library**. Then drag and drop a **VBox** from the **Containers** section onto the **Hierarchy** section or onto the content area, as shown in the following figure.

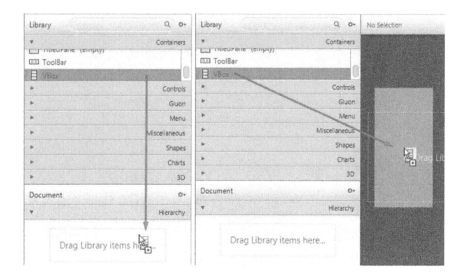

› Position the VBox's contents at the center of the screen, both vertically and horizontally. In the **Hierarchy** panel, select the **VBox** element. Locate the VBox's Alignment property in the **Properties** section of the **Inspector** panel, and select CENTER.

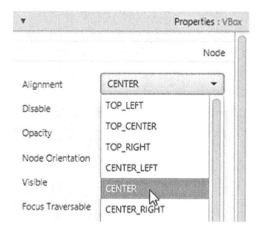

› In the **Hierarchy** panel, Select the **VBox** element, locate the VBox's `Pref Height` property in the **Layout** section of the **Inspector** panel. Type **300** for the `Pref Height` property value, and press Enter. Type **250** for the `Pref Width` property value, and press Enter.
› After that add a **TextField** component inside the **VBox** pane. Click the **Controls** section in the **Library** panel. Then drag and drop a **TextField** from the **Controls** section onto the **Hierarchy** section or onto the content area, as shown in the following Figure.

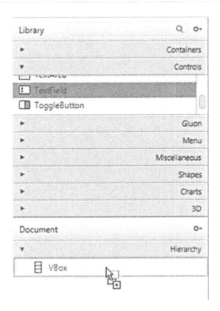

> In the **Hierarchy** panel, Select the **TextField** element and specify its properties according to the following table.

Property	Value
Properties section > Font > Size	18
Properties section > Alignment	CENTER_RIGHT
Properties section > nodeOrientation	RIGHT_TO_LEFT
Layout section > Pref Height	70
Code section > fx:Id	txtDisplay

> Add a **GridPane** to **VBox Pane** layout. Click the **Containers** section in the **Library** panel. Then drag and drop a **GridPane** from the **Containers** section onto the **VBox**, as shown the following Figure.

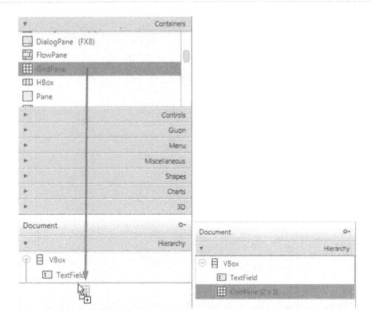

› Add four columns and five rows. You'll need to right-click on the **GridPane** in the **Hierarchy** section, and use the menus GridPane > Add Row Above and Add Column After to until you see a 4×6 grid as shown below.

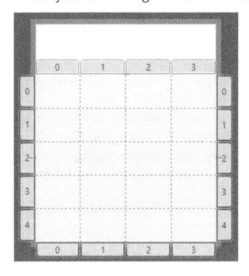

› Set the GridPane's **Vgrow**[1]. In the **Hierarchy** panel. Select the **GridPane** element, locate the GridPane's **Vgrow** property in the **Layout** section of the Inspector panel. Select **ALWAYS**.

---

[1] The hgrow and vgrow constraints specify the horizontal and vertical grow priorities for the entire column and row, even though it can be set for children individually.

› Add a **Button** inside each cell of **GridPane**. Next, select each Button control from the **Hierarchy**, and specify its properties according to the following table.

Property	Value
Properties section> Font > Size	14
Layout section > Pref Height	50
Layout section > Pref Width	60

› Change the text of each button to look like the following Figure.

› Now, specify the following values for the **fx:id** property of the **Button** controls from the **Code** section, according to the following table:

Control	fx:id value	Control	fx:id value
AC	btnAC	1	btnOne
%	btnPercent	3	btnThree
/	btnDivide	4	btnFour
X	btnMulti	5	btnFive
-	btnMinus	6	btnSix
+	btnPlus	7	btnSeven
=	btnEqual	8	btnEight
0	btnZero	9	btnNine
.	btnDot		

› Set the size of the scene to be large enough to accommodate your design. This is how my class `CalcMain.java` looks like:

```
01 package calculator;
```

```
02
03  import javafx.application.Application;
04  import javafx.fxml.FXMLLoader;
05  import javafx.scene.Parent;
06  import javafx.scene.Scene;
07  import javafx.stage.Stage;
08
09  public class CalcMain extends Application {
10
11      @Override
12      public void start(Stage primaryStage) throws Exception{
13          Parent root = FXMLLoader.load(getClass().getResource("Calc.fxml"));
14          primaryStage.setTitle("Calculator");
15          primaryStage.setScene(new Scene(root, 250, 300));
16          primaryStage.setResizable(false);
17          primaryStage.show();
18      }
19
20
21      public static void main(String[] args) {
22          launch(args);
23      }
24  }
```

Line 16: Don't allow the users to resize your calculator by invoking the method `setResizable` on the stage object.

› Save your design and close the **Scene Builder**.
› Run your project. Right-click the `CalcMain.java` file and select **Run 'Main'**. The result will be like this:

In the next section you'll learn how to make the buttons (or other components) to react to user actions, so you'll be able to complete the calculator.

Adding Events Handling for Calculator

> Create four separate event handler methods in the class `CalcController`. Name the first method `handlerDigit` - it will contain the code to process clicks on the digit buttons. Name the second method `handlerGeneral` it will contain the code to process clicks on such buttons as Plus, Minus, etc. Name the third method `handlerDecimal` - it will contain the code to process click on the (.) dot button. Name the fourth method `handlerEqual` -it will contain the code to process click on the (=) equal button.

> Assign the `CalcController.java` to the **VBox** element. Right-click the `Calc.fxml` file and select **Open In Scene Builder**. Click the **VBox** to select it. Now, specify the value `calculator.CalcController` for the **Controller class** property from the **Controller** section.

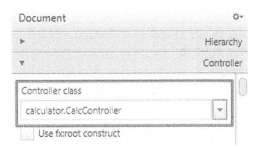

> Now, specify the following values for the **On Action** property of the button controls from the Code section, according to the following table:

Control	On Action property	Control	On Action property
1	handlerDigit	=	handlerEqual
2	handlerDigit	+'	handlerGeneral
3	handlerDigit	-'	handlerGeneral
4	handlerDigit	X	handlerGeneral
5	handlerDigit	+/-	handlerGeneral
6	handlerDigit	/	handlerGeneral
7	handlerDigit	AC	handlerGeneral
8	handlerDigit	.	handlerDecimal
9	handlerDigit		
0	handlerDigit		

Implementing 4 methods

Fields

```java
@FXML
private TextField txtDisplay;
private double decimalClick;
private String generalOperationObject;
private double firstDouble;
```

The `handlerDigit` method

```java
@FXML
public void handlerDigit (ActionEvent event){
    String digitObject = ((Button)event.getSource()).getText();
    String oldText = txtDisplay.getText();
    String newText = oldText + digitObject;
    txtDisplay.setText(newText);
}
```

The `handlerDecimal` method

```java
@FXML
public void handlerDecimal (ActionEvent event){
    if (decimalClick == 0) {
        String decimalObject =
((Button)event.getSource()).getText();
        String oldText = txtDisplay.getText();
        System.out.println(oldText);
        String newText = oldText + decimalObject;
        System.out.println(newText);
        txtDisplay.setText(newText);
        decimalClick = 1;
    }
}
```

The `handlerGeneral` method

```java
@FXML
private void handlerGeneralAction(ActionEvent event) {
    generalOperationObject = ((Button) event.getSource()).getText();
    switch (generalOperationObject) {
        case "AC":
            txtDisplay.setText("");
            decimalClick = 0;
            break;
        case "+/-":
            double plusMinus =
Double.parseDouble(String.valueOf(txtDisplay.getText()));
            plusMinus = plusMinus * (-1);
            txtDisplay.setText(String.valueOf(plusMinus));
            break;
        case "+":
```

```
                case "-":
                case "*":
                case "/":
                    String currentText = txtDisplay.getText();
                    firstDouble = Double.parseDouble(currentText);
                    txtDisplay.setText("");
                    decimalClick = ;
                    break;
                default:
            }
    }
```

The `handlerEqual` method

```
    @FXML
    public void handlerEqual (ActionEvent event){
        double secondDouble;
        double result = ;
        String secondText = txtDisplay.getText();
        secondDouble = Double.parseDouble (secondText);

        switch (generalOperationObject) {
            case "+":
                result = firstDouble + secondDouble;
                break;
            case "-":
                result = firstDouble - secondDouble;
                break;
            case "X":
                result = firstDouble * secondDouble;
                break;
            case "/":
                result = firstDouble / secondDouble;
                break;
            default:
        }
        String format = String.format(".1f", result);
        txtDisplay.setText(format);
    }
```

The `handlerGeneral` method

```
    @FXML
    public void handlerGeneral(ActionEvent event){
        generalOperationObject =
    ((Button)event.getSource()).getText();
        switch (generalOperationObject){
            case "AC":
                txtDisplay.setText("");
                decimalClick = ;
                break;
            case "+/-":
                double plusMinus = ;
                plusMinus =
    Double.parseDouble(String.valueOf(txtDisplay.getText()));
                plusMinus = plusMinus * (- );
                txtDisplay.setText(String.valueOf(plusMinus));
```

```
                break;
        case "+":
        case "-":
        case "*":
        case "/":
            String currentText = txtDisplay.getText();
            firstDouble = Double.parseDouble(currentText);
            txtDisplay.setText("");
            decimalClick = 0;
            break;
        default:
    }
}
```

Full Source Code

```
01  package calculator;
02
03  import javafx.event.ActionEvent;
04  import javafx.scene.control.Button;
05  import javafx.fxml.FXML;
06  import javafx.scene.control.TextField;
07
08
09  public class CalcController {
10      @FXML
11      private TextField txtDisplay;
12      private double decimalClick;
13      private String generalOperationObject;
14      private double firstDouble;
15
16
17      @FXML
18      public void handlerDigit (ActionEvent event){
19          String digitObject = ((Button)event.getSource()).getText();
20          String oldText = txtDisplay.getText();
21          String newText = oldText + digitObject;
22          txtDisplay.setText(newText);
23      }
24
25      @FXML
26      public void handlerDecimal (ActionEvent event){
27          if (decimalClick == 0) {
28              String decimalObject = ((Button)event.getSource()).getText();
29              String oldText = txtDisplay.getText();
30              System.out.println(oldText);
31              String newText = oldText + decimalObject;
32              System.out.println(newText);
33              txtDisplay.setText(newText);
34              decimalClick = 1;
35          }
```

```java
        }
        @FXML
        public void handlerGeneral(ActionEvent event){
            generalOperationObject =
((Button)event.getSource()).getText();
            switch (generalOperationObject){
                case "AC":
                    txtDisplay.setText("");
                    decimalClick = 0;
                    break;
                case "+/-":
                    double plusMinus = 0;
                    plusMinus =
Double.parseDouble(String.valueOf(txtDisplay.getText()));
                    plusMinus = plusMinus * (-1);
                    txtDisplay.setText(String.valueOf(plusMinus));
                    break;
                case "+":
                case "-":
                case "X":
                case "/":

                    String currentText = txtDisplay.getText();
                    firstDouble = Double.parseDouble(currentText);
                    txtDisplay.setText("");
                    decimalClick = 0;
                    break;
                default:
            }
        }
        @FXML
        public void handlerEqual (ActionEvent event){
            double secondDouble;
            double result = 0;
            String secondText = txtDisplay.getText();
            secondDouble = Double.parseDouble(secondText);

            switch (generalOperationObject) {
                case "+":
                    result = firstDouble + secondDouble;
                    break;
                case "-":
                    result = firstDouble - secondDouble;
                    break;
                case "X":
                    result = firstDouble * secondDouble;
                    break;
                case "/":
                    result = firstDouble / secondDouble;
                    break;
                default:
            }
            String format = String.format("%.1f", result);
            txtDisplay.setText(format);
```

```
89    }
90 }
```

Explanation (`handlerDigit` Method)

> Line 19: Get the value of the button's label and assign it to `digitObject` variable.

> Line 20: Get the current value from the Calculator's display field and assign it to the `oldText` variable.

> Line 21: Concatenate the `oldText`'s value and the `digitObject`'s value. Then assign the new value to the `newText` variable.

> Line 22: Assign the value of the `newText` variable back to the display field (`txtDisplay`), using the `setText(newText)` method.

Explanation (`handlerGeneral` Method)

> Line 40: Declare a variable, `generalOperationObject`, to remember the operation that the user wants to perform. For example, if the user clicked on +, store + in the variable `generalOperationObject`. Get the value of the button's label and assign it to `generalOperationObject` variable.

> Line 41: Using switch statement to dispatch execution to different parts of code based on the value of the expression, which is `generalOperationObject`.

> Line 42: In case a user clicked on the 'AC' button, execute the lines between 43 to 45.
> - Line 43: Set the value of the Calculator's display field, `txtDisplay`, to empty.
> - Line 44: Set the value of the `decimalClick` field to zero (0).
> - Line 45: Execute the `break` statement. When a break statement is reached, the `switch` terminates, and the flow of control jumps to the next line following the switch statement (in this case, line 64).

> Line 46: In case a user clicked on the '+/-' button, execute the lines between 47 to 51.

> Line 47: Variable initialization. Declares the `plusMinus` variable and initializes it with the value **0**.
> - Line 48: Assign the return value of `parseDouble()` method to the `plusMinus` variable
> - Line 49: If a value is positive, change it to negative and vise versa.
> - Line 50: Display the value of the `plusMinus` variable to the Calculator's display field (`textDisplay`) using the `setText()` method.
> - Line 51: Execute the `break` statement.

› Lines 52 to 56: Remember, as `break` statement is optional. If we omit the break, execution will continue on into the next case. In case a user clicked on one of the following buttons, +, -, X, /, execute the lines between 57 to 61.
  - Line 57: Get the current value from the Calculator's display field `txtDisplay` and assign it to the `currentText` variable.
› Line 58: Sends the value of the `currentText` variable to the `parseDouble()` method.
  - The `parseDouble()` method convert a String (the value entered into the display field - must be a number) to a primitive double value.
  - Then assign the value returned from the `parseDouble()` method to the `firstDouble` variable.
  - Note that, the conversion from String to primitive double may throw NFE (`NumberFormatException`) if the value in String - such as letters - is not convertible into a primitive double.
› Line 59: Set the value of the `txtDisplay` field to empty.
› Line 60: Set the value of the `decimalClick` field to zero.
› Line 61: Execute the `break` statement.
› Line 62: Execute the `default` statement. Default section is branched to if the user enters anything other than AC, +/-, +, -, X, or / . The default section does not need a break statement. It is optional, and it must appear at the end of the switch.

Explanation (`handlerEqual Method - When the (=) button is clicked`)
› Line 67: Variable declaration. Create a variable `secondDouble`, and assign a `double` data type for it.
› Line 68: Variable initialization. Declares the `result` variable, and initializes it with the value 0.
› Line 69: Get the current value from the Calculator's display field `txtDisplay` and assign it to the `secondText` variable.
› Line 70: Sends the value of the `secondText` variable to the `parseDouble()` method.
  - The `parseDouble()` method convert a String (the value entered into the display field - must be a number to a primitive double value.
  - Then assign the value returned from the `parseDouble()` method to the `secondDouble` variable.

- Note that, the conversion from String to primitive double may throw NFE (`NumberFormatException`) if the value in String - such as letters - is not convertible into a primitive double.
› Line 72: Using `switch` statement to dispatch execution to different parts of code based on the value of the expression, which is `generalOperationObject`.
› Lines 73 - 86: If the user clicks on the button =, get the value from `firstDouble` and from the display field `secondDouble` and perform the operation according to the value in `generalOperationObject`. Use the switch statement to perform different operations. Then assign the value in `result` variable.
› Line 87: Most common way of formatting a string in java is using `String.format()`.
  - Sends the value of the `result` variable to the `format()` method.
  - `"%.1f"` will print maximum one decimal digits of the number.
  - Then, assign the `String.format()`'s returned value to the `format` variable.
  - Summary: Store the calculated result in the variable `format` so the user can continue performing other operations. For example if the first operation was 2+5, the display shows 7, and the user can click on the buttons * followed by 2 requesting multiplication of 7 by 2.
› Line 88: Assign the value of the `format` variable to the display field by using the method `setText()`.

Summary

› We first instantiate a new VBox, and then set the alignment and padding properties. We also add gaps between columns and rows of the grid pane by setting Hgap and Vgap properties.
› We have also applied some column constraints to the grid pane. The `ColumnConstraints` constructor takes the min width, preferred width, and max width values.
› All the nodes in column one will have a `min-width` of 100, `pref-width` of 100 and `max-width` of `Double.MAX_VALUE`.
› Similarly, all the nodes in column two will have a `min-width` of 200, `pref-width` of 200 and `max-width` of `Double.MAX_VALUE`.

- Also, we have set the `Halignment` property to `HPos.RIGHT` in `columnOneConstraints` so that all the nodes in column 1 are right aligned.
- Moreover, by setting `Hgrow` property to `Priority.ALWAYS` in `columnTwoConstraints`, we're specifying that if the screen resizes, then column 2 should grow horizontally and fill in the extra space.

Leg. Dep. No: 2019/0526

Made in the USA
Monee, IL
21 June 2020